AF785117

The Role of Local Police:

Striking a Balance Between Immigration Enforcement and Civil Liberties

BY ANITA KHASHU

April 2009

POLICE FOUNDATION
Washington, DC

The Police Foundation is a national, nonpartisan, nonprofit organization dedicated to supporting innovation and improvement in policing. Established in 1970, the foundation has conducted seminal research in police behavior, policy, and procedure, and works to transfer to local agencies the best information about practices for dealing effectively with a range of important police operational and administrative concerns. Motivating all of the foundation's efforts is the goal of efficient, humane policing that operates within the framework of democratic principles and the highest ideals of the nation.

©2008 by the Police Foundation. All rights, including translation into other languages, reserved under the Universal Copyright Convention, the Berne Convention for the Protection of Literary and Artistic Works, and the International and Pan American Copyright Conventions. Permission to quote is readily granted.

ISBN 1-884614-23-X
978-1-884614-23-1

Library of Congress Control Number: 2009924868

POLICE FOUNDATION
1201 Connecticut Avenue, NW
Washington, DC 20036-2636
(202) 833-1460 voice
(202) 659-9149 fax
pfinfo@policefoundation.org
www.policefoundation.org

An executive summary and the full report of *The Role of Local Police: Striking a Balance Between Immigration Enforcement and Civil Liberties* are available online at http://www.policefoundation.org/strikingabalance/.

Table of Contents

Table of Contents

Table of Contents

Contributors

RAQUEL ALDANA
Professor of Law
William S. Boyd School of Law
University of Nevada
Las Vegas, Nevada

KAREN L. AMENDOLA
Chief Operating Officer
Research, Evaluation, and Professional Services
Police Foundation
Washington, DC

RANDOLPH CAPPS
Demographer and Senior Policy Analyst
Migration Policy Institute
Washington, DC

ALINA DAS
Immigrant Defense Fellow
New York University School of Law
New York, New York

SCOTT H. DECKER
Professor and Director of the School of Criminology and Criminal Justice
Arizona State University
Tempe, Arizona

ROBERTO G. GONZALES
Acting Assistant Professor
School of Social Work
University of Washington
Seattle, Washington

EDWIN E. HAMILTON
Professional Services Director
Police Foundation
Washington, DC

ANITA KHASHU
Former Director
Center on Immigration and Justice
The Vera Institute of Justice
New York, New York

PAUL G. LEWIS
Associate Professor of Political Science
Arizona State University
Tempe, Arizona

NANCY MORAWETZ
Professor of Clinical Law
New York University School of Law
New York, New York

JEFFREY S. PASSEL
Senior Demographer
Pew Hispanic Center
Washington, DC

DORIS M. PROVINE
Professor
School of Justice and Social Inquiry
Arizona State University
Tempe, Arizona

VERONICA PURYEAR
Senior Research Associate
Police Foundation
Washington, DC

RUBÉN G. RUMBAUT
Professor of Sociology
University of California
Irvine, California

MONICA W. VARSANYI
Associate Professor of Government
John Jay College of Criminal Justice
New York, New York

KRISTIN N. WILLIAMS
Research & Administrative Coordinator
Police Foundation
Washington, DC

EDITOR:
MARY MALINA
Communications Director
Police Foundation
Washington, DC

Foreword

America's efforts to find effective solutions to its undocumented immigration problem resulted in a series of debates at the federal, state, and local levels. These debates revealed the emotional intensity surrounding the issue and disclosed divisions in the political and social fabric of the country, all within the backdrop of a presidential election.

The failure of Congress to move forward with the development of a comprehensive national solution to this problem prompted states and localities to act unilaterally in passing legislation to curb immigration by penalizing employers who hire immigrants, prohibiting undocumented immigrant access to government benefits and services, and intensifying enforcement of immigration laws. These measures generated so much fear and uncertainty that large numbers of immigrants simply uprooted, leaving communities where they had lived for years.

This "immigration emergency" and demographic shift of the undocumented population resulted in an expansion of the role of federal immigration officials from maintaining the security of the borders to the enforcement of immigration laws in cities, towns, and villages throughout the United States. The relocation of immigrants from farming communities and predominately rural areas to cities and suburban communities has resulted in a cultural clash and generated a backlash against immigrants, who look different, speak foreign languages, and do not fit well within the social and political milieu of communities.

The influx of the immigrant population into cities and suburban communities has caused the federal government to reallocate a higher percentage of its resources to these areas and to encourage greater cooperation and support from state and municipal law enforcement agencies. Prior to 1996, the role of local police in immigration enforcement had been limited to such things as sharing information, providing back-up support for field operations, coordinating efforts, and holding and transferring prisoners. In 1996, when the Illegal Immigration Reform and Immigrant Responsibility Act added Section 287(g) to the Immigration and Nationality Act, local police, upon entry into a memorandum of agreement with the U.S. Department of Homeland Security (DHS), were granted the authority to enforce federal immigration laws.

Pursuant to Section 287(g) agreements, police who meet the requisite federal training standards are authorized to enforce federal immigration law under the supervision of DHS. Local police are provided direct access to DHS databases and authorized to initiate the deportation process. This enables local police to remove serious criminal offenders from the community more expeditiously and in a less costly manner by leveraging federal resources to deport them. Notwithstanding the benefits derived from Section 287(g), only a fraction of a percentage of police and sheriffs' departments has opted to participate.

There are good reasons for this. Police chiefs know that to be effective at crime control in this community-policing era, they must have public support. If local police are perceived as immigration enforcement officers, immigrants—both documented and undocumented—will avoid contact with police because of fear of arrest and deportation of themselves or a family member; 85 percent of immigrants in the U.S. live in mixed-status families. During our focus groups, representatives of the immigrant community told us that they avoided going outside of their homes whenever immigration authorities were in town. One mother said that she would not even go to the store to buy milk for her baby due to fear of arrest and deportation.

Foreword

The reluctance of local police to enforce immigration law grows out of the difficulty of balancing federal and local interests in ways that do not diminish the ability of the police to provide for public safety, which depends heavily on public trust. In communities where people fear the police, very little information is shared with officers, undermining the police capacity for crime control and quality service delivery. As a result, these areas become breeding grounds for drug trafficking, human smuggling, terrorist activity, and other serious crimes. As a police chief in one of the focus groups asked, "How do you police a community that will not talk to you?"

In order to overcome these obstacles, police departments should take appropriate measures to improve relationships with immigrant communities. They can do so by learning more about the cultures and traditions of immigrants who live within their jurisdictions. They should develop the capacity to communicate with immigrants more effectively by encouraging officers to become more proficient in Spanish and ensuring that department representatives who can speak other languages are available. The police need to pursue these goals so that they can tap into the wealth of information and knowledge about things that are going on within the immigrant community. This in turn facilitates their ability to control crime, maintain public safety, and provide meaningful support to DHS in its efforts to prevent another terrorist attack within the United States.

Local police chiefs recognize the importance of mutually cooperative and supportive relationships among law enforcement authorities, especially in efforts to remove violent offenders from communities. They understand such cooperation strengthens the capacity of government at all levels to ensure that our communities and our nation remain safe and secure. Nevertheless, the states, in establishing a federal government, determined immigration enforcement to be a federal responsibility. Hence, the enforcement of federal laws do not supersede the responsibilities of local police to enforce state statutes and provide for the public safety as derived from the police powers embodied within the reserve clause of the Tenth Amendment to the United States Constitution.

As the role of local police shifts from a concentration on public safety issues to immigration enforcement, the perception that immigrants have of police presence changes from protection and service to arrest and deportation. Police chiefs must carefully weigh and balance these divergent responsibilities to ensure that the primary mission and purpose of the police department is not compromised by the voluntary assumption of immigration enforcement responsibilities. Therefore, the question for local police is not merely what they do, but how they do it. To the degree that police departments can support the efforts of DHS without sending a message to the public that local police have become immigration enforcement officers and that contacts with them could result in deportation, mutual cooperation can be beneficial to all parties.

When local police execute the powers of immigration enforcement officers—as is the case when they check for green cards at roadblocks, or stop people for motor vehicle violations and request documentation or information associated with immigration status—they execute an immigration enforcement function in contacts with the general public. As a result, they assume all of the attendant risks and consequences associated with such activities. These risks are diminished considerably when the exercise of police authority does not involve contacts with the general public, such as would be the case when officers are processing prisoners in connection with

DHS to determine whether there are any outstanding warrants or holds against those individuals, or when transferring prisoners with warrants or holds into the custody of DHS.

Finally, local police are part of our nation's framework of institutions and organizations that insure the strength of our democratic republic by maintaining safe and secure communities. The effectiveness of the police is heavily dependent upon the nature of the relationship they have with the general public and the degree to which the police and community are able to work collaboratively to resolve crime problems. Every effort should be made to establish a mutually cooperative and supportive working relationship between local police and the immigrant communities they serve. Police departments that opt to enforce federal immigration law should do so in a manner that does not erode their relationship with immigrant communities or subordinate municipal interests to those of the federal government.

Hubert Williams
President
Police Foundation

Acknowledgments

As in any large-scale project, the Police Foundation owes a debt of gratitude to many people who shared their time, talent, insight, support, and experience to ensure its success. We are grateful to the Ford Foundation for its support and guidance. An advisory board of distinguished members of the legal, academic, and public policy communities guided the project from its inception and we gratefully acknowledge the following members for their contributions:

Pablo Alvarado
Executive Director
National Day Laborer Organizing Network

Professor Robert L. Bach
Center for Homeland Defense and Security
Naval Postgraduate School

George H. Bohlinger III
Managing Partner
Hanover Partners, LLP

Muzaffar Chishti
Director, Migration Policy Institute
at New York University School of Law

Professor David D. Cole
Georgetown University Law Center

Wade Henderson
Executive Director
Leadership Conference on Civil Rights

Professor Alex Piquero
Department of Criminology and Criminal Justice
University of Maryland-College Park

Honorable Vanessa Ruiz
District of Columbia Court of Appeals

Kareem Shora
National Executive Director
American-Arab Anti-Discrimination Committee

We learned a tremendous amount from the generous participation of all those who took part in our focus groups and especially thank the following law enforcement executives who organized participation in each of the sites: Chief Theron Bowman, Arlington (TX) Police Department; Sheriff Don Hunter, Collier County (FL) Sheriff's Office; Chief Ron Miller, Topeka (KS) Police Department; and Chief Richard Wiles, El Paso (TX) Police Department.

We thank the scholars, policy makers, law enforcement professionals, and immigrant community representatives from across the U.S. who participated in our national conference and greatly appreciate the distinguished assembly of conference presenters whose contributions informed both the conference and this report. The conference agenda and presenter information can be found in Appendix N. We appreciate Raquel Manso's work on the project, especially her efforts in coordinating the focus group process. We owe a special thanks to Anita Khashu, who carefully reviewed volumes of project material, data, and external resources to create both the focus group summary and final report narrative. We are grateful to Mary Malina, who served as editor and oversaw the production of the report.

Finally, this project, like all foundation projects, reflects the enormous talent, effort, and commitment of the staff of the Police Foundation.

Hubert Williams
President
Police Foundation

Executive Summary

In recent years, the United States has experienced historically high rates of immigration. Not only has the population of immigrants increased four-fold since the 1970s, in the last fifteen to twenty years immigrants have also settled away from traditional gateway cities and into new destinations throughout the country that have had very little experience with integrating new immigrants. The immigrant population has also grown more diverse, originating from all parts of the globe, in particular Latin America and Asia versus the predominantly Caucasian European migration of the early twentieth century. These demographic shifts have produced racial tensions, particularly in new destination communities, and given rise to contentious debate about the nation's immigration policies and practices, with long-standing resident communities demanding that government—federal, state, and local—more aggressively enforce immigration laws.

Traditionally, the prevailing view was that the responsibility for enforcing federal immigration laws was solely in the purview of the federal government. In recent years, however, local law enforcement agencies throughout the country have been drawn into the middle of the immigration debate, especially since 9/11, through pressure placed on them by their elected leaders, their communities, and the media to engage in federal immigration enforcement, a responsibility that has not traditionally been part of their organizational mandate. Beginning in the 1990s, federal immigration agencies, overwhelmed by the enormity of the task of apprehending, detaining, and deporting the country's almost twelve million unauthorized immigrants, launched programs and initiatives to induce the cooperation and assistance of the nation's approximately 18,000 state and local law enforcement agencies in identifying and deporting unauthorized immigrants living in the interior of the country. Prior to 1996, these programs were mostly directed at improving cooperation between local law enforcement and federal immigration authorities with respect to criminal detainees. In 1996, however, Congress passed legislation expanding the role of local law enforcement in federal immigration enforcement. The most well-known program is the U.S. Immigration and Customs Enforcement's (ICE) 287(g) program, which authorizes federal officials to enter into written agreements with state and local law enforcement agencies to carry out the functions of immigration officers, including investigation, apprehension, and detention.

While local law enforcement agencies collaborate with federal immigration authorities in a wide range of activities, most of this project's discussions focused on the ICE 287(g) program. Police executives have felt torn between a desire to be helpful and cooperative with federal immigration authorities and a concern that their participation in immigration enforcement efforts will undo the gains they have achieved through community oriented policing practices, which are directed at gaining the trust and cooperation of immigrant communities. Police are also concerned about the impact of local law enforcement of immigration law on already strained state and local resources, and particularly on the ability of local law enforcement to maintain its core mission of protecting communities and promoting public safety.

With support from the Ford Foundation, the Police Foundation launched a national effort to bring together law enforcement agencies, public officials, and community stakeholders to collaboratively examine the implications of local law enforcement of immigration laws. The main goal of the project was to provide local law enforcement with a venue to debate and disseminate their perspectives on the issue of their role in immigration enforcement so that they may have an influence in the national policy debate. A central project component was a series of focus groups held across the country that included local police, public officials, and representatives of immigrant communities and designed to elicit the perspectives and insights of those directly impacted by the issues surrounding immigration. The conversations and questions raised in the focus groups influenced the development of the agenda for a national conference in Washington in August 2008, at which scholars, policy makers, law enforcement professionals, and immigrant community representatives from across the U.S. participated in facilitated discussions and presented data and research on the issues involved in the debate. Finally, a short written survey was distributed to law enforcement executives who attended the national conference.

Although there were clearly differences of opinion among the diverse group of law enforcement representatives participating in the various project activities regarding the costs and benefits of local law enforcement participation in federal immigration enforcement, a majority of police chiefs seem to regard the costs of participation in civil immigration enforcement efforts, where there is no criminal nexus, as outweighing the potential benefits. In particular, many police executives were concerned with the impact on the relationship between immigrant communities and police and the probability of reduced cooperation of witnesses and victims of crime, thereby having a negative overall impact on public safety. They were also concerned about increased victimization and exploitation of immigrants, a possible increase in police misconduct, the fiscal impact on law enforcement budgets, the high possibility of error given the complexity of immigration law, the possibility of racial profiling and other civil lawsuits, and the effect on immigrant access to other municipal services. It also became clear, despite a healthy level of debate over specific issues, that certain recommendations and policy positions listed below were widely held among the group.

- The costs of participating in the U.S. Immigration and Customs Enforcement's (ICE) 287(g) program outweigh the benefits.
- Police officers should be prohibited from arresting and detaining persons to solely investigate immigration status in the absence of probable cause of an independent state criminal law violation.
- If a local agency nevertheless enters the 287(g) program, its participation should be focused on serious criminal offenders and should be limited to verifying the immigration status of criminal detainees as part of the 287(g) Jail Enforcement Officer program.
- Local and state authorities participating in federal immigration enforcement activities should develop policies and procedures for monitoring racial profiling and abuse of authority.
- In order to preserve the trust that police agencies have built over the years by aggressively engaging in community oriented policing activities, local law enforcement agencies should involve representatives of affected communities in the development of local immigration policies.
- There is a need for empirical research on ICE's 287(g) program and other methods of police collaboration with federal immigration authorities so that we have more objective data by which to better understand the way in which these programs are carried out in the field and their impact on public safety and civil liberties.
- Local law enforcement agencies should employ community-policing and problem-solving tactics to improve relations with immigrant communities and resolve tension caused by expanding immigration.

- Local law enforcement leaders and policing organizations should place pressure on the federal government to comprehensively improve border security and reform the immigration system, because the federal government's failure on both issues has had serious consequences in cities and towns throughout the country.

While much of the dialogue generated during the project centered on the specific benefits and costs of local law enforcement participation in immigration enforcement, the conversation often reverted to discussions about the core role of police and general principles of community policing. Local police must serve and protect *all* residents regardless of their immigration status, enforce the criminal laws of their state, and serve and defend the Constitution of the United States. As police agencies move away from their core role of ensuring public safety and begin taking on civil immigration enforcement activities, the perception immigrants have of the role of police moves from protection to arrest and deportation, thereby jeopardizing local law enforcement's ability to gain the trust and cooperation of immigrant communities. "How can you police a community that will not talk to you?" asked one police chief participating in the project. Without the cooperation of immigrant witnesses and victims of crime, local law enforcement's ability to identify, arrest, and prosecute criminals is jeopardized.

Over the past fifteen years, the community-policing movement has made significant gains in making communities safer, and police executives participating in the project expressed concern that local immigration enforcement efforts threaten to undo these gains. The community-policing movement has demonstrated that the effectiveness of police is heavily dependent on the relationships the police have with the communities they serve. Therefore, in developing and monitoring local immigration policies, it is critical that local law enforcement regularly communicate with affected communities and make every effort to establish a mutually cooperative and supportive relationship with immigrant communities.

The final project report presents the most salient arguments, positions, points of consensus, and recommendations that arose during the focus groups, conference presentations and discussions, and survey responses. Also included, as appendices to the report, are a comprehensive summary of the focus group discussions, results of the conference law enforcement executive survey, the conference agenda, presenters' bios, selected presentations, sample police department policies on immigration enforcement, and six papers (abstracts below) prepared specifically for the national conference by scholars from various academic disciplines.

Abstracts of Papers Prepared for This Project

Legal Issues in Local Police Enforcement of Federal Immigration Law

by Nancy Morawetz and Alina Das, New York University School of Law

As local police consider taking on enforcement of federal immigration law, they should carefully consider the legal complexity of their role and legal constraints on methods of enforcement in a legal and institutional system that operates quite differently from local criminal justice systems. Local police enforcement of federal immigration law must account for local, state, and federal laws that govern the rights of community residents and the obligations of localities. It must also account for the civil nature of most immigration violations. Most importantly, it must be conducted in a way that avoids several common misconceptions about the supposed targets of immigration law enforcement, including confusion over their rights, status, and place in the community. The risk of error is high, and already several localities have been subject to lawsuits over unlawful arrests and detentions, the use of racial profiling in enforcement, poor conditions of confinement, and other violations of law. This paper discusses the legal complexities of federal immigration law enforcement in the local setting and the changing demographics of communities. Risks of liability provide yet another factor for police departments to consider before making a decision about whether to tread into this new field of enforcement.

Making Civil Liberties Matter in Local Immigration Enforcement

by Raquel Aldana, William S. Boyd School of Law, University of Nevada-Las Vegas

The exponential rise in local law enforcement involvement in the enforcement of immigration laws raises significant questions regarding a state's source of power to enforce a traditionally federal power. As well, this trend presents local police with new challenges on how to protect the civil liberties and retain the trust of immigrant communities. In this paper, the author explains the unresolved controversy of the source and scope of local powers to enforce federal immigration laws and details the civil liberties concerns that arise from local law enforcement's involvement in immigration enforcement. The author then offers recommendations for ensuring greater civil rights compliance by local law enforcement agencies that still choose to enforce immigration laws, as well as explains immigrants' rights during these police encounters.

Undocumented Immigration and Rates of Crime and Imprisonment: Popular Myths and Empirical Realities

by Rubén G. Rumbaut, University of California-Irvine

The perception that the foreign-born, especially "illegal aliens," are responsible for higher crime rates is deeply rooted in American public opinion and is sustained by media anecdote and popular myth. In the absence of rigorous empirical research, stereotypes about immigrants and crime often provide the underpinnings for public policies and practices, and shape public opinion and political behavior. These perceptions, however, are not supported empirically; in fact, they are refuted by the preponderance of scientific evidence. In addition to reviewing previous literature on immigrant criminality, Rumbaut looks at national violent and property crime rates since the early 1990s, during the period of highest immigration. He then analyzes incarceration rates of young men eighteen to thirty-nine, comparing differences between the foreign-born and the U.S.-born by national origin and by education, and, among the foreign-born, by length of residence in the U.S. Rumbaut also examines findings from two major surveys (IIMMLA and CILS) in Southern California, the region of greatest immigrant concentration in the United States, and focuses comparative attention on those nationalities representing distinct modes of incorporation.

Executive Summary

Why Integration Matters: The Case of Undocumented Immigrant Youth and Moving Beyond Enforcement
by Roberto G. Gonzales, University of Washington-Seattle

Today's immigration debates have brought to the fore conflicting visions within the United States over how to address a population of eleven to twelve million undocumented immigrants. However, contemporary debates have yet to catch up to current realities and complexities of undocumented families and thus do not account, for the most part, for a growing population of undocumented children educated in the United States. Drawing upon three and a half years of fieldwork and over one hundred life histories with adult children of undocumented immigrants in Southern California, this paper seeks to address the complicated realities of contemporary immigration by examining the experiences of undocumented youth in the larger community context. It argues that while enforcement efforts are counterproductive, police and other community officials have an important role to play in the integration process of undocumented youth.

Local Enforcement of Immigration Laws: Evolution of the 287(g) Program and Its Potential Impacts on Local Communities
by Randolph Capps, Migration Policy Institute

By August 2008, sixty-two state and local agencies had entered into 287(g) agreements with U.S. Immigration and Customs Enforcement (ICE), although most were signed since 2005. Most of the jurisdictions adopting agreements are in southeastern and southwestern states, in conservative political areas, and in locations where recent growth in unauthorized immigration has been rapid. This paper begins with a brief timeline and overview of the 287(g) program and discusses some of the broad outlines of how it has been implemented to date. Then, for further background, population and political trends that underlie the adoption of 287(g) programs across the country are discussed. The third section of the paper relates preliminary findings about the implementation of 287(g) in Arkansas, based on a site visit there in June 2008. The site visit to the adjacent communities of Rogers and Springdale, Arkansas, confirmed that 287(g) officers there were checking immigration status in a variety of operations, including: routine traffic stops, worksite investigations, drug raids, and at the county jails in both communities. Several hundred immigrants had been arrested, detained, and sent into the custody of ICE for deportation over the course of the first six months. Latino community leaders who had originally supported the program in Springdale had withdrawn their support due to the wide net that the 287(g) officers had cast, and the program's broad impacts on local residents, including schoolchildren. The paper ends with policy recommendations and general observations about potential impacts of 287(g) operations on cities, immigrant communities, and children.

Immigration and Local Policing: Results from a National Survey of Law Enforcement Executives
by Scott H. Decker, Paul G. Lewis, Doris Marie Provine, Arizona State University, and Monica W. Varsanyi, John Jay College of Criminal Justice

One of the most important challenges for law enforcement agencies in many communities is how to respond to immigration and the presence of undocumented residents. Departments often face conflicting pressures from local politicians, federal authorities, community groups, and the private sector. Yet they have little available information to help them make sound policy decisions. This paper reports on the results of a recent nationwide survey of police executives on several issues, including differences between departments and communities and their attitudes about immigration and local law enforcement; relationships with federal immigration and customs enforcement authorities; and the range of policies on immigration policing being developed by cities and departments. The survey also explores levels of commitment to community policing practices and the potential for conflict with enforcement of immigration laws by local police.

About the Project

In recent years, the United States has experienced historic levels of immigration. During this time, not only did the immigrant[1] population increase significantly but it also became more dispersed. Prior to 1990, immigrants tended to settle in the major gateway cities; beginning in the 1990s, they began moving to regions that have not been traditional draws for immigration. In addition, unlike the last great period of immigration in the early twentieth century, when the vast majority of immigrants were of European origin, the current immigrant population arrives from all parts of the globe and they bring with them a host of new languages and cultures. As these demographic shifts started changing the racial and cultural landscape of communities throughout the country and as local governments were struggling to deal with the challenges of integrating these new immigrants into their communities, the public began to demand government do more to enforce immigration laws.

Even prior to the terrorist attacks of September 11, 2001, proponents of tightening immigration control measures have argued that greater investment in immigration reform will improve public safety by reducing crime, despite significant evidence to the contrary. Following the 9/11 attacks, public debate has become even more rancorous and has led to calls for greater involvement of local and state governments in immigration control. As the federal government struggles to resolve the complex and difficult issues surrounding immigration, local police are faced with a serious dilemma regarding their role and responsibility in this area. On the one hand, the federal government is telling them that the enforcement of immigration laws by state and local governments will assist the nation in controlling undocumented immigration. On the other hand, they realize that enforcing immigration laws could undermine their efforts to build trust with immigrant communities, whose cooperation they need to effectively provide public safety and policing services.

To address the dilemma facing so many local police agencies about how to balance civil rights protections, community-policing priorities, and immigration enforcement, the Police Foundation launched a national effort to bring together law enforcement leaders, public officials, scholars, and community stakeholders to collaboratively examine the implications of local law enforcement of immigration laws. The goals of the project were to review practices, constitutional issues, and budgetary factors; to provide state and local agencies with data and recommendations to inform policy; and to facilitate dialogue between immigrant communities and law enforcement in order to reduce fear and mistrust and enhance cooperation and improve public safety.

To accomplish these goals, the foundation hosted four sets of focus groups across the country that included law enforcement personnel, elected public officials, members of immigrant communities, and other interested groups. The hope was that by bringing immigrant communities together with local police to begin a dialogue on the role of police in immigration enforcement, we would also help to open up channels of communication and establish improved working relationships between local police and the immigrant communities they serve. A total of thirty-three local and state law enforcement agencies were represented in the four focus groups (see appendix A for a summary of focus group conversations).

The information derived from the focus groups was used to design an agenda for a national conference that was an invitation-only event at which over two hundred law enforcement leaders, policy makers, scholars, and community leaders participated in facilitated discussions geared toward generating concrete recommendations for how local law enforcement can strike a balance between civil liberties and immigration enforcement. (Photos from the conference illustrate this report. See appendix N for the conference agenda and presenters' bios.) National conference attendees included over one hundred law enforcement executives, many of whom were police chiefs or elected sheriffs, as well as fourteen federal, state, and local government representatives. The foundation also invited scholars and other immigration experts to present papers on specific topics relating to the role of local and state police in immigration enforcement. The topics of the papers included the rights of undocumented immigrants and the legal framework for the enforcement of immigration laws, demographic research, immigration and criminality, evaluation of federal efforts to collaborate with local police on immigration enforcement (287(g) program), a national survey of local police immigration policies, and the experience of undocumented youth (see appendices B-G).

The foundation also distributed a survey to law enforcement executives who attended the conference. Fifty-four attendees completed the survey: forty police chiefs, nine deputy or assistant police chiefs, two sheriffs, one police superintendent, a major, and a respondent who is both a sheriff and police chief. Most of the participants were from urban agencies (n=29), while many were from urban/suburban areas (n=19). The remaining six were from rural type areas. The size of the jurisdictions ranged from just under fifteen thousand to more than four million. Also, the majority of respondents (n=47) were from municipal or local law enforcement agencies, while one was from a county police department, four were from sheriffs' offices, one was from an urban county metropolitan area, and one was from both a sheriff's office and a municipal department (Amendola, Williams, Hamilton, and Puryear 2008) (see appendix H).

Police Foundation President Hubert Williams and Phoenix Mayor Phil Gordon share a moment before the conference convenes.

This report presents an accumulation of the conversations, findings, and recommendations derived from the focus groups, conference sessions, and academic papers prepared for the conference. The goal of the report is to discuss the implications of local police enforcing immigration laws with respect to building constructive relationships with minority communities, and to provide state and local law enforcement agencies with information and recommendations for reviewing their immigration law enforcement policies. Underlying the design of this project and report is a belief that encouraging dialogue between police and communities will enhance public trust in state and local law enforcement and promote a balanced approach to providing police services and protecting civil rights. The capacity of the police to prevent and respond to crime, including acts of terrorism, requires public cooperation that is anchored in public trust of the police.

History of the Role of Local Police in Immigration Enforcement

In 1952, Congress defined the nation's immigration laws in the Immigration and Nationality Act (INA), which contains both civil and criminal enforcement measures. Federal law, however, has never been clear about the role of local and state authorities in immigration enforcement; until recently, the prevailing position in the policing and immigration fields has been that enforcement of civil immigration laws is solely in the purview of the federal government and that local and state police have authority to make arrests for only a small subset of criminal immigration violations (Appleseed 2008, 11).

Federal law has never been clear about the role of local and state authorities in immigration enforcement.

The trend towards greater cooperation between local law enforcement and federal immigration officials began years before September 11, 2001, in the 1990s, when the United States began to experience historic levels of immigration. Overwhelmed by the task of detecting, arresting, and detaining the growing population of unauthorized immigrants in the United States, federal immigration authorities and proponents of greater immigration control began advocating for greater cooperation between local police and federal immigration authorities. Proponents argued that the nation's approximately 700,000 local and state police officers would be an effective "force-multiplier;" that is, they could dramatically increase the number of law enforcement officials who could detect undocumented immigrants in the interior of the country. In addition, proponents such as Alabama Senator Jeff Sessions argued that the failure of police to enforce immigration law created an incentive for greater inflows of unauthorized immigration into the United States (Venbrux 2006, 320).

Prior to legislative reforms of 1996, federal efforts towards increasing local law enforcement's role in immigration matters were limited to increasing communication and assistance to states regarding criminal detainees in violation of immigration law. For instance, in 1991, the legacy Immigration and Naturalization Service (INS) established the Alien Criminal Apprehension Program to foster greater cooperation between police and immigration authorities to deport criminal aliens. Under this program, state and local law enforcement officials would notify federal immigration officials of foreign-born nationals who had committed a crime and were taken into state or local custody (Seghetti, Viña, and Ester 2004, 3). Subsequently, in 1994, California politicians began advocating with the federal government for reimbursement of funds the state was expending to apprehend and incarcerate criminal aliens who had illegally reentered the country following a final order of deportation. Congress, in response to this advocacy, funded a program to reimburse states for costs incurred in the apprehension and incarceration of foreign nationals who had committed crimes (Appleseed 2008, 14).[2] Congress also appropriated funds to create the Law Enforcement Support Center (LESC) (Aldana 2008, 92).[3] The LESC's mission is to provide federal, state, and local law enforcement with information on immigration status of individuals arrested, suspected, or detained for a criminal offense. The LESC has operators working twenty-four hours a day, seven days a week answering inquiries from law enforcement. These operators use information gathered from various Department of Homeland Security (DHS) databases, the FBI's national database, and state criminal history databases (Appleseed 2008, 21).

In 1996, Congress expanded the role for state and local law enforcement in the Antiterrorism and Effective Death Penalty Act of 1996 (AEDPA) and the Illegal Immigration Reform and Immigrant Responsibility Act of 1996 (IIRIRA). Section 439 of the AEDPA amended federal immigration law to provide authority to states to arrest and detain an immigrant who had a previous order of deportation and had been previously convicted of a crime, to the extent authorized by state law (Appleseed 2008, 15). The law also required that state or local officials confirm immigration status with INS and prohibited detention for a period longer than necessary to transfer to federal custody (Appleseed 2008, 15). In addition, Section 372 of IIRIRA amendments to the INA provided authority to INS to deputize local and state law enforcement officials in the event of a mass influx of immigrants (Appleseed 2008, 15). IIRIRA also added section 287(g) to the INA, which authorized federal officials to

The trend toward greater involvement of state and local officials in federal immigration enforcement gained significant momentum after the terrorist attacks of September 11, 2001.

enter into written agreements with state and local law officials to carry out the functions of an immigration officer, including investigation, apprehension, and detention "at the expense of the State or political subdivision and to the extent consistent with State and local law" (ICE Fact Sheet: 287(g)). Moreover, by expanding the categories of criminal offenses that would subject immigrants (legal and unauthorized) to mandatory detention and deportation, IIRIRA reforms resulted in an increase in the number of criminal detainees subject to immigration deportation or removal proceedings (Chishti 2006, 462-463).

In 1999, INS Interior Enforcement Strategy included the tactic of developing partnerships with local and state law enforcement agencies to assist the INS with their interior immigration enforcement efforts (Chishti 2002, 372). In this same year, Congress appropriated funds for INS to create Quick Response Teams that responded to requests from state and local law enforcement officers who believed they had an unauthorized immigrant in custody. The INS established Quick Response Teams in regions that had experienced increases in the unauthorized immigrant population (Seghetti, Viña, and Ester 2004, 3).

The trend toward greater involvement of state and local officials in federal immigration enforcement gained significant momentum after the terrorist attacks of September 11, 2001, when federal, state, and local officials began to promote efforts at tightening immigration control as a counterterrorism measure (Venbrux 2006, 317). The most significant change that occurred in the aftermath of September 11 was the U.S. Department of Justice (DOJ) Office of Legal Counsel's (OLC) reversal of its long-standing position that involvement of state and local authorities in immigration enforcement should be limited, declaring that state and local police had inherent authority to make arrests for civil immigration violations (Chishti 2006, 467). Prior to 2002, DOJ officials had made statements and drafted memoranda arguing that state and local police did not have authority to enforce federal civil immigration law. In 1978, for instance, DOJ released a statement that, "INS officers are uniquely prepared for this law enforcement responsibility because of their special training, and because of the complexities and fine distinctions of immigration laws" (Appleseed 2008, 13). In 1983, the Reagan Justice Department encouraged a little more cooperation but limited that role to primarily informing INS about suspected deportable immigrants taken into police custody for state criminal violations (Seghetti, Viña, and Ester 2004, 7-8). The Reagan DOJ position also stated that where "state law authorizes local officers to enforce criminal provisions of federal law, "state and local police could exercise their authority to enforce criminal provisions of federal immigration law" (Appleseed 2008, 13). This position was confirmed as late as 1996, when the DOJ OLC issued an opinion concluding that state and local police do not have the authority to enforce civil immigration law violations (Seghetti, Viña, and Ester, 8). At a 2002 press conference, however, Attorney General John Ashcroft announced a reversal of DOJ's long-standing opinion, stating that state and local officials have inherent authority to enforce federal immigration law (Seghetti, Viña, and Ester, 8).

After September 11, in an effort to increase assistance from state and local police in the identification of unauthorized immigrants, DOJ also began putting information on civil immigration violations into the FBI's National Crime Information Center (NCIC) database. The NCIC database is a computerized index of criminal justice information operated by the FBI. In 1930, Congress first authorized the DOJ to maintain a clearinghouse for fingerprint records, rap sheets, and warrants (Gladstein, Lai, Wagner, and Wishnie 2005, 6-7). Over time, Congress has expanded the categories of records that can be included in the NCIC database. For the first time, in 1996, Congress authorized the entry of immigration records relating to previously deported felons (Gladstein et al. 2005, 6-7). Congress has never authorized entry of civil immigration records other than those relating to previously deported felons into the NCIC database (Gladstein et al. 2005, 6-7). Yet, as stated earlier, soon after September 11 the federal government began entering thousands of absconder records, most of which are purely civil violations. In December 2003, DHS officials stated intention to include student visa violators and persons deported for minor criminal offenses into NCIC (Gladstein et al. 2005, 6-7). Understanding that state and local law enforcement are the entities that mostly query the NCIC database, and given the federal government's interest in increasing involvement of state and local law enforcement as a "force multiplier" in immigration enforcement, it seems that the government's purpose in adding these immigration records to the database was a form of inducing local and state police to enforce immigration law when they routinely check the database in the course of regular police work (Kalhan 2008, 10). Policing organizations such as the International Association of Chiefs of Police (IACP) and the Major Cities Chiefs Association (MCCA) have criticized DOJ's decision to include civil warrants in the NCIC database because most state and local law enforcement agencies do not have authority to arrest for federal civil law violations according to state law governing the scope of their authority (IACP 2004, 4; MCC 2006, 10).

Since the 1996 immigration reforms, the federal government has had the authority to enter into agreements with state and local law enforcement agencies to train and then deputize local officers to perform immigration enforcement functions. However, prior to September 11, 2001, no state or local law enforcement agency had chosen to enter into such an agreement with the INS. Immediately after the terrorist attacks of September 11, the Florida State Police signed a memorandum of agreement with INS to train and deputize their officers. Since then, sixty-three law enforcement agencies in the country have taken advantage of the 287(g) program (ICE Fact Sheet: 287(g)).

For years, counter-balancing the movement toward greater federal/state/local cooperation on immigration enforcement, several states and municipalities throughout the country have passed local and state ordinances and laws limiting state and local government employees' ability to collaborate with federal immigration officials in the identification of unauthorized immigrants. In 1996, Congress passed two laws explicitly to counter such policies, by disallowing a federal, state, or local government entity from prohibiting their employees from communicating with federal immigration officials regarding the immigration status of any individual (Aldana 2008, 98). The legislative history, however, makes it clear that the purpose of this provision was not to require local or state governments to communicate with federal officials regarding immigration status (Pham 2005, 15). Since 1996, state and local governments have continued to limit their employees' ability to cooperate with federal immigration entities; however, rather than prohibiting communication with the federal government regarding immigration status, these state and local laws limit when employees can question individuals regarding their immigration status (Pham 2005, 23; Seghetti, Viña, and Ester 2004, 21). These municipalities have been labeled by many as "sanctuary cities." But as several conference participants argued, this term is a misnomer because these communities do not and cannot provide sanctuary for individuals from federal immigration enforcement officials. Moreover, many local and state law enforcement agencies not only do not provide sanctuary from federal immigration agents but indeed collaborate with federal officials to deport criminal aliens.

The Call for Greater Enforcement

During discussions, conference workshops, and presentations, participants provided various theories of factors influencing the movement towards greater participation in immigration enforcement by state and local officials. Some of these reasons are described below.

Demographic Changes

As stated early in this report, in the last fifteen to twenty years, the United States has experienced historically high levels of immigration. The immigrant population has quadrupled since 1970. In the 1990s, the size of the foreign-born population grew by 57.4 percent (Singer 2004, 1). By March 2008, the foreign-born population reached a historic high of 37.4 million people, or 12.5 percent of the population (Passel 2008) (see figure 1).

FIGURE 1. IMMIGRANT NUMBERS KEEP GROWING —PERCENT APPROACHES HISTORIC HIGHS

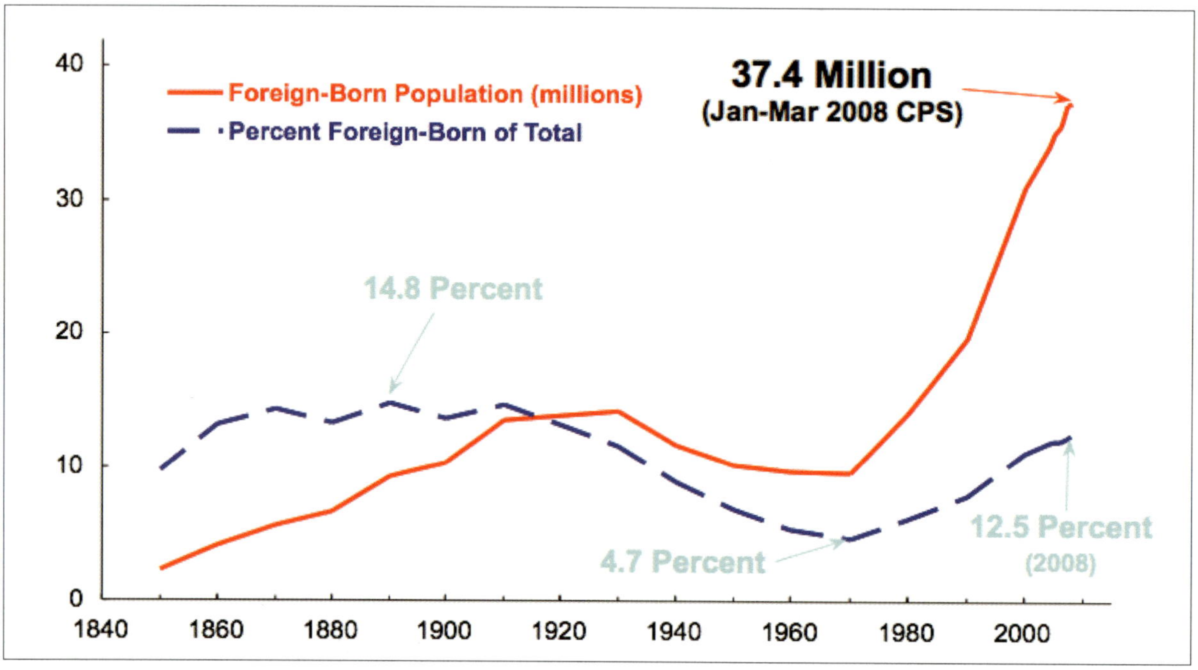

Source: *Unauthorized Immigrants: Trends, Characteristics, and Surprises.* Jeffrey S. Passel, Pew Hispanic Center. Presentation prepared for Police Foundation conference, The Role of Local Police: Striking a Balance Between Immigration Enforcement and Civil Liberties, Washington, DC, August 21, 2008 (see appendix I).

Not only is the number of immigrants in the United States reaching historically high levels, the population is also becoming more dispersed and areas of the country with no history of immigration are experiencing large influxes of immigrants (Singer 2007). In 1990, the top six immigrant states had 75 percent of the immigrant population. In 2008, these six states had merely 65 percent of the immigrant population (Passel 2008) (see figure 2).

The United States has also experienced great increases in the unauthorized population in recent years. Undocumented immigrants currently make up 30 percent of the foreign-born popu-

FIGURE 2. NEW IMMIGRATION GROWTH CENTERS

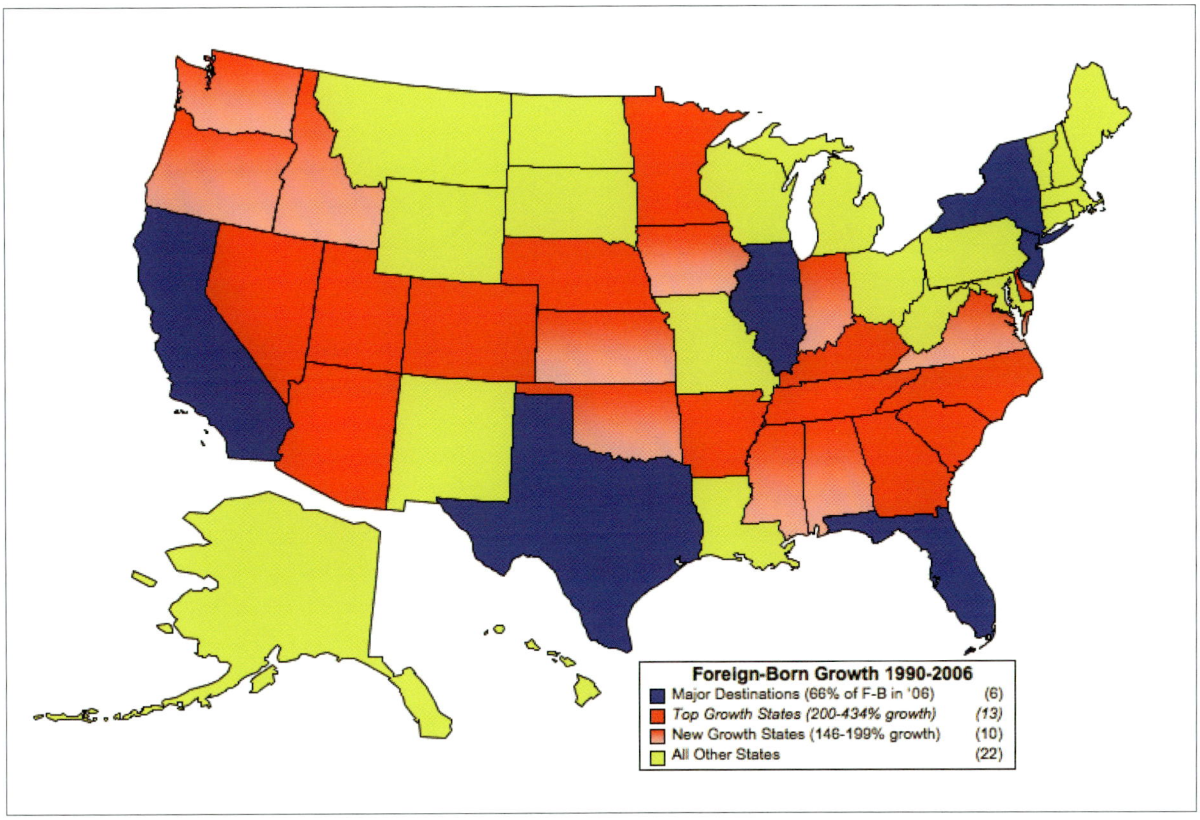

Source: *Unauthorized Immigrants: Trends, Characteristics, and Surprises.* Jeffrey S. Passel, Pew Hispanic Center. Presentation prepared for Police Foundation conference, The Role of Local Police: Striking a Balance Between Immigration Enforcement and Civil Liberties, Washington, DC, August 21, 2008 (see appendix I).

lation. Almost twelve million unauthorized immigrants were living in the United States in March 2008, constituting approximately four percent of the total U.S. population. Since the beginning of this decade, the unauthorized immigrant population increased by forty percent (Passel and Cohn 2008, i) (see figure 3).

The new emerging destination gateways tend to have immigrants who are from Asia and Mexico, are poorer than the native-born population, have low English proficiency, and lower rates of citizenship than traditional gateway cities that have longer-residing immigrant populations (Singer 2004, 1). New growth states are also seeing particularly high levels of unauthorized immigrants. Eighty percent of the undocumented population lived in six traditional immigrant gateway states in 1990, whereas in 2006 this percentage decreased to 60 percent (Passel 2008) (see appendix I).

In recent years, the average inflow of unauthorized immigrants appears to have slowed from 800,000 a year from 2000 to 2004 to approximately 500,000 yearly from 2005 to 2008. Yet, four out of ten unauthorized immigrants arrived in the United States since 2000. While growth of the unauthorized population may have slowed in recent years, the legal immigrant population inflow has now surpassed the undocumented population inflow, and thus communities continue to receive new immigrants (Passel and Cohn 2008, i-ii). The unauthorized population is largely Latino, with four out of five unauthorized immigrants originating from Latin America (Passel and Cohn 2008, iii).

FIGURE 3. UNAUTHORIZED NUMBER HIGH — TREND UNCERTAIN, BUT SLOWING (?)

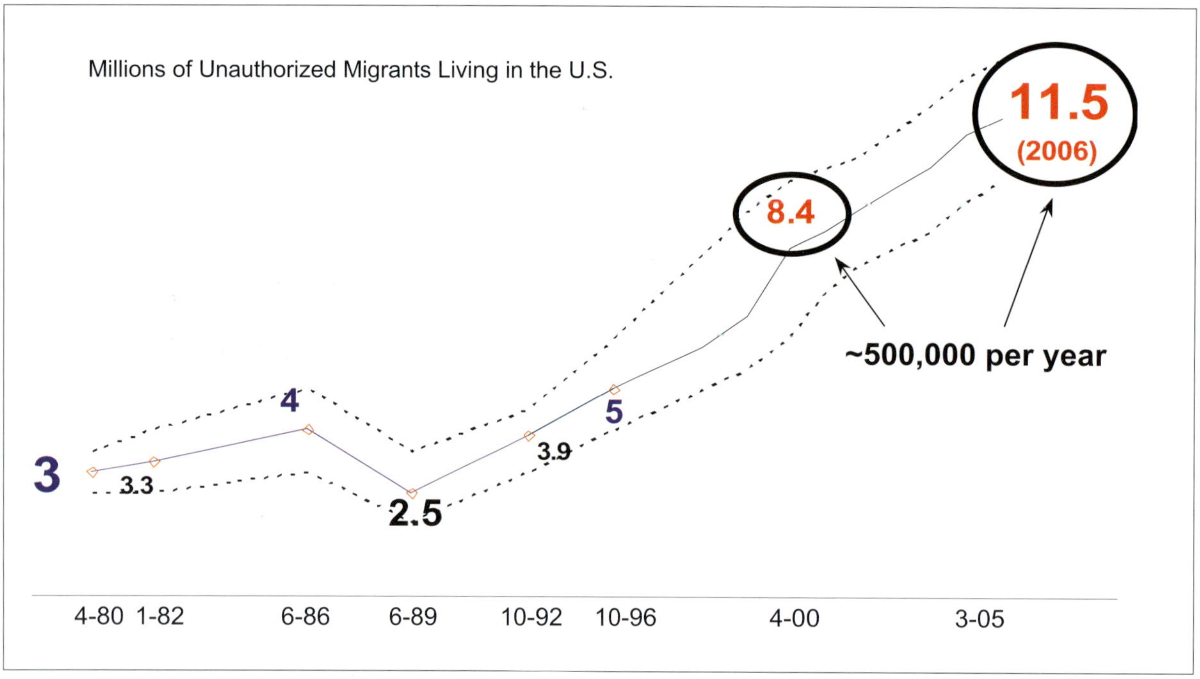

Source: *Unauthorized Immigrants: Trends, Characteristics, and Surprises.* Jeffrey S. Passel, Pew Hispanic Center. Presentation prepared for Police Foundation conference, The Role of Local Police: Striking a Balance Between Immigration Enforcement and Civil Liberties, Washington, DC, August 21, 2008 (see appendix I).

As the size of the immigrant population grows and immigrants move to new destination regions that have little or no experience with immigration, states and localities are struggling to figure out how to integrate these new residents. In the absence of a comprehensive and effective federal immigration policy, immigration becomes a local policy challenge (Chishti 2006, 464). Moreover, as the racial and cultural landscape of these communities change as a result of these new demographic trends, long-standing resident communities have begun to put pressure on local government, including police, to take measures to reduce levels of unauthorized immigration.

A significant share of unauthorized families can be characterized as "mixed status" in which there is one or more unauthorized parent and one or more children who are U.S. citizens by birth, according to Dr. Jeffrey Passel of the Pew Hispanic Center.

A biannually conducted national survey of the noninstitutionalized English-speaking population in the United States (General Social Survey) administered in 2000 confirmed that perceptions of increasing minority population size influenced attitudes towards immigration. The survey found that respondents tended to overstate the size of the minority population; roughly half of the respondents stated that Whites had become a numerical minority in the United States. Residents of rural areas were more likely to exaggerate minority-group size than urban residents. The survey also showed that perceptions of immigration issues become more unfavorable as the perception of group size moves away from Whites as a majority. In other words, the larger the non-Hispanic White population perceives minority-group size, the more it supports greater immigration restrictions. Moreover, respondents that overstated minority-group size also tended to believe that Blacks and Hispanics are more violent than other racial groups (Alba, Rumbaut, and Marotz 2005).

Law enforcement executives participating in the focus groups and the conference agreed that the changing demographics were driving the pressure from communities for a greater role for local police in federal immigration enforcement. As one police executive in the Arlington, Texas, session stated:

> **I don't think, generally speaking, people are complaining about the fact that someone is here in this country without official legal authorization to be here . . . All of a sudden their community is becoming more heavily populated with people who are different from them, who enjoy doing things that are unlike what other people in the community have historically done. And so rather than addressing the uneasy feeling about differences among the newcomers, they just cast this label "illegal immigration" over that, and then they want us to enforce immigration laws to get rid of the people who are different from what they are accustomed.**

Providing concrete evidence of the argument that racial tensions are underlying the anti-immigrant sentiment, one Dallas-Fort Worth Metroplex chief recounted that the morning of the focus group he received a complaint about a Puerto Rican family that had moved into his community and set up a landscaping business that they ran out of their home. Throughout the day, Puerto Rican workers were coming in and out of the house. Some neighbors complained to the police requesting that the police do something to deport these new residents. The community members clearly did not understand that these new residents were U.S. citizens. The chief provided this example to demonstrate that the problem with this family was not their immigration status but rather their race or ethnicity that disturbed other community members.

Several other participants in the focus groups and conference also strongly believed that attacks against "illegal immigration" are often motivated by racial discrimination. An El Paso participant stated, "It's been easy for them to hide this whole racism that is happening against the immigrant Mexicans, especially Latin America people, with the issue of the legality or illegality." As stated by a police chief from New Jersey:

> **Where I see it is [when] people come to council meetings and talk about [undesirable] people out in front of their homes or hanging out in a public park in a particular neighborhood. My question is, well, how do you define who is undesirable? And essentially what it comes down to when you cut through the veneer of the issue is there are people in front of their homes and in the parks who speak a different language, have different customs, and then also engage in some problematic behavior.**

Some participants expressed concern that racial tensions were going beyond mere pressure to control immigration into potentially violent and threatening behavior from a public safety perspective. In his conference keynote address (see appendix J), Phoenix Mayor Phil Gordon reported that public protests over immigration are a regular occurrence in Arizona and participants are sometimes armed with knives and guns, thereby requiring a strong police presence to ensure that demonstrations do not spin out of control and turn violent. He displayed a protester's sign with a swastika at the bottom that stated: "Hooray for the slaughtering of the illegals. Boo to the Beaners!!"

Phoenix Mayor Phil Gordon shows conferees an anti-immigrant sign, which says, "Hooray for the slaughtering of the illegals. Boo to the Beaners!!".

Mayor Gordon also reported an incident in which a United States Marine, in full uniform, was harassed, insulted, and called a traitor by a group of protestors, who shouted at the marine, "It's too bad you didn't die in the war; you're a disgrace to your uniform. Go back to your own country." Mayor Gordon added:

> **Well, this American hero of Hispanic heritage is in his own country. He fought for this country. These stories have nothing to do with green cards. They have everything to do with brown skin. They were about racism and nothing else.**

Mayor Gordon also warned that if the federal government fails to reform the immigration system, communities in the interior of the country would begin to experience the racial tension they do on the border. In fact, communities throughout the nation are already experiencing a rise in hate crimes. Recently in Patchogue, New York, for instance, an Ecuadorian man was murdered by a group of teenagers looking for Latino immigrants to beat up (Macropoulos 2008). At the conference, a representative of the National Council of La Raza, Clarissa Martinez De Castro, stated that in recent years the organization has observed a rise in anti-immigration groups with direct links to hate groups.

Perceptions of Immigrant Criminality

Despite considerable empirical evidence to the contrary, much of the public believes that immigrants are more prone to engage in criminal behavior than the native-born population, which many project participants contended influenced the debate on the role of police in immigration enforcement. Seventy-three percent of respondents to the 2000 General Social Survey believed that immigration is causally related to more crime (Rumbaut 2008, 119). Stereotypes of immigrant criminality are enforced through the media, in particular coverage of singular criminal events involving immigrant perpetrators (Rumbaut 2008, 119). Several focus group participants provided examples of singular criminal events or actors resulting in community pressure on local police to "do something about the immigration issue." For example, a Dallas-Fort Worth Metroplex chief gave the example of a drug-trafficking cartel setting up base in his city, and the public's outrage that immigration had brought this problem to their community.

Several studies, however, have demonstrated evidence contrary to this perspective (Rumbaut 2008, Butcher and Piehl 2007, Nadler 2008). Rubén Rumbaut, professor of sociology at the University of California at Irvine, presented findings from his research on immigrants and crime at the national conference (see appendix D). He argued that empirical evidence has consistently refuted the popular myth that influxes of immigrants lead to increases in crime. Since the early 1990s, over the same time period as legal and especially illegal immigration was reaching and surpassing historic highs, crime rates have *declined*, both nationally and most notably in cities and regions of high immigrant concentration (including cities with large numbers of undocumented immigrants such as Los Angeles and border cities like San Diego and El Paso, as well as New York, Chicago, and Miami). The FBI Uniform Crime Reports showed a decline in both violent and property crime during the era of mass migration of the 1990s. Data from the National Crime Victimization Survey showed even more significant decreases in violent crime during this period of time (Rumbaut 2008).

This period of time also coincided with an era of mass incarceration; the number of incarcerated adults in U.S. federal or state prisons quadrupled from 500,000 in 1980 to over 2.2 million in 2006. The incarcerated population is composed of mostly young men from ethnic minority groups, who are low-wage workers and have low levels of education. These characteristics are also common among the immigrant population in the United States, in particular the undocumented population; and thus logic would suggest that immigrants would have higher incarceration rates. To the contrary, Rumbaut's analysis of incarceration rates of males between the age of eighteen and thirty-nine who were in federal or state prisons at the time of the 2000 U.S. Census showed lowest rates of incarceration for the foreign-born population. The incarceration rate for the U.S.-born population (3.51 percent) was five times the rate of the foreign-born (.68 percent). The foreign-born incarceration rate was less than half the incarceration rate for non-Hispanic Whites (1.71 percent). Rumbaut's research also points out that in the state of California, which has higher overall incarceration rates than the rest of the country (4.5 versus 3.4 percent) and the largest percentage foreign-born population, the foreign-born incarceration rates are lower than they are nationally (.4 to 1.0 percent) (Rumbaut 2008). A study of the Americas Majority Foundation disaggregated data by states, finding that from 1999 to 2006 the total crime rate declined 13.6 percent in the nineteen highest immigration states as compared to a 7.1 percent decline in the other thirty-two states (Nadler 2008, 9).

Although deeply rooted in American public opinion and sustained by media anecdote and popular myth, the perception that the foreign-born, especially "illegal aliens," are responsible for higher crime rates is not supported empirically, according to research by Professor Rubén Rumbaut and others.

Further evidence was presented at the national conference by Mayor John Cook of El Paso, who pointed out that El Paso—with its large immigrant population and proximity to the border—has been named the second safest city with 500,000 or more people in the United States.

Economic Costs and Benefits of Migration

One of the arguments put forth by proponents of immigration enforcement is that immigration, and in particular undocumented immigration, places financial burdens on government services because undocumented immigrants do not pay their fair share of taxes. In Collier County, Florida, participants cited the costs of undocumented immigration to include the drains to school budgets to support bilingual education, emergency medical costs for undocumented who are uninsured, and law enforcement costs. One participant stated that because the vast majority of undocumented he arrests do not have social security numbers, he assumed they did not pay taxes.

Professor Stephen Legomsky presented an overview of undocumented immigration and Professor Raquel Aldana discussed civil liberties concerns that arise from local law enforcement's involvement in immigration enforcement.

At the conference, Professor Stephen Legomsky of Washington University School of Law, in his overview of the current debate surrounding immigration, argued that, to the contrary, studies show that a majority of undocumented immigrants do pay income taxes, although they pay a below-average amount because of their relatively low incomes. He explained they can pay taxes using either a false social security number or under an individual tax identification card.

A tax attorney who was a participant in the Topeka focus group confirmed that he often prepares tax returns for undocumented immigrants without social security numbers. Additionally, the U.S. Social Security Administration has estimated that three quarters of undocumented immigrants pay payroll taxes, and that they contribute six to seven billion dollars in social security funds that they will be unable to claim (Capps and Fix 2005; Porter 2005).

Experts have also argued that undocumented immigrants pay the same real estate taxes—whether as homeowners or through their rent payments—and the same sales and other consumption taxes as everyone else (Immigration Policy Center 2007). Most state and local services, such as schooling, are paid through these taxes.

A study by the Americas Majority Foundation showed that regions with high resident population growth and high inflows of immigrants tend to have high levels of growth in gross state product, personal income, per capita personal income, disposable income, per capita disposable income, median household income, and median per capita income. By 2006, high immigrant jurisdictions also had lower rates of unemployment, individual poverty, and total crime than other states (Nadler 2008, 7-9).

Political Pressure

Conference and focus group law enforcement participants spoke openly about the political pressures that politicians and communities place on local police to enforce immigration law. Some participants attributed the rise in this political pressure in part to the media's sensationalized coverage of immigration issues. Other commentators have noted that conservative media's coverage of immigration and its ability to connect with the public's frustration on the issue have been particularly influential in pushing for stronger enforcement policies (Rodriguez, Chishti, and Nortman 2007, 2).

A study conducted by a media watchdog organization of three conservative news programs, Lou Dobbs Tonight, The O'Reilly Factor, and Glenn Beck, showed that during 2007 the allegation that undocumented immigrants drain social services and/or do not pay taxes was discussed on seventy-one episodes of Lou Dobbs Tonight, thirteen episodes of Glenn Beck, and eight episodes of The O'Reilly Factor. Dobbs and Beck have also repeatedly discussed two myths—that there are plans to construct a NAFTA superhighway running from Mexico to Canada, and there are plans to join Mexico, Canada, and the U.S. into a North American Union. Dobbs discussed the North American Union on fifty-six separate programs during the past two years (Media Matters Action Network 2008).

Media pressure and the public's frustration with the federal government's inability to control unauthorized immigration have led to elected officials placing pressure on their police chiefs to

> **Media pressure and the public's frustration with the federal government's inability to control unauthorized immigration have led to elected officials placing pressure on their police chiefs to enforce federal immigration law.**

enforce federal immigration law. Law enforcement participants noted that while some of these politicians are merely responding to the political pressures they are facing from the public and media, others cynically use the immigration issue to gain votes. One participant recounted an incident in which a local politician in his community "was quoted in the media as saying that we should sit at the border and shoot the illegal immigrants as they come across the border." Another participating police chief noted:

> **Immigration was not such a big problem until the last national election . . . when the Republicans were worried about losing control of Congress. Then, all of a sudden, we have this big problem and we need to fix it and they were thinking, where are we going to find the people to do it because we do not have the people in the federal government. Oh, we will get state and local law enforcement involved.**

Another law enforcement participant in the Arlington, Texas, focus group explained:

> **In my city and in other cities around here, [people] are getting elected and unelected on this issue alone. It's that big . . . So people at the municipal level are running scared on this issue and are just trying to find their way, regardless of what their personal beliefs are . . . You have to figure out how far you are willing to go and what you are willing to get fired for on this issue.**

Seventy-four percent of participants responding to the conference survey (Amendola et al. 2008) stated that they are facing changing expectations and new demands as a result of the immigration issue, and forty-four percent stated that they are responding to political pressure in their communities as a result of the immigration issue. While few law enforcement agencies represented in the focus groups and conference were in favor of entering agreements with federal immigration officials to deputize their officers to perform immigration enforcement functions, many explained that they have increased collaboration with DHS in recent years because of the politics surrounding the immigration issue. For instance, one Texas police chief explained that his agency has had a policy of asking detainees their citizenship status since 1991 to ensure compliance with consular notification requirements. If they would encounter someone who they believed was illegally present in the United States, they would on an ad hoc basis check the NCIC database for possible detainers. Occasionally, they would find a detainer and contact immigration officials. More recently, because there has been so much focus on the department's immigration policy, they formalized the process of questioning persons arrested and detained in the jail about whether they are U.S citizens or were born in the U.S.; if the detainee answers "no" to either question, they check the NCIC database. In sum, it seems as if many police departments have begun to formalize their processes of checking status of arrestees due to political pressure and media attention being paid to the immigration issue.

Since the terrorist attacks of September 11, 2001, the federal government has made use of immigration law as a tool to identify or investigate suspected terrorists.

A survey of police chiefs in large and medium-sized jurisdictions (60,000 residents or more), conducted by researchers at Arizona State University (ASU) and presented at the conference, provides some insight into the reasoning behind the political pressure police are under to engage in civil immigration enforcement and why they are more resistant than many of their communities and politicians to engage in immigration enforcement. The survey found that on the question of immigration enforcement, there was a difference of opinion between community members and police, with police executives more frequently responding that immigration was a controversial topic within their community versus within the department. The survey also found that, according to police executives, community members are more likely than police to believe that it is simple to determine a person's immigration status. Finally, chiefs also reported that gaining the trust of unauthorized immigrants is a much greater priority for their department than for their community (Decker, Lewis, Provine, and Varsanyi 2008) (see appendix G).

Professors Scott Decker, Doris Marie Provine, Paul Lewis, and Monica Varsanyi present findings from their national survey of law enforcement executives on immigration and local policing.

Counterterrorism

Prior to September 11, 2001, economic and social concerns were driving the debate about unauthorized immigration. After the terrorist attacks, however, with immigration law becoming a tool in the fight against terrorism, those who had long opposed rising levels of immigration from Latin America reframed their arguments in terms of the counterterrorism and national security objectives (Harris 2006, 19).

Since the terrorist attacks of September 11, 2001, the federal government has made use of

Clarissa Martínez De Castro, National Council of La Raza, and Kareem Shora, American-Arab Anti-Discrimination Committee, discuss the community impact of local immigration enforcement.

immigration law as a tool to identify or investigate suspected terrorists. Because violations of civil immigration law are not criminal, the government does not have to respect the same constitutional protections they would for a criminal defendant and thus can detain suspects while seeking removal, without any proof of involvement in terrorist activities. However, according to Kareem Shora, national director of the American-Arab Anti-Discrimination Committee, who presented at the conference, federal counterterrorism programs using immigration tools have in practice become just another tool in immigration law enforcement of noncriminal members of particular nationalities (see appendix L).

Do Local and State Police Have Legal Authority to Enforce Federal Immigration Law?

While the proposition that Congress has exclusive authority to regulate immigration is uncontroverted, courts have had few opportunities to address the authority of state and local officials in the realm of immigration enforcement (Venbrux 2006, 312-313). Many legal experts believe that federal immigration law preempts local police from engaging in immigration enforcement (Rodriguez, Chishti, and Nortman 2007, 34-35). While Congress has never explicitly prohibited state or local involvement in federal immigration enforcement, these experts contend that where Congress demonstrates intent to preempt a field of legislation, state and local governments may be preempted from acting on this area of legislation (Appleseed 2008, 12). These experts argue that Congress's express delegation of authority to state and local officials to enforce immigration law under a narrow set of circumstances implicitly preempt state and local enforcement of immigration violations (civil and criminal) that fall outside this narrow scope (Rodriguez, Chishti, and Nortman 2007, 35).

Congress has expressly authorized state and local police to arrest for violations of certain criminal violations of the Immigration and Nationality Act (INA). Specifically, they can make arrests for the federal immigration crimes of smuggling, transporting, or harboring illegal immigrants (§ 274 of the INA) and illegal reentry after a final order of removal (§ 276 of the INA) (Aldana 2008, 92). Congress has also authorized federal immigration officials to deputize state and local law enforcement in the event of a mass influx of immigrants (§ 103 of the INA) Aldana 2008, 92). As stated earlier, in the AEDPA of 1996 Congress authorized state and local law enforcement to arrest and detain an individual who is illegally present in the United States and has been previously convicted of a felony and deported or left the United States after such conviction (§ 8 U.S.C. § 1252c) (Seghetti, Viña, and Ester 2004). Finally, the 1996 IIRIRA reforms amended the INA to include section 287(g) that gave the legacy INS authority to

Whether or not local police have inherent authority under federal law to enforce immigration laws, they must still abide by state laws regarding the scope of their arrest authority.

enter into formal agreements with state and local law enforcement agencies to train and deputize some of their officers to perform immigration enforcement functions (Rodriguez, Chishti, and Nortman 2007, 34). Given these statutory provisions, legal experts have argued that state and local activity that extends beyond the scope of these narrow express delegations of authority are likely preempted (Rodrigez, Chishti, and Nortman 2007, 34-35). Courts, however, have diverged on the question of whether state and local authorities have inherent authority to arrest apart from these express grants of authority (Seghetti, Viña, and Ester 2004, 9-13).[4] But even the attorney general, who in his 2002 legal opinion reversing the long-standing opinion of the federal government that civil immigration enforcement was solely a federal function, argued that local police's inherent authority to arrest is limited to a narrow set of circumstances. According to the attorney general's public statement in 2002:

> **When federal, state and local law enforcement officers encounter an alien of national security concern who has been listed on the NCIC for violating immigration law, federal law permits them to arrest that person and transfer him to the custody of the INS. The Justice Department's Office of Legal Counsel has concluded that this narrow, limited mission that we are asking state and local police to undertake voluntarily—arresting aliens who have violated criminal provisions of the Immigration and Nationality Act or civil provisions that render an alien deportable, and who are listed on the NCIC—is within the inherent authority of states (Seghetti, Viña, and Ester 2004, 8).**

Much of the police activity in the realm of immigration enforcement occurs in the course of routine policing duties, rather than in the course of patrolling for immigration violators. Under such circumstances, police typically stop or arrest an individual upon suspicion of violation of a state law, and thus they do not need to rely on inherent authority to arrest or detain for violations of immigration law (Aldana 2008, 93). It is important to note, however, that such inquiries must not prolong the duration of detention beyond that necessary for criminal law enforcement purposes (unless the federal government places a detainer on the detainee), and individuals have the right to refuse to answer police questions and to request an attorney (Rodriguez, Chishti, and Nortman 2007, 36).

Whether or not local police have inherent authority under federal law to enforce immigration laws, they must still abide by state laws regarding the scope of their arrest authority. For this reason, many state attorneys general have issued legal memoranda on the issue of the authority of police working within their state to make arrests for immigration violations. The New York attorney general, for example, opined that state law on warrantless arrests would apply to the realm of federal immigration enforcement, which requires that criminal immigration offenses occur in the presence of the officer in order to make a warrantless arrest. The New York attorney general also stated that police in New York State do not have authority to arrest for purely civil violations. The

Ohio attorney general concluded that Ohio sheriff offices may arrest and detain someone for violation of criminal provisions of federal immigration law but not for purely civil violations, based on an interpretation of state law defining the general powers and duties of a county sheriff. South Carolina's attorney general concluded that state law authorizes law enforcement officers to enforce state criminal laws, and thus no inherent authority to enforce immigration law exists in the state of South Carolina. (Aldana 2008, 94).

Is Immigration Enforcement a Federal or Local Responsibility? The Local Police Perspective

While there is clearly a significant difference of opinion among this nation's approximately 18,000 law enforcement agencies regarding whether state and local police share responsibility for immigration enforcement, a majority of police chiefs seem to regard immigration enforcement as the responsibility of the federal government.

The ASU study found that 72 percent of police chiefs surveyed stated immigration enforcement was a responsibility of the federal government (Decker et al. 2008, 175). Some policing experts believe that strains on local policing budgets, particularly as homeland security responsibilities have increased and as state and local budgets have shrunk, have contributed to this opposition (Harris 2006, 7). But much of the opposition is due to a shift in the policing field in the past fifteen to twenty years towards more community- or problem-oriented policing, which requires the cooperation and participation of communities in ensuring public safety (Harris 2006, 7). While the number of 287(g) agreements has increased in recent years, the number (sixty-three) (ICE Fact Sheet: 287(g)) is still very small compared with the total number of law enforcement agencies in the country (nearly 18,000). Most police chiefs believe that local police activity in the realm of immigration enforcement would make communities less safe (Harris 2006, 37).

The majority of respondents to the conference survey felt that local law enforcement should not even be partially responsible for enforcement of immigration laws (54 percent), whereas 24 percent said they should. The remaining 22 percent neither agreed nor disagreed that local law enforcement had at least partial responsibility. However, the majority (62 percent) of law enforcement leaders believed that officers should ask for documentation of citizenship status when in contact with those who break the law (including those violating traffic laws). Only 17 percent agreed they should do so when in contact with crime witnesses, and even fewer (15 percent) when in contact with crime victims. While 13 percent of respondents felt such decisions should be at the discretion of officers, just 7 percent said that officers should *never* ask for proof of citizenship (Amendola et al. 2008).

The Various Ways in Which Local Law Enforcement and Federal Immigration Officials Collaborate

Most conversations and dialogues on the role of state and local police in immigration enforcement during the focus groups, at the conference, and in the media have focused on ICE's 287(g) program of deputizing local and state police to perform immigration enforcement functions. However, as we learned from project participants, state and local police collaborate with federal immigration officials in a wide range of activities. Some of these activities only incidentally involve immigration enforcement, while having a principally criminal law enforcement purpose (such as joint anti-gang task forces), while other methods of collaboration involve local and state officials performing in the role of immigration enforcement agents (such as the 287(g) program). Some agencies collaborate with federal immigration officials in a formal program,

FIGURE 4. PERCENTAGE OF POLICE DEPARTMENTS THAT TYPICALLY CHECK IMMIGRATION STATUS AND/OR CONTACT ICE WHEN ENCOUNTERING POSSIBLE UNAUTHORIZED IMMIGRANTS IN THESE SITUATIONS

Source: *Immigration and Local Policing: Results from a National Survey of Law Enforcement Executives* (Decker et al. 2008). Presentation prepared for Police Foundation conference, The Role of Local Police: Striking a Balance Between Immigration Enforcement and Civil Liberties, Washington, DC, August 22, 2008 (see appendix G).

whereas others collaborate more informally and in a more ad hoc manner.

The most common forms of collaboration take place in the regular course of criminal law enforcement. Either on a formal or informal basis, most agencies participating in the Police Foundation project check the status of individuals arrested and detained for a criminal law offense and inform ICE when they encounter noncitizens. Feedback at the conference suggests that this form of collaboration has always existed to some extent but not in such a systematic or formalized manner as in recent years. Participants cited political pressure as the reason behind the trend towards formalization of the process of verification of immigration status of criminal detainees. They also stated that this political pressure sometimes is sparked by media attention on cases where unauthorized immigrants have committed serious crimes after being released upon a prior arrest.

The ASU survey of police executives found that the more serious the violation of criminal law, the more likely responding agencies were to contact ICE regarding criminal detainees in violation of immigration law (see figure 4). Thus, for instance, only slightly more than 20 percent of respondent agencies check immigration status of traffic violators, whereas over 80 percent check immigration status of those arrested for a violent crime.

Only state and local agencies that participate in the 287(g) program have direct access to DHS immigration databases. However, non-participating state and local law enforcement officials can contact the LESC to query its databases to check the status of an arrestee. In the El Paso law enforcement focus group, one small police agency with few resources mentioned it has on occasion also called U.S. Customs and Border Protection (CBP) to run a check on an arrestee or detainee because the agency does not have access to criminal justice databases and needs to confirm identity. This has on occasion resulted in deportation. In addition, as described above in the section describing the history of local law enforcement's role in immigration, many law enforcement officers do not make an affirmative decision to cooperate with federal immigration efforts but end up doing so as a result of running a check on criminal detainees in the FBI's NCIC database.

Some law enforcement agencies, such as the Phoenix Police Department, have chosen to embed ICE officers within the police department, rather than have the local police be responsible for verification of immigration status and other immigration enforcement functions. At the conference, Mayor Gordon of Phoenix contended that in terms of cost and effectiveness, this model of collaboration makes more sense than turning police officers into immigration agents. Many departments, such as the Houston Police Department, have also collaborated with ICE on interagency task forces, such as the Houston Police Department's collaboration with ICE and other federal agencies on an anti-gang task force. The federal government has also signed on state and local police in various joint operations, such as the Absconder Apprehension Initiative, in which local police assist DHS in identifying and arresting individuals with outstanding removal orders (Seghetti, Viña, and Ester 2004, 3).

DHS also collaborates with state and local law enforcement to address criminal activity associated with border security. Some of the participants in the El Paso focus group discussed DHS's Border Enforcement Security Task Force initiative (BEST), whose mission is to disrupt criminal organizations posing threats to border security. Operation Community Shield, an ICE anti-transnational gang initiative, also sometimes engages local police in joint operations (ICE Fact Sheet: Operation Community Shield).

Finally, the most intensive immigration enforcement role for state and local law enforcement occurs as part of the ICE 287(g) program. As discussed above, this section authorizes DHS to enter into formal agreements with state and local law enforcement agencies to deputize local and state officers to perform immigration law enforcement functions, under the supervision of sworn ICE officers. Each agency that enters the 287(g) program must sign a memorandum of agreement (MOA) that defines the scope and limitations of the authority designated to the local or state officers. These agreements also must articulate a supervisory and monitoring structure for the program. Section 287(g) also requires that state and local officers are trained in the enforcement of immigration laws (ICE Fact Sheet: 287(g)).

Not until after September 11, 2001, did any state or local agency sign a 287(g) agreement with the federal government. In 2002, the Florida State Police became the first 287(g) partner (Capps 2008, 156) (see appendix F). Florida described the intent behind the agreement as to "address the counter-terrorism and domestic security needs of the nation and the state of Florida by enhancing those efforts through the authorization of selected state and local law enforcement officers ... to perform certain functions of an immigration officer." In 2003, the Florida MOA eliminated the emphasis on counterterrorism in favor of greater emphasis on general domestic security (Appleseed 2008, 23).

In 2003, the state of Alabama followed Florida, and then there were a half dozen more agreements signed in 2005 and 2006 in Arizona, California, and North Carolina. The number of local and state agencies joining the 287(g) program started to increase more rapidly in 2007 when twenty-six law enforcement agencies signed MOAs, and during the first seven months of 2008 when twenty-eight more agencies entered agreements with ICE (Capps 2008, 156). Currently, there are sixty-three local and state law enforcement agencies participating in the 287(g) program. The program has identified more than 70,000 people suspected of violating immigration law and trained more than 840 officers (ICE Fact Sheet: 287(g)).

Geographically, agencies that have chosen to join the 287(g) program seem to be disproportionately located in regions with large immigrant populations or are emerging gateways that have recently begun seeing large influxes of immigrants. Forty-one out of sixty-two programs (as of August 2008) were located in the twenty-two new immigrant destination states (see figure 5).

FIGURE 5. 1990-2000 IMMIGRATION GROWTH PATTERNS AND LOCATION OF 287(G) PROGRAMS ACROSS THE STATES

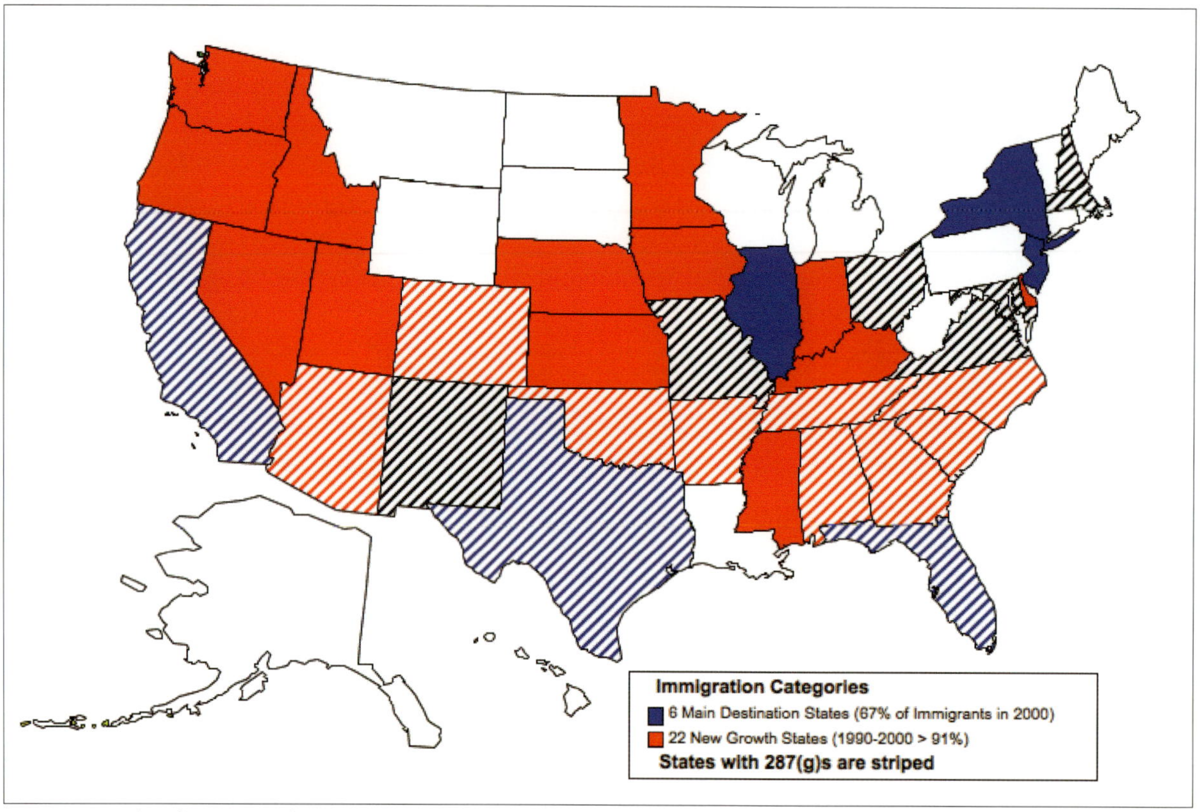

Source: *Local Enforcement of Immigration Laws: Evolution of the 287(g) Program and Its Potential Impacts on Local Communities.* Randolph Capps, The Urban Institute. Presentation prepared for Police Foundation conference, The Role of Local Police: Striking a Balance Between Immigration Enforcement and Civil Liberties, Washington, DC, August 21, 2008 (see appendix F).

These new growth states tend to also have large unauthorized immigrant populations, high numbers of Latin American immigrants, and fewer citizens. In August 2008, thirty-seven of the 287(g) participating agencies were located in the Southeastern part of the United States, eighteen in the Southwest, five in the Northeast, and two in the Midwest (Capps 2008, 160).

The 287(g) program has two categories of agreements or classes of trained officers, Jail Enforcement Officers (JEO) and Task Force Officers (TFO). JEOs are trained solely to verify legal status of detainees in local jails, whereas TFOs can verify legal status of persons encountered in their regular policing duties and can participate with ICE in joint enforcement operations. As of August 2008, there were twenty-three law enforcement agencies with Task Force agreements, twenty-seven with Jail Enforcement agreements, and twelve with joint Task Force/Jail Enforcement agreements (Capps 2008, 159).

Conference presenter Raquel Aldana, a University of Nevada Professor of Law, reviewed thirty-four of fifty-five 287(g) agreements. Aldana found that the agreements varied in nature and scope. Some granted a broad range of powers to local officers, while others were more restrictive (see appendix C for descriptions of these powers) (Aldana 2008, 95).

Forty-six percent of respondents to the ASU survey reported that their local government had no official policy on immigration enforcement, while 12 percent reported that their local government expects that the police take a proactive role in immigration enforcement. Four percent of respondents reported that they had an agreement with ICE for local police officers to investigate and arrest immigration law violators and three percent had jail-based 287(g) programs. Eight percent reported that they had ICE officers embedded within one or more units of the police department. Only 4 percent of chiefs reported that their local governments have openly declared themselves as "sanctuary cities" for unauthorized migrants who are not engaged in criminal activities, while another 15 percent report that their cities unofficially operate under a "don't ask-don't tell" policy (Decker et al. 2008).

State and Local Law Enforcement of Immigration Law: Benefits and Costs

During the conference and the focus groups, there was a healthy level of debate over the role of local law enforcement in enforcing federal immigration law. Law enforcement participants, community members, elected officials, and researchers presented varying arguments on the benefits and costs associated with immigration enforcement. The great majority of comments made during the focus groups and at the conference opposed local law enforcement's participation in purely civil immigration enforcement. However, some participants in the Collier County focus group and at the conference also articulated some of the benefits of state and local law enforcement sharing responsibility with the federal government for immigration enforcement. Below we describe the main arguments for and against local participation in federal immigration enforcement that were raised during project activities.

Sheriff Don Hunter discusses his agency's participation as a 287(g) partner.

Benefits

1. Reduce Jail Population and Save Detention Costs

Sheriff Don Hunter of Collier County, Florida, stated that Collier County decided to participate in the 287(g) program as part of their overall strategy to reduce jail crowding. The sheriff's office had conducted a study of its jail population and found that 25 percent were removable aliens. Twenty-seven officers from the sheriff's office were trained to identify, arrest, and detain immigration law violators. As a result, Sheriff Hunter argued, the jail population had dropped 14 percent between July 2007 and July 2008 (the program did not begin until October 2007) (see appendix K). It is not clear if there were other factors contributing to the decline in jail population.

2. Deterrent to Unauthorized Immigration

One argument mentioned during the focus groups in favor of local participation in federal immigration efforts, in particular the 287(g) program, is that communities where agencies participate in the program receive a lot of media attention as places where unauthorized immigration is not tolerated. This reputation, they argue, could serve as a deterrent to unauthorized immigrants settling in the area and/or could lead to unauthorized immigrants moving out of these regions. But as one Collier County focus group participant pointed out, this deterrent effect would merely displace unauthorized immigrants from a pro-enforcement community to one in which the police and local government do not engage in immigration enforcement. For this reason, the participant argued, there is a need for a nationally consistent policy or approach.

Another project participant, who favored local participation in immigration enforcement, stated that the size of the undocumented population in the United States is simply too large for federal law enforcement agencies to manage; therefore, without the assistance of state and local police, the federal government will never be able to solve its undocumented immigration problem. One law enforcement conference participant challenged this argument, stating, "If you have people who are undocumented but are good, law-abiding, contributing citizens, I'm not sure all the negative impacts of this issue are worth removing a law-abiding person. There are other ways to work with federal agents than to use 287(g) to arrest otherwise good citizens."

3. Criminal Enforcement Tool

Proponents of local police participation in immigration enforcement, such as some of the Collier County focus group participants, argue that immigration enforcement, and in particular the 287(g) program, could serve as a criminal enforcement tool. A Collier County participant argued that when sophisticated criminals successfully evade criminal prosecution, an agency could use immigration enforcement as a tool to rid that community of the individual if he or she is unauthorized to be present in the United States. James Pendergraph, executive director of ICE's Office of State and Local Coordination, also asserted that deportation of a person who has previously committed a crime would reduce overall crime rates. Conference survey participants were also asked to describe the advantages and disadvantages of local participation in immigration enforcement; merely nine stated that it would help fight crime (Amendola et al. 2008).

4. Counterterrorism

Proponents of increased immigration enforcement, such as Kris Kobach, former counsel to Attorney General John Ashcroft, have argued that because several of the September 11 terrorist attackers had overstayed their visas without significant interference from federal or local law enforcement, the abuse of U.S. immigration laws was responsible for the deaths resulting from those attacks (Olivas 2007, 47). Others have criticized this argument, stating that the real failure, as pointed out by the bipartisan 9/11 Commission, was the failure of the federal government's various intelligence offices to collaborate and to take seriously radical Islamic movements following the earlier bombing of the World Trade Center in New York (Olivas 2007, 50).

These proponents argue that increased local immigration enforcement may identify individuals suspected of engaging in terrorist activities. For instance, in the course of routine policing, police may encounter an immigrant with an individual warrant in the NCIC database, and who may have plans at some point to engage in terrorist activities. However, as stated by Kareem Shora during his presentation at the national conference, a local department's participation in immigration enforcement efforts may result in isolating communities, making them less willing to provide intelligence to police on possible terrorist and other criminal activity (see appendix L).

5. Access to Federal Databases to Verify Identity

Some participants who favored local police immigration enforcement argued that participation in the 287(g) program has the advantage of giving local agencies access to federal databases to verify identity of suspects. One participant claimed that undocumented immigrants often give false names but that through the use of federal immigration databases it might be possible to accurately identify a suspect. As James Pendergraph noted, an agency has access to the various federal immigration databases only if it is a 287(g) partner. However, a non-participating agency can always contact the LESC if it needs additional information, and ICE is currently piloting an integration of the NCIC database with federal immigration databases so that when an agency runs a check on NCIC, it automatically searches federal immigration databases as well (Carroll 2008).

Policing experts and project participants have expressed concern that local police involvement in immigration enforcement could have a chilling effect on immigrant cooperation.

6. Immigration Violators are Lawbreakers

A common argument heard in the media and mentioned during project conversations is that, like criminal law violators, those individuals who have violated federal immigration law are lawbreakers. Some participants argued that police are bound to enforce federal immigration laws just as they are violations of criminal law and cannot pick and choose which laws to enforce. Conference participants engaged in lively discussion about whether police have discretion to choose which laws to enforce. While some argued police have no discretion, others disagreed, maintaining that police everyday make choices about which laws to enforce. Furthermore, some pointed out, police officers take an oath to uphold state not federal law.

Costs

1. Reduced Trust and Cooperation in Immigrant Communities Would Undermine Public Safety

Policing experts and project participants have expressed concern that local police involvement in immigration enforcement could have a chilling effect on immigrant cooperation. Immigrant witnesses and victims of crime, many of whom already bring with them fear and mistrust of police due to experiences with authorities in their home countries, would be less likely to report crimes and cooperate as witnesses. Without this cooperation, law enforcement will have difficulty apprehending and successfully prosecuting criminals, thereby reducing overall public safety for the larger community. Immigrants need assurances that they will not be subject to deportation proceedings if they cooperate with police.

To demonstrate the fragility of the relationship between the police and immigrants, one midwestern police chief recounted an incident where an unauthorized immigrant was a witness to a crime and agreed to testify in a criminal case. The witness's name appeared on a witness list in preparation for the trial. As the court began to vet the background of this witness, defense attorneys revealed that he was an undocumented alien. A few days after the witness testified in the court case, ICE arrested him and initiated deportation proceedings. Word of this incident rapidly spread throughout the immigrant community and, as a result, the police have had difficulty securing the cooperation of other immigrant witnesses. Even residents who were victimized and exploited feared approaching the police because trust between the immigrant community and the police had been destroyed.

El Paso focus group participants and Mayor John Cook in his conference presentation also reported a similar experience. Years earlier, the El Paso Police Department had a practice of conducting joint patrol operations with CBP in El Paso City. They later discontinued this practice because the joint operations had a chilling effect on immigrant communities. In particular, in the context of domestic violence, they found a troubling decrease in reports.

Mayor John Cook of El Paso, where the population is over 80% Hispanic and there are 8.3 million pedestrian border crossings annually between the U.S. and Juarez, Mexico.

The Police Foundation has done much of the research that led to a new view of policing—one emphasizing a *community* orientation—that is widely embraced today, and has played a principal role in the development of community policing research, training, and technical assistance. Over the past fifteen to twenty years, community policing and problem-solving policing initiatives—a philosophy of policing that requires significant collaboration and cooperation with community members—have become increasingly commonplace in the policing profession (Harris 2006, 7). Community policing is an approach to policing where police officers engage communities in a working partnership to reduce crime and promote public safety. It thus requires police to interact with neighborhood residents in a manner that will build trust and improve the level of cooperation with the police department (Moore 1992, 123). Proponents of community policing have expressed concern that policies and practices that sanction police officers to act as immigration agents will undo the successes they have gained over years of developing police relations with immigrant communities (Appleseed 2008, 8). As pressure for local police to proactively get involved with immigration enforcement increases, the public safety gains achieved through the community-policing movement are placed in jeopardy, particularly in communities and cities with significant immigrant populations.

The majority of respondents to the conference survey indicated that aggressive enforcement of immigration law would have a negative impact on community relationships by decreasing (1) community trust of the police (74 percent), (2) trust between community residents (70 percent), and (3) reporting of both crime victimization (85 percent) and criminal activity (83 percent). Adding to those concerns are beliefs that aggressive enforcement of immigration laws would weaken (1) public trust initiatives (77 percent), (2) community-policing efforts (77 percent), (3) youth outreach (74 percent), (4) intelligence/information gathering (63 percent), (5) criminal investigations (67 percent), and (6) even recruitment (31 percent), thereby impacting operations significantly (Amendola et al. 2008).

Project participants expressed concerns that the loss of trust and cooperation would not be limited to undocumented immigrants. Eighty-five percent of immigrant families are mixed-status families, families with a combination of citizens, undocumented immigrants, and documented immigrants (Morawetz and Das 2008, 73). The loss of cooperation resulting from local police involvement in immigration enforcement would extend to authorized immigrants living in mixed-status households who fear contact with police would lead to deportation of family members and other loved ones (Harris 2006, 39). A recent Pew Hispanic Center survey found that the majority of Latinos in the United States worry about deportation of themselves, a family member, or a close relative (Lopez and Minushkin 2008, ii).

2. Increased Victimization and Exploitation of Undocumented Immigrants

Many law enforcement participants also emphasized their duty as police executives to ensure public safety for all community members, regardless of legal status, and expressed their concerns that criminal predators take advantage of undocumented immigrants' fear and tendency not to report crimes. As one northeastern city police chief stated:

> **They [undocumented immigrants] refer to themselves as walking ATMs because everybody knows that they don't have documentation enough to get bank accounts, checking accounts, and those kinds of things, and that their savings and whatever they have is on their person, not anywhere else. First of all, they live in an apartment with eight other people, so you can't leave it behind. They carry it with them and the people who seek to victimize them take advantage of that.**

Fifty-three percent of respondents to the ASU survey stated that undocumented immigrants are more likely to be victims of theft or robbery (Decker et al. 2008). Similarly, respondents to the conference survey were asked whether undocumented immigrants were likely or unlikely to be crime perpetrators and crime victims. As figure 6 shows, respondents believed that undocumented immigrants were more likely to be crime victims (81 percent) than crime perpetrators (39 percent) (Amendola et al. 2008).

Any police actions that result in exacerbating fear of police in immigrant communities could lead to increased victimization and exploitation of immigrants as perpetrators of crime take advantage of heightened immigrant fear to target them for criminal activity. At least one El Paso focus group participant believed that more enforcement would specifically lead to more human trafficking, as smugglers or traffickers are more able to use the threat of deportation to coerce undocumented immigrants into situations of forced labor. Several participants also believed there would be an aggravation of employer abuse and exploitation of undocumented immigrants.

FIGURE 6. LIKELIHOOD OF CRIME PERPETRATION AND VICTIMIZATION

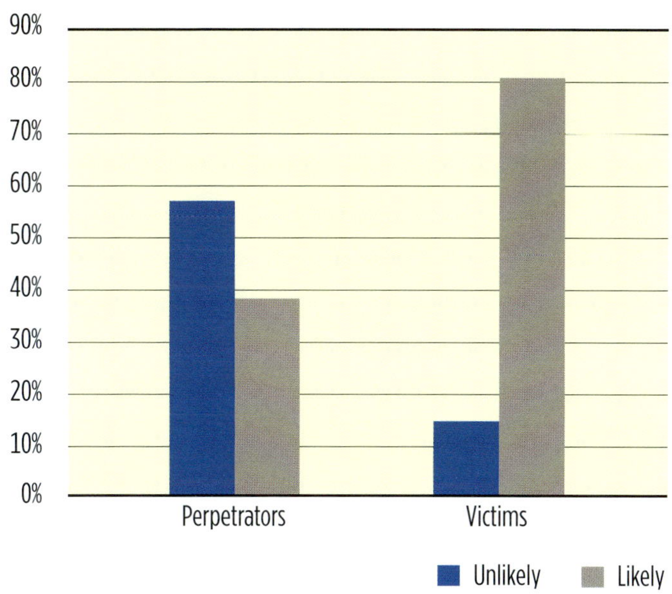

Source: *Law Enforcement Executive Views: Results from the Conference Survey* (Amendola et al. 2008) (see appendix H).

Participants' perceptions of immigrant victimization were confirmed by research conducted in Memphis, Tennessee, on victimization of undocumented immigrants and their interaction with police. The study found that undocumented workers experienced high rates of victimization, yet they were unlikely to report the crimes to law enforcement officials. The study also found perceived deportation risk to be a factor driving both undocumented workers' particular risk of victimization and their reluctance to report crimes. Memphis is a city that reports interactions with undocumented victims and perpetrators to immigration officials (Bucher, Tarasawa, and Manasse 2007).

3. Police Misconduct

For similar reasons that immigration enforcement by local police could lead to increased victimization and exploitation of undocumented immigrants (fear of police and deportation), some participants expressed concern that it could lead to an increase in police misconduct. As one El Paso focus group law enforcement executive stated, "I might have issues out in the field with officers who are doing things they're not supposed to be doing, but people are afraid to tell us, simply because they're afraid." At the conference, Professor Raquel Aldana also argued that the extremely limited application of the exclusionary remedy in immigration court proceedings creates an additional risk of abuses of power not subject to judicial review and oversight (Aldana 2008, 99). In another project that brought together police officials from the New York/New Jersey metropolitan area, one police official working in a jurisdiction that in the past collaborated with federal immigration officials confirmed that his agency's prior involvement in immigration enforcement had indeed led to corruption and extortion (King 2006, 25).

4. Large Financial Costs of Immigration Enforcement Divert Resources from Traditional Law Enforcement Activities

In recent years, police departments throughout the country have experienced budget cuts because of the diversion of federal funds from traditional law enforcement funding streams, such as the Office of Community Oriented Police Services (COPS) and Bureau of Justice Assistance (BJA) Byrne grants, to homeland security programs, while simultaneously their workloads have increased as a result of current homeland security and counterterrorism responsibilities (Harris 2006, 12). In addition to having to take on additional counterterrorism responsibilities, local law enforcement has to make up for reductions in federal law enforcement manpower that was previously devoted to federal criminal enforcement, such as drug trafficking and bank robbery (MCC 2006, 6). In this fiscal environment, local law enforcement simply does not have the resources to add immigration enforcement responsibilities (MCC 2006, 10). As one participant stated, "Law enforcement is struggling just to keep up with the things [we] need to do every day. So taking on an additional responsibility is probably impossible."

Federal immigration enforcement agencies contend they do not have adequate resources to accomplish their immigration enforcement mandate. Local agencies have even fewer resources given all their competing demands (MCC 2006, 6). Moreover, focus group participants warned that were the federal government to change its current practice and begin funding local agencies to collaborate in immigration enforcement, those resources should not come at the expense of traditional crime fighting resources, such as what little is left in the COPS and BJA Byrne grant funding streams.

Indeed, respondents to the conference survey ranked resources as their highest agency concern, followed by staffing. Immigration ranked merely seven after the concerns listed above (see table 1) (Amendola et

TABLE 1. HIGHEST RANKED AGENCY CONCERNS

In general, what do you consider to be the most critical issues facing you and your agency? Please list them in priority order, from highest to lowest.

1. Resources
2. Staffing
3. Violent Crime
4. Gangs
5. Community Relations; Drugs (tie)
6. Property Crime
7. Immigration Issues

Rankings were based on a weighted scoring system. Those ranked first were given a score of 5, second scored 4, third scored 3, and so forth.

Source: *Law Enforcement Executive Views: Results from the Conference Survey* (Amendola et al. 2008) (see appendix H).

Federal immigration law is very complicated, technical, and constantly changing.

al. 2008). One of the biggest concerns discussed in policing today—as confirmed by the choice of staffing as the second most urgent agency concern—is the challenge of police officer recruitment (Raymond, Hickman, Miller, and Wong 2005). Therefore, even if the federal government provided financial resources for local immigration enforcement, many police agencies would have difficulty hiring quality police recruits to meet the additional workload demands of enforcing immigration law.

Because of the resource issues above, opponents of local law enforcement participation in federal immigration enforcement contend that there could be a diversion of police resources away from criminal investigations to immigration enforcement (Seghetti, Viña, and Ester 2004, 25). Financial costs listed by conference and focus group participants included the patrol resources and overtime costs resultant from arresting and processing immigration detainees, costs of providing temporary detention space, transportation costs, and potential medical costs incurred during detention. This diversion of resources, participants argued, could have a negative public safety impact. Mayor Gordon gave the example of the immigration enforcement initiatives of the Maricopa County Sheriff's Office being responsible for its failure to investigate at least thirty violent crimes, including a dozen sexual assaults, in the past year in a small city of 32,000 people. "He [sheriff of Maricopa County] allows sexual assaults, homicides, and other serious crimes to go unsolved, by arresting victims and witnesses and sending them to jail for violating immigration statutes. That's a direction that makes our community less safe."

5. Complexity of Federal Immigration Law and Difficulty in Verifying Immigration Status

One of the arguments articulated against local participation in federal immigration enforcement is that federal immigration law is very complicated, technical, and constantly changing. Indeed, it has often been compared to the tax code in complexity (Harris 2006, 36). A conference participant who supports local enforcement of immigration law argued that police are used to enforcing all types of laws and that immigration would be no different. However, IACP has stated that immigration enforcement would require specialized knowledge of "suspect's status and visa history and the complex civil and criminal aspects of the federal immigration law and their administration. This is different from identifying someone suspected of the type of criminal behavior that local officers are trained to detect" (IACP 2004, 4). MCCA has also said that immigration law is very complicated and nothing like criminal violations, such as murder, assaults, narcotics, robberies, burglaries, and so forth (MCC 2006, 7). If police departments employ insufficiently trained officers to perform federal immigration enforcement duties, they may also risk exposing themselves to substantial civil liability (Venbrux 2006, 330).

At the conference, Nancy Morawetz, New York University Professor of Clinical Law, presented a paper that describes in detail some of the complexities of immigration law enforcement and reveals the challenges to local police participation in immigration enforcement activities (see appendix B). Professor Morawetz begins by challenging the assumption that the immigration status of an individual is easy to identify. Firstly, she points out that approximately 70 percent of the foreign born in the United States are legal permanent residents or citizens. Of the remaining 30 percent, substantial numbers have some form of lawful status or are in the process of obtaining lawful status. About 300,000 of these immigrants have temporary protected status (TPS), which allows them to live and work in the United States; and 617,000 are in the process of applying for legal permanent residency and have official permission to work. Every year, approximately one million people receive legal permanent resident status. In addition, there are millions of people each year who are present in the United States with a lawful business, visitor, or student visa. The challenge this creates for police engaging in immigration enforcement is that there are no distinguishable factors that allow police to distinguish between the authorized and unauthorized immigrant population.

Professor Nancy Morawetz describes the legal complexity of local law enforcement's role in immigration enforcement and legal constraints on methods of enforcement in a legal and institutional system that operates quite differently from local criminal justice systems.

Furthermore, Professor Morawetz notes that police will have difficulty verifying immigration status because many people do not have the necessary documentation to prove their lawful status, in part because immigration documents were not designed to function as identity documents. Thirteen million U.S. citizens lack papers proving they are citizens, permanent residency card ("green card") renewals are frequently delayed, and there is no national database of citizens and the status of other people.

Both Professors Morawetz and Aldana also observed that federal immigration databases are notoriously inaccurate; thus, police reliance on these databases will most likely lead to error. The DHS Inspector General estimates that the immigration records relied upon by ICE's fugitive teams are inaccurate in up to 50 percent of cases (Morawetz and Das 2008, 82). DHS also commissioned a study of Social Security Administration (SSA) databases and found that they were able to verify employment eligibility in less than 50 percent of work-authorized noncitizens (Aldana 2008, 101). The SSA itself has estimated that 17.8 million of its records contain errors with respect to name, date of birth, and citizenship status; and that 4.8 million of 46.5 million noncitizen records in its database contain errors (Aldana 2008, 101). A mismatch between employee records when checked against the SSA databases can turn into an immigration administrative warrant (Aldana 2008, 101). Immigration warrants and information contained in the NCIC database have also proven to be inaccurate. A study by the Migration Policy Institute of calls to the LESC showed that 42 percent of all police inquiries to the LESC were false positives that DHS was unable to confirm (Gladstein et al. 2005, 3).

6. Racial Profiling and Other Civil Litigation Costs

Because local law enforcement agencies lack sufficient and ongoing training in federal immigration law, are prohibited from racial profiling, lack clear authority to enforce civil immigration laws, and are limited by state law on making warrantless arrests, those police agencies that get involved in civil immigration law enforcement risk being subject to civil litigation (MCC 2006, 8). Prohibitions on racial profiling and state laws limiting the scope of police authority exist to protect community members from being victim to police error or abuse. Were these laws to be violated in the context of immigration enforcement, and given the complexity of federal immigration law, it is likely that citizens and immigrants with lawful status would be arrested and detained. These errors are then likely to result in litigation.

Prohibitions on racial profiling and state laws limiting the scope of police authority exist to protect community members from being victim to police error or abuse.

Indeed, there have been several lawsuits where citizens or legal permanent residents have been arrested, detained, and in some cases deported. For instance, Pedro Guzman, a cognitively-impaired U.S. citizen who had been arrested and detained in a Los Angeles County jail for misdemeanor charges, has sued the sheriff of Los Angeles County who erroneously identified Mr. Guzman as an unauthorized immigrant and turned him over to federal immigration officials who later deported him to Mexico. It took months for Mr. Guzman's family to locate him after he was deported to Mexico (Morawetz and Das 2008, 78).

The likelihood of error in the context of immigration enforcement is higher for poor and minority communities. A recent study showed that citizens with incomes under twenty-five thousand dollars are twice as likely to lack citizenship documents as those earning more than twenty-five thousand dollars. Twenty-five percent of African Americans lack any form of government-issued photo identification. As many as thirty-two million American women do not have citizenship documents reflecting their current name. And, as stated above, there is no national database of citizens to verify status (Morawetz and Das 2008, 77).

Even well-intentioned police officers risk racial profiling and resultant lawsuits in the course of enforcing immigration laws. As stated above, there are no discernible indicators of immigration status; thus, it is difficult for police officers to observe behavior that indicates immigration status as they would be able to observe criminal activity. As a result, police officers may use ethnic or racial characteristics as a basis for stopping and questioning, and possibly detaining, people from certain racial and ethnic groups (Chishti 2002, 374). The practice of using race or ethnic characteristics to determine whether to investigate immigration status also wastes valuable law enforcement resources. The number of erroneous stops or detentions resulting from false positives will be particularly high in regions with high Hispanic and Asian populations (Harris 2006, 51). Furthermore, many communities of color already have strained relations with police, which will be further exacerbated as they feel targeted by immigration enforcement efforts (Appleseed 2008, 10). A recent survey of Hispanic residents in the United States found that nearly one out of ten Hispanic adults (native-born 8 percent and immigrants 10 percent) have been stopped and questioned about their immigration status in the past year (Lopez and Minushkin 2008, i). Thus, it seems the trend towards greater participation by local law enforcement in federal immigration enforcement has already begun to impact the Hispanic community.

Professor Morawetz emphasized during her conference presentation that 287(g) agreements contain language clarifying that officers are bound by federal civil rights statutes and regulations and specifically prohibit the practice of racial profiling. The 287(g) agreements are also narrowed to authorize behavior only to the extent that it is consistent with state and local law (Morawetz and Das 2008, 76). Some state and local law enforcement officials participating in the project were under the impression that the federal government would assume liability under the Federal Tort Claims Act (FTCA) . However, because 287(g) limits police behavior as described above, local agencies will not be protected or covered by the agreement where they have violated federal civil rights statutes, state or local law, or engaged in racial profiling in the course of immigration enforcement (Morawetz and Das 2008, 76).

Several major lawsuits have already been filed alleging racial profiling by police departments engaging in immigration enforcement. For instance, residents, alleging racial profiling among other violations, sued the Chandler, Arizona, Police Department as a result of a joint operation with CBP. Complainants alleged that police officers were stopping and questioning dark-skinned, Spanish-speaking residents (who appeared "Mexican") and requesting proof of citizenship (Venbrux 2006, 327-328). In addition to costing the city money as a result of the lawsuits, the police department created deep distrust in the Latino community, harming its ability to effectively police the city.

Sheriff Joe Arpaio of the Maricopa County, Arizona, Sheriff's Office (an ICE 287(g) partner) has faced several lawsuits, the allegations of which include racial profiling (Aldana 2008, 105). Mayor Gordon commented during his conference remarks that the sheriff, himself, says he can identify an unauthorized immigrant "by the way they dress and where they are coming from." As Mayor Gordon stated, that is "the very definition of racial profiling." Mayor Gordon further explained that sheriff's deputies are stopping citizens in Maricopa County because they are brown and detaining them, even when they have documentation proving their legal status. Even a member of Mayor Gordon's staff and her husband, who are third-generation Latino citizens, were stopped and asked for their social security cards by Maricopa sheriff deputies.

7. Immigrants Will Fear Accessing Other Municipal Services

The increased fear of deportation resulting from local law enforcement participation in immigration enforcement will not only impact police-community relations with immigrant communities but might also lead to fear among immigrant communities of accessing other state and local government services. Several focus group participants who worked for city agencies discussed the difficulty they already have encouraging immigrants to access municipal services. In a paper presented at the conference, Professor Roberto Gonzales of the University of Washington discusses the impact of immigration enforcement efforts on schools, including increased absences and students distracted by their anxiety over deportation (Gonzales 2008, 142) (see appendix E).

Striking a Balance Between Immigration Enforcement and Civil Liberties: Recommendations

The goal of the Police Foundation project was to begin a dialogue among police executives and professionals, scholars, public policy and community groups over the role of local law enforcement in federal immigration law enforcement, in order to improve law enforcement's understanding of the issue and to begin to develop some consensus on how to strike the balance between the competing federal need of immigration enforcement with local public safety priorities and civil liberties. As stated earlier in the About the Project section, the foundation conducted a series of focus groups throughout the country with police executives, local government officials, and community members; convened a national conference of leaders in the policing, public policy, academic, and immigrant communities; commissioned academic papers on pertinent topics; and conducted a written survey of police executives. Throughout this process, there was a healthy level of dialogue and disagreement about specific questions and issues. However, it also became clear that certain recommendations and policy positions were widely held among the group. In this section of the report, we describe some of these positions and recommendations.

Almost all project participants agreed that agencies should not be patrolling for immigration violators and that immigration enforcement activity should be limited to contacts incidental to a lawful arrest for a state criminal law violation.

The Costs of the 287(g) Program Outweigh the Benefits

As outlined earlier, the majority of police executives participating in the project did not see the benefits to local agencies of participating in the 287(g) program. They felt that the 287(g) program created substantial additional work for local agencies to fulfill a federal mandate for which they would not receive any compensation or funding and, therefore, would divert resources from traditional law enforcement functions. Because of the complexity of immigration law, they would have to invest significant labor hours and resources to provide and update training on developments in immigration law. They also were concerned that public safety would suffer because of destroyed trust and cooperation with immigrant communities. Participation in the 287(g) program, or at least the media coverage and fear generated by it, would undermine years of community-policing efforts, which in turn would compromise public safety. Finally, police leaders were concerned about racial profiling and litigation costs: if state and local law enforcement officers engage in racial profiling, violate federal civil rights laws, or violate state and local law defining the scope of police authority, 287(g) agreements will not protect them from liability.

Police Officers Should be Prohibited from Arresting and Detaining Persons to Solely Investigate Immigration Status in the Absence of Probable Cause of an Independent Crime

Almost all project participants agreed that, at the very least, local law enforcement agencies should not be patrolling for immigration violators and that immigration enforcement activity should be limited to contacts incidental to a lawful arrest for a state criminal law violation. Even under the best of circumstances, many participants expressed the concern that the use of racial profiling is almost inevitable where local police patrol for immigration violations. One police chief from Arizona stated that in many parts of the country, particularly Arizona, race is being used as a predictor of criminal behavior, which violates the equal protection clause of the Constitution. He explained that citizens and legal residents are being targeted by local immigration enforcement efforts because of the color of their skin. Many participants contended that there are no objective, visibly discernible factors indicating immigration status. "You cannot see immigration status," one participant stated. Therefore, Chief Harold Hurtt of Houston contended that were local law enforcement to begin engaging in civil immigration enforcement activities, they would have to ask everyone they stop for proof of citizenship. For example, he stated, the Caucasian wife of a member of the chamber of commerce is pulled over for a traffic violation and is without proof of citizenship. The police officer would have to ask her about her citizenship status and, in the absence of such proof, arrest and detain her. "Imagine," Chief Hurtt said, "the community outrage you would get then."

Chief Harold Hurtt describes the Houston Police Department's policy of focusing on the criminal nexus in immigration enforcement.

If a Local Agency Enters the 287(g) Program, it Should Limit Participation to Serious Criminal Offenders and Jail-Based Programs

Many participants believed that if state and local law enforcement agencies were to enter a 287(g) agreement with the federal government, it should be limited to jail-based programs and that the delegated immigration enforcement powers should be selectively used to target serious felony offenders. One former INS official mentioned that, in response to political pressure to deport more unauthorized immigrants and the lack of available federal resources to do so, federal immigration officials designed the 287(g) program initially with the intent to focus on jails and prisons.

Implement Policies and Procedures for Monitoring and Enforcing Racial Profiling Violations

Because of grave concerns about racial profiling, in particular in jurisdictions operating 287(g) programs in the patrol context (versus solely in the jail), it is important that both local agencies themselves and the federal government implement policies and procedures for monitoring and enforcing civil rights violations. While 287(g) agreements contain provisions prohibiting racial profiling, comments at the conference seem to suggest that the federal government has not been effectively policing compliance with these provisions of the 287(g) agreements. Indeed, Mayor Gordon of Phoenix stated that he had written a complaint letter to the U.S. Department of Justice's Civil Rights Division arguing that the Maricopa County Sheriff's Office has been using racially-biased enforcement practices, but the mayor stated that the federal government had not yet taken any steps towards investigating the allegations. Participants recommended that agencies engaging in immigration enforcement activities need to put into place their own racial profiling and civil rights violation self-monitoring policies and practices to prevent potential abuses of immigrant rights.

Involve Community Members in Developing Immigration Policies

Local law enforcement agencies depend on the trust and cooperation of immigrant communities to effectively police these communities. In order to preserve this trust that they built over the years by aggressively engaging in community-oriented policing trust-building activities, state and local law enforcement agencies should open lines of communication with immigrant communities to establish collaborative partnerships for public safety and crime control purposes and to obtain input from the immigrant community on the impact of police department policies. Police departments should regularly meet with representatives of immigrant communities to educate them about their immigration policies, obtain their perspectives on immigration enforcement and other issues involving immigrant communities, and to monitor impact of their efforts. As a result of efforts by the Houston Police Department to educate the immigrant community on the content and purpose of department policies and the rationale necessitating changes, a more aggressive posture in the enforcement of immigration laws adopted by the department had no discernible negative effects on police-community relations.

> **Whether or not a local agency is involved in immigration enforcement, it is important that it make efforts to build trust with immigrant communities and ease tensions between different communities.**

Evaluation Research Should be Conducted of the 287(g) Program and Other Local Immigration Enforcement Initiatives

Several participants suggested that there was very little research and empirical evidence of the costs and benefits of the different forms of local law enforcement collaboration in federal immigration enforcement efforts. As a result, we are asked to rely on subjective perspectives of law enforcement executives and politicians who may be influenced by a need to support their own policies. There is a great need for evaluation research of these programs, their outcomes, and their impact. Some research questions suggested by program participants included (1) who conducts the immigration status inquiry, (2) who is being arrested and detained, (3) who is being questioned but released, (4) is there any racially disparate impact, (5) how often is error occurring, (6) how often do civil rights violations occur, (7) what happens to those agencies that violate 287(g) agreements, and (8) how many people are being jailed and deported because of these efforts.

Employ Community-Policing and Problem-Solving Tactics to Improve Police-Community Relations with Immigrant Communities and Resolve Tension Caused by Expanding Immigration

Whether or not a local agency is involved in immigration enforcement, it is important that it make efforts to build trust with immigrant communities and ease tensions between different communities. Rapidly changing demographics, tougher enforcement of immigration laws, and stricter limitations on the privileges and benefits authorized by the government for undocumented immigrants have created an environment in which increased tension between communities and police exist. In this environment, police-community relations will be impacted regardless of what local policy is. Several participants provided some good examples of strategies that not only improved police-community relations but also diffused local tensions over immigration.

For instance, one northeastern city police executive reported that they were experiencing tensions between communities over concerns attributed to increased immigration. The police department, in response, organized dialogues in various neighborhoods, including representatives of new immigrant communities and established communities. In these dialogues, using problem solving policing techniques, the police department facilitated discussions that led communities and police to jointly work out resolutions to neighborhood problems. In other words, they focused the energy of the group on specific behavioral issues and jointly problem-solved. Overtime, the police executive stated, "We're not yelling. They're not yelling anymore. They know each other's names now. They know the children. They know the teenagers. And we're working at it. And it's not solved. And it probably never will get solved because they're opposing cultures.

We're like a mediator. But it's not a crime problem. It's a community problem and that's how we're dealing with it."

Another police chief from an east coast beach city gave a similar example. They were having trouble with complaints about migrant workers coming to town during weekends, when they get a very large Hispanic population at the beach. These migrants sometimes would hang up hammocks underneath the pier and they would drink and bring their own food, at times creating a trash problem. For years, the police department had received complaints from the business community but since there was no real crime problem, there was little they could do. A few years ago, the department put up signs in Spanish explaining that drinking in public was illegal and could lead to arrest, placed garbage bins along the beach, and added showers to the beach. As a result, the chief explained, "Now we don't have the same complaints we had before. We used problem solving to help overcome some of the complaints that citizens were having."

Most of the conference participating agencies engaged in some form of outreach to immigrant communities. Respondents to the conference survey were asked to describe the strategies they have developed or would develop to engage the immigrant community. The most frequently cited strategies in the forty-five received responses were: organizing and/or attending community meetings, events, and forums (n=19), establishing community outreach programs or using community liaisons (n=17), attempting to educate the community through the media and bilingual pamphlets (n=13), or creating specialized department positions or programs to focus on the immigrant community (n=13) (Amendola et al. 2008).

The Federal Government Must Enact Comprehensive Border Security and Immigration Reforms

One of the most universal recommendations made during the project was for police organizations to urge Congress and the federal government to make a real commitment to comprehensive border security and immigration reform. Participants expressed their frustration with Congress's inability to comprehensively reform the immigration system. They explained that Congress's failure has had severe consequences on cities and towns throughout the country that struggle to deal with the fiscal and administrative challenges of integrating immigrant communities and must figure out how to manage the racial and ethnic tension generated by the presence of an increasingly large population of immigrants.

Mayor Gordon, for instance, stated:

> **I am calling upon this Congress and the next one, this president and the next one, to make the dual issues of border security and immigration reform their first order of national business. I don't believe that certain members of Congress understand...the impact of their neglect...on cities. They don't see the hate. They don't see the division. They don't hear the rhetoric. They don't see the civil rights violations. And they don't understand the costs.**

At the conference, Julie Erfle, the widow of a Phoenix police officer killed by an unauthorized immigrant who had previously been deported, discussed the psychological and social costs of Congress's failure to pass comprehensive immigration reform, not only on law enforcement and their families but also on the undocumented and their families. She, like Mayor Gordon, suggested, "My solution is comprehensive immigration reform....It is time to stop pandering and time to stop talking about the issue and time to start enacting a real policy" (see appendix M).

Conclusion

Julie Erfle, an advocate for comprehensive immigration reform, told conferees, "We need to put compassion and humanity on an equal footing with immigration enforcement."

Immigration issues are some of the most contentiously debated in the United States today. Increasing levels of immigration, the dispersal of immigrants to communities throughout the country that have no experience with immigration, and the federal government's failure to secure the borders and comprehensively reform the immigration system have created tensions between communities in regions throughout the country and the resultant pressure on state and local law enforcement to control unauthorized immigration. As one police chief stated, "Once again we [police] are found to be in between. In fact, much of the civil unrest in this country goes back to some conflict that erupted in one of our communities across this country, where police were at the fulcrum." During conversations throughout the project, we repeatedly heard law enforcement officials discuss the pressure they are feeling to take sides in the immigration debate.

One of the ultimate goals of the foundation project was to give police a voice on this critical issue. And, indeed, during much of the national conference, participants openly and passionately discussed a range of issues relating to the role of local police in federal immigration enforcement: from the legal rights of the unauthorized immigrant population; to empirical evidence and research conducted on the demographic characteristics of the population, immigrant criminality, the experience of the undocumented, and the impact of immigration enforcement programs; to the diverse perspectives of law enforcement executives and community leaders on the issue. The conversations were always lively but respectful and they included specificity, empirical evidence, and detail often absent in national conversations about immigration enforcement.

Ultimately, however, the conversations at the conference always came back to the core role of local police and core principles of community policing. One police chief quoted the police officer's oath of office: "To support and defend the Constitution of the United States and to be faithful and bear true allegiance to state laws, and to the best of our skill and judgment diligently and faithfully without prejudice or partiality execute the office of the police officer." As this chief and many other law enforcement executives stated, police have a duty to uphold state and local laws but must do so while respecting and protecting the Constitution. This includes the equal protection clause, which prohibits racially discriminatory enforcement practices. In fact, great concern was expressed throughout the conference about the impact on the Latino community, in particular, and the risks of racial profiling where local law enforcement becomes involved in immigration

Coatesville, PA, Chief of Police William Matthews moderates the open forum on the final day of the conference.

As one police chief asked,
"How do you police a community
that will not talk to you?"

enforcement. Moreover, the participants generally agreed that their duty as a police executive is to provide public safety to *all* residents in their community, whether documented or undocumented. One police chief stated, "We need to draw the line and stand for justice and civil liberties. This has to be done by the police because others will not do it. It goes back to our oath of office to uphold the Constitution and justice."

Many police executives, particularly those working in communities with significant immigrant populations, also expressed concern that police participation in immigration enforcement efforts has threatened to undo years of community oriented policing efforts to build trust with immigrant communities. Police participants discussed the difficulties they have gaining the trust and cooperation of immigrant communities because of fears of deportation and imported distrust and perceptions of police from their home country. Participants felt that they needed the support of these communities in order to effectively provide public safety. As one police chief asked, "How do you police a community that will not talk to you?" For this reason, one of the core recommendations discussed in this report is that law enforcement agencies engage communities in the process of developing immigration policies and educate them about agency policy and practices. By inviting communities to participate in the process of generating policies, agencies can make great headway towards striking a balance between immigration concerns, civil liberties, and maintaining public safety.

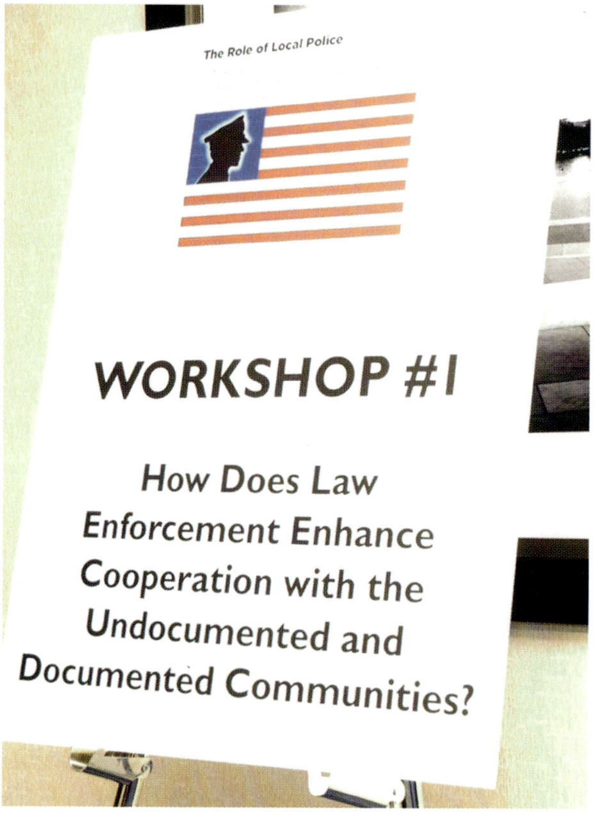

Endnotes

[1] The terms "immigrant" and "foreign-born" are used interchangeably throughout the report to describe individuals who were not born in the United States, including unauthorized immigrants, legal permanent residents, and naturalized citizens.

[2] The Bureau of Justice Assistance of the U.S. Department of Justice administers the State Criminal Alien Assistance Program (SCAAP), in conjunction with the Bureaus of Immigration and Customs Enforcement and Citizenship and Immigration Services, Department of Homeland Security (DHS). SCAAP provides federal payments to states and localities that incurred correctional officer salary costs for incarcerating undocumented criminal aliens with at least one felony or two misdemeanor convictions for violations of state or local law and incarcerated for at least four consecutive days during the reporting period. In 1995, Congress appropriated $130,000,000 to the program, Public Law 104-208 accessed at http://www.lib.umich.edu/govdocs/text/104208.txt. SCAAP awards totaled $377,323,723 in 2007, $287,143,095 in 2005, $281,605,292 in 2004, $239,999,996 in 2003, and $545,090,055 in 2002. Accessed at http://www.ojp.usdoj.gov/BJA/grant/scaap_site.html. Totals not posted for 2000, 2001, and 2006.

[3] In 2005 alone, LESC responded to 676,502 inquiries by state and local law enforcement officials (Aldana 2008).

[4] Citing *Gonzalez v. City of Peoria*, 722 F.2d 468 (9th Cir. 1983) (Court held that local police have authority to arrest for criminal provisions of INA but no inherent authority to arrest for civil violations.); *United States v. Vasquez-Alvarez*, 176 F.3d 1294 (10th Cir. 1999) (Court held state and local law enforcement officers have the general authority to investigate and make arrests for federal immigration law. Case premised on Oklahoma law allowing local officers to make arrests for violations of federal law.); and *United States v. Santana-Garcia*, 264 F.3d 1188 (10th Cir. 2001) (Court held local law enforcement had authority to investigate and make arrests for violations of immigration law, relying partially on Utah statute defining scope of authority of peace officers.).

References

Alba, Richard, Rubén Rumbaut, and Karen Marotz. 2005. "A Distorted Nation: Perceptions of Racial/Ethnic Group Size and Attitudes toward Immigrants and Other Minorities." *Social Forces* 84: 901-919.

Aldana, Raquel. 2008. "Making Civil Rights Matter in Local Immigration Enforcement." Paper presented at the Police Foundation conference, The Role of Local Police: Striking a Balance Between Immigration Enforcement and Civil Liberties, Washington, DC, August 21-22, 2008.

Amendola, Karen L., Kristin N. Williams, Edwin E. Hamilton, and Veronica Puryear. 2008. "Law Enforcement Executive Views: Results from the Conference Survey." Survey from the Police Foundation conference, The Role of Local Police: Striking a Balance Between Immigration Enforcement and Civil Liberties, Washington, DC, August 21-22, 2008.

Appleseed. 2008. "Forcing Our Blues into Gray Areas: Local Police and Federal Immigration Enforcement." Appleseed: Washington, DC. http://neappleseed.org/docs/local_police_and_immigration_enforcement.pdf.

Bucher, Jacob, Beth Tarasawa, and Michelle Manasse. 2007. "Hidden Victims: An Examination of Crimes Against Illegal Immigrants." Paper presented at the annual meeting of the American Society of Criminology, Atlanta, Georgia, November 14.

Butcher, Kristin F. and Anne Morrison Piehl. 2007. "Why are Immigrants' Incarceration Rates So Low? Evidence on Selective Immigration, Deterrence, and Deportation." NBER Working Paper No. 13229. National Bureau of Economic Research: Cambridge, MA, July. http://www.nber.org/papers/w13229.

Capps, Randolph. 2008. "Local Enforcement of Immigration Laws: Evolution of the 287(g) Program and Its Potential Impacts on Local Communities." 2008. Paper presented at the Police Foundation conference, The Role of Local Police: Striking a Balance Between Immigration Enforcement and Civil Liberties, Washington, DC, August 21-22, 2008.

Capps, Randolph and Michael E. Fix. 2005. "Undocumented Immigrants: Myths and Reality." Urban Institute: Washington, DC, November 1. http://urban.org/publications/900898.html.

Carroll, Susan. 2008. "Harris County Jailers Can Access Huge Immigration Database." *Houston Chronicle*, October 27.

Chishti, Muzaffar. 2002. "The Role of States in U.S. Immigration Policy." *NYU Annual Survey of American Law* 58: 371-376.

Chishti, Muzaffar. 2006. "Enforcing Immigration Rules: Making the Right Choices." *NYU Journal of Legislation and Public Policy* 10: 451-471.

Decker, Scott H., Paul G. Lewis, Doris Marie Provine, and Monica W. Varsanyi. 2008. "Immigration and Local Policing: Results from a National Survey of Law Enforcement Executives." Paper presented at the Police Foundation conference, The Role of Local Police: Striking a Balance Between Immigration Enforcement and Civil Liberties, Washington, DC, August 21-22, 2008.

Gladstein, Hannah, Annie Lai, Jennifer Wagner, and Michael Wishnie. 2005. "Blurring the Lines: A Profile of State and Local Police Enforcement of Immigration Law Using the National Crime Information Center Database, 2002-2004." Migration Policy Institute: Washington, DC, December. http://www.migrationpolicy.org/pubs/MPI_report_Blurring_the_Lines_120805.pdf.

Gonzales, Roberto G. 2008. "Why Integration Matters: The Case of Undocumented Immigrant Youth and Moving Beyond Enforcement." Paper presented at the Police Foundation conference, The Role of Local Police: Striking a Balance Between Immigration Enforcement and Civil Liberties, Washington, DC, August 21-22, 2008.

Gordon, Phil. 2008. Keynote address at the Police Foundation conference, The Role of Local Police: Striking a Balance Between Immigration Enforcement and Civil Liberties, Washington, DC, August 21-22, 2008.

Harris, David A. 2006. "The War on Terror, Local Police, and Immigration Enforcement: A Curious Tale of Police Power in Post-9/11 America." *Rutgers Law Journal* 38: 1-60.

Immigration Policy Center (IPC). 2007. "Undocumented Immigrants as Taxpayers." Immigration Policy Center: Washington, DC, November 29. http://immigration. server263.com/images/File/factcheck/ Undocumented%20as%20 Taxpayer%2011-29-07.pdf.

International Association of Chiefs of Police (IACP). 2004. "Enforcing Immigration Law: The Role of State, Tribal, and Local Law Enforcement." International Association of Chiefs of Police: Alexandria, VA. http://www.theiacp.org/Portals/0/pdfs/Publications/ImmigrationEnforcementconf.pdf.

Kalhan, Anil. 2008. "Immigration Enforcement and Federalism After September 11, 2001." In *Immigration, Integration, and Security: America and Europe in Comparative Perspective*, edited by Arianne Chebel d'Appollonia and Simon Reich. Pittsburgh: University of Pittsburgh Press. http://papers.ssrn.com/sol3/papers.cfm?abstract_id=1145666#.

King, Martha, ed. 2006. *Justice and Safety in America's Immigrant Communities*. Policy Research Institute for the Region, Woodrow Wilson School of Public and International Affairs. Princeton University: Princeton, NJ.

Lopez, Mark Hugo and Susan Minushkin. 2008. "2008 National Survey of Latinos: Hispanics See Their Situation in U.S. Deteriorating; Oppose Key Immigration Enforcement Measures." Pew Hispanic Center: Washington, DC, September 18. http://pewhispanic.org/reports/report.php?ReportID=93.

Macropoulos, Angela. 2008. "In Mourning an Immigrant, a Call for Unity on Long Island." *The New York Times*, November 15. NY/Region section.

Major Cities Chiefs Association. 2006. *MCC Immigration Committee Recommendations for the Enforcement of Immigration Laws by Local Police Agencies*, June. http://www.majorcitieschiefs. org/pdfpublic/mcc_position_statement_revised_cef.pdf

Media Matters Action Network Report. 2008. "Fear & Loathing in Prime Time: Immigration Myths and Cable News," May 21. http://mediamattersaction.org/reports/fearandloathing/online_version.

Moore, Mark H. 1992. "Problem-Solving and Community Policing." In *Modern Policing*, edited by Michael Tonry and Norval Morris, 99-158. Chicago: University of Chicago Press.

Morawetz, Nancy and Alina Das. 2008. "Legal Issues in Local Police Enforcement of Federal Immigration Law." Paper presented at the Police Foundation conference, The Role of Local Police: Striking a Balance Between Immigration Enforcement and Civil Liberties, Washington, DC, August 21-22, 2008.

Nadler, Richard. 2008. "Immigration and the Wealth of States." Americas Majority Foundation: Overland Park, KS, January. http://www.amermaj.com/ImmigrationandWealth.pdf.

Olivas, Michael. 2007. "Immigration-Related State and Local Ordinances: Preemption, Prejudice, and the Proper Role for Enforcement." *University of Chicago Legal Forum* 27-56.

Passel, Jeffrey. 2008. "Unauthorized immigrants: Trends, characteristics, and surprises." Presentation at the Police Foundation conference, The Role of Local Police: Striking a Balance Between Immigration Enforcement and Civil Liberties, Washington, DC, August 21-22, 2008.

Passel, Jeffrey and D'Vera Cohn. 2008. "Trends in Unauthorized Immigration: Undocumented Inflow Now Trails Legal Inflow." Pew Hispanic Center: Washington, DC, October 2. https://pewhispanic.org/files/reports/94.pdf.

Pham, Huyen. 2005. "The Constitutional Right Not to Cooperate? Local Sovereignty and the Federal Immigration Power." *bepress Legal Series*, Working Paper 771, September 11. http://law.bepress.com/expresso/eps/771.

Porter, Eduardo. 2005. "Illegal Immigrants Are Bolstering Social Security With Billions." *The New York Times*, April 5, Business/Financial Desk.

Raymond, Barbara, Laura J. Hickman, Laura Miller, and Jennifer S. Wong. 2005. "Police Personnel Challenges After September 11: Anticipating Expanded Duties and a Changing Labor Pool." RAND Occasional Paper. RAND Corporation: Santa Monica, CA. http://www.rand.org/pubs/occasional_papers/2005/RAND_OP154.pdf.

Rodriguez, Cristina, Muzaffar Chishti, and Kimberly Nortman. 2007. "Testing the Limits: A Framework for Assessing the Legality of State and Local Immigration Measures." Migration Policy Institute: Washington, DC. http://www.migrationpolicy.org/pubs/NCIIP_Assessing%20the%20Legality%20of%20State%20and%20Local%20Immigration%20Measures121307.pdf.

Rumbaut, Rubén. 2008. "Undocumented Immigration and Rates of Crime and Imprisonment: Popular Myths and Empirical Realities." Paper presented at the Police Foundation conference, The Role of Local Police: Striking a Balance Between Immigration Enforcement and Civil Liberties, Washington, DC, August 21-22, 2008.

Seghetti, Lisa M., Stephen R. Viña, and Karma Ester. 2005. "Enforcing Immigration Law: The Role of State and Local Law Enforcement." Congressional Research Service, updated October 13.

Singer, Audrey. 2004. "The Rise of New Immigrant Gateways." Center on Urban and Metropolitan Policy, The Brookings Institution: Washington, DC, February. http://www.brookings.edu/reports/2004/02demographics_singer.aspx.

Singer, Audrey. 2007. "The Impact of Immigration on States and Localities." Testimony presented before the House Committee on the Judiciary, Subcommittee on Immigration, Citizenship, Refugees, Border Security, and International Law, May 17. http://www.brookings.edu/testimony/2007/0517demographics_singer.aspx.

U.S. Immigration and Customs Enforcement (ICE). 2008. "Delegation of Immigration Authority Section 287(g) Immigration and Nationality Act," last modified November 17. http://www.ice.gov/partners/287g/Section287_g.htm.

U.S. Immigration and Customs Enforcement (ICE). 2008. "Operation Community Shield: Targeting Violent Transnational Street Gangs," last modified November 12. http://www.ice.gov/pi/news/factsheets/opshieldfactsheet.htm.

Venbrux, Greg K. 2006. "Devolution or Evolution? The Increasing Role of the State in Immigration Law Enforcement." *UCLA Journal of International Law and Foreign Affairs* 11.

APPENDICES

APPENDIX A

Focus Group Summary

Table of Contents

APPENDIX A

Focus Group Summary

Introduction

The primary goal of the Police Foundation project, *The Role of Local Police: Striking a Balance Between Immigration Enforcement and Civil Liberties,* was to bring together law enforcement agencies, public officials, and community stakeholders to collaboratively examine one of the most timely and controversial topics in policing today—how local and state police strike the balance between civil liberties and federal immigration enforcement. One of the principal activities the Police Foundation undertook was to host a series of focus groups across the country including representatives of law enforcement, elected officials, and immigrant[1] communities. Focus groups were held in Topeka (KS), El Paso (TX), Arlington (TX), and Collier County (FL). The objective of the focus groups was to elicit the perspectives and insights of those directly impacted by the issues surrounding immigration. As stated by the president of the Police Foundation, Hubert Williams, "It's absolutely critical from our perspective that the people who are most directly affected at the ground level have their voices heard at the policy-making level and have some impact and discussion related to this issue."

The information derived from focus groups is cited at various points in the final project report, was influential in the development of the agenda for the national conference, and is one of the main sources of data upon which the ultimate recommendations proposed were based. Because of the key role played by focus groups, this summary of the conversations is included here as an appendix.

This summary begins with an overview of focus group methodology, followed by a review of general themes raised across all or the majority of sites. Presented next is a description of each of the four focus group sites, including any issues unique to a specific site.

Methodology

In choosing focus group sites, the Police Foundation wanted to include a varied set of law enforcement agencies and geographic locations so that recommendations would reflect the diversity of this nation and the different environments in which law enforcement agencies throughout the country operate. Criteria established for selecting a host agency for each focus group included the police executive's willingness to work with the Police Foundation, the makeup and size of the jurisdiction's immigrant population, and the agency's experience in confronting issues related to serving an immigrant population. Agencies directly involved in litigation were not selected. The local host law enforcement agency was responsible for assisting the Police Foundation in selecting a location that could accommodate focus group discussions.

Two ninety-minute sessions were conducted at each site. Law enforcement executives and officers of varying ranks attended the first session, scheduled from 11:00 a.m. to 1:00 p.m. Policy makers, legislators, community groups, service providers, and community members at large generally attended the second session, held from 6:30 p.m. to 8:30 p.m. The chief executive of the host law enforcement agency or his designee also attended the evening civilian session as an observer. A member of the Police Foundation staff with knowledge of policing and immigration facilitated the sessions. The foundation contracted with a local professional transcriber to record the conversation. As needed, the moderator or a participant interpreted for limited-English proficient participants.

The Police Foundation president and each host law enforcement executive jointly signed a letter of invitation mailed to service providers, policy makers, special interest groups, ad hoc committees, coalitions, and associations. The foundation also requested that host agencies draw from diverse neighborhoods, government departments, and organizations in order to obtain a varied set of viewpoints and experiences at the civilian sessions. Finally, the foundation specifically requested that invitations be sent to representatives of minority groups and others impacted by immigration issues. The designated point of contact invited selected, potential participants telephonically and by a letter drafted by the Police Foundation, which included information about the nature of the meeting but not focus group questions. Names of those confirming their intention to attend were forwarded to the Police Foundation. Once the maximum number of twenty attendees was reached, the process was closed and additional persons were not permitted to attend. The host agency also invited representatives of neighboring law enforcement agencies to attend the morning law enforcement sessions. As a result, thirty-three local and state agencies were represented in the four law enforcement focus groups.

Each civilian and law enforcement session began with an introduction from the host chief and from the president of the Police Foundation, who explained to participants the purpose of the focus group. The facilitator then provided a short briefing on the process and set the ground rules for discussion. The questions asked were open-ended and designed to elicit opinions, experiences, and perspectives from participants regarding the following topics: challenges and opportunities presented serving immigrant communities, agency practices and policies on immigration enforcement and police-immigrant community relations, benefits and costs of local involvement in immigration enforcement, political and economic factors involved with immigration enforcement, constitutional and civil liberty implications, and recommended approaches to striking the balance between immigration enforcement and civil liberties.

General Themes Discussed in Focus Groups

Challenges faced by communities adapting to a changing population

In all sites except El Paso, participants discussed challenges associated with growth in the population, or a shift in the composition, of immigrant communities and the tensions produced by this change. In Arlington, for instance, law enforcement executives mentioned that the Dallas-Fort Worth Metroplex area has seen enormous population increases, which some participants attributed to growth in immigrant communities and "ethnic minorities." In Topeka, where immigration is relatively new and immigrants are still a very small part of the population, participants expressed concern about the resultant budgetary burdens of a large growth in the immigrant population. In Collier County, as well, participants discussed the growth in immigrant population and the resulting fiscal burdens placed on public services.

This growth in immigrant communities produces challenges for immigrants, long-standing residents, and police departments serving them because immigrants bring with them new cultures, languages, and lifestyles. Some participants, both civilian and law enforcement, felt that the introduction of these cultural differences can produce tensions with other communities. As one police executive in the Arlington session stated:

> **I don't think, generally speaking, people are complaining about the fact that someone is here in this country without official legal authorization to be here... All of a sudden their community is becoming more heavily populated with people who**

> **are different from them who enjoy doing things that are unlike what other people in the community have historically done. And so rather than addressing the uneasy feeling about differences among the newcomers, they just cast this label "illegal immigration" over that, and then they want us to enforce immigration laws to get rid of the people who are different from what they are accustomed.**

Arlington and Topeka law enforcement participants also talked about challenges presented by language barriers, in particular that some officers become frustrated when they cannot communicate with witnesses or victims and that Hispanic officers often are overburdened by responding to the language barrier. In El Paso, a participant mentioned that because of language barriers it is difficult for different ethnic communities to communicate, thereby creating challenges to resolving differences or creating mutual understanding.

In all sites except Collier County, many participants believed that attacks against "illegal immigration" are often motivated by racial discrimination. One Arlington participant stated:

> **When the public talks about the open problem with illegal immigration, the focus is really on the Latino community. That same level of concern does not extend to the Asian population. And then I think the perception of the Muslim population is not that they're really illegal immigrants as much as they are terrorists or potential terrorists.**

An El Paso participant stated, "It's been easy for them to hide this whole racism that is happening against the immigrant Mexicans, especially Latin America people, with the issue of the legality or illegality." Topeka participants characterized the current anti-immigrant environment as a continuation of a historical pattern of racism against African Americans in Topeka. This perspective could be due to the composition of the civilian group or the historical significance that the antiracism movement has played in Topeka, the home of *Brown v. Board of Education*.

One police executive from the Dallas-Fort Worth Metroplex provided an anecdote demonstrating that racial discrimination is underlying the immigration debate. The morning of the focus group, he had received a report that a predominantly White neighborhood was incensed that a Puerto Rican family had moved into a home there, out of which they ran a landscaping business. The homeowner employs predominantly Puerto Rican workers who come and go from the home throughout the day. Unaware that the family and their workers are Puerto Rican or that they are U.S. citizens, the community demanded that the police take action towards deporting the family and their workers. A Topeka participant, who works with youth, gave another example indicative of the racial undercurrent to the debate. He was transporting a group of Latino youth to a Hispanic orientation at a college and, while he was standing away from the group, some locals mistook the group of Latino youth for gang members. El Paso was different from other sites in that it has traditionally been a Latino-dominated city and therefore there was less discussion of local racial tension; however, participants felt the national discourse on immigration often stemmed from racist attitudes towards Latinos.

In Collier County, there was no discussion of racism against Latinos or the challenges of integrating new cultures and differences. The participants, however, discussed the financial challenges public agencies face integrating the needs of these new communities and commented on the belief that immigrants often do not contribute proportionately into the system by paying taxes. A law enforcement official mentioned that the majority of arrested immigrants do not have social security numbers, which he assumed meant they were not paying taxes. Other participants explained that when the costs of immigration outweigh tax revenue, it provokes a very emotional response in the community, particularly as the economy takes a downturn. In Topeka, one participant suggested that as state and local budgetary burdens resultant from increased migration rise, the local debate on immigration enforcement might grow more contentious. He believed once Midwesterners "see their emergency rooms close, as they see their school district costs go up 30 percent or 40 percent to deal with bilingual education, and as they see or perceive that they see an increase in crime based on immigrant population, then [their] attitudes [are] going to change too." In El Paso, representatives of several law enforcement agencies talked about the additional law enforcement resources needed to address the challenges produced by the changing dynamics of migration across the southern border. For example, one officer explained that they are encountering more corpses in the desert and that additional police resources are required to deal with these bodies appropriately.

The relation of immigration to crime was discussed in some of the sessions. Many participants spoke of the public's perception that crime problems were caused in part by immigration. A Dallas-Fort Worth Metroplex chief gave the example of a drug-trafficking cartel setting up a base in his city and the resultant public outrage and perception that immigration had brought this problem to their community. The police executive, on the other hand, did not believe there was a connection between immigration and the drug traffickers' decision to set up in his community. There were, however, different viewpoints on the relation of gang activity to immigration. In Collier County, one participant said "immigration exacerbates the gang problem," versus an Arlington participant who said the two issues are not connected. In El Paso, the sentiment was expressed more generally that homegrown American problems are being blamed on Mexico. In Arlington, one police chief stated that he regularly receives complaints about a day labor hiring site in his city where typically twenty to forty "Latino-looking" workers congregate, which community members fear is a threat to public safety.

A couple of participants also attributed some of the tensions mentioned above not only to the growth in immigrant communities but also to the growth in their visibility politically. For instance, some Arlington law enforcement participants felt that large immigrant marches, where thousands of Latinos and other immigrants publicly demonstrated in favor of immigrant rights, exacerbated racial tensions. In addition, a Topeka participant expressed the belief that the relative youth of the Latino community also causes fear and, consequently, racial tension.

The role of politics and media in influencing local immigration enforcement policy

In every site, law enforcement complained that media coverage of the immigration debate and the role of law enforcement is often sensationalized and has exacerbated an already sensitive environment. On both sides of this highly emotional and contentious debate, law enforcement participants felt that media coverage was often inaccurate and that advocates manipulate media coverage to advance their agenda. To demonstrate this position, one Topeka participant recounted the story of an accident that occurred involving a van of undocumented immigrants. The driver of the vehicle had a Mexican driver's license and since the officers had no database to verify the validity of the document, they called Immigration and Customs Enforcement (ICE). ICE advised that it did not have resources available at that moment to respond to the scene and, since no criminal law had been violated, the deputies released the driver and the passengers. Subsequently, the police executive received a lot of criticism in the media about the decision of his officers to release the passengers. On the other side of the immigration debate, a Collier County law enforcement participant related his experience with the media publishing inaccurate stories, namely that the Collier County Sheriff's Office was preparing to initiate immigration sweeps of undocumented immigrant communities, which he felt was an inaccurate portrayal of their 287(g) program. The participant stated that advocates for immigrants used the media to advance their agenda and, in the process, created fear in immigrant communities. In El Paso, one participant also commented that the media coverage of the border after the attacks of September 11 was highly sensationalized and unnecessarily intensified the immigration debate.

This hyped media coverage, combined with the racial tensions resulting from the demographic changes, can generate a lot of political pressure on local police to expand their activities into the immigration enforcement arena. In all but the Collier County focus group, law enforcement participants candidly talked about the pressures they face from politicians to be more aggressively involved in immigration enforcement. It is possible that this topic did not arise in Collier County because many of the participants were themselves elected officials, including three sheriffs. Some police executives also said that often they feel pulled in opposite directions; they need to preserve good police-community relations with a Caucasian majority community that often wants them to enforce immigration law, while simultaneously building trust in a minority immigrant community whose cooperation is essential to maintaining public safety. Some felt that many local politicians are under similar pressures. In fact, one sheriff, who is currently campaigning for reelection, stated that immigration is a big issue raised by constituents. Voters frustrated by the demographic changes in their communities put pressure on local politicians, such as mayors, city council representatives, and county commissioners, and these politicians in turn place pressure on police executives, some of whom were hired by those very same politicians. As one Arlington law enforcement participant stated:

> **In my city and in other cities around here, [people] are getting elected and unelected on this issue alone. It's that big. . . So people at the municipal level are running scared on this issue and are just trying to find their way, regardless of what their personal beliefs are. . . .You got to figure out how far you are willing to go and what you are willing to get fired for on this issue.**

Some law enforcement participants noted that, while some politicians are merely responding to political pressure they feel from the media and the public, other politicians use the immigration debate and emotions surrounding it to win elections. One Arlington participant recounted, in outrage, an incident where a local politician in his community "was quoted in the media as saying that we should sit at the border and shoot the illegal immigrants as they come across the border." Some participants noted that the politics surrounding immigration enforcement do not always reflect overall public sentiment on the issue, because a large proportion of Latinos are either ineligible to vote or do not choose to vote.

Focus Group Summary

The costs and benefits of local police enforcement of federal immigration law: Is it a federal or local responsibility?

Focus group participants disagreed over whether immigration enforcement is and should be solely a federal responsibility or a dual responsibility of federal and local law enforcement. Generally speaking, the law enforcement perspective in three of the sites (all but Collier County) was that immigration enforcement is a federal responsibility. One law enforcement official in the Arlington session explained that local law enforcement's authority to enforce laws comes from the state. While he agreed that local law enforcement sometimes collaborates with federal authorities on specific investigations, he stated that they must be cautious when doing so and those police officials who sit on federal task forces often become federal officers to do so. When asked whether immigration enforcement is a federal or local responsibility, one law enforcement official in the El Paso group stated, "[I]f everybody does their own job and quits trying to be something that they're not, we could get a lot more done. Border Patrol doesn't answer calls in my community. They don't go and patrol neighborhoods and stuff like that. But I've got to go and patrol their border?"

Throughout the discussions, many arguments against and in favor of local enforcement of federal immigration laws were discussed. Prior to discussing these costs and benefits, it would be helpful to deconstruct the differing perspectives on what constitutes "immigration enforcement" because the variations in definitions often result in miscommunication. Frequently, law enforcement agencies assert they are not involved in immigration enforcement, while the immigrant communities served disagree, insisting that their community members have been deported as a result of law enforcement's actions.

For instance, in the El Paso and Doña Ana County sessions, where law enforcement participants across the board seemed to have a policy of nonenforcement of immigration laws, many community members complained that police were indeed enforcing immigration law and had examples to support their claim. Part of the reason for these diverging perspectives might be attributed to differing conceptions of what is "immigration enforcement." For instance, a representative of the Socorro Police Department explained that they do not ask immigrants or visitors for their immigration documentation: "These are people; they deserve to be served." But at the same time, another representative of the Socorro Police Department stated that they do not have the kind of databases that a larger agency, such as the El Paso Police Department, has to verify the identity of people who have perpetrated a crime. Therefore, they sometimes contact Customs and Border Protection (CBP), which has access to more sophisticated criminal databases, e.g., EPIC, after which CBP typically takes steps towards deporting the undocumented immigrant. This, the speaker explained, perpetuates the perception that they work with CBP. Another police representative explained that once they arrest someone, CBP might interview the arrestee and later initiate removal proceedings. This participant also complained that the community blames the law enforcement agency for deportation of these detainees. From the community's perspective, however, these actions described by police participants might constitute "immigration enforcement."

Even a participant from the Collier County Sheriff's Office, a law enforcement agency that has signed a memorandum of agreement with ICE as part of its 287(g) program (arguably the highest level of involvement of local law enforcement in immigration control), stated that the 287(g) program is not really an immigration enforcement program. "It is simply just so we can access the database so we [can] document the people we're encountering who have already committed criminal law violations and informing ICE, filling out the paperwork, and subjecting those people to removal. So it's not really performing all the duties of the ICE agency."

In the three sites where participants considered immigration enforcement solely a federal responsibility (Topeka, El Paso, and Arlington), participants provided numerous examples of the costs of local involvement in immigration enforcement. Many believed the little trust immigrant communities have in police would disappear were local police to assist federal authorities deport unauthorized immigrants. Because so many families are mixed-status (they include both documented and undocumented members), not only would undocumented immigrants become difficult for police to work with, but also legally present relatives would be hesitant to cooperate. This reduced trust would lead to an underreporting in crime and less cooperation from witnesses, which in turn would make it more difficult to prosecute cases successfully. As one Topeka law enforcement participant expressed, "How do we police a community that won't talk to us?" Moreover, civilian participants explained that when one victim or witness is deported, this information spreads rapidly within the social networks of immigrant communities and fear proliferates. As a result of the lack of cooperation, the decrease in crime reporting, and the challenges this lack of cooperation presents to successful prosecutions, some participants believed that ultimately it would lead to an increase in crime.

Many participants also believed that increased fear of police and deportation would lead to increased victimization and exploitation of undocumented immigrants. While there was a general consensus across sites that criminals already target undocumented immigrants, believing that they will not report the offense to police, many felt this dynamic would worsen. In particular, participants expressed concern that victims of domestic violence would not come forward and that batterers would not only use the threat of deportation of the victim but also use the threat that the principal earner in the family—the batterer—would be deported after arrest. One participant in El Paso also believed that more enforcement would lead to more human trafficking, as smugglers or traffickers are better able to use the threat of deportation to coerce undocumented immigrants into situations of forced labor. In Collier County, one participant, while agreeing that undocumented immigrants are often targets of crime, had a slightly different perspective on immigrant victimization and stated that the increased patrol resources needed to deal with this increased victimization is another cost of undocumented immigration borne by local law enforcement agencies. Several participants also believed that there would be increased employer abuse and exploitation of undocumented immigrants. In addition, these fears, some participants believed, will deter immigrants from accessing other municipal services, such as health care and education.

During the El Paso sessions, the issue of police misconduct arose. Participants supposed that immigrants' fear of police and the threat of possible deportation would lead to an increase in police misconduct. As one police executive stated, "I might have issues out in the field with officers who are doing things that they're not supposed to be doing, but people are afraid to tell us, simply because they're afraid."

Many law enforcement participants stated that the economic and labor costs of police involvement in immigration enforcement were high and would divert scarce resources from traditional law enforcement activities. Those costs include the funds needed to temporarily detain immigrants, medical costs for those in need of care while being detained by local authorities, and transportation costs to the jail. Moreover, an agency would need to invest patrol resources to arrest, to await federal response, and to process paperwork required by ICE. The federal 287(g) program merely pays for training local officers; the federal government does not cover all of these other costs. One participant explained, "You can't deficit spend in Kansas but the federal government can."

In the two Texas locations, participants also talked about the possibility of the federal government distributing funds to local agencies to enforce immigration laws. In the Arlington law enforcement session, some participants felt the price to pay for accepting these funds was not worth the gains. One participant noted federal funds are already being diverted to the Department of Homeland Security from funds that used to be allocated to assist law enforcement with traditional crime control efforts. He stated, "How many of you are getting money from Homeland Security for that stuff that absolutely makes no sense in a rational world? . . . COPS grants have gone . . . We don't have our local law enforcement block grants. The [Byrne] grant situation is just appalling. You have to get an earmark from a senator to get a grant."

Participants also discussed the impact of increased deportation on children and families. When the principal earner is deported, how will those families manage? Will those families who are eligible require assistance from the state? Citizen children of deported parents might need to enter the foster care system if they do not have a legal relative that could care for them. One participant believed that because of poor outcomes in the foster care system, these children might eventually end up in the juvenile delinquency system.

Another cost of immigration enforcement many law enforcement officials raised was potential litigation costs, especially those resulting from racial-profiling and civil rights lawsuits. Across sites, law enforcement participants agreed that they could not legally arrest someone solely on the basis that they look Latino. Participants in every site also agreed that police could not just stop people on the street and ask about immigration status during a casual encounter. As one Collier County participant stated, "If you start picking them up sitting on the sidewalk because they look illegal, then I got a problem." One Collier County law enforcement official acknowledged that the department would be exposed to litigation were it to use the 287(g) program to patrol for immigration violators. For this reason, the sheriff has limited the use of the 287(g) program to target criminals who the department has already arrested and are detained in their jails and those who are the subject of an ongoing criminal investigation. An El Paso participant also noted that local agencies would expose themselves to litigation when officers mistakenly arrest a citizen or legal permanent resident. Finally, one of the Topeka participants explained that consequences of racial profiling extend beyond civil litigation in Kansas, which has a state statute prohibiting the use of race or ethnicity as the sole criteria for arrest.

Participants in Collier County, where the sheriff's office participates in ICE's 287(g) program, raised most of the benefits of local enforcement of immigration laws. The Collier County Sheriff's Office did an analysis of jail costs and found that approximately 24 percent of its jail population was immigration violators and that the pure jail costs associated with their cases cost the county approximately nine million dollars. This was the principal argument they gave county officials for entering into the 287(g) program. Currently, ICE removes one out of five detainees, which they contend saves the county jail costs.

The sheriff also views immigration enforcement as a criminal enforcement tool to remove criminals from his community. As he explained, the Collier County sheriff limits 287(g) activity to immigrants arrested for an independent state law violation and those who are targets of criminal investigations. Another Collier County participant contended that sophisticated criminals are not going to get caught committing crimes but, if the agency discovers that they are unauthorized residents, they could be removed from the community through deportation.

In Topeka, one participant articulated his unease with releasing undocumented immigrants on bond because they may provide false identities and because of the difficulties police agencies have verifying their addresses due to a shortage of interpreters. Another participant in Topeka also feared the establishment of vigilante movements if local and federal government do not control immigration and, in fact, provided an example of a town in Kansas where a group of citizens made such threats.

While law enforcement participants in Topeka clearly were opposed to sharing responsibility for immigration enforcement with the federal government, they seem to make an exception for immigrants who commit criminal law violations, in particular gang members. Some felt it was important for criminals to serve their criminal sentence in a state or local correctional facility prior to deportation. On the other hand, another participant explained that at times during criminal prosecutions, the defendant is offered the option to voluntarily agree to deportation in exchange for a dismissal of charges. As this participant explained, if the defendant then returns to the country, he or she can be prosecuted on the federal charge of illegal reentry. Another Topeka participant pointed out the complexity of the issue of deportation of criminal law violators, stating that while all agree that murderers should be deported, the issue becomes complicated with an undocumented immigrant who uses false documents to work in the country and has thus technically committed a felony offense.

Interestingly, in all conversations about criminal aliens, they were referred to as "illegal immigrants" who commit crimes. At no point did they mention legal permanent residents who are deported upon conviction of a crime; therefore, it is not clear if the participants' opinions on the issue would vary based on the legal status of the immigrant.

Counterterrorism and immigration enforcement

While the topic of the attacks of September 11 and counterterrorism was surprisingly infrequently mentioned during the sessions, a few participants commented on changes that have occurred post 9/11 and the relation between immigration enforcement and counterterrorism efforts. Due to changes that have occurred as a result of the increase in the budget and resources dedicated to homeland security and immigration enforcement, participants felt that ICE is much more responsive than the legacy Immigration and Naturalization Service (INS). Prior to 2001, it was very difficult to get INS to deport a criminal alien. Since then, at least regarding gang members, participants believed that ICE is more responsive. Moreover, comments were made that the federal government also has offered funds to local agencies to get them involved in border security and immigration enforcement. As stated above, in Arlington, the participants warned that taking these funds diverts resources from traditional criminal law enforcement funding streams, such as the COPS and Byrne grants.

There was some disagreement between the various sites about the link between terrorism and immigration. In Arlington, a participant stated that there was no relationship between terrorism and the Hispanic community. In El Paso, one participant questioned the emphasis of newer security measures on the U.S.-Mexico border versus the Canadian border. The participant maintained that if counterterrorism were the primary objective, the government would not make such a distinction. Participants in the El Paso civilian session related an incident where the Uvalde County sheriff publicly stated that there were al Qaeda training camps on the other side of the border, to justify seeking federal border security funds and actively participating in immigration enforcement. When asked to substantiate his claim, the sheriff stated, "Well, that's the whole point. They're terrorists." The El Paso participants also recounted an incident where an ICE official, attempting to justify raids in a town located in the region, alleged that a group of al Qaeda operatives crossed the border with a group of undocumented Mexican migrants. When a local congressional representative confronted the ICE official about the veracity of this claim, the ICE official backed down. In sum, participants in these two Texas locations generally felt that there was no connection between terrorism and immigration and that the government used fear of terrorism to justify immigration enforcement initiatives.

In the Collier County sessions, on the other hand, some expressed the position that failure to enforce our nation's immigration laws is a threat to national security. One of the law enforcement participants suggested that potential terrorists might be coming in through Mexico, adopting Spanish surnames, learning Spanish and a Cuban accent, and being granted permission to stay in the United States under sanctuary policies directed at Cubans. This participant also stated that both President Chavez of Venezuela (who he claimed gave Venezuelan national identity cards to all that apply) and Fidel Castro are known to have close relations with foreign terrorist organizations. Also, one participant stated that they do not have access to government databases of many countries either because of the lack of technology or privacy rights (as is the case with Europe) and, therefore, are unable to verify identity of immigrants from these countries. This, the participant felt, was a national security threat.

Should undocumented immigrants and their children be entitled to public benefits?

During the civilian sessions of the focus groups, a question posed was, "What type of benefits, if any, do you think the government should provide to the undocumented immigrant who pays taxes? What about those who do not pay taxes?" In all but Collier County, the participants believed that undocumented immigrants were entitled to certain health and education benefits (to the extent that U.S. citizens are entitled to these benefits) and that such a public policy would generally benefit the country. Firstly, some participants explained that children have a constitutional right to education, regardless of their immigration status. Moreover, in the event that the federal government deports parents of U.S. citizen children, some commented that the government has an obligation to provide support to that child. Even in Collier County, where participants generally felt that immigrants should not receive government benefits, one participant stated that it would be morally difficult to deny benefits to a child but simultaneously argued that providing children with benefits could provide an incentive to the undocumented to migrate to the United States.

There was much debate during several sessions over whether the undocumented pay taxes and whether these taxes outweigh public expenditures on the undocumented. One tax attorney in Topeka stated that he often prepares taxes for undocumented immigrants. An El Paso participant contended that anyone who pays rent is indirectly paying property taxes and undocumented immigrants at the very least pay sales taxes when they purchase items. Another participant argued that it would be very difficult to identify which undocumented immigrants pay taxes. In Collier County, on the other hand, several participants claimed that the expenses incurred in serving the undocumented outweigh the revenue gained through taxes.

Proposed solutions and recommendations

While there may have been disagreement on the central question of whether local law enforcement shares responsibility for enforcing federal immigration laws, common to both sides of the debate was a call for a national policy to provide policy consistency from locality to locality. As one Collier County participant stated, "How would we resolve what is fundamentally a national problem when each jurisdiction deals with it differently?" In Arlington, law enforcement participants felt a national policy, or at least a regional one, would protect police chiefs against political pressure to enforce immigration laws. With a national policy (or at least regional), the public or politicians would not be able to pressure police chiefs using a comparison to a neighboring police chief's policy of collaboration with ICE. Moreover, participants in Arlington felt that the impact of an agency's decision to actively participate in immigration enforcement is felt in neighboring cities and counties and, therefore, it is important to have a uniform regional policy. In Topeka, where neighboring states such as Colorado, Oklahoma, and Nebraska have passed measures against unauthorized immigrants, concern was raised whether these states' undocumented population would move to Kansas in the absence of similar Kansas state laws. One Arlington participant stated that Congress and the attorney general did an extreme disservice to local law enforcement agencies when giving them authority to enforce federal immigration laws. "The federal government needs to come in and say that enforcement of federal laws is our purview."

Across sites, there was also a general frustration with Congress's inability to pass immigration reform and a belief that many of the problems associated with undocumented immigration could be resolved through both administrative and legislative reform of the federal immigration benefits and enforcement system. In Topeka and Collier County, some participants stated that Congress should increase funding to the various immigration departments within the Department of Homeland Security, including CBP, ICE, and U.S. Citizenship and Immigration Services, so that they can more effectively fulfill their respective missions. Others felt that Congress should create a pathway to legalization for the millions of undocumented immigrants currently in the country. Many also believed that the government must make the process easier for migrants to come legally to the United States and for the undocumented to adjust their status. In Collier County, one participant, who had experience hiring temporary seasonal workers, argued that the federal government should make the process easier for businesses to hire temporary lawful workers.

Several recommendations were mentioned to improve the working relationship between police and immigrant communities. In Topeka, the law enforcement group agreed that bilingual-pay incentives would help attract more bilingual officers. They also believed that police departments should offer Spanish-language training to officers. A couple of participants in different sites suggested cultural sensitivity training for police officers. And in Arlington, participants also said that police should teach immigrants about police and public safety issues.

Several participants raised additional recommendations. In Collier County, for instance, a law enforcement participant suggested broadening the T visa and U visa programs to include a broader range of crimes (these are visas for victims of trafficking and victims of certain serious crimes that assist in prosecutions). Also, they suggested that since it would be impractical to deport all undocumented immigrants in the country, local and federal government should focus on the criminal alien population. One civilian participant in Collier County suggested taking away all incentives for undocumented migration, including jobs and benefits. In El Paso, where participants expressed concern about civil rights abuses and misconduct of federal immigration officials, a participant recommended creating civilian oversight commissions to oversee federal and local law enforcement agencies involved in immigration enforcement. In Arlington, one participant suggested legislation that would shield police executives from political influence.

Focus Group Sites

Topeka, Kansas

FIGURE 1. TOPEKA FOCUS GROUP SITE MAP

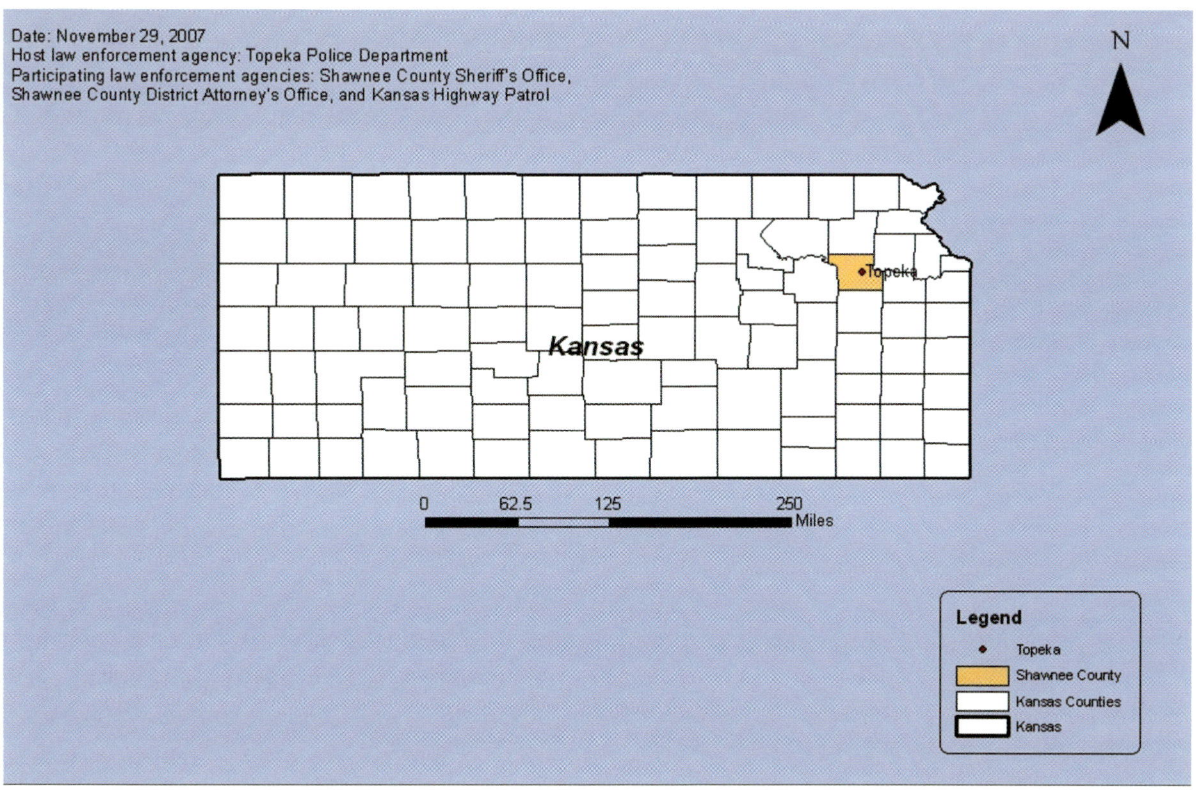

APPENDIX A

Focus Group Summary

Topeka is the capital of Kansas and the most populous city in Shawnee County. The Census Bureau estimated Shawnee County's population at 172,529 on average from 2005 to 2007,[2] with Topeka's at 121,184.[3] The location is unique in that it was the only Midwest site of the focus group project and has a relatively small population compared with the other sites. Besides providing desired geographical diversity, Topeka was chosen because of the importance of the immigration issue there and the Police Foundation's prior history working with its police chief, Ron Miller. Chief Miller invited other law enforcement officials, including the Shawnee County Sheriff and members of his agency and a representative of the Shawnee County District Attorney and Kansas Highway Patrol.

For the civilian session, the Topeka Police Department contacted community partners, such as the Law Enforcement Partnership Panel, the NAACP, and a number of Hispanic organizations, which were asked to extend invitations to their members. Once people started learning about the event, a number of additional people called the police department to request permission to attend. Ultimately, representatives attended the civilian session from the Topeka City Council, Kansas Human Rights Commission, Kansas Hispanic and Latino Commission, the NAACP, League of United Latin American Citizens, community-based organizations, private business, and the clergy. Given that Topeka is the most populous part of Shawnee County and the Topeka Police Department organized the event, it was no surprise that all of the community focus group participants were from the city of Topeka.

During focus group discussions, reference was made to Topeka's racial history. One of Topeka's school districts was the defendant in *Brown v. Board of Education*, the landmark Supreme Court case requiring racial integration of American public schools. In addition, in the late 1980s, a group of citizens calling themselves the Task Force to Overcome Racism in Topeka formed to address the problems associated with racism in the city, including housing segregation, disproportionate minority incarceration, and continuing school segregation.

Of all the project sites, Topeka had the smallest immigrant population. According to the U.S. Census Bureau American Community Survey three-year estimates of 2005 to 2007, approximately 5 percent of the population of Topeka[4] and 4 percent of the population of Shawnee County[5] was foreign born. Of Topeka's foreign-born residents, approximately 33 percent were naturalized citizens and 35 percent entered in the year 2000 or later.[6] In both locations, only a slightly larger percentage of the population five years or older spoke a language other than English at home: 12 percent in Topeka[7] and 8 percent in Shawnee County.[8] In addition, approximately 11 percent of Topeka's population identified as Hispanic or Latino of any race, 12 percent Black or African American, 1 percent Native American, and a little less than 2 percent Asian.[9] Similarly, in Shawnee County, approximately 9 percent of the population identified as Hispanic or Latino of any race, 9 percent Black or African American, and a little over 1 percent identified as Asian and Native American.[10] Shawnee County saw a 58.4 percent increase in its Hispanic or Latino population between 1990 and 2000, which is slightly above the national average growth rate of 57.6 percent.[11] From 2005-2007, median household income in Topeka was $36,071 and median family income was $46,500; median household income was $45,274 and median family income was $57,636 in Shawnee County.[12]

The Topeka Police Department is a medium-size police force with 338 full-time employees, 283 of whom are sworn personnel. Of the sworn officers, 89 percent are White, 4 percent Black, 6 percent Hispanic or Latino, and 1 percent Native American.[13] The Topeka Police Department saw slightly lower rates of reported violent and property crime in 2006 than in 1985 (see table 1), although the number of those crimes increased during the period. For the Shawnee County Sheriff's Office, the rate of reported violent crimes decreased slightly while the rate of reported property crimes increased considerably. See table 1 for more detailed statistics.[14]

TABLE 1. CRIME STATISTICS FOR TOPEKA PARTICIPATING AGENCIES

Agency	1985 Violent Crime Rate	1985 Property Crime Rate	2006 Violent Crime Rate	2006 Property Crime Rate
Topeka Police Department	580.6	7,180	544.8	7,123.4
Shawnee County Sheriff's Office	226.7	1,476.1	205.2	3,310.6

Data Source: U.S. Department of Justice, Bureau of Justice Statistics, *Crime & Justice Data Online*, and *Crime Trends* from *FBI Uniform Crime Reports*. Violent and property crime rates are number of crimes reported per 100,000 population. Data are unavailable for some of the smaller agencies that participated. Violent crimes include murder and non-negligent homicide, forcible rape, robbery, and aggravated assault. The definition of property crimes includes burglary, larceny/theft, motor vehicle theft, and arson.

Overall, during the Topeka law enforcement session, participants made more comments about lack of ICE responsiveness than during the other sessions. To support this claim, a representative of the Kansas Highway Patrol related an incident involving seizure of two hundred and fifty thousand dollars worth of marijuana from undocumented immigrants. The officer called ICE to respond but ICE did not have officers available to do so. Some participants felt that if ICE did not respond to such a serious incident, it certainly would not have the resources to respond to all calls for service were local law enforcement to start actively enforcing immigration law. Moreover, because of ICE's inability to respond in a timely manner, the local law enforcement agency would incur significant detention (seventy-two dollars per day) and labor costs. The local agency would also be forced to allocate valuable beds in the detention center to immigration detainees. If the agency no longer had the space to detain all criminal law violators, it would be forced to pay another jurisdiction to hold the prisoners. The reason this issue mainly arose in this site is unclear, but perhaps it is due to the relatively fewer immigration resources allocated to this region.

APPENDIX A
Focus Group Summary

El Paso, Texas

FIGURE 2. EL PASO FOCUS GROUP SITE MAP

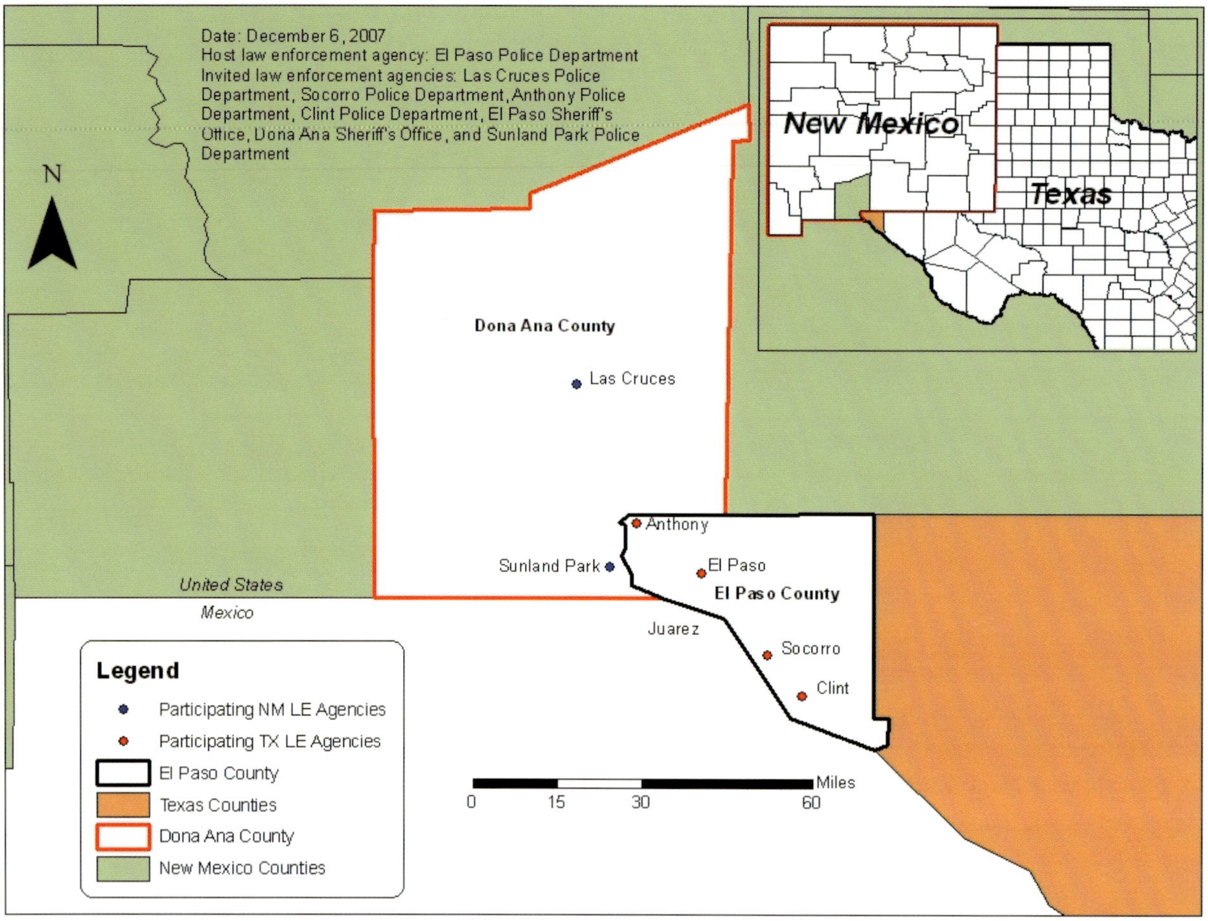

El Paso County, the westernmost county in Texas, borders New Mexico and the Mexican state of Chihuahua. El Paso City shares a border with Ciudad Juarez (the largest city in Chihuahua), which together make up the El Paso/Juarez Borderplex, the largest population center on any international border in the world. About 2.2 million live in the area.[15] In the Borderplex region, there are four major border points of entry and pedestrian traffic of approximately 8.3 million annually.[16] With a population of 609,415, El Paso is the twenty-first largest city in the nation and was the seventh fastest growing large city (cities with a population over 500,000) in the nation from 2000-2006.[17] From 2005 to 2007, El Paso County had an estimated population of 724,217.[18] El Paso County includes El Paso City, Horizon City, Socorro, Anthony, Clint, and Vinton.

Chief Richard Wiles of the El Paso Police Department, the host agency, invited law enforcement representatives from both El Paso County and bordering Doña Ana County, New Mexico. Doña Ana County includes the cities of Las Cruces and Sunland Park and borders the U.S.-Mexico border state of Chihuahua. A large number of the law enforcement session attendees were chiefs of police from these agencies. For the civilian session, Chief Wiles worked with community-based organizations to support efforts to get community participation. The final list of civilian session participants included representatives from the Border Network for Human Rights, Centro Mujeres de la Esperanza, Paseo del Norte Civil Rights Project, Diocesan Migrant and Refugee Services, and a local private attorney; most of the civilian participants were based in El Paso County.

In addition to being border counties, El Paso County, and to a slightly lesser extent Doña Ana County, compared with other selected sites, are unique in that Latinos are the majority population and a significant percentage of them are eligible to vote (citizens). While the population of Latinos is very high in the region—approximately 81 percent of El Paso County[19] and 65 percent of Doña Ana County identified as Hispanic or Latino according to three-year estimates from 2005 to 2007 of the American Community Survey[20]—the growth rate in the Hispanic or Latino population in both counties was lower than the national average of 58 percent.[21] El Paso County saw a 29 percent increase in Hispanic or Latino population between 1990 and 2000,[22] while Doña Ana County saw a 45 percent increase.[23]

Both El Paso County and Doña Ana County also have a foreign-born population well above the national rate of 12.5 percent. From 2005 to 2007, the U.S. Census Bureau estimated that approximately 27 percent of residents of El Paso County were born outside the United States or its territories. Of the foreign born, approximately 41 percent were naturalized U.S. citizens and 18 percent entered the United States after 2000.[24] In the same time period, the Census Bureau estimated that approximately 19 percent of Doña Ana County's 193,888 residents were foreign born. Of the foreign born, 31 percent were naturalized U.S. citizens and 22 percent entered the United States in 2000 or later.[25]

In both counties, the majority of the population speaks a language other than English at home—approximately 76 percent in El Paso and 54 percent in Doña Ana County from 2005 to 2007. During this period, median household income in El Paso was $33,684 and median family income was $36,817. In Doña Ana County, median household income was $34,118 and median family income was $39,453.[26, 27]

The El Paso Police Department is the largest law enforcement agency in the region and has by far the largest percentage of Hispanic or Latino officers of all agencies participating in the focus groups. As of 2000, the El Paso Police Department had 1,351 full-time employees, 1,057 of whom were sworn. Of the full-time sworn personnel, 24 percent were White (non-Hispanic), 2 percent Black (non-Hispanic), 72 percent Hispanic, 1 percent Asian, and 1 percent Native American. The second largest agency present at the El Paso law enforcement session was the Las Cruces Police Department, which had 199 full-time employees, 141 of whom were sworn personnel. Of sworn full-time personnel, 46 percent were White (non-Hispanic), 7 percent Black (non-Hispanic), 45 percent Hispanic, and 1 percent Native American.[28]

In the past twenty years, the rate of both violent and property crimes reported in El Paso City declined considerably despite an appreciable increase in population size and despite focus group comments that in recent years crimes relating to drug trafficking increased significantly and became more violent. The El Paso County sheriff reported a slight increase in the violent crime rate, most of this increase caused by a rise in aggravated assault charges. Murder/non-negligent manslaughter, forcible rape, and robbery rates all declined. The other agencies with available data for the past twenty years saw slight increases in the rate of violent crimes reported but large decreases in property crime rates. Despite proximity to the border, El Paso City was named the second safest city in America (of cities with a population of 500,000 or more).[29] See table 2 for more detailed statistics.[30]

TABLE 2. CRIME STATISTICS FOR SOME EL PASO PARTICIPATING AGENCIES

Agency	1985 Violent Crime Rate	1985 Property Crime Rate	2006 Violent Crime Rate	2006 Property Crime Rate
El Paso Police Department	771.2	6,324.9	393.5	3,370.6
El Paso Sheriff's Office	243.7	2,549.8	266.4	1,486.1
Las Cruces Police Department	504.8	8,749.9	614.6	4,661.4
Doña Ana County Sheriff's Office	289.5	2,231.1	331	1,367.3

Data Source: U.S. Department of Justice, Bureau of Justice Statistics, *Crime & Justice Data Online* and *Crime Trends* from *FBI Uniform Crime Reports*. Violent and property crime rates are number of crimes reported per 100,000 population. Data are unavailable for some of the smaller agencies that participated. Violent crimes include murder and non-negligent homicide, forcible rape, robbery, and aggravated assault. The definition of property crimes includes burglary, larceny/theft, motor vehicle theft, and arson.

Because El Paso is situated on the U.S.-Mexico border, participants had particular perspectives, issues, and concerns relating to the border that were not raised in other sessions. In El Paso, law enforcement interacts with immigrant residents, undocumented migrants who have recently crossed the border and are heading to the interior of the country, and Mexican visitors legally present in the United States with a border-crossing card. Furthermore, many residents of El Paso have family on both sides of the border, which influences their viewpoints on migration issues.

El Paso and Doña Ana County law enforcement agencies, particularly those located in rural border cities, often must respond to criminal activity specific to border communities, such as drug and human trafficking and the resulting violence. Some law enforcement participants expressed concern that these criminal problems have worsened in recent years. One participant contended that the Juarez and Sinaloa drug cartels have begun to enter the human trafficking business. These local law enforcement agencies feel overwhelmed by criminal enforcement demands placed on them, and for this reason the Border County Sheriff's Coalition sought federal funds to address border criminal activity and to deter criminal activity by having more of a presence in the rural areas of the county. One participant reported a decline in trespass and burglary complaints from farmers since more deputies were placed in these areas.

The discussions in El Paso often included comments about the role and presence of CBP in the region. In the past, as one civilian participant mentioned, the agency did not patrol beyond three miles of the border. Now, however, it is conducting enforcement activities further inland, patrolling public areas such as shopping malls. On occasion, some police agencies in the area have collaborated with CBP on criminal investigations, particularly in jurisdictions where patrol resources are limited. For example, an officer in a more rural area may call CBP for backup.

Arlington, Texas

FIGURE 3. ARLINGTON FOCUS GROUP SITE MAP

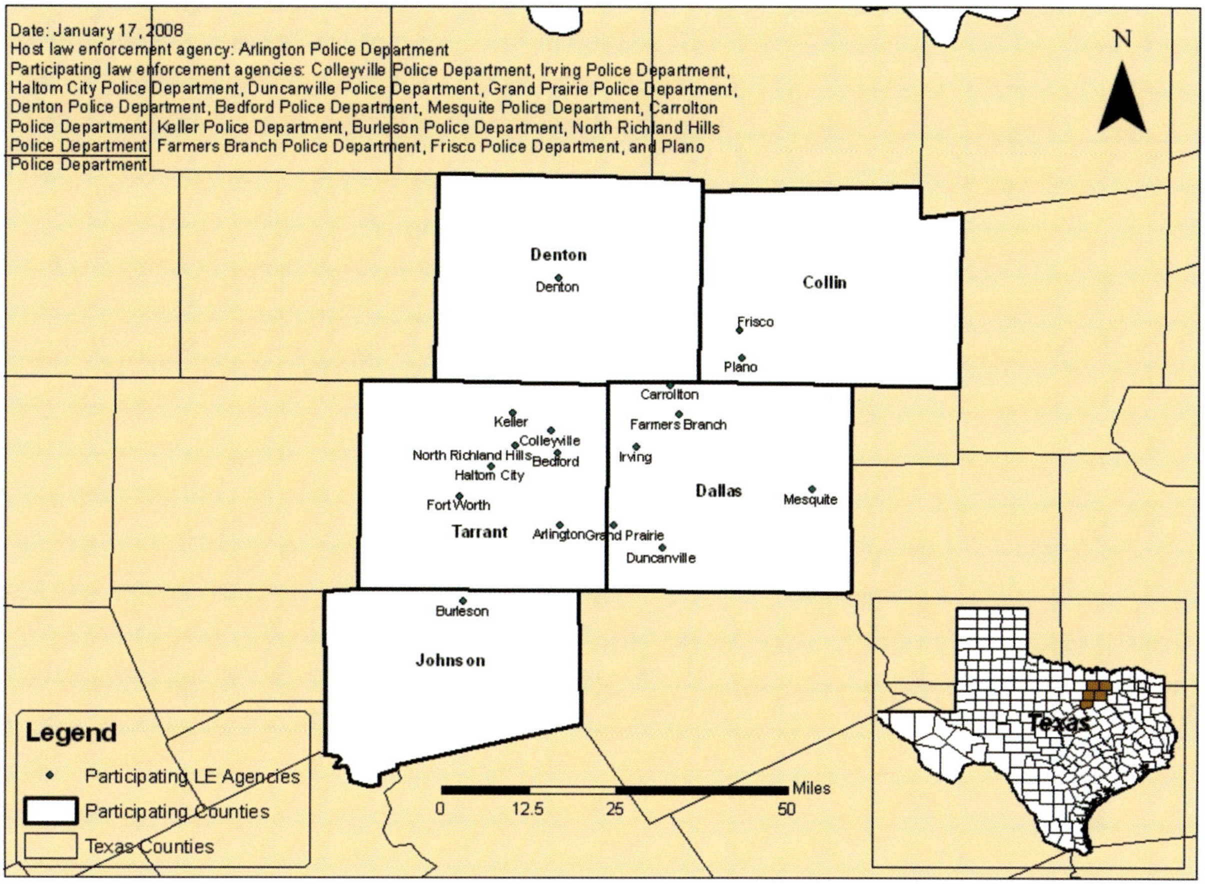

Arlington, Texas, is part of the Dallas-Fort Worth-Arlington Metropolitan area, as named by the U.S. Census Bureau, or as it is commonly named in the region, the Dallas-Fort Worth Metroplex. In 2006, the population of the Metroplex reached almost six million, making it the fourth-largest metropolitan area in the United States.[31] It is an enormous geographic area covering 9,286 square miles, which includes the third and fifth largest cities in Texas (Dallas and Fort Worth). Fort Worth was the fastest growing city in the nation from July 2000 to July 2006, having increased its population by more than 20 percent.[32] The Dallas-Fort Worth Metroplex includes the following counties that were represented in the law enforcement focus group: Dallas, Tarrant, Collin, Johnson, and Denton. Parker, Rockwall, Kaufman, Hunt, Ellis, and Wise counties, also located in the metropolitan area, did not have their law enforcement agencies represented at the law enforcement focus group session.

According to estimates of the 2006 American Community Survey, the foreign-born population of the Metroplex area was estimated at approximately 18 percent.[33] In 2006, 56 percent of foreign-born residents were born in Mexico and 67 percent came from Latin America.[34] In addition, approximately 29 percent of the metropolitan area spoke a language other than English at home.[35]

APPENDIX A

Focus Group Summary

Chief Theron Bowman of the Arlington Police Department invited local area police executives on the basis of their proximity to Arlington, agency size, and community similarities. Because this group regularly meets twice a month, they have had a lot of experience discussing complex issues, including challenges associated with immigration. Moreover, unlike other sites, almost all participants were chiefs of police. Sheriff's offices in the metropolitan area were not represented nor were the larger police departments in the region, specifically the Dallas Police Department and the Fort Worth Police Department.

The Arlington Police Department collaborated with a variety of local-area partners, including faith-based organizations, police partners, and residential communities, to whom they drafted an invitation letter describing the purpose of the event and requesting that the community partners invite residents to attend. They used this approach to establish a layer of trust with members of the community who might normally feel uncomfortable attending an event hosted by a police agency. Many participants were too frightened to give their name and contact information, preferring to remain anonymous; thus, we do not have specific information about the composition of this group, unlike the other sites.

Since the Arlington Police Department invited focus group participants by using organizations it worked with in the past, most civilian participants were from that city. Therefore, a more detailed description of its population is available. Arlington is a suburb of Fort Worth in Tarrant County. The demographic profile for Arlington is quite similar to the entire metropolitan area. From 2005 to 2007, the U.S. Census Bureau estimated Arlington's foreign-born population at 19 percent, and 30 percent of the population five years old or over was estimated to speak a language other than English at home.[36] Of the 30 percent, 71 percent spoke Spanish and approximately 51 percent reported that they did not speak English "very well."[37] From 2005 to 2007, 32 percent of the foreign-born population were naturalized citizens and 32 percent entered in 2000 or later.[38] Of the estimated 356,764 residents in Arlington from 2005 to 2007, 62 percent were White, 17 percent Black, 6 percent Asian, and less than 1 percent was Native American. Approximately 26 percent reported they were Hispanic or Latino (of any race). The city is relatively prosperous, with a median household income of $50,582 and median family income of $60,364.[39] According to Chief Bowman, Arlington's population has almost doubled in the past twenty to twenty-five years, and most of that growth is due to increases in ethnic minority communities. Specifically, Arlington's Hispanic population growth is significant, as is the unauthorized portion of this community, according to the chief.

Table 3 presents brief demographic statistics of the five counties that had at least one police department represented in the law enforcement session and gives the reader a brief overview of the population served by this large number of police agencies. Important to note in this table is that a significant portion of the immigrant population possibly resides in the cities of Dallas and Fort Worth; those cities were not represented in the law enforcement session. All five counties experienced tremendous growth in the Latino community between 1990 and 2000. Tarrant County's Latino population grew 104 percent; Dallas County's, 110 percent; Collin County's, 178 percent; Denton County's, 177 percent; and Johnson County's, 106 percent.[40] Some law enforcement group participants discussed growth not only in the Latino community but in various Asian and Middle Eastern communities as well.

TABLE 3. DEMOGRAPHIC STATISTICS FOR ARLINGTON REPRESENTED COUNTIES - 2006

County	Population	Foreign Born (percent)	Speak a Language Other than English (percent)	Hispanic (percent)	Asian (percent)
Dallas	2,336,012	24	40	37	4
Tarrant	1,668,042	16	26	25	4
Collin	695,317	17	23	14	10
Johnson	146,663	6	14	15	.4
Denton	585,139	13	20	16	5

Data Source: U.S. Census Bureau, *American FactFinder, 2005-2007 American Community Survey 3-Year Estimates: Data Profile Highlights*.

The Arlington Police Department was the largest agency represented in the law enforcement session, with 643 full-time employees (485 sworn) in 2000 and the largest proportion of Hispanic sworn officers, 13 percent. Sixty-nine percent of sworn full-time employees were White (non-Hispanic), 12 percent Black (non-Hispanic), 3 percent Asian, and 3 percent Native American. Hispanic composition of sworn personnel in the other police departments for which data on racial makeup were available was less than 10 percent. See table 4 for more detailed statistics.[41]

TABLE 4. RACIAL MAKEUP OF ARLINGTON PARTICIPATING AGENCY SWORN PERSONNEL - 2006

Agency	White (non-Hispanic) (percent)	Black (non-Hispanic) (percent)	Hispanic (percent)	Asian (percent)	Native American (percent)
Arlington PD	69	12	13	3	3
Irving PD	87	4	6	1	1
Plano PD	88	5	5	0	1
Grand Prairie PD	86	7	8	0	0
Mesquite PD	94	3	4	0	1
Carrollton PD	91	2	7	0	0
Denton PD	91	2	5	0	2

Data Source: U.S. Department of Justice, Bureau of Justice Statistics, *Crime & Justice Data Online, Law Enforcement Management and Administrative Statistics 2000* (LEMAS).

All police departments participating in the Arlington focus group, except for the Frisco Police Department, saw a decrease in property crime rates between 1985 and 2006. A little more than half of participating police departments also saw a decrease in violent crime rates. See table 5 for more detailed statistics.[42]

TABLE 5. CRIME STATISTICS FOR ARLINGTON PARTICIPATING AGENCIES

Agency	1985 Violent Crime Rate	1985 Property Crime Rate	2006 Violent Crime Rate	2006 Property Crime Rate
Arlington PD	507	8,461.1	731.2	5,271.2
Bedford PD	198.6	6,414.4	510.4	3,239.5
Burleson PD	157.2	6,137	187.2	3,881.5
Carrollton PD	195.5	5,930.5	187.3	3,093.9
Colleyville PD	50.5	3,398.6	39.1	1,311.4
Denton PD	666.8	8,398.3	310.9	3,001.7
Duncanville PD	222.2	6,059.4	304.3	4,014.3
Farmers Branch PD	210.7	6,534.9	238.6	4,376.2
Frisco PD	598.1 (1988)	3,646.5	134.6	4,375.1
Grand Prairie PD	629.2	8,162.2	330.1	5,038.8
Haltom City PD	342.8	8,722	463.4	5,689.6
Irving PD	687.4	9,095.3	426.8	4,842.9
Keller PD	264.8	4,583.4	68.1	1,497.9
Mesquite PD	588.8	8,315.7	371.3	4,023
North Richland Hills PD	316.8	6,724.6	299.1	3,758.3
Plano PD	167.4	5,973.2	287.7	3,338.1

Data Source: U.S. Department of Justice, Bureau of Justice Statistics, *Crime & Justice Data Online*, and *Crime Trends* from *FBI Uniform Crime Reports*. Violent and property crime rates are number of crimes reported per 100,000 population. Data are unavailable for some of the smaller agencies that participated. Violent crimes include murder and non-negligent homicide, forcible rape, robbery, and aggravated assault. The definition of property crimes includes burglary, larceny/theft, motor vehicle theft, and arson.

Collier County, Florida

FIGURE 4. COLLIER COUNTY FOCUS GROUP SITE MAP

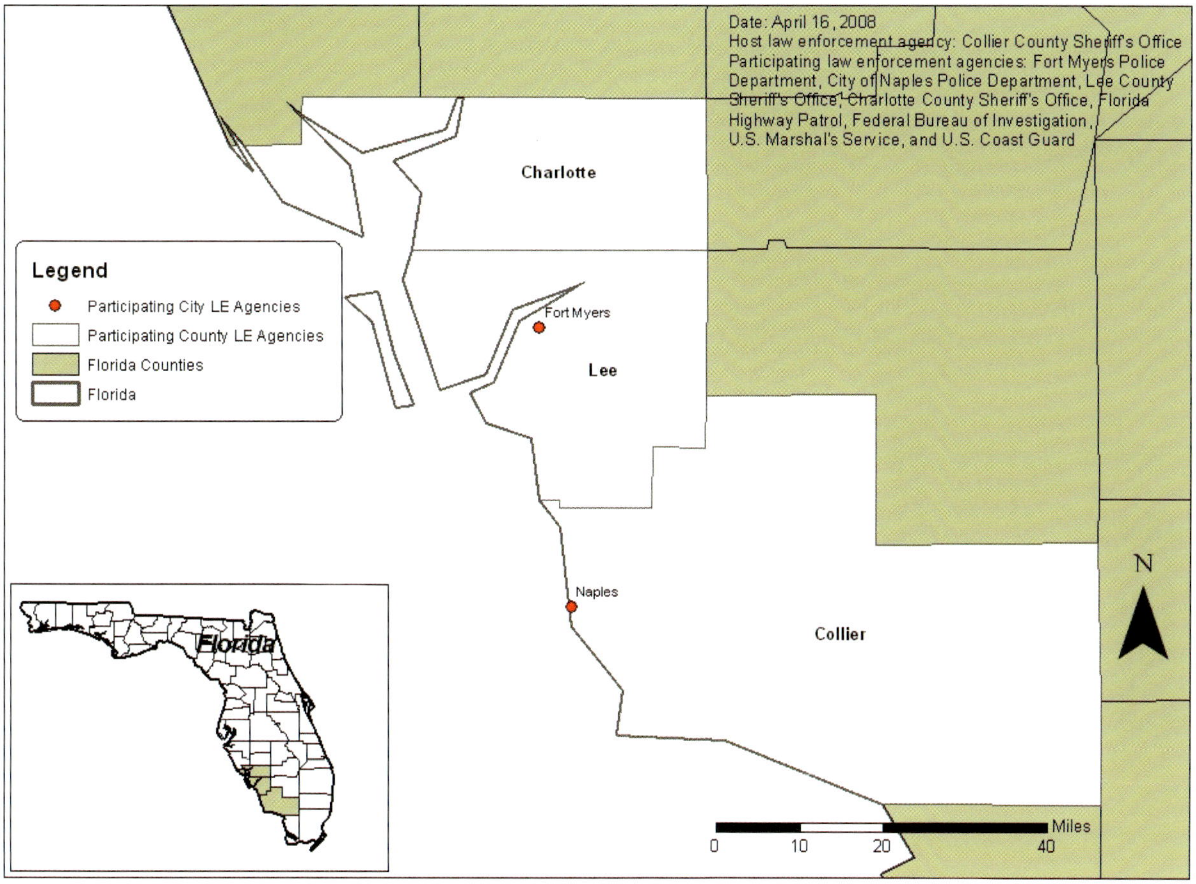

With the exception of a few representatives, law enforcement and civilian participants of the Collier County focus group sessions were largely from two counties, Collier County and Lee County, both located in Southwest Florida. In 1923, Collier split from Lee County and includes the incorporated cities of Everglades City, Marco Island, and the City of Naples. The unincorporated areas of the county include Immokalee and East Naples (both had representatives at the focus group). The population of Collier County from 2005 to 2007 was 311,926;[43] Lee County's was 567,711.[44]

Both counties saw a more than doubling of their Hispanic or Latino populations from 1990 to 2000, well above the national average. The growth rate in the Hispanic or Latino population was 137.8 percent in Collier County and 178.5 percent in Lee County.[45] The U.S. Census Bureau American Community Survey 2005-2007 3-Year Estimates also indicate that 25 percent of Collier County and 16 percent of Lee County were Hispanic or Latino (of any race). In addition, 24 percent of the population of Collier County was foreign born. Of the 76 percent of the population born in the United States, merely 21 percent was born in Florida.[46] During this same period of time, 14 percent of the population of Lee County was foreign born. Of the 86 percent born in the United States, 24 percent was born in Florida (similar to Collier County).[47] Thirty percent of the population five years or over spoke a language other than English at home in Collier County; 19 percent in Lee County did also. Median household income in Collier County from 2005 to 2007 was $57,166, and median family income was $66,846.[48] In Lee County, median household income in 2006 was $49,742, and median family income was $57,475.[49]

When county statistics for Collier and Lee Counties are disaggregated into smaller geographical areas, there is much variation in racial and ethnic makeup, median income, place of birth, and languages spoken. Included within Collier County, for instance, is Immokalee, where, in 2000, 46 percent of the population was foreign born, 71 percent was Hispanic or Latino, and 78 percent spoke a language other than English at home. Immokalee is also a very poor community, with median household income of $24,315 and a median family income of $22,628 in 2000.[50] In contrast, in this same year, Naples City, also in Collier County, had a foreign-born population of only 9 percent, a Hispanic or Latino population of 2 percent, and only 10 percent of the population spoke a language other than English at home. Naples is also a wealthier municipality than Immokalee, with a median household income of $65,641 and median family income of $83,831.[51]

Immokalee is the home base of the Coalition of Immokalee Workers (CIW), a community-based worker organization whose members are largely Latino and Haitian immigrants. It is well known nationally for boycotts against Taco Bell and McDonald's, resulting in both companies agreeing to pay a higher price for tomatoes in order to increase workers' wages. The CIW is also well known for its antitrafficking and antislavery programs with farm workers.

Sheriff Don Hunter and his staff coordinated participation in the Collier County focus group. Twelve of the twenty-one law enforcement session participants were from the Collier County Sheriff's Office. Seven members of the sheriff's office attended the afternoon civilian session, six merely as observers. The civilian session included representatives from the Collier County School Board, East Naples Civic Association, Collier County Board of County Commissioners, City of Bonita Springs, Florida Fish and Wildlife Commission, Collier County government, Greater Naples Chamber of Commerce, Golden Gate Fire Commission, Collier County School District, and Marco Island City Council.

No immigrant community representatives or organizations participated in the Collier County focus group. This site was added later in the project and there was a relatively short amount of time to organize the civilian session compared with the other focus group sites. Also, the Police Foundation had requested that elected and appointed government officials were included in the civilian session.

In 2000, the Collier County Sheriff's Office had 915 employees, 504 being full-time sworn personnel. Of full-time sworn personnel, 87 percent were White (non-Hispanic), 2 percent Black (non-Hispanic), 11 percent Hispanic, and 1 percent Asian. The Lee County Sheriff's Office had 910 full-time employees, 410 of whom were full-time sworn personnel. Of full-time sworn personnel, 94 percent were White (non-Hispanic), 3 percent Black (non-Hispanic), and 2 percent Hispanic. The Fort Myers Police Department had 238 full-time employees, 152 of whom were full-time sworn personnel. Of full-time sworn personnel, 84 percent were White (non-Hispanic), 11 percent Black (non-Hispanic), 5 percent Hispanic, and 1 percent Asian.[52]

The Collier County Sheriff's Office had a higher violent crime rate in 2006 than in 1985, although the rates have been decreasing slowly since 1999 (around the period when violent crime rates were relatively high in the jurisdiction). The county has seen consistent decreases in property crime rates since 1996. The Naples Police Department's violent and property crime rates both dropped during this period. As noted in table 6, the Lee and Charlotte County Sheriff's Offices saw increases in violent crime rates and barely any change in property crime rate between 1985 and 2006. The Fort Myers Police Department's property crime rate decreased; and while the violent crime rate was slightly higher in 2006 than in 1985, the violent crime rate has been steadily decreasing since 1992, when violent crime was at a high.

TABLE 6. CRIME STATISTICS FOR COLLIER COUNTY PARTICIPATING AGENCIES

Agency	1985 Violent Crime Rate	1985 Property Crime Rate	2006 Violent Crime Rate	2006 Property Crime Rate
Collier County Sheriff's	383.2	4,823.9	477.4	1,873.2
Lee County Sheriff's	188.4	3,230	522.6	3,420.6
Naples PD	500.2	7,218.8	240.1	3,891.3
Fort Myers PD	1,229.3	9,241.2	1,577.1	4,897.9
Charlotte County Sheriff's	182.9	3,360.6	483.9	3,505.8

Data Source: U.S. Department of Justice, Bureau of Justice Statistics, *Crime & Justice Data Online*, and *Crime Trends* from *FBI Uniform Crime Reports*. Violent and property crime rates are number of crimes reported per 100,000 population. Data are unavailable for some of the smaller agencies that participated. Violent crimes include murder and non-negligent homicide, forcible rape, robbery, and aggravated assault. The definition of property crimes includes burglary, larceny/theft, motor vehicle theft, and arson.

Because of the large Cuban population in Florida, participants in Collier County discussed special immigration benefits and privileges granted to Cubans. Unlike immigrants from other countries, ICE will not initiate removal proceedings against a Cuban who has committed a criminal law violation. One participant expressed his belief that Cubans should not receive such special treatment because they are no worse off than immigrants from many other countries. Some participants also claimed that the Castro administration provides support to Cuban smugglers, who are smuggling not only Cubans but also other foreign nationals. One member of the U.S. Coast Guard supported this claim, stating that the Coast Guard had recently intercepted a boat coming from Cuba where nine out of eleven of the passengers were Chinese nationals. Others claimed that Cubans are now entering the United States through the U.S.-Mexico border, and that their smuggling networks are training migrants from other countries on Cuban accents and mannerisms so that they can benefit from the immigration privileges extended to Cubans.

Endnotes

[1] Throughout this report, the term "immigrant" is used to describe any foreign-born resident, including legal permanent residents and other legally present foreign nationals, naturalized citizens, undocumented immigrants, and out-of-status immigrants.

[2] U.S. Census Bureau. *American FactFinder, 2005-2007. American Community Survey 3-Year Estimates Data Profile Highlights, Shawnee County, Kansas.* http://factfinder.census.gov/servlet/ACSSAFFFacts?_event=Search&geo_id=&_geoContext=&_street=&_county =Shawnee+County&_cityTown=Shawnee+County&_state=04000US20&_zip=&_lang=en&_sse=on&pctxt=fph&pgsl=010.

[3] U.S. Census Bureau. *American FactFinder, 2005-2007. American Community Survey 3-Year Estimates Data Profile Highlights, Topeka, Kansas.* http://factfinder.census.gov/servlet/ACSSAFFFacts?_event=Search&geo_id=05000US20177&_geoContext=01000US%7C04000US20%7C05000US20177&_street=&_county=Topeka&_cityTown=Topeka&_state=04000US20&_zip=&_lang=en&_sse=on&ActiveGeoDiv=geoSelect&_useEV=&pctxt=fph&pgsl=050&_submenuId=factsheet_1&ds_name=ACS_2007_3YR_SAFF&_ci_nbr=null&qr_name=null&reg=null%3Anull&_keyword=&_industry=.

[4] *Id.*

[5] U.S. Census Bureau. *American FactFinder, 2005-2007. American Community Survey 3-Year Estimates Data Profile Highlights, Shawnee County, Kansas.* http://factfinder.census.gov/servlet/ACSSAFFFacts?_event=Search&geo_id=&_geoContext=&_street=&_county=Shawnee+County&_cityTown=Shawnee+County&_state=04000US20&_zip=&_lang=en&_sse=on&pctxt=fph&pgsl=010.

[6] U.S. Census Bureau. *American FactFinder, Selected Social Characteristics in the United States: 2005-2007, 2005-2007 American Community Survey 3-Year Estimates, Topeka, Kansas.* http://factfinder.census.gov/servlet/ADPTable?_bm=y&-geo_id=16000US2071000&-qr_name=ACS_2007_3YR_G00_DP3YR2&-ds_name=ACS_2007_3YR_G00_&-_lang=en&-_sse=on.

[7] *Id.*

[8] U.S. Census Bureau. *American FactFinder, 2005-2007. American Community Survey 3-Year Estimates Data Profile Highlights, Shawnee County, Kansas.* http://factfinder.census.gov/servlet/ACSSAFFFacts?_event=Search&geo_id=&_geoContext=&_street=&_county=Shawnee+County&_cityTown=Shawnee+County&_state=04000US20&_zip=&_lang=en&_sse=on&pctxt=fph&pgsl=010.

[9] U.S. Census Bureau. *American FactFinder, Selected Social Characteristics in the United States: 2005-2007, 2005-2007 American Community Survey 3-Year Estimates, Topeka, Kansas.* http://factfinder.census.gov/servlet/ADPTable?_bm=y&-geo_id=16000US2071000&-qr_name=ACS_2007_3YR_G00_DP3YR2&-ds_name=ACS_2007_3YR_G00_&-_lang=en&-_sse=on.

[10] *Id.*

[11] http://www.hablamosjuntos.org/latinos/statetable.asp?st=kansas.

[12] U.S. Census Bureau. *American FactFinder, 2005-2007. American Community Survey 3-Year Estimates Data Profile Highlights, Shawnee County, Kansas.* http://factfinder.census.gov/servlet/ACSSAFFFacts?_event=Search&geo_id=&_geoContext=&_street=&_county=Shawnee+County&_cityTown=Shawnee+County&_state=04000US20&_zip=&_lang=en&_sse=on&pctxt=fph&pgsl=010.

[13] U.S. Department of Justice, Bureau of Justice Statistics, *Crime & Justice Data Online, Law Enforcement Management and Administrative Statistics, 2000* (LEMAS), *Law Enforcement Agency Profile for Topeka Police Department, KS*. There were no LEMAS data available for Shawnee County Sheriff's Office. http://bjsdata.ojp.usdoj.gov/dataonline/Search/Law/Local/RunLawLocalAgencyProfile.cfm.

[14] U.S. Department of Justice, Bureau of Justice Statistics, *Crime & Justice Data Online*, and *Crime Trends* from *FBI Uniform Crime* Reports. The *FBI Uniform Crime Reports* began reporting on crime rates for individual agencies in 1985 and the most current data available are for 2006. http://www.fbi.gov/ucr/cius2006/data/table_08_tx.html, http://www.fbi.gov/ucr/cius2006/data/table_08_nm.html.

[15] http://www.elpasoinfo.com.

[16] Data provided by Mayor John Cook of El Paso City in his presentation at the Police Foundation national conference on August 21, 2008.

[17] Les Christie, "The Fastest Growing U.S. Cities," CNNMoney.com, June 28, 2007. http://money.cnn.com/2007/ 06/27/real_estate/fastest_ growing _cities/.

[18] U.S. Census Bureau. *American FactFinder, 2005-2007. American Community Survey 3-Year Estimates Data Profile Highlights, El Paso County, Texas.* http://factfinder.census.gov/servlet/ACSSAFFFacts?_event=Search&geo_id=16000US4824000 &_geoContext =01000US%7C04000US48%7C16000US4824000&_street=&_county=El+Paso+County&_cityTown=El+Paso+County&_state=04000US48&_zip=&_lang=en&_sse=on&ActiveGeoDiv=geoSelect&_useEV=&pctxt=fph&pgsl=160&_submenuId=factsheet_1&ds_name=ACS_2007_3YR_SAFF&_ci_nbr=null&qr_name=null&reg=null%3Anull&_keyword=&_industry=.

[19] *Id.*

[20] U.S. Census Bureau. *American FactFinder, 2005-2007. American Community Survey 3-Year Estimates Data Profile Highlights, Doña Ana County, New Mexico.* http://factfinder.census.gov/servlet/ACSSAFFFacts?_event=Search&geo_id=&_geoContext=&_street=&_county=Dona+Ana+County&_cityTown=Dona+Ana+County&_state=04000US35&_zip=&_lang=en&_sse=on&pctxt=fph&pgsl=010.

[21] U.S. Census Bureau, *Hispanics in the United States*. http://www.census.gov/population/www/socdemo/hispanic/files/ Internet_Hispanic_in_US_2006.pdf.

[22] "Growth in Latino Population," table accessed at http://www.hablamosjuntos.org/latinos/statetable.asp?st=texas.

[23] "Growth in Latino Population," table accessed at http://www.hablamosjuntos.org/latinos/statetable.asp?st=newmexico.

[24] U.S. Census Bureau, *American FactFinder, Selected Social Characteristics in the United States: 2005-2007, 2005-2007 American Community Survey 3-Year Estimates, El Paso County, Texas.* http://factfinder.census.gov/servlet/ADPTable?_bm=y&-geo_id=05000US48141&-qr_name=ACS_2007_3YR_G00_DP3YR2&-ds_name=ACS_2007_3YR_G00_&-_lang=en&-redoLog=false&-_sse=on.

[25] U.S. Census Bureau, *American FactFinder, Selected Social Characteristics in the United States: 2005-2007, 2005-2007 American Community Survey 3-Year Estimates, Doña Ana County, New Mexico.* http://factfinder.census.gov/servlet/ADPTable?_bm=y&-geo_id=05000US35013&-qr_name=ACS_2007_3YR_G00_DP3YR2&-ds_name=ACS_2007_3YR_G00_&-_lang=en&-redoLog=false&-_sse=on.

[26] U.S. Census Bureau. *American FactFinder, 2005-2007. American Community Survey 3-Year Estimates Data Profile Highlights, El Paso County, Texas.* http://factfinder.census.gov/servlet/ACSSAFFFacts?_event=Search&geo_id=16000US4824000&_geoContext=01000US%7C04000US48%7C16000US4824000&_street=&_county=El+Paso+County&_cityTown=El+Paso+County&_state=04000US48&_zip=&_lang=en&_sse=on&ActiveGeoDiv=geoSelect&_useEV=&pctxt=fph&pgsl=160&_submenuId=factsheet_1&ds_name=ACS_2007_3YR_SAFF&_ci_nbr=null&qr_name=null&reg=null%3Anull&_keyword=&_industry=.

[27] U.S. Census Bureau. *American FactFinder, 2005-2007. American Community Survey 3-Year Estimates Data Profile Highlights, Doña Ana County, New Mexico.* http://factfinder.census.gov/servlet/ACSSAFFFacts?_event=Search&geo_id=&_geoContext=&_street=&_county=Dona+Ana+County&_cityTown=Dona+Ana+County&_state=04000US35&_zip=&_lang=en&_sse=on&pctxt=fph&pgsl=010.

[28] U.S. Department of Justice, Bureau of Justice Statistics, *Law Enforcement Management and Administrative Statistics, 2000* (LEMAS). Statistics are available only for local police and sheriffs' agencies with one hundred or more sworn officers and fifty or more uniformed officers assigned to respond to calls for service, which is why data were unavailable for other police participating agencies. http://www.ojp.usdoj.gov/bjs/pub/pdf/lemas00.pdf.

[29] Mayor John Cook's presentation at the Police Foundation's national conference on August 21, 2008, citing 12th Annual America's Safest (and Most Dangerous) Cities, Morgan Quitno Awards.

[30] U.S. Department of Justice, Bureau of Justice Statistics, *Crime & Justice Data Online*, and *Crime Trends* from *FBI Uniform Crime Reports*. http://www.ojp.usdoj.gov/bjs/data/lgcithom.csv, http://www.fbi.gov/ucr/cius2006/data/table_08_tx.html, http://www.fbi.gov/ucr/cius2006/data/table_08_nm.html.

[31] U.S. Census Bureau, *Estimates of Population Change for Metropolitan Statistical Areas and Rankings: July 1, 2006, to July 1, 2007.* http://www.census.gov/popest/metro/CBSA-est2007-pop-chg.html.

[32] Les Christie, "The Fastest Growing U.S. Cities," CNN.com, June 28, 2007. http://money.cnn.com/2007/06/27/real_estate/fastest_growing_cities/.

[33] U.S. Census Bureau, *United States—Metropolitan and Micropolitan Statistical Area; and for Puerto Rico, Percent of People Who are Foreign Born: 2006.* http://factfinder.census.gov/servlet/GCTTable?_bm=y&-geo_id=01000US&-_box_head_nbr=GCT0501&-ds_name=ACS_2006_EST_G00_&-_lang=en&-redoLog=false&-format=US-35&-mt_name=ACS_2006_EST_G00_GCT0703_US35&-CONTEXT=gct..

[34] U.S. Census Bureau, *United States—Metropolitan and Micropolitan Statistical Area; and for Puerto Rico, Percent of People Born in Mexico: 2006: Percent of People Born in Latin America: 2006.* http://factfinder.census.gov/servlet/GCTSubjectShowTablesServlet?_lang=en&_ts=255556846835.

[35] U.S. Census Bureau, *United States—Metropolitan and Micropolitan Statistical Area; and for Puerto Rico, Percent of People 5 and Over Who Speak a Language Other than English at Home: 2006.* http://factfinder.census.gov/servlet/GCTSubjectShowTablesServlet?_lang=en&_ts=255556846835.

[36] U.S. Census Bureau, *American FactFinder, 2005-2007. American Community Survey 3-Year Estimates Data Profile Highlights, Arlington, Texas.* http://factfinder.census.gov/servlet/ACSSAFFFacts?_event=Search&geo_id=&_geoContext=&_street=&_county=Arlington&_cityTown=Arlington&_state=04000US48&_zip=&_lang=en&_sse=on&pctxt=fph&pgsl=010.

[37] U.S. Census Bureau, *American FactFinder, Population and Housing Narrative Profile: 2005-2007, 2005-2007 American Community Survey 3-Year Estimates.* http://factfinder.census.gov/servlet/NPTable?_bm=y&-geo_id=16000US4804000&-qr_name=ACS_2007_3YR_G00_NP01&-ds_name=&-redoLog=false.

[38] U.S. Census Bureau, *American FactFinder, Selected Social Characteristics in the United States: 2005-2007, Arlington, Texas.* http://factfinder.census.gov/servlet/ADPTable?_bm=y&-geo_id=16000US4804000&-qr_name=ACS_2007_3YR_G00_DP3YR2&-ds_name=ACS_2007_3YR_G00_&-_lang=en&-redoLog=false&-_sse=on.

[39] U.S. Census Bureau, *American FactFinder, 2005-2007. American Community Survey 3-Year Estimates Data Profile Highlights, Arlington, Texas.* http://factfinder.census.gov/servlet/ACSSAFFFacts?_event=Search&geo_id=&_geoContext=&_street=&_county=Arlington&_cityTown=Arlington&_state=04000US48&_zip=&_lang=en&_sse=on&pctxt=fph&pgsl=010.

[40] "Growth in Latino Population," tables accessed at http://www.hablamosjuntos.org/latinos/statetable.asp?st=texas.

[41] U.S. Department of Justice, Bureau of Justice Statistics, *Law Enforcement Management and Administrative Statistics, 2000* (LEMAS). Statistics are only available for local police and sheriffs' agencies with one hundred or more sworn officers and fifty or more uniformed officers assigned to respond to calls for service, which is why data were unavailable for other police participating agencies. http://www.ojp.usdoj.gov/bjs/pub/pdf/lemas00.pdf.

[42] Where statistics were unavailable for 1985, the comparison year is provided.

[43] U.S. Census Bureau, *American FactFinder, 2005-2007 American Community Survey 3-Year Estimates, Data Profile Highlights, Collier County.* http://factfinder.census.gov/servlet/ACSSAFFFacts?_event=Search&geo_id=&_geoContext=&_street=&_county=Collier+County&_cityTown=Collier+County&_state=04000US12&_zip=&_lang=en&_sse=on&pctxt=fph&pgsl=010.

[44] U.S. Census Bureau, *American FactFinder, 2005-2007 American Community Survey 3-Year Estimates, Data Profile Highlights, Lee County, Florida.* http://factfinder.census.gov/servlet/ACSSAFFFacts?_event=Search&geo_id=&_geoContext=&_street=&_county=Lee+County&_cityTown=Lee+County&_state=04000US12&_zip=&_lang=en&_sse=on&pctxt=fph&pgsl=010.

[45] http://www.hablamosjuntos.org/latinos/statetable.asp?st=florida.

[46] U.S. Census Bureau, *American FactFinder, Selected Social Characteristics in the United States: 2005-2007, Collier County, Florida.* http://factfinder.census.gov/servlet/ADPTable?_bm=y&-geo_id=05000US12021&-qr_name=ACS_2007_3YR_G00_DP3YR2&-ds_name=ACS_2007_3YR_G00_&-_lang=en&-redoLog=false&-_sse=on.

[47] U.S. Census Bureau, *American FactFinder, Selected Social Characteristics in the United States: 2005-2007, Lee County, Florida.* http://factfinder.census.gov/servlet/ADPTable?geo_id=05000US12071&ds_name=ACS_2007_3YR_G00_&qr_name=ACS_2007_3YR_G00_DP3YR2&_lang=en&_sse=on.

[48] U.S. Census Bureau, *American FactFinder, 2005-2007 American Community Survey 3-Year Estimates, Data Profile Highlights, Collier County, Florida.* http://factfinder.census.gov/servlet/ACSSAFFFacts?_event=Search&geo_id=&_geoContext=&_street=&_county=Collier+County&_cityTown=Collier+County&_state=04000US12&_zip=&_lang=en&_sse=on&pctxt=fph&pgsl=010.

[49] U.S. Census Bureau, *American FactFinder, 2005-2007 American Community Survey 3-Year Estimates, Data Profile Highlights, Lee County, Florida.* http://factfinder.census.gov/servlet/ACSSAFFFacts?_event=Search&geo_id=&_geoContext=&_street=&_county=Lee+County&_cityTown=Lee+County&_state=04000US12&_zip=&_lang=en&_sse=on&pctxt=fph&pgsl=010.

[50] U.S. Census Bureau, *Fact Sheet, Immokalee CDP, Florida, 2000.* Data is unavailable for the year 2005-2007. http://factfinder.census.gov/servlet/SAFFFacts?_event=Search&geo_id=&_geoContext=&_street=&_county=Immokalee&_cityTown=Immokalee&_state=04000US12&_zip=&_lang=en&_sse=on&pctxt=fph&pgsl=010&show_2003_tab=&redirect=Y.

[51] U.S. Census Bureau, *Fact Sheet, Naples City, Florida, 2000.* Data is unavailable for the year 2005-2007. http://factfinder.census.gov/servlet/SAFFFacts?_event=&geo_id=16000US1247625&_geoContext=01000US|04000US12|16000US1247625&_street=&_county=Naples+City&_cityTown=Naples+City&_state=04000US12&_zip=&_lang=en&_sse=on&ActiveGeoDiv=&_useEV=&pctxt=fph&pgsl=160&_submenuId=factsheet_1&ds_name=ACS_2007_3YR_SAFF&_ci_nbr=null&qr_name=null&reg=&_keyword=&_industry=.

[52] U.S. Department of Justice, Bureau of Justice Statistics, *Crime & Justice Data Online, Law Enforcement Management and Administrative Statistics, 2000* (LEMAS). http://www.ojp.usdoj.gov/bjs/pub/pdf/lemas00.pdf.

APPENDIX B

Legal Issues in Local Police Enforcement of Federal Immigration Law

BY NANCY MORAWETZ AND ALINA DAS

Introduction

The question of whether and to what extent local police should be involved in the enforcement of federal immigration law has sparked considerable debate in the current political climate. Local police departments are no doubt fielding concerns from political leaders and residents about this issue and are struggling to determine how to respond. Some police departments may view civil violations of immigration law as being similar to violations of criminal laws, and thus consider immigration enforcement as inherent in their law enforcement role. They may also welcome a closer collaboration with federal authorities on these issues. At the same time, however, some police departments may view direct involvement in federal immigration law enforcement as being in tension with their traditional models of policing. Local enforcement of immigration law also does not mesh well with public safety models of policing, since immigrants commit criminal offenses at lower rates than their citizen neighbors[1] and local police are already charged with the task of arresting individuals who do violate criminal laws. In addition, local enforcement of immigration law does not appear to fit neatly into community-based models of policing. As many police departments and community advocates have observed, fear of deportation undermines the ability of police to garner trust in immigrant communities and dissuades residents from contacting the police to report crime or otherwise engage in problem-solving partnerships.[2]

Despite these disconnects, some localities have chosen to get involved in the direct enforcement of immigration law, either by asserting that they have the inherent authority to enforce federal immigration law or by entering into agreements with federal agencies. They have revised their policing model to focus on the enforcement of an entirely different set of laws. In doing so, however, some localities have not fully considered the legal challenges inherent in federal immigration law enforcement and the very real possibility that their actions may violate the rights of the residents in their communities.

This paper seeks to address these issues by delving into the legal complexities of local enforcement of immigration law and their implications for local liability. Who is directly affected by the local enforcement of immigration laws and what rights do they have? What legal issues do local police face if they become involved in enforcing immigration law on the street, in people's homes and workplaces, and in local jails? How is immigration enforcement different from criminal law enforcement? What kind of liability do localities expose themselves to by taking on immigration enforcement duties? To what degree can police count on other institutions to provide checks and balances that will mitigate these potential liabilities?

As this paper will show, immigration enforcement is a complex business. The nuances of immigration law and the changing demographics of American communities create an environment ripe for violation of the myriad rights of both immigrants of any status as well as citizens. The

Nancy Morawetz is a Professor of Clinical Law at New York University School of Law.
Alina Das is an Immigrant Defense Fellow at New York University School of Law.

arrest, detention, and/or transfer of custody of citizens and residents with lawful immigration status, the use of racial profiling to target immigrants without status, and the unlawful arrests, stops, and searches of immigrants in their homes and communities all raise real risks of liability for localities. The role of enforcing federal immigration law essentially requires localities to become familiar with a completely different set of rules of engagement by officers, thereby blurring lines about permissible police action and leading to the violation of the rights of the residents of the communities they seek to protect and serve.

The ultimate choice of any locality on its role in immigration enforcement will involve a wide range of factors. As part of the calculus, localities should weigh the complexity of the immigration law enforcement task, the real risk that their actions will violate the rights of people in the community, and the resulting potential exposure to liability.

I. Rights, Status, and the Changing Demographics of Immigrants in the United States

Popular discussions of immigration enforcement tend to make three false assumptions about the people who will be affected by local enforcement of immigration law. First, they assume that noncitizens have little or no rights under local, state, and federal law. Second, they assume that the precise immigration status of individuals in the community will be easy to identify. Third, they assume that if enforcement does target an individual who has violated immigration law, only that individual will be affected by the enforcement action. Because of these false assumptions, the debate over local enforcement of immigration law fails to consider significant potential of liability for violations of the rights of community residents. This section of the paper clarifies the underlying misconceptions that frame the debate.

A. The Rights of Immigrants in the United States

Regardless of status in the United States, immigrants have numerous rights protected under the U.S. Constitution and local, state, and federal laws. Some people mistakenly believe that noncitizens have no rights under the U.S. Constitution because they lack citizenship. This is incorrect. Provisions under the U.S. Constitution that refer to "persons" rather than "citizens" apply to individuals regardless of immigration status. As the Supreme Court has explained, "[t]hese provisions are universal in their application, to all persons within the territorial jurisdiction, without regard to any differences of race, of color, or of nationality."[3] Immigrants in the U.S. are considered "persons" within the territorial jurisdiction for purposes of constitutional protections regardless of how they entered the U.S. or whether they have lawful immigration status.[4] Under this reasoning, the Supreme Court has had occasion to uphold noncitizens' rights under a variety of provisions for over a century, including but not limited to the Fourth Amendment,[5] the Fifth and Sixth Amendments,[6] and the Due Process and Equal Protection clauses of the Fourteenth Amendment.[7]

Some of the misconceptions over the constitutional rights of noncitizens may be due to a much more narrow debate over how the Fourth Amendment applies in immigration courts. For example, a split Supreme Court addressed the degree to which suppression rules would be relaxed in the immigration court context.[8] The majority denied suppression in the specific case, but went on to say that it did "not condone any violations of the Fourth Amendment that may have occurred" and explained that its "conclusions concerning the exclusionary rule's value [in immigration court] might change, if there developed good reason to believe that Fourth Amendment violations by INS officers were widespread."[9] It further noted that there had been no assertion that officers had violated the agency's internal regulations or that there were any egregious violations of the Fourth Amendment or other rights involved in that particular case. Thus, as immigration enforcement has changed since this 1984 opinion, immigration practitioners still bring motions to suppress in immigration court, addressing the issues outlined by the Supreme Court. In any event, the decision was limited to the issue of suppression in immigration court. Nothing in the opinion addressed application of the Fourth Amendment to damage actions, and recent lawsuits have raised claims under the Fourth Amendment and other rights in the U.S. Constitution.

In addition to the rights under the U.S. Constitution, numerous rights and obligations also flow from federal statutes, from civil rights legislation such as the Civil Rights Act of 1964[10] to immigrant-specific legislation such as discrete provisions within the Immigration and Nationality Act that specify rights and/or provide limits on government authority.[11] Federal regulations under these laws also provide immigrants with specific protections. At the state level, many states have constitutional provisions that may be more expansive than U.S. constitutional rights.[12] In addition, many states and localities have enacted laws to protect their residents that do not distinguish on the basis of immigration status. Local ordinances and regulations may also provide strict guidelines delineating permissible actions towards residents and their rights to redress violations.

Thus, local police departments will have to account for a plethora of constitutional provisions and laws that govern both the rights of immigrants and the obligations of law enforcement officials if they seek to expand their enforcement goals into the realm of immigration. To say that immigration enforcement is somehow made easier by differences in the rights of immigrants and citizens is extremely misleading. In many ways, law enforcement officers will have to contend with a more complex set of laws and regulations governing immigration enforcement and permissible state action than they usually contend with in their traditional criminal law enforcement activities.

B. Status and the Changing Demographics of Immigrants in the United States

Another common misconception that has framed the debate over local enforcement of federal immigration law is the idea that the changing demographic Americans are witnessing in their communities involves only immigrants without status and thus such individuals will be easy to target through police efforts. This idea is flawed for two interrelated reasons. First, most new immigrants in the U.S. have some form of legal status. Second, the status of each specific individual is not easily discernable.

Contrary to popular belief, much of the changing demographic that Americans have witnessed in recent years deals primarily with legal immigration to the United States. While the percentage of foreign-born individuals in the United States has risen dramatically in the last thirty years, the vast majority of these individuals have lawful immigration status or citizenship. The percentage of foreign born in the United States population reached an historic low of 4.7 percent in 1970; today that share has climbed to approximately 12.5 percent of the population, or 38 million persons residing in the U.S.[13] The U.S. Department of Homeland Security (DHS), which administers the programs that provide immigration status and citizenship to the foreign born, does not maintain statistics about the size of the different components of this population.[14] However, reliable estimates place the percentage of citizens or lawful permanent residents at approximately 70 percent of the foreign born.[15] The remaining 30 percent are unauthorized immigrants who overstayed their visas or those who entered the United States without permission. But even within this group, there are substantial numbers who have a form of lawful status or are on the verge of obtaining lawful status. About 300,000 have or will soon have Temporary Protected Status, a form of status that allows the person to work legally in the United States and that precludes detention.[16] An additional 617,000 have completed every step of the legal immigration process, have official permission to work, and are on the verge of being provided with lawful permanent resident status.[17] Thus, even among those who are labeled as "undocumented" or "illegal," many have important intermediate forms of status.

These numbers call into question whether a community is correctly characterizing the new immigrants that are residing in or passing through their neighborhoods. Legal immigration continues at historically high levels. Each year, there are approximately one million new lawful permanent residents in the U.S.[18] Added to these are 320,000 temporary workers and dependents on a path to legal residence.[19] Over 72 percent of new immigrants each year have lawful status.[20] On top of these numbers of permanent residents, there are millions of foreign born who come to the United States on temporary visas, such as student visas, business visas, and tourist visas. Approximately 1.1 million students study each year on student visas.[21] Tourism varies by the time of the year, but the latest statistics are a reminder of how many foreign born visit each year. In February 2008, hardly the top tourist month of the year, there were 3.3 million international visitors to the United States, a 15 percent increase over the previous year.[22]

There is no doubt that in some parts of the country the demographic shifts from immigration are striking, and residents are grappling with these demographic changes[23]. However, the changes may not reflect unauthorized immigration. In Virginia, for example, the fiscal years 2005 through 2007 brought in almost one hundred thousand new lawful permanent residents.[24] That number constitutes 1.2 percent of the entire population of the state of Virginia.[25] But these numbers are of lawful immigrants. While local residents might attribute changes in their environment to popular press discussions of illegal immigration, much of what they observe is legal immigration.

Moreover, there are no readily discernable factors that accurately indicate a person's immigration status. Some people may believe that foreign language use, or a lack of English skills, is necessarily a sign of unauthorized immigration. However, foreign language use is high across the foreign-born population. The vast majority of the foreign born use a language other than English in the home.[26] In addition, foreign language use is high among citizens. Nine percent of the native-born population over the age of five—twenty-three million Americans—speaks a language other than English at home.[27] Of these native-born citizens, most speak English. But 4.7 million report that they do not speak English "very well."[28] Thus, use of a foreign language or lack of English skills does not necessarily mean that a person is likely to lack immigration status. Similarly, a person's surname is also not an accurate indicator of unauthorized immigration. For example, while some localities particularly along the southern border might assume that a Spanish surname is an indicator of unauthorized immigration, such an assumption is baseless—nearly 15 percent of the U.S. population is of Hispanic origin and the majority of Hispanic residents are native-born U.S. citizens.[29]

In summary, the categories of lawful immigration status are complex and commonly used indicators to determine which individuals fall into which categories will often prove false. Treading into the local enforcement of federal immigration law will therefore entail a significant risk of targeting residents with lawful status, including U.S. citizens, and may be motivated by false assumptions about the demographic changes in the community.

C. Mixed-Status Families and the Ripple Effect of Immigration Enforcement

Another common misconception related to the debate over local immigration enforcement is that the purported targets of these efforts are somehow isolated from the rest of the community by their lack of immigration status. There is no clear dividing line between citizens and noncitizens within most communities, however. Nearly one in ten U.S. families with children is a "mixed-status" family, i.e., a family with at least one noncitizen parent and at least one citizen child.[30] One in ten children living in the U.S. is a part of a mixed-status family.[31] Approximately 85 percent of immigrant families (families with one noncitizen parent) are mixed-status families.[32]

Thus, the arrest and detention of an immigrant may very well affect a citizen spouse or child. Recent studies and reports have noted the harms that U.S. citizen children have experienced when a parent is arrested and detained during a home raid or workplace raid.[33] The immediate harms may include unlawfully detaining U.S. citizen children[34] or leaving children unsupervised while their primary caregivers are detained.[35] Longer term effects for children and families may include socioeconomic hardship, school disruptions, and emotional trauma.[36]

As a matter of liability, mixed-status families present local officials engaged in immigration enforcement with two kinds of problems. First, they may improperly detain citizens or lawful residents in the course of seeking a person without proper status. If they do so, they will be held accountable for treading on these residents' right to liberty. Second, they may leave minors unsupervised as they detain their parents and thereby violate their general responsibility for the care and well-being of the children residing in the community. Simply put, immigration enforcement cannot proceed on the assumption that these U.S. citizen children will not be affected by their attempts to enforce immigration law.

Thus, immigration enforcement is made infinitely more complex by misconceptions about the well-ingrained legal rights of immigrants, the changing demographics of the immigrant population, and the intertwined nature of immigrants and citizens in local communities. The complexities of immigration law make it very difficult for even the most experienced and well-trained federal immigration officers to follow the letter of the law. These underlying complexities are important for localities to consider when evaluating the legal risks of undertaking immigration enforcement.

II. Liability Issues in Local Police Enforcement of Immigration Laws

In the past year, as both the federal government and local authorities have stepped up immigration arrests, the methods for identifying, arresting, and detaining those charged with violations of the immigration laws have sparked significant litigation. These lawsuits range from class actions that challenge methods for arresting people in their homes or workplaces, to actions focused on the wrongful detention or deportation of a specific individual. Some of these actions involve police action outside of a correctional institution. Some involve sheriffs or wardens who are identifying or detaining suspected immigration law violators in the local jail.

This section of the paper serves to unpack the potential liability of state and local officials. First, it addresses the interplay between local and federal liability and how agreements between localities and the federal government affect local liability. Second, it takes a closer look at the specific liability risks inherent in the local enforcement of federal immigration law and describes some of the lawsuits that community members and their advocates have initiated to challenge unlawful actions in the recent raids, arrests, detentions, and deportations.

A. The Interplay Between Local and Federal Liability

Police departments that engage in the enforcement of federal immigration law face potential damages, actions, and other lawsuits similar to those faced by federal authorities. A person who feels that a local law enforcement officer or police department violated his or her rights may sue to address those violations. The plethora of laws that may be at issue in a lawsuit may include but are not limited to numerous local and state laws, state constitutional provisions, Title VI of the Civil Rights Act of 1964, and various provisions of the U.S. Constitution, including the Fourth, Fifth, and Fourteenth Amendments. The exact contours of liability may depend both on the nature of the violations and the scope of the relationship between local and federal authorities.

States and localities that act on their "inherent authority" to enforce immigration law, i.e., independent immigrant enforcement efforts without a formal agreement with federal immigration authorities, also risk challenges to the underlying validity of their actions. Although this issue continues to be debated, there is substantial support for the view that localities are simply not permitted to engage in most forms of immigration law enforcement in the absence of a specific agreement with federal immigration authorities.[37] There are two interrelated bases for this view.

The first is the argument that states and localities have inherent authority to enforce federal law only as it pertains to criminal violations. Under this reasoning, states do not have inherent authority to enforce most immigration law because most immigration violations are civil, not criminal.[38] The second argument is focused on the issue of federal preemption. Given that the federal government has a comprehensive scheme for enforcing immigration law, there is a strong argument that direct local enforcement of the immigration law is preempted by federal law.[39] The only forms of federal criminal enforcement that states and localities are arguably authorized to engage in under this scheme are for specific federal crimes related to smuggling, transporting or harboring,[40] and illegal presence following reentry after a deportation order.[41] But notably, even in these areas, Congress has imposed limitations. With respect to reentry, Congress included specific limitations on the reentry arrests, requiring that state and local officials first "obtain appropriate confirmation from the Immigration and Naturalization Service of the status of such individual and only for such period of time as may be required for the Service to take the individual into federal custody for purposes of deporting or removing the alien from the United States."[42] Indeed, the legislative history shows that Congress was careful not to provide broader state and local authority to enforce immigration laws.[43] As to smuggling, harboring, and transporting, there are arguments that these provisions are meant to be interpreted narrowly to reach classic smuggling operations and the harboring and transportation related to these operations. Localities that seek to enforce federal immigration law through their "inherent authority" risk making arrests that fall outside the scope of their actual legal authority.

For these reasons and others, some states and localities seek to establish an agreement with federal immigration authorities in an effort to prevent challenges to their authority. Section 287(g) of the Immigration and Nationality Act, a provision that Congress enacted as part of the Illegal Immigration Reform and Immigrant Responsibility Act, authorizes the federal government to enter into written memoranda of agreement (MOAs) with states and localities to provide for the local enforcement of federal immigration law.[44] These "287(g) agreements" permit "an officer or employee of the State or subdivision" to carry out the "function[s] of an immigration officer in relation to the investigation, apprehension, or detention of aliens . . . ."[45] An officer or employee "acting under color of authority" of a 287(g) agreement may be treated as federal employees for purposes of litigation under the Federal Tort Claims Act (FTCA), which provides for the United States to assume tort liability for actions taken by federal employees under the scope of their employment.[46]

At first blush, these 287(g) agreements seem to provide some measure of protection for state and local resources if facing suit over unlawful acts stemming from federal immigration law enforcement. However, the devil is in the details. The FTCA does not cover claims that are brought directly under constitutional guarantees distinct from torts under state law.[47] In addition, FTCA protections do not extend to "discretionary functions" or actions taken outside the scope of the officer's employment.[48]

Thus, lawsuits challenging a locality's actions will inevitably focus on activities that lie outside the 287(g) agreement. The DHS Bureau of Immigration and Customs Enforcement (ICE) has specified that the "287(g) program is not designed to allow state and local agencies to perform random street operations" and "is not designed to impact issues such as excessive occupancy and day labor activities."[49] ICE guidelines have clarified that "[p]olice cannot randomly ask for a person's immigration status or conduct raids" and may not use traffic offenses as a pretext for questioning individuals about their immigrations status.[50] Furthermore, 287(g) agreements do not cover conduct that constitutes racial profiling.[51] State officers operating under a 287(g) agreement will not be treated as federal officers for purposes of the FTCA if they fail to follow these guidelines.

Thus, as a whole, 287(g) provides very limited protection to localities and their officers, and may even introduce new dangers in liability. Section 287(g) provides that states and localities may carry out its functions only "at the expense of the State or political subdivision" and only "to the extent consistent with State and local law."[52] At the same time, however, the officer or employee taking on this role will be "subject to the direction" of the Attorney General.[53] If federal officers, untrained in state and local law, direct a state or locality to participate in an operation or series of arrests in a way that is inconsistent with state and local law, there are no protections under 287(g). Thus, regardless of federal officials' involvement, states and localities must assure that their practices comport with local and state laws, including state court rulings on state constitutional analogs to the Fourth and Fifth amendments, as well as other requirements under federal guidelines, federal statutes, and the U.S. Constitution.

B. Liability Risks: An Overview of Recent Lawsuits Challenging Immigration Enforcement Actions

As the overview above describes, the local enforcement of federal immigration law involves a minefield of potential litigation and liability for police departments and localities. The Lawyers Committee in San Francisco alone reports that it has settled eight cases over the last ten years for a total of $642,500.[54] This section of the paper describes some of the most recent public lawsuits in varying locales that have exposed unlawful actions by states and localities, often in cooperation with or under direction of the federal government, when engaging in immigration law enforcement whether on the street, in people's homes or workplaces, or in the local jail.

1. Liability Stemming from the Arrest and Detention of U.S. Citizens and Other U.S. Residents

Several localities have been sued in recent years due to the arrest and detention of U.S. citizens, lawful permanent residents, and other immigrants with lawful status. As explained above, immigration law is incredibly complex. Officers who make immigration arrests or detain individuals on the street, workplace, home, or jail will rarely have firsthand evidence of the status of a person. Instead, assuming there is a lawful basis for a stop or other questioning, they will be making judgments about whether the person is a citizen, an immigrant with some other form of lawful status, or an individual who lacks status altogether. These are not easy judgments and erroneous determinations create a risk of liability.

The first danger is of targeting U.S. citizens. This occurs when law enforcement officers improperly arrest and detain U.S. citizens for immigration violations or misidentify U.S. citizens in the local jail as noncitizens, holding and transferring them into immigration custody. While shocking, such occurrences are not uncommon. Citizenship law is complicated. Many persons born abroad are citizens as a result of the status of their parents or grandparents.[55] They may not know the details of their citizenship, or even that they are citizens. Other citizens do not carry or possess any proof of their status. As many as 13 million Americans do not have ready access to proof of citizenship (such as a birth certificate, U.S. passport, or naturalization certificate).[56] The problem is more pronounced for various segments of the population. Citizens with incomes under $25,000 are twice as likely to lack citizenship documents as citizens with incomes above $25,000.[57] Twenty-five percent of African Americans lack any form of government-issued photo identification.[58] As many as 32 million American women who have married do not have citizenship documents reflecting their current name.[59] Thus, lack of documentation does not necessarily mean that an individual is not a U.S. citizen. When a question about citizenship arises, however, there is no national database of citizens to resolve those questions. DHS can only answer questions about people who have been processed by that agency. Most citizens, however, have never had a file with DHS. DHS itself has reportedly detained and even deported U.S. citizens despite its own purported expertise in this area of law.[60] Similarly, local jails that attempt to engage in screening make the predictable error of issuing detainers on some citizens, improperly holding them for transfer into immigration custody instead of releasing them.[61]

A second danger is of arresting, detaining, holding, and transferring into immigration custody some immigrants with lawful immigration status who are not subject to removal. Immigrants who have been granted lawful permanent residence, for example, maintain that status regardless of whether their permanent resident card (or "green card") itself is expired; only a final removal order can terminate lawful permanent residence status.[62] Thus, many individuals with expired lawful permanent resident cards have diligently applied for and are still awaiting their replacement cards due to the government's delay, as described in a recent lawsuit challenging DHS's failure to provide cards in a timely manner for certain individuals.[63] In any event, such individuals still have lawful status and any false arrest and unlawful detention would be grounds for a lawsuit.

Similarly, individuals without lawful permanent residence status may nonetheless have other forms of immigration status that would make their arrest and detention on immigration grounds unlawful. For example, many individuals have been granted Temporary Protected Status (TPS), which is granted to persons who are from countries that are suffering from natural disasters or ongoing armed conflict or other extraordinary conditions.[64] It is available to persons who crossed the border without inspection and even to those with outstanding removal orders if they otherwise meet eligibility requirements.[65] The documentation for TPS, however, is chronically out of date. Each year, applicants must apply to renew their status.[66] The government does not process their applications in time, however, for them to have a new document before their current documents expire. Nonetheless, their status is considered valid and the government posts a notice in the federal register stating that employment authorization is automatically extended beyond the date on their existing cards.[67] Individuals with TPS are statutorily prohibited from being detained based on status.[68]

Given the serious violations inherent in the arrest and detention of U.S. citizens and residents with lawful immigration status in the name of immigration enforcement, such actions carry serious liability risks. Recent lawsuits that have been made public chronicle outrageous cases of botched federal and local enforcement of immigration law against U.S. citizens and other residents. In one recent case, federal and local Los Angeles officials, including the sheriff, were sued for improperly causing the detention and deportation of Pedro Guzman, a cognitively impaired United States citizen.[69] Mr. Guzman was serving time for a misdemeanor charge in a local jail when local criminal justice officials, through a special pilot project established through an MOA with DHS, misidentified Mr. Guzman as a noncitizen, placing an immigration detainer on him in the local jail and then transferring him to ICE, which eventually deported him—despite the fact that Mr. Guzman was born in the U.S.[70] Pedro Guzman's case was a major news story since it took months for Mr. Guzman to be located and returned to his family.[71] The particular facts of his case have yet to be fully developed, but it is possible that his cognitive impairment played some role in his deportation. If so, it would follow a reported pattern in which the cognitively impaired or mentally ill are misidentified as noncitizens.[72]

In addition to actions resulting in unlawful deportation, unlawful stops, searches, questioning, arrests, and detention of U.S. citizens and residents also carry serious liability risks. In one recent case, filed as a class action against Maricopa County, Arizona, Maricopa County Sheriff's Office, and Maricopa County Sheriff Joe Arpaio, four U.S. citizens and one individual with lawful status at the time of his arrest describe having been unlawfully stopped, detained, and questioned by Maricopa County Sheriff's Office officials based on their efforts to enforce immigration laws through a 287(g) agreement.[73] In New Jersey, several U.S. citizens, lawful permanent residents, and an individual with TPS joined other immigrants challenging home raids conducted by ICE and the Penns Grove Police Department, describing the raids, questioning, seizure of documents, and/or arrests in their homes despite their lawful status.[74]

These are only a few public examples of the myriad cases involving lawsuits against localities attempting to enforce complex immigration law. They add to the already long list of lawsuits against ICE practices that ensnare people with lawful status, including highly publicized lawsuits such as a damages action following the wrongful arrest and detention of a nine-year-old U.S. citizen[75] and a damages action with 114 administrative complaints challenging a workplace raid that involved the detention and search of scores of U.S. citizens and lawful permanent residents.[76] Police departments that engage in federal immigration law enforcement can hardly expect to be better at identifying individuals without lawful immigration status than federal immigration agents, and open themselves up to liability for violating the rights of community residents.

2. Liability Stemming from the Use of Racial Profiling as a Method of Enforcing Federal Immigration Law

Racial and ethnic profiling is a real risk in state and local immigration enforcement of federal immigration law. Enforcement without profiling requires some individualized suspicion related to the individual who is stopped and questioned or otherwise investigated. But what will constitute individualized suspicion? As explained above, immigration status is a complex legal issue. Local officers will not be able to "observe" an immigration violation the way they might observe a violation of criminal law. Under such circumstances, there is a serious risk that the grounds for suspicion will in fact be nothing more than a series of assumptions that begin with a profile about people who speak another language or have a particular racial or ethnic profile. Indeed, the federal government has long been criticized for using racial profiling in its efforts to enforce immigration law.[77] A statistical study of data gathered through the Freedom of Information Act found substantial evidence of profiling in the New York office of the Immigration and Naturalization Service, the precursor agency to DHS.[78] Such tactics may well be ingrained in certain federal immigration enforcement efforts.

Despite its ubiquitous nature, racial profiling is unlawful and has subjected law enforcement officers to liability.[79] Even localities engaged in racial profiling under the direction of federal immigration agents will not escape liability for these actions. Under 287(g) agreements, localities have no protection from claims that they have engaged in racial profiling. The 287(g) agreements have specifically provided that officers exercising authority under the MOA are bound by all federal civil rights statutes and regulations, explicitly including the U.S. Department of Justice 2003 guidance, "Guidance Regarding the Use of Race by Federal Law Enforcement Agencies."[80] As the federal guidance states: "Reliance upon generalized stereotypes is absolutely forbidden. Rather, use of race or ethnicity is permitted only when the officer is pursuing a specific lead concerning the identifying characteristics of persons involved in an identified criminal activity."[81]

In the lawsuit against Maricopa County, its Sheriff's Office, and Sheriff Arpaio, allegations of racial profiling are front and center. The plaintiffs allege that the defendants have engaged in a pattern and practice of racial profiling that includes the use of sweeps involving "pretextual and unfounded stops, racially motivated questioning, searches and other mistreatment, and often baseless arrests" as well as "widespread, day-to-day targeting and mistreatment of persons who appear to be Latino."[82] The named plaintiffs in the complaint detail several disturbing incidents where police officers targeted individuals with Latino appearance during sweeps and arrests.[83] The plaintiffs allege that these actions violate the civil and constitutional rights of the class, citing violations of constitutional rights including the right to equal protection and the prohibition against unreasonable search and seizure; violations of the prohibition against racial discrimination by federally funded programs in Title VI of the Civil Rights Act of 1964, 42 U.S.C. § 2000d and its implementing regulations; and violations of the Arizona State Constitution Art. II, § 8, which provides that "No person shall be disturbed in his private affairs, or his home invaded, without authority of law."[84]

Similarly, several immigrant plaintiffs brought a lawsuit against ICE agents and the mayor, police chief, and individual police officers in Danbury, Connecticut, raising claims under state and federal law.[85] The lawsuit challenges the "discriminatory and unauthorized enforcement of federal immigration laws against Latino residents" and alleges that the police "have repeatedly and knowingly made illegal civil immigration arrests, engaged in impermissibly discriminatory law enforcement, and retaliated against residents for expressive activities secured by the First Amendment."[86] The lawsuit challenges the city's discriminatory targeting of a group of day laborers as well as its use of racial profiling and pretextual stops to enforce civil immigration law, particularly in terms of the use of civil immigration violations found in the National Crime Information Center database to make unauthorized civil immigration arrests.[87] Because Danbury has taken on these actions without engaging in any 287(g) agreement with federal immigration officials, the lawsuit raises federal preemption arguments in addition to the other legal claims.[88]

Racial profiling is also the focus of a lawsuit against Sonoma County and the Sonoma County Sheriff's Department in Sonoma County, California. The lawsuit, brought by several individuals and the Committee for Immigrant Rights of Sonoma County, alleges that sheriff's deputies, both with and without assistance from DHS immigration agents, "use race as a motivating factor in traffic stops and other detentions," unlawfully targeting, interrogating, and detaining Latino residents of Sonoma County for purposes of immigration enforcement.[89] The lawsuit challenges the authority of the county to engage in this immigration enforcement as well as the county's denial of the constitutional, statutory, and regulatory rights of immigrants once held in the county jail for immigration purposes.[90]

Allegations of racial profiling and bias have also been raised in the context of identifying—and misidentifying—individuals as deportable immigrants while in criminal custody in local jails. The lawsuit against the Los Angeles County Sheriff's Department for the deportation of a U.S. citizen alleges that the plaintiff, Mr. Guzman, "was selected for interview [by the local law enforcement officer who works with DHS] based solely on his perceived race, ethnicity and national origin" and that that the Los Angeles County Sheriff's Department thus "unconstitutionally discriminated against plaintiff Guzman on the basis of his race and ethnicity...by causing or participating in the illegal deportation of Mr. Guzman."[91] The lawsuit also alleges inadequate training of the local law enforcement officials.[92]

Given the complexities of immigration law, it may not be uncommon for federal immigration agents and local police officers alike to fall back on racial profiling tactics to identify people who may be in violation of civil immigration law. Once such tactics are used, the violations may be widespread, as the plaintiffs in these lawsuits attest. Thus, states and localities that are considering whether to engage in federal immigration law enforcement must question how their officers will be able to conduct these activities and identify individuals who have violated immigration law without engaging in racial profiling.

3. Liability Stemming from Unlawful Arrests, Searches, and Seizures and Other Common Immigration Enforcement Tactics

In addition to the problems described above, local police also face a substantial risk of liability in performing immigration tasks due to the differing rules of engagement between traditional police work and immigration law enforcement. As police departments are well aware, the laws of criminal enforcement are complex and regular training is essential to ensure that rights are respected and evidence is admissible in any subsequent prosecution. Adding immigration enforcement into this mix, which differs in substantial ways from what is considered permissible police conduct in the criminal investigation context, changes the rules of engagement. Violating these complex rules could lead to significant liability for localities.

A key area of confusion for local police who have been involved in home raids and arrests involves the scope of the arrest warrant. In the criminal sphere, an arrest warrant is issued by a judge upon a showing of probable cause.[93] The underlying information for the warrant is likely to be supplied by an affidavit of an officer who has investigated the case and can provide sworn testimony about the probable cause for believing that the target has committed a crime.[94] The arresting officer may go to the home to execute the warrant and is expected to follow a knock and announce procedure.[95] If the suspect does not open the door, the officer may force open the premises and arrest the individual named in the warrant.[96] Once arrested, the individual is provided with a right to counsel and will be arraigned within a short time.[97] If there is a major mistake in the original ground for the arrest, it may well be discovered by the prosecutor and defense lawyer, and lead to a dismissal of the charges.

Consider the contrasting rules and institutional structure for an immigration arrest. An administrative warrant is issued by one of a wide array of immigration officers, often on the basis of limited paper information. There is no process for a sworn statement reviewed by a neutral judge or other officer. The warrant may be based on data that is old and out of date.[98] Once the warrant is prepared, the officers may go to the place believed to be the home of the person named in the warrant. They do not have the right, however, to enter the home without consent.[99] Once they arrest the individual on civil immigration grounds, they may detain the person and there is no right to an attorney at government expense.[100] As a result, it is very possible that a mistake will go undetected and that an individual who was not in fact subject to arrest will remain detained.

Because officers do not have the right on an administrative warrant to enter a home without consent, the key to the execution of an immigration home arrest focuses on the issue of consent. When an individual sees a police officer at her door, however, she may assume that she has no choice in the matter. A person who consents believing that the police would otherwise be authorized to gain entry forcibly cannot be said to have consented. Police officers may face similar confusions, not understanding the limitations of an administrative warrant. When the target of a warrant does not answer the door, for example, local police might presume that they are free to force their way into a home. Similarly, they may presume that the warrant bears the safeguards and relative reliability of the criminal law system and may be surprised to find that the person specified in the administrative warrant is not the person they find in the targeted home. Simply put, the "warrant" for an immigration arrest—a defining instrument of police authority under other regimes—is a highly misleading document for police who are accustomed to enforcing criminal laws.

Thus, it comes as no surprise that home raids have sparked litigation over the tactics in executing administrative immigration warrants or otherwise attempting to enter homes and arrest individuals without a valid warrant. In Minnesota, a group of U.S citizens, lawful permanent residents, and other immigrants filed a lawsuit challenging the legality of methods used by ICE and several local law enforcement officials as part of "Operation Crosscheck."[101] Through this operation, an officer with Kandiyohi County Probation Service "collected information regarding persons under her supervision who, in her determination, had been 'born in foreign countries' and concluded were 'here illegally.'"[102] She contacted ICE officials in Minnesota with a "'dossier of foreigners' for their inspection."[103] ICE and local law enforcement officers from several area police departments used this information to engage in warrantless home raids that resulted in the unlawful arrest and detention of numerous individuals, including children.[104] The lawsuit asserts that ICE and the local law enforcement officers violated the plaintiffs' constitutional and statutory rights through these warrantless arrests, searches, and seizures and other unlawful practices during the raids.[105]

Similar lawsuits have also arisen in response to home raids as part of "Operation Return to Sender," a "fugitive" enforcement action that targets immigrants who have been ordered deported but have not left the country. In New Jersey, for example, a group of U.S. citizens, immigrants with lawful status, and other immigrants filed a lawsuit challenging the legality of methods used by ICE and local police in carrying out "Operation Return to Sender."[106] According to the lawsuit, the operation was carried out unlawfully and in fact did not target these alleged absconders. The complaint alleges that the agents used deceptive tactics or force to gain entry into the home and proceeded to interrogate everyone in the home without any individualized suspicion.[107] The complaint further alleges that these operations are conducted without adequate prior investigation, thereby leading to the harassment of people without reasonable cause to expect a "fugitive" to be in the relevant location.[108] Many of the individuals were wrongly arrested despite having valid status and/or otherwise treated harshly while detained.[109] For these violations of their rights, the plaintiffs are seeking compensatory and punitive damages as well as injunctive relief under federal and state constitutional law.

A similar lawsuit was filed in New York as a class action, also challenging ICE's tactics against residents under "Operation Return to Sender."[110] The complaint alleges that the agents used deceptive tactics—including announcing themselves as "police"—during predawn raids in people's homes.[111] The complaint further notes the lack of consent in ICE's entry as well as the agents' questioning and rough treatment of residents who were not listed as "fugitives."[112] Notably, the complaint cites the statements of public officials within Nassau County government expressing their frustration with ICE. In a public letter to the local Agent-In-Charge of ICE, Nassau County Commissioner of Police Lawrence W. Mulvey stated that ICE had misled the Nassau County Police about the nature of the raids and that the people arrested were not the purported targets of the raids.[113] Noting that the ICE agents acted with a "cowboy mentality," Police Commissioner Mulvey criticized the inaccurate information they used for the investigation, including their use of incorrect addresses for the targeted homes and, in one instance, their attempt to look for a 28-year-old suspect using a photograph of the suspect when he was seven years old.[114]

The inaccuracies that plagued these home raids described in these lawsuits are not isolated. A study by the DHS Inspector General has observed that the data relied upon by ICE's fugitive teams is inaccurate in up to 50 percent of cases.[115] Community groups have struggled to educate residents about their rights under the varying laws, but as the lawsuits demonstrate, many individuals are afraid and feel coerced when confronted with predawn operations at their homes. Local police departments may seek to consider whether to get involved in any such operations given the inaccurate and incomplete information and unlawful practices that are often involved.

4. Other Areas of Local Involvement in Potential Litigation

While many of the most recent lawsuits have focused on the problems described above, the local enforcement of federal immigration law may lead to numerous other types of unforeseen areas of liability and increased involvement in litigation. These include but are not limited to litigation over the conditions of confinement, the treatment of minors, the release of information about the policies and practices of the police department, and increasing involvement in immigration court litigation.

First, localities face considerable litigation concerning the conditions of confinement in local area jails that hold immigrant detainees. While localities may enter into formal agreements with the federal government to hold immigrant detainees, the federal government has pointedly argued that the states and localities that agree to hold detainees are solely responsible for the quality of their care under applicable intergovernmental service agreements and contracts.[116] They argue that these state and local facilities are "independent contractors" and are therefore not within the scope of the FTCA.[117]

Second, localities must face the real and pressing question of how children will be treated if and when police conduct arrests and raids. ICE has been highly criticized for detaining sole caregivers and children present during raids. For example, during a workplace raid in New Bedford, Massachusetts, community residents complained that ICE had given little notice to social welfare agencies and a significant number of children were left unsupervised while their parents were detained and even transferred out of state.[118] In another example involving a highly publicized home raid that resulted in a lawsuit, ICE agents arrested and detained a nine-year-old U.S. citizen for twelve hours, after his father showed the agents the child's U.S. passport and asked to arrange for someone to watch him.[119] In the Minnesota lawsuit challenging "Operation Crosscheck," sixteen children are included as plaintiffs challenging warrantless home raids in which the children themselves were arrested and detained.[120] These types of acts have instigated lawsuits and will no doubt result in liability risks for states and localities that engage in similar practices.

Third, many localities have been drawn into "freedom of information" litigation. In the Danbury lawsuit, for example, the immigrants' lawyers filed a state freedom of information law request to obtain documents related to the arrest of a group of day workers.[121] The hearing on the request involved testimony by the city police chief, the chief of detectives, the mayor's chief of staff, and the deputy corporation counsel.[122] In some of these freedom of information cases, the state may not be free to defend the action as it sees fit. In one case, the federal government appeared in the state freedom of information action to present the position of the United States in opposition to release of the records that the sheriff used to place an immigration detainer on an individual who had a "hit" on the NCIC database.[123] Ultimately the state was ordered to make the disclosure.[124] But in the meantime, the litigation was prolonged by the federal position against release of information.

Fourth, localities may find themselves being drawn increasingly into immigration court. Immigration proceedings differ significantly from criminal proceedings. In most cases, the court decides a binary question—whether to deport or not deport. There is no opportunity to plead to reduced charges or otherwise achieve compromise. That means that in cases where the immigration law offers no relief if the case goes forward, there is a premium on proving that the arresting officers violated applicable regulations or otherwise made a wrongful arrest. Police errors are therefore more likely to be at the center of attention. This issue may arise in two different ways. First, an individual may move to terminate the proceedings based on an argument that the officer violated applicable regulations.[125] This kind of claim necessarily involves questions about what happened in connection with the arrest. It is therefore standard procedure in these kinds of cases to subpoena the officer to testify about the arrest. Secondly, immigration cases, like criminal cases, may involve motions to suppress evidence, such as statements made by the person arrested or documents obtained through the arrest.[126] These motions also involve subpoenas of the arresting officers to inquire into the circumstances surrounding the particular arrest but may also involve an inquiry into the general practices of the arresting agency. Thus localities may find the actions of their officers and their general practices and policies increasingly at issue in immigration court.

Conclusion

Many of the issues surrounding state and local liability for immigration enforcement have yet to be resolved. Indeed, some of these issues may not be resolved for many years as immigration enforcement practices change and as cases work their way through the courts. But the risks for states and localities are very real. These risks must be considered as states and localities decide whether to take on enforcement of immigration law.

Endnotes

[1] *See* Kristin F. Butcher & Anne Morrison Piehl, *Crime, Corrections, and California: What Does Immigration Have to Do With It?* California Counts: Population Trends and Profiles (Feb. 2008), *available at* http://www.ppic.org/content/pubs/cacounts/CC_208KBCC.pdf (last visited July 25, 2008); Kristin F. Butcher & Anne Morrison Piehl, *Why Are Immigrants' Incarceration Rates So Low? Evidence on Selective Immigration, Deterrence, and Deportation* (Nat'l Bureau of Econ. Research, Working Paper No. 13229, 2007); Daniel Mears, *Immigration and Crime: What's the Connection?* 14 Fed. Sent. Rep. 284 (2002).

[2] Appleseed, Forcing Our Blues into Grey Areas: Local Police and Federal Immigration Enforcement 10 (2008), *available at* http://www.appleseednetwork.org/Portals/0/Reports/Forcing_Our_Blues_Into_Gray_Areas 2008.pdf (last visited July 25, 2008).

[3] *Yick Wo v. Hopkins*, 118 U.S. 356, 369 (1886).

[4] *See Plyer v. Doe*, 457 U.S. 202, 210-212 (1982).

[5] *See, e.g., Almeida-Sanchez v. United States*, 413 U.S. 266 (1973).

[6] *See, e.g., Wong Wing v. United States*, 163 U.S. 228, 237 (1896).

[7] *See, e.g., Plyer*, 457 U.S. at 202-230; *Graham v. Richardson*, 403 U.S. 365, 370 (1971); *Yick Wo*, 118 U.S. at 369.

[8] *I.N.S. v. Lopez-Mendoza*, 468 U.S. 1032, 1050 (1984).

[9] *Id.*

[10] *See Lau v. Nichols*, 414 U.S. 563 (1974).

[11] *See Zadvydas v. Davis*, 533 U.S. 678 (2001).

[12] *See* Michael J. Gorman, *Survey: State Search and Seizure Analogs*, 77 Miss. L. J. 417 (2007) (identifying differences between federal and state search and seizure law).

[13] Aaron Terrazas, Jeanne Batalova, & Velma Fan, Migration Policy Institute, Frequently Requested Statistics on Immigrants in the United States (Oct. 2007), *available at* http://www.migrationinformation.org/USfocus/display.cfm?id=649#1.

[14] Nancy F. Rytina, U.S. Dept. of Homeland Security, Office of Immigration Statistics, Estimates of Legal Permanent Resident Population and Population Eligible to Naturalize in 2004, 1 (Feb. 2006), *available at* http://www.dhs.gov/xlibrary/assets/statistics/publications/LPRest2004.pdf (last visited July 25, 2008).

[15] *See* Terrazas et al., *supra* note 13.

[16] *See* David A. Martin, Migration Policy Institute, Twilight Statuses: A Closer Examination of the Unauthorized Population (June 2005) at 7-8, *available at* http://www.migrationpolicy.org/pubs/MPI_PB_6.05.pdf (last visited July 25, 2008).

[17] *See id.* at 6.

[18] Migration Police Institute, Annual Immigration to the United States: The Real Numbers (May 2007) at 1, *available at* http://www.migrationpolicy.org/pubs/FS16_USImmigration_051807.pdf (last visited July 25, 2008).

[19] *Id.*

[20] *Id.*

[21] U.S. Dept. of Homeland Security, Yearbook of Immigration Statistics: 2006, Temporary Admissions Table 32, available at http://www.dhs.gov/ximgtn/statistics/publications/YrBk06NI.shtm (last visited July 25, 2008).

[22] U.S. Dept. of Commerce, Office of Travel & Tourism Industries, International Visitation Up 15 Percent in February 2008 (May 20, 2008), *available at* http://tinet.ita.doc.gov/tinews/archive/tinews2008/20080520.html (last visited July 25, 2008).

[23] *See* Cristina M. Rodríguez, *The Significance of the Local in Immigration Regulation*, 106 Mich. L. Rev. 567, 593-595 (2008).

[24] KELLY JEFFERYS & RANDALL MONGER, U.S. DEPT. OF HOMELAND SECURITY, OFFICE OF IMMIGRATION STATISTICS, US LEGAL PERMANENT RESIDENTS: 2007 (Mar. 2008), *available at* http://www.dhs.gov/xlibrary/assets/statistics/publications/LPR_FR_2007.pdf

[25] U.S. CENSUS BUREAU, STATE & COUNTY QUICK FACTS, VIRGINIA (2006), *available at* http://quickfacts.census.gov/qfd/states/51000.html (last visited July 25, 2008).

[26] U.S. CENSUS BUREAU, 2006 AMERICAN COMMUNITY SURVEY, TABLE B16005, NATIVITY BY LANGUAGE SPOKEN AT HOME BY ABILITY TO SPEAK ENGLISH FOR THE POPULATION 5 YEARS AND OLDER (2006), *available at* http://factfinder.census.gov/http://factfinder.census.gov/home/saff/main.html?lang=en (last visited July 25, 2008) (reporting that 84.4 percent of the foreign born speak a language pother than English at home).

[27] *Id.* (reporting that 23.4 million Americans over the age of five speak a language other than English at home).

[28] *Id.*

[29] PEW HISPANIC CENTER, STATISTICAL PORTRAIT OF HISPANICS IN THE UNITED STATES, 2006 (January 23, 2008), *available at* http://pewhispanic.org/factsheets/factsheet.php?FactsheetID=35 (last visited July 25, 2008).

[30] MICHAEL E. FIX & WENDY ZIMMERMAN, ALL UNDER ONE ROOF: MIXED-STATUS FAMILIES IN AN ERA OF REFORM 1 (Oct. 6, 1999), *available at* http://www.urban.org/UploadedPDF/409100.pdf (last visited July 25, 2008).

[31] *Id.* at 2.

[32] *Id.*

[33] *See, e.g.,* David B. Thronson, *Creating Crisis: Immigration Raids and the Destablization of Immigrant Families,* 43 WAKE FOREST L. REV. 391, 403-406 (2008); RANDY CAPPS, ROSA MARIA CASTAÑEDA, AJAY CHAUDRY, & ROBERT SANTOS, NAT'L COUNCIL OF LA RAZA & THE URBAN INST., PAYING THE PRICE: THE IMPACT OF IMMIGRATION RAIDS ON AMERICA'S CHILDREN (2007), *available at* http://www.urban.org/UploadedPDF/411566_immigration_raids.pdf (last visited July 25, 2008).

[34] *See, e.g., Reyes v. Alcantar*, No. 4:07-cv-022771 (N.D. Cal., filed Nov. 19, 2007) (damage action involving the unlawful detention of a U.S. citizen child when his father was arrested during a home raid).

[35] *See* CAPPS ET AL., *supra* note 33, at 37-38 (describing cases in which children were left unsupervised when their parents were detained during raids).

[36] *See id.* at 43-54 (describing the long-term effects of immigration enforcement on children and families); Thronson, *supra* note 33, at 403-418 (same).

[37] For further discussion of the legality of state and local enforcement in the absence of a specific agreement under INA 287(g), see LISA M. SEGHETTI, STEPHEN R. VINA, & KARMA ESTER, CONGRESSIONAL RESEARCH SERVICE, ENFORCING IMMIGRATION LAW: THE ROLE OF STATE AND LOCAL ENFORCEMENT (August 14, 2006), available at http://www.ilw.com/immigdaily/news/2006,0912-crs.pdf (last visited July 25, 2008); Michael J. Wishnie, *State and Local Police Enforcement of Immigration Laws,* 6 U. PENN. J. CONST. L. 1084 (2004).

[38] *See* APPLESEED, *supra* note 2, 13-16.

[39] *See, e.g.,* CRISTINA RODRÍGUEZ, MUZAFFAR CHISHTI, & KIMBERLY NORTMAN, MIGRATION POLICY INSTITUTE, TESTING THE LIMITS: A FRAMEWORK FOR ASSESSING THE LEGALITY OF STATE AND LOCAL IMMIGRATION MEASURES 32-37 (2007); Wishnie, *supra* note 37.

[40] 8 U.S.C. § 1324(c). But note that it is debatable whether this provision extends to state and local officers since the provision does not mention state and local officers and could be read as reaching federal officers other than immigration agents.

[41] 8 U.S.C. § 1252c(a).

[42] *Id.*

[43] *See* Wishnie, *supra* note 37, at 1092-93.

[44] 8 U.S.C. § 1357(g)(1).

[45] *Id.*

[46] *Id.*§ 1357(g)(7).

[47] *See* Jeremy Travis, *Rethinking Sovereign Immunity After Bivens,* 57 N.Y.U.L. Rev. 597,650-51 (1982).

[48] 28 U.S.C. § 2680(a); *see also* Travis, *supra* note 47, at 650-51.

[49] *Ortega et al. v. Arpaio et al.*, No. CV 07-02513-PHX-MHM (D. Ariz., filed July 16, 2008) (quoting U.S. Dept. of Homeland Security, Bureau of Immigration and Customs Enforcement, Fact Sheet: Section 287g of the Immigration and Nationality Act (September 24, 2007)).

[50] *Id.*

[51] *Id.; see also* section B.2 *infra.*

[52] 8 U.S.C. § 1357(g)(2).

[53] *Id.* § 1357(g)(3).

[54] Stephanie Ward, *Illegal Aliens on I.C.E: Tougher Immigration Enforcement Tactics Spur Challenges*, ABA Journal (June 2008), *available at* http://www.abajournal.com/magazine/illegal_aliens_on_ice/ (last visited July 25, 2008).

[55] SungJee Lee, *The Parent/Child Relationship: Derivative Citizenship Through Parents,* 16 J. Contemp. Legal Issues 43 (2007).

[56] The Brennan Center for Justice, Citizens Without Proof: A Survey of Americans' Possession of Documentary Proof of Citizenship and Photo Identification 2 (Nov. 2006), *available at* http://www.brennancenter.org/page/-/d/download_file_39242.pdf (last visited July 25, 2008).

[57] *Id.*

[58] *Id.* at 3.

[59] *Id.*at 2.

[60] *See* Anna Gorman, *Immigration officials held U.S. citizen for two weeks,* LA Times (Oct. 28 2008), *available at* http://www.latimes.com/news/printedition/california/la-me-deport28-2008oct28,0,4273833.story (last visilted November 19, 2008);, Sandra Hernandez, *Detainee Tries To Prove He Is a U.S. Citizen; Birth Certificate Isn't Enough to Win Man's Release* (Nov. 4, 2008), *at* http://www.ijjblog.org/2008/11/_detainee_tries_to_prove_he_is.html; Daryl Fears, *Immigration Is Snaring U.S. Citizens In Its Raids*, Washington Post (Aug. 16 2008), *available at* http://www.washingtonpost.com/wp-dyn/content/article/2008/08/15/AR2008081503208.html; Jacqueline Stevens, *Thin ICE*, The Nation (June 5, 2008), *available at* http://www.thenation.com/doc/20080623/stevens (last visited July 25, 2008) (chronicling specific instances of U.S. citizens being detained and/or deported and estimating that "since 2004 ICE has held between 3,500 and 10,000 US citizens in detention facilities and deported about half"); *see also* Northwest Immigrant Rights Project, U.S. Citizen and Army Veteran Spends Nine Months in Detention While U.S. Immigration and Customs Enforcement Denies Detaining Citizens (July 21, 2008) (describing the experience of Rennison Castillo, a U.S. citizen and veteran who was detained in a local detention facility, and noting that the Northwest Immigrant Rights Project has seen fourteen cases of U.S. citizens being detained by federal immigration officials in that local detention center alone since 2005); Marisa Taylor, *Feds admit mistakenly jailing citizens as illegal immigrants*, Houston Chronicle (Feb. 14, 2008).

[61] *See, e.g.*, Rucks Russell, *American citizen held in county jail as illegal immigrant*, KHOU-TV (Oct. 17, 2008), *at* http://www.khou.com/topstories/stories/khou081017_mp-american-held-as-immigrant.121b56a52.html (last visited November 18, 2008); Paloma Esquivel, *Suit filed over disabled U.S. citizen's deportation ordeal*, LA Times (Feb. 28, 2008), *available at* http://articles.latimes.com/2008/feb/28/local/me-guzman28.

[62] *See Matter of Lok,* 18 I&N Dec. 101 (BIA 1981), *aff'd, Lok v. INS*, 681 F.2d 107 (2d Cir. 1982).

[63] *See Pantoja-Castillo et al. v. Sanchez et al.*, No. 07-204 (S.D. Tex., filed Aug. 2, 2007).

[64] 8 U.S.C. § 1254a.

[65] *Id.*; 8 C.F.R. §§ 244.2, 244.3.

[66] 8 U.S.C. § 1254a.

[67] For example, in the recent extension of TPS for Somalis, the U.S. Citizenship and Immigration Service posted a notice in the Federal Register stating: "Given the timeframes involved with processing TPS re-registration applications, the Department of Homeland Security (DHS) recognizes the possibility that re-registrants may not receive a new EAD until after their current EAD expires on March 17, 2008. Accordingly, this Notice automatically extends the validity of EADs issued under the TPS designation of Somalia for 6 months, through September 17, 2008 and explains how TPS beneficiaries and their employers may determine which EADs are automatically extended." 73 Fed. Reg 13245-01 (Mar. 12, 2008).

[68] 8 U.S.C. § 1254a(d)(4) (providing that a person with TPS "shall not be detained on the basis of the alien's immigration status").

[69] *Guzman v. Chertoff et al.*, No. 2:08-cv-01327-GHK-SS (C.D. Cal., filed Feb. 27, 2008).

[70] *Id.*

[71] *See* Randal C. Archibold, *Deported in Error, Missing and Months Later Home*, N.Y. TIMES (Aug, 8, 2007); Stevens, *supra* note 60.

[72] *See* Stevens, *supra* note 60 (reporting that the author identified thirty-one cases of citizens charged with removal, fourteen of whom were deported, and describing a case of a mentally ill woman who claimed to have been born in Paris); *see also* TESTIMONY OF KARA HARTZLER, FLORENCE IMMIGRANT AND REFUGEE PROJECT, U.S. HOUSE OF REPRESENTATIVES, SUBCOMMITTEE ON IMMIGRATION 14 (Feb. 13, 2008) (reporting that her office sees 40 to 50 detainees a month with possible citizenship claims).

[73] *Ortega et al. v. Arpaio et al.*, No. CV 07-02513-PHX-MHM (D. Ariz., filed July 16, 2008).

[74] *Argueta v. ICE*, No. 2:08-cv-01652-PGS-ES (D. N.J., filed May 22, 2008).

[75] *Reyes v. Alcantar*, No. 4:07-cv-022771 (N.D. Cal., filed Nov. 19, 2007).

[76] *United Food and Commercial Workers International Union v. DHS*, No. 2:07-cv-00188 (N.C.D. Tex., filed Sept. 12, 2007).

[77] *See, e.g.*, Wishnie, *supra* note 37, at 1102-1113; Susan M. Akram & Kevin R. Johnson, *Race, Civil Rights, and Immigration Law After September 11, 2001: The Targeting of Muslims and Arabs*, 58 N.Y.U. ANN. SURV. AM. L. 295, 316-355 (2002) (describing the targeting of Arabs and Muslims in immigration enforcement); Kevin R. Johnson, "The Case Against Race Profiling in Immigration Enforcement," 78 WASH. U. L.Q. 675, 697-705 (2000) (describing the racial profiling of Mexicans and Central Americans in immigration enforcement)

[78] Wishnie, *supra* note 37, at 1109-1113.

[79] Michele Waslin, *Immigration Enforcement by Local Police: The Impact on the Civil Rights of Latinos*, NAT'L COUNCIL OF LA RAZA ISSUE BR. NO. 9 (Feb. 2003), *available at* http://www.nclr.org/content/publications/detail/1390/ (last visited July 25, 2008) (outlining incidents of racial profiling by federal and local officials and listing successful lawsuits filed on behalf of the targets of racial profiling).

[80] *See Ortega et al. v. Arpaio et al.*, No. CV 07-02513-PHX-MHM (D. Ariz., filed July 16, 2008); *see also* U.S. DEP'T OF JUSTICE. CIVIL RIGHTS DIV., GUIDANCE REGARDING THE USE OF RACE BY FEDERAL LAW ENFORCEMENT AGENCIES (June 2003), *available at* www.usdoj.gov/crt/split/documents/guidance_on_race.pdf (last visited July 25, 2008) [hereinafter "GUIDANCE"].

[81] *See* GUIDANCE, *supra* note 80, at 5.

[82] *See Ortega et al. v. Arpaio et al.*, No. CV 07-02513-PHX-MHM (D. Ariz., filed July 16, 2008).

[83] *See id.*

[84] *Id.*

[85] *Barrera v. Boughton*, No. 3:07-cv-01436-RNC (D. Conn., filed Sept. 26, 2007).

[86] *Id.*

[87] *Id.* Data indicate that police are on particularly shaky ground when relying on National Crime Information Center data in order to make an arrest. *See* HANNAH GLADSTEIN, ANNIE LAI, JENNIFER WAGNER, & MICHAEL J. WISHNIE, BLURRING THE LINES: A PROFILE OF STATE AND LOCAL POLICE ENFORCEMENT OF IMMIGRATION LAW USING THE NATIONAL CRIME INFORMATION CENTER DATABASE, 2002-2004, 3 (Dec. 2005) (concluding that "[f]orty-two percent of all [National Crime Information Center] immigration hits in response to a police query were 'false positives,' where DHS was unable to confirm that the individual was an actual immigration violator").

[88] *Id.*

[89] *Committee for Immigrant Rights of Sonoma County et al. v. County of Sonoma et al.*, No. 08-CV-4220-PJH (N.D. Cal., filed Sept. 5, 2008).

[90] *Id.*

[91] *Guzman v. Chertoff et al.*, No. 2:08-cv-01327-GHK-SS (C.D. Cal., filed Feb. 27, 2008).

[92] *Id.*

[93] *See* 1-2 CRIM. CONST. L. § 2.05.

[94] *See id.*

[95] *See id.* § 2.08

[96] *See id.*

[97] *See* 3-13 CRIM. CONST. L. § 13.03.

[98] *See* Raquel Aldana, *Of Katz and "Aliens": Privacy Expectations and the Immigration Raids*, 41 U.C. DAVIS L. REV. 1081, 1111-1113 (2008) (describing the inaccuracies in immigration records that often form the basis for administrative warrants, including those based on records of individuals with old deportation orders entered into the National Crime Information Center database); GLADSTEIN ET AL., *supra* note 87, at 3 (noting inaccuracies in information found on immigration violators in the National Crime Information Center database).

[99] *See* Letter of Michael Chertoff to Senator Christopher J. Dodd (June 14, 2007) (on file with author) ("[A] warrant of removal is administrative in nature and does not grant the same authority to enter dwellings as a judicially approved search or arrest warrant.")

[100] *See* 8 U.S.C. §§ 1226 (providing Attorney General with authority to arrest and detain immigrants pending a decision on removal), 1362 (providing a statutory right to counsel "at no expense to the government").

[101] *Arias v. ICE*, No. 07-cv-01959-ADM-JSM (D. Minn., filed July 27, 2007).

[102] *Id.*

[103] *Id.*

[104] *Id.*

[105] *Id.*

[106] *Argueta v. ICE*, No. 2:08-cv-01652-PGS-ES (D. N.J., filed May 22, 2008)

[107] *Id.*

[108] *Id.*

[109] *Id.*

[110]*Aguilar v. ICE*, No. 07-cv-8224 (S.D.N.Y., filed Sept. 20, 2007).

[111] *Id.*

[112] *Id.*

[113] *Id.*

[114] *Id.*

APPENDIX B

Legal Issues in Local Police Enforcement of Federal Immigration Law

[115] *See* U.S. Dept. of Homeland Security, Office of the Inspector General, Assessment of United States Immigration and Customs Enforcement's Fugitive Operations Teams 15 (Mar. 2007), *available at* http://www.dhs.gov/xoig/assets/mgmtrpts/OIG_07-34_Mar07.pdf (last visited on July 25, 2008).

[116] *See Barrera v. Boughton*, No. 3:07-cv-01436-RNC, Federal Defendants' Memorandum in Support of Motion to Dismiss (Feb. 1, 2008).

[117] *Id.*

[118] *See* Thronson, *supra* note 33, at 405-406.

[119] *Reyes v. Alcantar*, No. 4:07-cv-022771 (N.D. Cal., filed Nov. 19, 2007).

[120] *Arias v. ICE*, No. 07-cv-01959-ADM-JSM (D. Minn., filed July 27, 2007).

[121] *See Junta for Progressive Action et al. v. Danaher*, No. FIC 2007-416 (Conn. Freedom of Information Comm., filed Aug. 2, 2007) (on file with author).

[122] Conversation with Michael J. Wishnie, June 16, 2008.

[123] Letter of Victoria Shin, Assistant United States Attorney to Mary E. Schwind, Freedom of Information Commission, re Dkt. No. FIC2007-136 (July 18, 2007).

[124] El Badrawi v. Commission, State of Connecticut, Department of Correction, (Freedom of Information Comm'n of the State of Connecticut, Dkt FIC 2007-136, Jan. 9, 2008) (on file with author).

[125] *See, e.g., Accardi v. Shaughnessy*, 347 U.S. 260, 268 (1954); *Waldron v. INS*, 17 F.3d 511, 518 (2d Cir. 1994)

[126] *See, e.g., Almeida-Amaral v. Gonzales*, 461 F.3d 231 (2d Cir. 2006).

APPENDIX C

Making Civil Liberties Matter in Local Immigration Enforcement

BY RAQUEL ALDANA

Every month, the United States Immigration and Customs Enforcement (ICE) Law Enforcement Support Center (LESC) responds to over 60,000 queries from local law enforcement about foreign nationals they encounter in the course of their daily duties.[1] In fiscal year 2005 alone, LESC responded to 676,502 such immigration queries,[2] representing an exponential increase from only 4,000 queries nearly a decade earlier.[3] This trend coincides with the "force multiplier" that has resulted from the involvement of local law enforcement in enforcing federal immigration laws, particularly post 9/11.[4] Thousands of local police, state troopers, correctional facilities staff, and other law enforcement personnel assist ICE to detect, arrest, detain, and turn over foreign nationals who are present in the United States in violation of civil or criminal immigration laws. To do so, local law enforcement agencies either rely on express statutory authority or claim inherent powers to enforce federal immigration laws. The claimed source of power to enforce immigration laws is relevant to assess local law enforcement's legality and scope of authority to enforce federal immigration laws. In this paper, therefore, I first address the issue of source and scope of local powers to enforce federal immigration laws, as this is also pertinent to the discussion of civil liberties that belong to immigrants and citizens alike who encounter these practices. Next, I explain the civil liberties concerns that arise from local law enforcement's involvement in immigration enforcement and offer recommendations for ensuring greater civil rights compliance by law enforcement agencies if they choose to enforce immigration laws. Finally, I explain immigrants' rights during these police encounters.

I. The Source and Scope of Local Law Enforcement Agencies' Power to Enforce Federal Immigration Law

Congress cannot compel local law enforcement to enforce immigration laws, but it can and has conferred express authority to permit federal local law enforcement officers to voluntarily enforce certain provisions of the Immigration and Nationality Act (INA). To date, Congress has chosen to confer this power only with respect to a limited number of criminal provisions in the INA (*see* subpart A below). In addition, in 1996, Congress authorized cooperation agreements between federal immigration and state law enforcement agencies, which have in some cases significantly expanded the scope of local immigration enforcement authority (*see* subpart C below). The newness of these cooperation agreements and the limited resources for their implementation are the reasons why most local law enforcement agencies still rely on claims of inherent authority to make arrests for violations of most federal immigration laws. This claimed inherent local law enforcement power to enforce federal immigration laws minimally is plagued with lack of clarity and, worse, its legality *per se* is still in question (*see* subpart B below).

In understanding this debate, therefore, it is important to understand the legality—and consequently the implicated civil rights of immigrants in relation to local law enforcement—of immigration laws. Finally, not all localities have heeded the call to enforce immigration laws for various policy reasons, including limited resources and concerns over hurting local police community relations with immi-

Raquel Aldana is a Professor of Law at the William S. Boyd School of Law, University of Nevada, Las Vegas.

grant communities. Some of these cities, thus, have opted instead to enact so-called "sanctuary laws" to forbid all or certain types of local police collaboration with ICE. Since 1996, however, federal law bans state laws that seek to forbid state employees from reporting immigration violations to ICE (*see* subpart D below). The issue therefore becomes the need for local law enforcement to resolve these seeming conflicts between state and federal law.

A. Congressional Delegation of Authority to Local Law Enforcement to Enforce Specific Immigration Violations

Most provisions of the INA codifying immigration violations do not delineate which law enforcement officers have the authority to enforce them. A few sections, however, expressly assert that state and local officers have the authority to enforce them. These sections are:

- INA § 274: Arrest authority to enforce prohibitions against transporting and harboring certain aliens.[5]
- INA § 276: Authority to arrest and detain re-entry offenders; that is, previously deported immigrants with a felony conviction who are found present in the United States.[6]
- INA § 103(a)(8): Confers emergency powers on the Secretary of Homeland Security (DHS) to authorize "any State or local law enforcement officer" to enforce federal immigration laws in the event the Secretary certifies that "an actual or imminent mass influx of aliens arriving off the coast of the United States or near a land border" exists.[7]
- INA § 287(g): Authorizes immigration enforcement agreements between the Immigration and Customs Enforcement (ICE) and local law enforcement agencies (*see* subpart C below).

In addition to these provisions delegating specific immigration enforcement powers to local law enforcement, Congress has provided some resources to defer costs and for information sharing to facilitate cooperation between local and federal agencies. In 1994, Congress appropriated funds for the creation of the LESC to serve as the point of contact between police who apprehended possible noncitizen felons and ICE.[8] In 1996, Congress authorized the Attorney General (now the Secretary of DHS) to make payments to the states for the detention of undocumented immigrants in nonfederal facilities.[9] Then in 1998, Congress established Quick Response Teams (QRTs), used by INS and then ICE to respond to immigration arrests made by state and local police.[10] Eventually, ICE discontinued QRTs, as such, and now offers states and localities enforcement assistance through various programs.

The selective nature of congressional delegation of immigration enforcement powers strongly suggests that Congress did not intend for local law enforcement to possess broader authority than that expressly provided. If such broader authority exists, then the express delegation would be superfluous.[11] The issue of whether states possess inherent authority to enforce immigration laws other than the authority expressly delegated by Congress is not settled, however. As the next section explains, the lack of clarity in this area of the law has led states and localities to reach contradictory conclusions on the issue.

B. Local Law Enforcement's Inherent Authority to Enforce Immigration Law?

The question on inherent authority asks whether states have the power to make arrests for violations to either criminal or civil federal immigration law or both without express congressional authorization. To date, there is fierce disagreement on the legal response. While some defend states' inherent right to make both civil and criminal immigration arrests,[12] others conclude that no such state inherent power exists because the enforcement of immigration law is an exclusive federal power that must be enforced uniformly by one sovereign in light of immigration laws' implications on foreign policy.[13] At a minimum, these scholars maintain that states can enforce federal immigration laws only to the degree that express congressional delegation authorizes.[14]

In practice, the legal resolution regarding the scope and nature of inherent local immigration enforcement authority does not apply to every encounter between noncitizens and local law enforcement. Much of local immigration enforcement occurs in the course of ordinary local policing work; e.g., during traffic stops or in the course of community policing functions or other criminal investigations. Thus, local law enforcement officers possess an independent state ground, even if pretextual, for detaining or even arresting the immigrant. As such, local law enforcement need not rely on any inherent immigration law enforcement authority to effectuate the detention or arrest. Moreover, almost always courts will treat inquiries, including by local law enforcement agents, into the detainees' immigration status as consensual encounters. Therefore, such inquiries do not constitute a separate immigration-related seizure, at least not under the Fourth Amendment. (*see* Part II.) Thus, in cases in which the immigrant is detained or arrested pursuant to independent state grounds, local law enforcement officers need not rely on the inherent authority doctrine at all to collaborate with ICE. Pretextual challenges to these types of encounters, moreover, are unlikely to succeed, at least under the Fourth Amendment (*see* Part II.) There may be other challenges to these types of encounters, such as the legality of including civil immigration violations in the NCIC databases, or racial profiling challenges under federal civil rights statutes (*see* Part II).

Still, generally, the relevance of inherent authority to enforce immigration law violations arises only when local law enforcement officers detain or arrest a person solely on the basis of an immigration violation. Such would be the case, for example, when police encounter passengers in a car during a routine traffic stop and detain or arrest the passengers, in addition to the driver, for immigration violations unrelated to the traffic stop. In such cases, neither Congress nor the courts, nor immigration federal agencies for that matter, have provided clear guidance to states on the issue of inherent authority.[15]

Congress's delegation of some immigration enforcement powers to states, without more, does not put to rest whether states are able to act beyond those delegated powers. The Supreme Court[16] and several federal appellate courts, including the Second,[17] Fifth,[18] and Seventh Circuits,[19] have long recognized that state law controls the validity of state law warrantless arrests for federal crimes, even when Congress has not directly authorized it. In the immigration context, however, only three federal circuit courts, the Ninth, the Tenth, and the Fifth, have weighed on the specific question of whether local law enforcement possesses inherent authority to make arrests for immigration offenses which have not been preempted by federal law.[20] A circuit split exists between the Ninth Circuit recognizing an inherent, nonpreempted local law enforcement power to make such arrests, but restricting it to violations of federal criminal immigration laws[21] and the Fifth[22] and Tenth Circuits[23] subsequently concluding similarly on the preemption issue, but without drawing the same distinction between civil and criminal offenses. In addition, the Third

Circuit has recently upheld the legality of a warrantless arrest executed by local law enforcement for an immigration criminal violation without expressly addressing local law enforcement's authority to engage in that type of law enforcement in the first place.[24]

The uncertainty of states' authority to make arrests for immigration violations has been made worse by conflicting opinions issued by the Office of Legal Counsel (OLC) on the issue. In 1996, after the Ninth and Fifth, but before the Tenth Circuit, opinions, the OLC accepted the Ninth Circuit limits and concluded that state and local police may constitutionally detain or arrest persons who have violated criminal provisions of the Immigration and Nationality Act (INA), subject to state law, but may not do so solely for civil violations.[25] After the September 11 attacks on the World Trade Center and the Pentagon, however, the OLC issued a new 2002 opinion retracting its earlier position and concluding that state and local police possess inherent authority to make arrests for both criminal and civil violations that would render that person removable.[26] The 2002 OLC opinion remained unpublished until July 2005 when it was released after the Second Circuit granted a FOIA request,[27] although allowing some redactions to the opinion.[28]

Given this lack of clarity in the law, it should not be surprising that state attorneys general continue to receive requests for advisory opinions on the nature and scope of states' inherent powers to enforce immigration laws. Nor should the varied responses be a surprise. In 2007, for example, the Virginia attorney general responded to an inquiry by two state legislators as follows:

> **It is my opinion that Virginia law-enforcement officers have authority to detain and arrest individuals who have committed violations of the laws of the United States and other states, subject to federal and state limitations. It further is my opinion that such authority extends to violations of federal criminal immigration law. Finally, because the federal appellate courts are ambiguous regarding state's authority to arrest individuals for civil violations of federal immigration law, until the law is clarified, it would not be advisable to enforce such violations outside of the scope of an agreement with federal authorities.**[29]

In addition, some attorneys general are turning to state statutes to decide the issue, given that state law controls on the question of when it is legal for states to arrest for federal offenses.[30] In 2007, for example, the attorney general of Ohio concluded that a county sheriff may arrest and detain persons suspected of violating a criminal provision of federal immigration law but may not do so if the violation is purely civil, given that state statutes define the general powers and duties of a county sheriff as "preserving the peace," a phrase that pertains only to criminal enforcement.[31] South Carolina's attorney general went even further and concluded that since South Carolina statutes only authorize state and local officers to enforce state criminal laws, no inherent authority to enforce federal immigration law exists in the state.[32] In an earlier opinion, in fact, the South Carolina attorney general had concluded that "any authority to empower state and local law enforcement officers to arrest and detain individuals for violation of the criminal provisions of federal immigration law would have to be provided by enactment of the General Assembly."[33]

Another layer of complexity is the relationship between a state's arrest warrant requirement and the inherent authority of local law enforcement to enforce immigration laws. The issue is that since some state statutes authorize warrantless arrests for misdemeanors solely when the crime is committed in the presence of the arresting officer, then warrantless arrests of noncitizens for federal immigration violations, whether for civil or minor crimes, violate this law.[34] When presented with the question, the New York attorney general, for example, concluded that the power to make warrantless arrests for federal immigration crimes more likely would be upheld, but subject to the requirements of state arrest requirements such that "offenses" would need to be committed in the presence of the officer and no arrest authority would exists for purely civil violations.[35]

Warrantless arrests that do not comply with state law requirements have been challenged in motions to suppress in federal criminal cases when defendants have been arrested by local law enforcement based solely on immigration violations. At least the Third Circuit, however, has denied remedy, even after it recognized that a violation to the state law has occurred. That case involved a member of the Marine Unit of the Virgin Islands Police Department (VIPD), who arrested the defendants and turned them over to ICE to be tried for alien smuggling offenses.[36] The Third Circuit affirmed the district court's finding that the arrest was illegal under state law because it was for a misdemeanor, which required the crime to be committed in the presence of the officer to justify a warrantless arrest.[37] Nevertheless, the Third Circuit reversed the initial grant of a motion to suppress on the basis that "an arrest that is unlawful under state or local law is [not] unreasonable *per se* under the Fourth Amendment."[38] As part of its rationale, the Third Circuit noted that a different holding would lead to the anomaly that the same arrest would be legal so long as local police conduct it jointly with ICE, given that ICE must not comply with the same presence requirement under federal law.[39] This type of potential watering down of state criminal procedural requirements as a result of local law enforcement of immigration laws is a civil rights concern I highlight in Part II.

C. INA § 287(g) Agreements

The Illegal Immigration Reform and Immigrant Responsibility Act of 1996 (IIRIRA) added Section 287(g) to the INA. This provision authorizes the Secretary of DHS to enter into an agreement, known as a Memorandum of Agreement (MOA), with a state or local law enforcement agency and to permit trained officers to perform immigration enforcement functions under the supervision of ICE officers, at the expense of the state or political subdivision and to the extent consistent with state and local law.[40] As of June 2008, 55 local law enforcement agencies, 765 officers in all, in 18 states have entered into such agreements, with approximately 80 more with pending requests.[41] ICE credits the program with identifying more than 60,000 persons since January of 2006, mostly in jails, who are suspected of being in the country without authorization.[42]

I have reviewed thirty-four of the fifty-five MOA agreements to date, which are available online after the Yale Law School Clinic filed a FOIA request with ICE.[43] ICE has entered into these MOAs directly with police departments, departments for public safety or state patrol, sheriff's offices, jails or correctional facilities, or with the city, the county, or the state. These MOAs reveal that Section 287(g) allows ICE to confer on local law enforcement nearly all of its enforcement powers under the INA. There are essentially eight types of immigration law enforcement functions that have been delegated to local law enforcement through these MOAs:

1. The power and authority to interrogate any person believed to be an alien as to his right to be or remain in the United States (INA § 287(a)(1) and 8 C.F.R. § 287.5(a)(1)) and to process for immigration violations those individuals who are convicted of state and federal felony offenses;
2. The power to arrest without warrant any alien entering or attempting to unlawfully enter the United States, or any alien in the United States, if the officer has reason to believe that the alien to be arrested is in the United States in violation of the law and is likely to escape before warrant can be obtained. INA § 287(a)(2) and 8 C.F.R. 287.5(c)(1);
3. The power and authority to arrest without warrant for felonies which have been committed and which are cognizable under any law of the United States regulating the admission, exclusion, expulsion, or removal of aliens, if there are reasons to believe that the person so arrested has committed such felony and if there is likelihood of the person escaping before a warrant can be obtained. INA § 287(a)(4) and 8 C.F.R. § 287.5(c)(2). Notification of such arrest must be made to ICE within twenty-four (24) hours;
4. The power and authority to serve warrants of arrest for immigration violations pursuant to 8 C.F.R. § 287.5(e)(3);
5. The power and authority to administer oath and to take and consider evidence (INA § 287(b) and 8 C.F.R. § 287(a)(2)), to complete required criminal alien processing, including fingerprinting, photographing, and interviewing of aliens, as well as the preparation of affidavits and the taking of sworn statements for ICE supervisory review;
6. The power and authority to prepare charging documents (INA Section 239, 8 C.F.R. § 239.1; INA Section 238; 8 C.F.R. § 238.1; INA Section 241(a)(5), 8 C.F.R. § 241. INA Section 235 (b)(1), 8 C.F.R. § 235.3), including the preparation of a Notice to Appear (NTA), application or other charging document, as appropriate, for the signature of an ICE officer for aliens in categories established by ICE supervisors;
7. The power and authority to issue immigration detainers (8 C.F.R. § 287.7) and I-213 Record of Deportable/Inadmissible Alien, for processing aliens in categories established by ICE supervisors; and
8. The power and authority to detain and transport (8 C.F.R. § 287.5(c)(6)) arrested aliens to ICE-approved detention facilities.[44]

The MOAs greatly differ in terms of their nature and scope. The broadest of them take on all of the eight powers/functions to allow trained local law enforcement officers to enforce both civil and criminal immigration laws.[45] Others also pertain to all types of immigration violations but may exclude certain of the delegated powers, usually the power to serve immigration warrants or the power to conduct warrantless arrests.[46] One MOA, that of Mecklenburg County, North Carolina, stands out because while it deals with all immigration violations, it includes only five of the eight powers (to interrogate; to administer oaths; to issue detainers; to prepare charging documents; and to transport aliens).[47] Most MOAs, however, restrict the cooperation agreement to assist ICE with criminal investigations in general; to certain types of criminal investigations, such as human trafficking, gangs, drugs, to identity theft; to capture "criminal aliens;" or to address counterterrorism and domestic security needs.[48] Florida, which opted not to include the power to serve warrants, is an exception to all other MOAs that include all power/functions.[49] There were also quite a few agreements with detention facilities, most of which did not include arrest powers in the MOAs as their purpose was to identity and process immigration violators already in detention.[50]

Thus, the MOA itself defines the scope and limitations of the authority to be designated to the local law enforcement agency, as well as the number of local officers trained and authorized to enforce federal immigration laws. Some MOAs are quite broad and grant all available powers to the local officers, while others are restricted to specific types of enforcement and adopt only some or a few of the enforcement powers. No one is monitoring how these agreements are actually being implemented, however, which raises concern over potential enforcement of immigration laws beyond those expressly spelled out in the agreement.[51]

Another issue is whether state law permits localities and/or local law enforcement agencies to enter into MOAs with ICE. Responses by the states attorneys general on the issue have varied among the states. In Ohio, for example, the attorney general concluded that a county sheriff lacked state statutory authority to enter into agreements with ICE for the enforcement of civil provisions of federal immigration law.[52] In contrast, Virginia's attorney general concluded that current Virginia law already authorized localities to enter into an agreement with ICE under the terms prescribed by INA § 287(g).[53]

The distinction between civil and criminal immigration enforcement continues to be relevant not only to the question of inherent local authority to enforce federal immigration laws but also to the permissible and/or actual scope of MOAs under INA § 287(g). However, in many instances this dichotomy under federal immigration law is unworkable as increasingly what were once treated as purely civil immigration violations now also result in criminal penalties, subject to the discretion of ICE. In fact, there are at least forty-seven criminal provisions in the sections of federal immigration law.[54] In addition, increasingly, ICE is relying on federal identity theft or fraud statutes to charge noncitizens for the possession or use of false or a third party's immigration documents or social security numbers.[55] Thus, while ICE is likely to simply institute removal proceedings against most persons apprehended through collaboration with local law enforcement, the potential applicability of a federal crime to any or most actions by the noncitizen is likely to conflate civil and criminal immigration enforcement to such degree as to make the distinction untenable. The conflation of civil and criminal immigration violations also has implications for civil liberties concerns, which I explore in Part II.

D. Conflict with State Law: "Sanctuary Cities"

At the same time that localities and/or local law enforcement agencies are engaging in the enforcement of immigration laws, other local entities, including state and city governments, have adopted "sanctuary policies" restricting local law enforcement collaboration with ICE on the detection and detention of unauthorized immigrants. Most of the largest cities in the United States today have some variation of such sanctuary policies.[56] In all, about forty-nine cities and towns and about three states have some type of sanctuary law.[57] Such sanctuary policies are generally of three types: (1) they limit inquiries into a person's immigration status (don't ask); (2) they limit arrests or detention for violation of immigration law (don't enforce); and (3) they limit provision to federal authorities of immigration status information (don't tell).[58] Localities promulgate these policies through various means, including by adopting city council resolutions, municipal ordinances, mayoral executive orders, and police chief memoranda.[59] The issues that arise with sanctuary policies are whether they are preempted by federal immigration law, as well as whether they are invalidated or made moot by conflicting local policies that seek greater local enforcement of immigration laws, including through adoption of INA § 287(g) agreements.

Several potential conflicts exist between sanctuary policies and federal law. Some suggest, for example, that sanctuary policies violate the federal anti-harboring provision.[60] The resolution is likely to depend on the federal court that decides the issue given that circuit courts interpret the harboring provision quite differently.[61] The issue might turn on whether courts view "sanctuary policies" as active concealment, as has been required by the Sixth Circuit, as opposed to most other circuits (the Second, the Fifth, the Eighth, and the Ninth) that include in the definition of harboring the provision of services and the mere omission to report that person to immigration authorities.[62] From a political perspective, however, such challenge is unlikely.[63]

Congress, however, passed two laws in 1996 explicitly to counter local sanctuary policies.[64] The first, Section 1373, mandates that "a Federal, State, or local government entity or official may not prohibit, or in any way restrict, any government entity or official from sending to, or receiving from, [ICE] information regarding the citizenship or immigration status, lawful or unlawful, of any individual."[65] Section 1644 includes much of the same language as Section 1373, and states that "no State or local government entity may be prohibited, or in any way restricted, from sending to or receiving from the Immigration and Naturalization Service information regarding the immigration status, lawful or unlawful, of an alien in the United States."[66] Essentially, the broader provision, Section 1373, prohibits a government entity or official from restricting disclosure of immigration status to ICE. Section 1644 only prohibits the proscription as applied to government entities. In 1999, the Second Circuit decided the only case to date that assesses the application of these provisions to sanctuary policies (*City of New York v. United States*).[67] In that case, the Giuliani administration sought to enjoin the 1996 laws, arguing that these laws violated the Tenth Amendment because they forced New York City to collaborate with federal immigration enforcement and the Guarantee Clause of the Constitution by interfering with the city's chosen form of government.[68] The Second Circuit disagreed and found that the federal provisions preempted the city's sanctuary policy, which proscribed voluntary cooperation with ICE by local police in immigration enforcement.

Essentially, "don't tell" sanctuary policies are vulnerable to preemption challenges in light of the Second Circuit opinion.[69] In contrast, "don't ask" and "don't enforce" sanctuary policies are not vulnerable to preemption.[70] Federal prohibition of such sanctuary policies, moreover, would run afoul of the anti-commandeering doctrine, under which the federal government could not require that state and local officials engage in immigration law enforcement.[71]

Local protection against immigration enforcement by local police responds to the strong policy objective of building trust and cooperation between immigrant communities and police.[72] Unfortunately, the effectiveness of the so-called sanctuary policies is weak for several reasons, including that violations of these policies by local police are not enforced, and that the policies do not prevent removal of individual immigrants once they have been turned over to ICE.[73]

II. The Civil Liberties Pitfalls of Localized Immigration Enforcement

Localizing immigration enforcement also means that local law enforcement agencies assume immigration enforcement powers generally available only to ICE under the INA. Indeed, in some localities this is already happening. Local law enforcement officers are not only asking all persons detained and/or arrested during their routine police work for their immigration status,[74] but they are, alone or in collaboration with ICE, executing immigration raids,[75] or conducting raids,[76] road blocks,[77] street sweeps, or other investigations that target noncitizens for violations of the federal immigration laws.[78] Moreover, this localized policing work is being conducted with increasingly greater access to immigration databases and immigration information, either directly or though requests to the LESC. As a result, the very same civil liberties concerns over trends in federal immigration enforcement by federal agents are simply transferred to local agents who essentially take on the role of ICE. In other words, the more local police act like ICE agents, the more the same civil liberties concerns will plague local immigration enforcement. These civil liberties concerns include: the transference of immigration enforcement's Fourth Amendment exceptionalism and flexible administrative enforcement tools to local law enforcement; the increased criminalization of immigration law in the context of few privacy protections; and racial profiling.

A. Fourth Amendment Exceptionalism in Immigration Enforcement

The extremely limited application of the exclusionary remedy and the flexible application of the consent doctrine to immigration enforcement practices risk creating a culture of aggressive local law enforcement where abuses of power occur without judicial oversight. Essentially, the deterrence rationale behind the exclusionary remedy is almost absent from immigration law enforcement, given its nonapplication to nearly all immigration encounters, even when Fourth Amendment violations have occurred. For this reason, ICE is criticized for committing many civil rights violations in the course of immigration enforcement. Recently, ICE has been the subject of much litigation, particularly in the way it has executed raids.[79] Complaints against ICE, for example, have included the dragnet-like and intimidating execution of warrants in people's homes and in the workplace, which have devastating effects on families and communities.[80] In other cases, ICE has been accused of conducting forcible warrantless raids in people's homes, claiming they were police and aggressively interrogating all residents about their immigration status.[81] Still, more abuses include the racially charged nature in which these raids are being executed, mostly against Latinos.

Since 1984, the United States Supreme Court precluded the Fourth Amendment's exclusionary remedy in immigration proceedings, except within the narrow "egregious violations" exception.[82] Also, the exclusionary remedy does not apply to suppress the identity of the person arrested even in criminal trials, which has allowed ICE to successfully convict immigrants for certain immigration crimes, such as re-entry. In these cases, exclusion of any unlawfully seized evidence does not remedy the Fourth Amendment violation because the defendant's identity is never suppressible as the fruit of an unlawful arrest and because the government can prove its case simply by providing proof of a prior removal order and the defendant's renewed presence in the United States.[83]

Moreover, the application of the consent doctrine in immigration enforcement under the most coercive circumstances increasingly defies the premise that reasonable people feel free to walk away from law enforcement encounters. In immigration enforcement, the Fourth Amendment doctrine assumes that a reasonable person is free to refuse questions of immigration agents at immigration checkpoints.[84] The same assumption applies during unannounced workplace raids conducted by dozens of armed immigration agents, some of whom question workers while other agents guard the exits.[85]

At the local level, the assumption has often applied when local police question drivers and passengers about their immigration status during traffic stops[86] or roadblocks[87] even when, for instance, the encounter is prolonged when police seek information or direct assistance from ICE on the scene. The assumption has even applied during the execution of warrants in person's home when the person who has been handcuffed and detained for more than two hours was asked, by local law enforcement this time, about her immigration status.[88]

As a result, immigrants targeted for immigration enforcement have had almost no protection under the Fourth Amendment, either because the exclusionary rule has no application in removal proceedings or because it is limited in certain criminal trials. Moreover, even when the exclusionary rule does apply in removal proceedings, no Fourth Amendment protection is offered because most encounters are deemed nonseizures and nonsearches.

A related concern involves the transfer of ICE's broad regulatory and enforcement powers to local law enforcement, particularly through INA § 287(g) agreements. These transferred powers could have substantial adverse effects on privacy, especially through the increased use by local police of immigration databases and civil warrants to conduct law enforcement. ICE's regulatory arm reaches into employer hiring practices, university requirements (for foreign students), the government's distribution of public benefits, and driver's licenses, among other areas.

The regulatory function, in turn, has caused the proliferation of databases that, in most cases, grant ICE easy access to information about a person's immigration status as a worker, student, or driver. With easy access to these databases, ICE can arm itself with civil warrants even where no particularized probable cause exists to conduct raids in private or quasi-private spaces. Similarly, the proliferation of local ordinances that, for example, make it illegal for undocumented immigrants to loiter in public spaces, occupy housing, procure employment, or conduct business transactions,[89] is possibly expanding the administrative policing arm of local law enforcement against noncitizens and could lead to the creation of immigrant databases and to the issuance of civil warrants similar to those already available to ICE and some local law enforcement though INA §287(g) agreements.

The immigration warrants currently available to ICE are not that different from the general warrants that originally inspired the Fourth Amendment. The infamous general search warrants in early United States history were issued by executives and legislators, without judicial intervention, with neither a probable cause requirement or oath, nor a description of the particular places to be searched and persons or things to be seized.[90] Courts have upheld the constitutionality of immigration administratively issued warrants that lack particularized suspicion, such as workplace warrants based on general reasonable belief that unauthorized workers may be present, without having to name any particular worker.[91] This is a very low threshold given that ICE can establish a generalized reasonable suspicion of the presence of unauthorized persons in many contexts given the spread of immigration databases. Today, immigration laws authorize the compelled collection of information in ever-expanding databases over which persons retain no expectation of privacy and which become the basis for the issuance of warrants. Moreover, these databases, which were not intended to have a law enforcement purpose, often contain flawed information such that warrants are issued with significant errors, which are also shielded from any exclusionary remedy based on the "good faith" exception.[92]

One prominent example of immigration databases that provide easy access to immigration warrants are the databases established pursuant to the Immigration Reform and Control Act of 1986 ("IRCA")[93] to permit employer verification of immigration documents provided to employers by their employees at the time of hiring. In 1996, Congress created the Basic Pilot Employment Eligibility Verification Program (Basic Pilot), an electronic employment eligibility verification program which permits employers to match employee provided immigration information against the United States Citizenship and Immigration Services (CIS) and the Social Security Administration (SSA) databases for verification.[94] Basic Pilot is today known as E-Verify and contains over 444 million records in the SSA database and more than sixty million records in the DHS immigration databases.[95] Today, more than 69,000 employers are enrolled in E-Verify, with over four million queries executed so far in fiscal year 2008.[96]

IRCA data collection, along with E-verify, provide ICE with readily accessible information to procure warrants to execute immigration raids. In some cases, to avoid IRCA liability, employers voluntarily report to ICE discrepancies in their employee records when checked against the CIS and SSA databases.[97] As well, IRCA authorized DHS access to examine evidence of any person or entity under investigation for immigration violations and to compel such participation by subpoena.[98] Essentially, ICE can compel an employer to turn over all of its IRCA-mandated employee records, which ICE then runs through the databases. Any mismatch becomes a ground for an administrative warrant. Both the immigration and SSA databases are notoriously inaccurate, however. A 2004 report commissioned by DHS, for example, noted that the SSA databases are able to verify employment eligibility in less than 50 percent of the work-authorized noncitizens.[99] The SSA itself estimates that 17.8 million of its records contain discrepancies related to name, date of birth, or citizenship status.[100] SSA further notes that 4.8 million of the approximately 46.5 million noncitizen records contained in the SSA's database contain discrepancies.[101] Also, a government report reviewing immigration agencies' records (the then INS and the Executive Office of Immigration Review) found name, nationality, and case file number discrepancies, as well as cases missing from electronic files.[102]

Yet another database created to facilitate the execution of immigration warrants is based on ICE's implementation of its absconder initiatives in 2002 to arrest persons with a removal order who are still in the country.[103] The implementation of the absconder initiatives involved several preliminary steps. First, the government prepared the cases of immigration absconders, also called fugitives, for entry into the National Crime Information Center (NCIC) database,[104] an

FBI-operated federal criminal database containing individuals' criminal histories. In 1996, Congress authorized the inclusion of deported "felons" records in the NCIC database to help authorities identify and prosecute persons for illegal re-entry.[105] Until then, the long-standing policy had been to keep immigration law enforcement information separate from that of criminal law enforcement. Since 2001, the then INS also began including absconders' names and information, of whom there are more than 465,000, into the NCIC system.[106]

Now the NCIC database contains records of persons with civil immigration removal orders, regardless whether they also have a criminal history. The database contains around 247,500 immigration warrants, more than half of which are for people with old removal orders, while the rest are records of persons removed for the commission of crimes.[107] The presence of these names in the NCIC database gives local police the necessary information to make immigration arrests during the course of routine traffic stops since most police vehicles are equipped with laptop computers connected to the NCIC system.[108]

Unfortunately, much of the information that forms the basis for these fugitive warrants is unreliable. Immigration agencies have been notorious for atrocious record-keeping and faulty databases, including errors in removal order files.[109] A 2003 study of immigration removal records revealed that discrepancies in the identity and address information occurred in 7 percent of the 308 cases of immigrant files with final orders reviewed, and 11 percent of the 470 cases of aliens from countries believed to sponsor terrorism.[110]

Absconder warrants are also served in people's homes, relying on the final address recorded in immigration files. Several other factors, however, contribute to incorrect records. First, many of the removal orders date back for years,[111] which increases the probability that persons other than the person subject to the removal order live at the address when the warrant is finally executed. Second, DHS relies on the addresses provided by noncomplying immigrants, who often move to avoid immigration authorities. Third, address changes reported to immigration agencies often are not recorded in the databases.[112] As a result of these factors, the administrative warrants are often issued on the basis of incorrect information about a person's place of residence.

Reliance on faulty databases to issue immigration warrants could become a ground for a Fourth Amendment challenge, when a motion to suppress is available. Courts, however, have not required foolproof evidentiary reliability to substantiate probable cause and may tolerate some degree of database inaccuracy. In fact, challenges to the NCIC database have been upheld, despite their noted inaccuracies.[113] In addition, the good-faith exception could very well provide an exception to the exclusionary rule.[114] Finally, recent challenges by civil rights groups to the inclusion of immigration information in the NCIC databases have been dismissed for lack of standing.[115]

An additional concern over immigration warrants pertains to their indiscriminate and dragnet-like execution. The problem with general workplace immigration warrants, for example, is precisely their undefined scope. Thus, what constitutes a reasonable execution of these warrants remains vague but is likely to lie somewhere between consensual encounters and indiscriminate seizures.

Consider workplace raids, during which it is not uncommon for ICE to interrogate all workers about their immigration status. The *INS v. Delgado* precedent involving consensual encounters during workplace raids already offers ICE significant flexibility to question the workers and, through the questioning, to acquire reasonable suspicion of unlawful presence.[116] In *Delgado*, the INS moved systematically through a garment factory, asked employees to identify themselves, and asked the employees one to three questions about their citizenship.[117] During the interrogations, armed INS agents were stationed near the exits while other agents moved throughout the factory and questioned workers at their work areas.[118] The agents showed badges, had walkie-talkies, and carried arms, though they never drew their weapons.[119] Despite all these facts, the court still considered the encounter consensual.

Usually, courts have drawn the line into nonconsensual encounters when immigration agents specifically have targeted Latinos or persons who simply looked "foreign" for more than brief questioning.[120] With absconder warrants executed in people's homes, ICE strategic practice has been to send several armed ICE agents to people's homes at the crack of dawn and aggressively interrogate everyone present about their immigration status and arrest those unable to provide it.[121]

B. The Criminalization of Immigration Law

A significant explanation for the Fourth Amendment exceptionalism in immigration enforcement is early treatment by courts of immigration law as civil as opposed to criminal enforcement.[122] The characterization of immigration enforcement as administrative, which has allowed more flexible law enforcement practices, however, is becoming increasingly difficult to justify. In the last twenty years, immigration control has increasingly adopted the practices and priorities of the criminal justice system.[123] Yet, the criminal justice parallels in immigration enforcement have not resulted in correspondingly greater constitutional protections for immigrants, at least not in those protections that traditionally apply to criminal investigations and trials.

Professor Stephen H. Legomsky has called this trend "the asymmetric importation of the criminal justice norms into immigration law."[124] In other words, the enforcement aspects of criminal justice have been imported but without the bundle of procedural and substantive rights recognized in criminal cases.[125] The danger therefore is that law enforcement agencies are left without a legal obligation to balance immigrants' interests against the government's interest to control immigration, despite the large liberty stakes involved for immigrants.

Increasingly, what were once solely civil immigration violations have been criminalized, resulting in an unprecedented cooperation between criminal and immigration law enforcement agencies. Congress has created a host of new immigration crimes, ranging from illegal re-entry to the most recent attempt to criminalize mere immigration presence.[126] Further, criminal prosecution for immigration violations has increased rapidly. A recent study by Syracuse University's Transactional Records Access Clearinghouse documented that in March 2008, of 16,298 federal criminal prosecutions recorded, more than half (9,350) were for immigration violations.[127] The increase is part of DHS Operation Streamline, which seeks to deter undocumented migration through harsher criminal sanctions.[128]

Moreover, ICE is increasingly targeting for criminal prosecution persons who use false documents or documents belonging to third parties to procure work. An increasing number of persons arrested during workplace raids are being criminally prosecuted and face felony charges with a real threat of jail time for violating immigration or other United States laws related to identity theft. In 2006, for example, the number of those criminally charged was 716 (or 16 percent of the total number), up from only twenty-five (or 5 percent) in 2002.[129] Then, in July 2008, in an unprecedented move, ICE criminally charged over 90 percent of the nearly 400 workers during the largest single-site workplace raid in the history of the United States at Postville, Iowa.[130] Also, at the local level, states are increasingly legislating to criminalize the aliens and those who associate with them. States are adopting laws, for example, that duplicate federal crimes, including in areas of human trafficking and document fraud.[131] States have also passed ordinances that impose criminal penalties on landlords who rent to undocumented immigrants or on employers who hire undocumented workers.[132]

Civil immigration enforcement, moreover, has become more punitive and difficult to distinguish from criminal enforcement. Mandatory immigration detention, previously reserved for the most dangerous persons, is now broadly applied in almost all removal cases.[133] Indeed, immigration detainees are currently the fastest growing segment of the jail population in the United States.[134] Most persons picked up in the latest wave of immigration raids have been detained, for example. Only a few are released for humanitarian reasons or because they were eligible for some other type of immigration relief. Those charged with any immigration crime or those with a criminal history are not eligible, however, for bond or any other avenue of relief from detention.[135]

Further, even when immigrants are criminally charged rather than placed in removal proceedings, the Fourth Amendment exceptionalism that characterizes immigration enforcement still applies. Pretextual doctrines permit prosecutors to rely on the significantly more relaxed immigration-related Fourth Amendment doctrines to justify reasonableness of searches and arrests. Consider, for example, the workplace raids. ICE has made the detection of identity theft during these raids a priority, such that most who are arrested are being criminally charged, rather than put in removal proceedings.[136] Still, ICE is conducting these raids, relying on its broad administrative law enforcement powers. The pretextual Fourth Amendment doctrine will likely preclude a motion to suppress remedy even in the limited cases where it is available, however. In parallel cases, where the argument has been that the administrative function is only a pretext for criminal law enforcement, motions to suppress have not succeeded.[137]

In *Whren v. United States*, the United States Supreme Court refused to consider whether the true motives of police officers who detained a group of young men for a traffic infraction were to investigate them for drug possession.[138] The Court's position instead was to avoid guessing the intent or motivation of the law enforcement officers when acting and to approve the action as long as the officers had "objective" Fourth Amendment grounds.[139] Thus, even when many of the workers are being criminally charged, despite the evidence that DHS is shifting policy to criminalize the undocumented worker, the motion to suppress, when available, will likely fail, so long as removal proceedings are plausible when instituted.

Pretextual claims have been successful only when the government's stated primary purpose cannot be justified as administrative. For example, in *City of Indianapolis v. Edmond*, which involved random stops at a checkpoint to investigate drug crimes, police conceded that the checkpoint was primarily for the detection of drugs, which the Court considered primarily a criminal law enforcement purpose.[140] Immigration enforcement, however, in the majority of cases carries both civil and criminal penalties, and it is unclear whether that fact alone would trigger a different holding from the courts on the continued use of the administrative function to conduct criminal immigration enforcement.

Some of the factors that a court may consider to distinguish *Whren* are that, unlike traffic enforcement, which is predominantly civil, the transformation of immigration enforcement to a dual civil/criminal system argues for a different result. Consider the absconder initiative, for example, which has a clear criminal law enforcement purpose. Absconders are not solely immigration violators but also criminals *per se*, as they could face up to four years of incarceration for failure to depart after a removal order.[141] The entry of absconders' names into the NCIC database, moreover, indicates immigration agencies' shift to treat absconders as criminal, rather than solely civil immigration violators. This interrelatedness of civil/criminal sanctions in the absconder initiative could distinguish *Whren*. Until that happens, however, *Whren* is controlling in immigration enforcement and is likely to shield against motions to suppress with regard to the enforcement of immigration law during traffic stops, in the context of home raids, or in other types of investigative practices, whether conducted by ICE or by local law enforcement.

C. Racial Profiling

Another looming civil liberties concern of immigration law enforcement has been its racially charged execution. Racial profiling in immigration enforcement in the form of the disproportionate targeting of Latinos occurs in several contexts. ICE is commonly accused of racial profiling in the execution of raids, for example. Consider the absconder initiative. When initially implemented, the then INS specifically targeted "priority absconders," a category that included persons with removal orders from countries with an al Qaeda presence, namely Muslims and Arabs. As such, the national origin discrimination was explicit.[142] The program then included persons with a criminal history and ultimately, in May 2006, DHS launched Operation Return to Sender, which casts a wider net and targets all persons with preexisting removal orders.[143] As such, the program now is at least facially neutral. Its disparate targeting of Latino immigrants, however, is documented in nearly all media stories detailing the raids.[144] The disparate targeting of Latino workers is also evident in workplace raids, which primarily occur in segregated workspaces occupied primarily by brown or Latino workers.[145] Allegations of racial profiling, moreover, are also present in the "driving while brown" phenomena, insofar as immigration enforcement occurs in the context of routine traffic stops disproportionately against Latinos.[146]

Sheriff Joe Arpaio's street raids in Arizona cities have also been heavily criticized for their racially charged execution. Similar street raids conducted in Arizona by local police jointly with immigration agents in the 1990's, known as the "Chandler Roundup," cost the city $400,000 as part of a settlement of lawsuits in which plaintiffs alleged they were stopped and questioned based exclusively on their apparent Mexican descent.[147] Not surprisingly, Sheriff Arpaio faces today similar lawsuits.[148] Indeed, in that litigation, allegations include Arpaio's reliance on citizen "tips" to single out alleged undocumented immigrants, which are often placed with biased and racialized stereotypes of who is or is not legally in the U.S.[149] The complaint also documents indiscriminate street sweeps that target "Latinos," and the use of private volunteers to execute the raids.[150] Finally, even consensual encounters that fall beyond the scope of Fourth Amendment seizures do not escape racial targeting to the extent that Latinos are disproportionately targeted for questioning about their immigration status.

In racial profiling, too, few remedies are available, however. Courts are unlikely to consider these challenges, at least in the context of Fourth Amendment motions to suppress. First, the Court has directed parallel cases that have raised disproportionate law enforcement practices—such as in the "driving while black" phenomena away from Fourth Amendment challenges and into civil rights lawsuits.[151] Yet, a civil rights remedy for selective immigration enforcement is unlikely to be available under equal protection grounds, absent a clear showing of intentionality, which evidentiarily is nearly impossible to establish.[152]

Second, the United States Supreme Court has tolerated racial targeting in immigration enforcement, at least at immigration checkpoints and as a factor in the determination of reasonable suspicion in traffic enforcement.[153] The Court has justified a degree of ethnic profiling flexibility in immigration enforcement based partly on the questionable premise that civil immigration enforcement is less intrusive of liberty interests than in the criminal context.[154]

In addition, *in dictum* the Court noted that reliance on "Mexican appearance" as a factor for immigration law enforcement makes sense given that numerically it is largely Latinos, and primarily Mexican, who comprise the undocumented population.[155] The problem with this approach is twofold. First, ICE's enforcement statistics reveal that there is a notable disproportionate over-enforcement of immigration laws against Mexicans and other Latinos, even taking into account the large number of undocumented persons from these countries.[156] Second, the number of Latinos in the United States who are either citizens (by birth or naturalization) or possess immigration authorization to be in the United States is much larger than the number of unauthorized Latinos. A May 2008 press release by the United States Census Bureau puts the population of Hispanic origin at 45 million, a group still constituting the largest minority in the nation and totaling more than four times the number of unauthorized (and uncounted) persons of Hispanic origin.[157]

At least the Ninth Circuit in 2000 rejected the Court's dictum that Mexican appearance can be a factor to establish reasonable suspicion and reasoned that the much higher Latino percentage of the local population now makes demographic links between Latino ethnicity and unlawful status unreliable and that racial profiling unfairly stigmatizes.[158] In addition, the Ninth and the Third Circuits have found that stopping someone solely or partly because the driver is of Latino appearance constitutes "egregious" conduct, such that a motion to suppress is permitted in removal proceedings.[159]

D. Civil Liberties Recommendations for Local Immigration Law Enforcement

In light of the foregoing, I offer the following recommendations to states to improve civil liberties in immigration law enforcement:

- States should exercise immigration enforcement powers only with express legislative approval, preferably by Congress. The lack of clarity regarding inherent authority to enforce immigration laws contributes to confusion and chaos about the nature and scope of this authority, such that it is best if the political branches of the government make the determinations. The legislative process also has the potential of providing adequate airing into the public and public participation about the policy reasons for and against authorizing local immigration enforcement.

- Legislative authority should be clearly defined and monitored. As is the case of INA § 287(g) agreements, their nature and scope vary widely, with some containing a greater degree of specificity and outlining clear priorities. Localities and law enforcement agencies that choose to enter into such agreements for collaboration with ICE should aim to be as specific as possible regarding priorities and should detail as much as possible the scope and types of enforcement authorized. Ideally, localities should weigh the civil liberties implications of authorizing flexible immigration enforcement functions too broadly. For example, localities may wish to avoid local law enforcement collaborations in raids given the heightened civil liberties concerns that have been raised regarding their execution by ICE. Moreover, states should monitor and assure that the execution of the 287(g) agreements does not exceed the scope of their terms and establish complaint mechanisms through which civil rights groups may direct their concerns.
- Localities and/or agencies who enter into law enforcement collaboration agreements with ICE should also adopt policies to improve civil liberties in their execution, particularly taking into account the Fourth Amendment exceptionalism that characterizes immigration law enforcement and the particular civil liberties concerns that are implicated with such enforcement. In other words, localities cannot rely on federal courts to offer the civil liberties protections they may find desirable but can prevent violations to civil liberties by adopting good practice policies to preempt concerns. Some of these policies could include:
    - Restrict the enforcement of immigration warrants in the NCIC database, particularly given the database inaccuracies. Localities might, for example, prioritize enforcing cases involving only persons with a felony criminal record.
    - Disallow questioning of persons regarding their immigration status without reasonable suspicion. So-called consensual encounters involving immigration inquiries into a person's immigration status raise a host of civil liberties concerns that include judicial acquiescence into their voluntary nature under coercive circumstances and racial profiling.
    - Do not authorize the enforcement of immigration civil warrants. These immigration warrants are plagued with too many privacy violations, beginning from faulty databases, to their generalized character, and relatedly to their undefined scope of enforcement.
    - Disallow local enforcement participation in certain types of immigration enforcement, including raids, when such practices have been implicated in civil rights litigation.

III. Immigrants' Rights During Immigration Encounters

Pro-immigrant groups, when devising strategies for immigrants on what to do to protect their civil liberties during immigration encounters, whether with ICE or local law enforcement, are aware of the following two circumstances: (1) too many immigrants "waive" their constitutional rights by "voluntarily" even if unwittingly cooperating with law enforcement during consensual encounters; and (2) even if a violation occurs, there is almost never an effective remedy that could offer relief for the damage caused. As a result, civil rights groups follow two principal strategies, both of which are focused on prevention. The first is to seek to enjoin law enforcement from certain practices that raise civil liberties concerns through civil rights litigation. The second is to train individual immigrants to assert their rights better during personal encounters with law enforcement. Below, I detail the list of rights that immigrants do possess when confronting law enforcement on immigration matters.

A. The Right to Refuse Cooperation

1. During Consensual Encounters or Nonconsensual Encounters Unrelated to Immigration Enforcement

Immigrants should assume that most encounters, irrespective of how coercive, are consensual and should always seek clarification about (1) whether they are being detained and (2) if so, why they are being detained. If they are not being detained or if the detention is unrelated to an immigration matter, then it is very likely that police are asking about their immigration status without reasonable suspicion. For this reason, as a general rule, civil rights groups advise immigrants to remain silent during all law enforcement encounters, under the assumption that these are consensual or that the inquiry into a person's immigration status exceeds the reasonable scope of the seizure.

Importantly, then, immigrants have a right not to cooperate with law enforcement by divulging their immigration status or providing identification in the absence of reasonable suspicion. Some have suggested that foreign nationals must produce immigration documents when requested in the course of consensual encounters and in the absence of individualized suspicion.[160] This argument is based on the fact that all foreign nationals over the age of 14, except temporary immigrants, must register with immigration agencies and be fingerprinted if they have been in the country more than 30 days.[161] Failure to register constitutes a misdemeanor offense, punishable by a $100 fine, 30 days maximum jail time, or both.[162] Yet, in the absence of individualized suspicion, compelling identification would violate Fourth Amendment principles. In *Hiibel v. Sixth Judicial District Court of Nevada*,[163] the United States Supreme Court upheld a Nevada statute that compelled having to identify oneself to the police but only when the police had reasonable suspicion for the stop. In contrast, consensual encounters have always presumed voluntariness, and, in fact, refusal to cooperate cannot then become the basis for reasonable suspicion.[164]

2. During Nonconsensual Encounters Related to Immigration Enforcement

a. Workplace Raids

If ICE is executing a generalized immigration warrant and the person encountered or seized is not named in the warrant, then that person too has a right to remain silent and to refuse to cooperate. Here, too, refusal to cooperate cannot become the basis for reasonable suspicion, and persons over whom no legal justification to detain them exists should be allowed to leave. Moreover, it is not entirely clear that law enforcement can compel disclosure of identity under the warrant of persons not named in the warrant for purposes of locating the persons actually named in the warrant. Law enforcement could argue that finding the workers named in the warrant requires engagement of all workers in brief questioning and that such questioning could potentially be permitted if done in an indiscriminate fashion. The legality of such approach, provided the validity of the warrant is upheld, is still being decided in current litigation against ICE.

b. Home Raids

Often, immigration raids in people's homes are under the absconder program. As such, the immigration warrant being executed is against a person or persons with prior removal orders. Immigrants have a right to see a copy of the warrant before opening the door to their homes and to refuse to answer the door if the person/s listed in the warrant does not live in the house or is not present at the time. Several questions arise here. The first question involves the constitutional "know and announce" requirement before the execution of warrants.[165] With criminal warrants, the knock-and-announce requirement only requires law enforcement to wait a reasonable time for occupants to respond to their knock, after which law enforcement may enter by force.[166] In contrast, ICE's administrative warrants do not require immigrants to answer the door or allow entry.[167]

If the person named in the warrant is present in the home, then during the execution of the warrant immigrants who are not named in the warrant, like the workers during a workplace raid, have a right to refuse cooperation. Again, it is unclear, however, if ICE can compel that those present disclose their identity unless it is necessary to identify the person named in the warrant. Once that person has been identified, law enforcement's justification for compelling the identity and/or immigration status of the rest of the persons present is questionable.

B. The Right against Self-Incrimination and to an Attorney While in Custody

The *Miranda* warnings required in criminal proceedings are not required in removal proceedings, and the absence of a warning does not preclude use of the statement in removal proceedings.[168] However, immigration regulations provide that a foreign national shall be advised of the reason for his arrest, informed of his right to be represented by counsel of his own choice at no expense to the government, provided with a list of available free legal services, and advised that any statement he makes may be used against him.[169] Thus, unlike defendants in a criminal trial, immigrants in removal proceedings or facing civil immigration charges do not have a right to an attorney provided by the state, but they do possess a statutory right to counsel at their own expense.[170] By requesting an attorney, foreign nationals in custody foreclose further questioning by law enforcement and law enforcement should offer the foreign national the opportunity to call his or her attorney.[171]

Motions to suppress are also available to immigrants when law enforcement has procured the statements illegally through coercion.[172] In such a case, quite apart from the benefit of deterring official lawlessness, the statement will be suppressed simply because of the dubiousness of its probative value.

IV. Conclusion

The civil rights costs of local immigration enforcement can be high and localities should duly weigh these costs when deciding how and whether to enforce federal immigration laws.

Endnotes

[1] *287(g) Program: Ensuring the Integrity of America's Border Security System Through Federal-State Partnerships: Before the House Committee on Homeland Security Committee on Management, Integration, and Oversight*, July 27, 2005, at 5 (statement of Paul M. Kilcoyne, Deputy Assistant Director of Investigative Serv. Div., USCIS), http://www.ice.gov/doclib/pi/news/testimonies/050727kilcoyne.pdf.

[2] ICE, Partners, Law Enforcement Support Center, www.ice.gov/partners/lesc/.

[3] ICE Law Enforcement Support Center, Fact Sheet, http://www.ice.gov/pi/news/factsheets/081204lesc.htm.

[4] *See* Kris W. Kobach, *The Quintessential Force Multiplier: The Inherent Authority of Local Police to Make Immigration Arrests*, 69 ALB. L. REV. 179 (2005).

[5] The statute reads in pertinent part:

> No officer of person shall have the authority to make any arrests for a violation of any provision of this section except officers and employees of the Service designated by the Attorney General, either individually or as a member of a class, *and all other officers whose duty it is to enforce criminal laws.*

8 U.S.C § 1324 (2000) (emphasis added).

[6] Congress enacted amendment to grant local law enforcement authority to make arrests under INA § 276 as part of the 1996 broad immigration reform laws. The relevant provision reads:

In general

> Notwithstanding any other provisions of law, to the extend permitted by relevant State and local law, State and local law enforcement officials are authorized to arrest and detain an individual who:

is an alien illegal present in the United States; and (2) has previously been convicted of a felony in the United States and deported or left in the United States after such conviction, but only after the States or local law enforcement officials obtain appropriate confirmation from [ICE] of the status of such individual and only for such period of time as may be required for the Service to take the individual into Federal custody for purposes of deporting or removing the alien from the United States.

> The Attorney General shall cooperate with the States to assure that information in the control of the Attorney General, including information in the National Crime Information Center, that would assist the State and local law enforcement officials in carrying duties under subsection (a) of this section is made available to such officials.

8 U.S.C. 1256(c) (2000), *amended by* Illegal Immigration Reform and Immigrant Responsibility Act of 1996 (IIRIRA), Pub. L. No. 104-208, § 372(3), 110 Stat. 3009.

[7]Said provision reads:

> In the event that the Attorney General determines that an actual or imminent mass influx of aliens arriving off the United States or near a land border present urgent circumstances requiring an immediate Federal response, the Attorney General may authorize any State or local law enforcement officer, with the consent of the head of the department, agency or establishment under whose jurisdiction of the individual is serving, to perform or exercise any of the power, privileges or duties conferred or imposed by the Act or regulations issued thereunder upon officers or employees of the service.

8 U.S.C. § 1103(a)(8) (2000), *amended by* Illegal Immigration Reform and Immigrant Responsibility Act of 1996 (IIRIRA), Pub. L. No. 104-208, § 372(3), 110 Stat. 3009.

[8]*See Department of Commerce, Justice, and State, the Judiciary, and Related Agencies Appropriations for 1997: Hearings Before a Subcomm. of the H. Comm. on Appropriations*, 104th Cong. 1140 (1996) (testimony of Doris Meissner, INS Comm'r).

[9] 8 U.S.C. § 1103(a)(9) (2000).

[10] *INS and the Executive Office for Immigration Review: Hearing Before the Subcomm. on Immigration and Claims of the H. Comm. on the Judiciary*, 107th Cong. 10 (2001) (prepared statement of Kevin D. Rooney, Acting INS Comm'r).

[11] Michael J. Wishnie, *State and Local Police Enforcement of Immigration Law*, 6 U. Pa. J. Const. L. 1084, 1095 (2004). *But see* Kobach, *supra, note* at 4, 202-08 (listing other congressional actions as evincing an intent to preserve inherent state arrest authority, including the establishment in 1994 of the Law Enforcement Support Center (LESC) to respond to local police who make immigration arrests or the establishment in 1998 of QRTs for the express purpose of responding to immigration arrests made by state and local police).

[12] *See, e.g.*, Kobach, *supra* note 4.

[13] *See, e.g.*, Huyen Pham, *The Inherent Flaws in the Inherent Authority Position: Why Inviting Local Enforcement of Immigration Laws Violates the Constitution*, 31 Fla. St. U. L. Rev. 965, 978-1000 (2004). *See also* Wishnie, *supra* note 11, at 1092-95.

[14] Wishnie, *supra* note 11, at 1092-95.

[15] *See, e.g.*, U.S. Senator Jeff Sessions & Cynthia Hayden, *The Growing Role for State & Local Law Enforcement in the Realm of Immigration Law*, 16 Stan. L. & Pol'y Rev. 323 (2005).

[16] *U.S. v. Di Re*, 332 U.S. 581, 591 (1948) ("No act of Congress lays down a general federal rule for arrest without a warrant for federal offenses. None purports to supersede state law. And none applies to this arrest which, while for a federal offense, was made by a state officer accompanied by federal officers who had the power to arrest. Therefore the New York statute provides the standard by which this arrest must stand or fall."). *See also Miller v. U.S.*, 357 U.S. 301, 305 (1958) (in the circumstance of an arrest for violation of federal law by state peace officers, "...the lawfulness of the arrest without warrant is to be determined by reference to state law")

[17] *U.S. v. Haskins*, 228 F.3d 151, 152 (2d Cir. 2000), *cert denied*, 531 U.S. 1175 (2001).

[18] *U.S. v. Bowdach*, 561 F.2d 1160, 1168 (5th Cir. 1977).

[19] *U.S. v. Janik*, 723 F.2d 537, 548 (7th Cir. 1983).

[20] Sessions and Hayden, *supra* note 15, at 332-336.

[21] *Gonzalez v. City of Peoria*, 722 F.2d 468, 475-77 (9th Cir. 1983). The Ninth Circuit held, for example, that the enforcement authority must distinguish illegal entry, which is a criminal immigration violation, from illegal presence, such as overstaying a visa, which is only a civil violation. *Id.* at 477.

[22] *Lynch v. Cannatella*, 810 F.2d 1363, 1366, 1371 (5th Cir. 1987).

[23] *See* U.S. *v. Vasquez-Alvarez*, 176 F.2d 1294, 1295-1300 (10th Cir. 1999); *U.S. v. Santana-Garcia*, 264 F.3d 1188, 1190-1194 (10th Cir. 2001).

[24] *U.S. v. Laville*, 480 F.3d 187 (2007). *See infra* notes 35-36 and accompanying case for a discussing of the case.

[25] Theresa Wynn Roseborough, Deputy Assistant Att'y Gen., Office of Legal Counsel, U.S. Dep't of Justice, *Assistance by State and Local Police in Apprehending Illegal Aliens* (memorandum opinion for U.S. Attorney, S.D. Cal.) (Feb. 5, 1996), http://www.usdoj.gov/olc/immstopo1a.htm.

[26] Sessions and Hayden, *supra* note 15, at 337.

[27] *Nat'l Council of La Raza v. Dep't of Justice*, 411 F.3d 350 (2nd Cir. 2005).

[28] Dep't of Justice, Office of Legal Counsel, *Non-preemption of the Authority of State and Local Law Enforcement Officials to Arrest for Immigration Violations* (Apr. 3, 2002), *available at* www.aclu.org/FilesPDFs/ACF27DA.pdf.

[29] Op. Va. Att'y Gen. No. 07-086 (2007), 2007 *1 WL 3120673 (Va. A.G.).

[30] See *supra* note 6 and accompanying text.

[31] Op. Ohio Att'y Gen. No. 2007-018 (2007), 2007 WL 1953424 * 2 (Ohio A.G.).

[32] Op. S.C. Att'y Gen. (2003), 2003 WL 21471506 (S.C. A.G).

[33] Op. S.C. Att'y Gen. (2002), 2002 WL 399643 *1 (S.C. A.G.).

[34] *See, e.g.*, Cecilia Renn, *State and Local Enforcement of the Criminal Immigration Statutes and The Preemption Doctrine*, 41 U. Miami L. Rev. 999, 1005 (1987).

[35] Informal Op. N.Y. Att'y Gen. No. 2000-1 2(000), 2000 WL 420372 (N.Y. A.G.).

[36] *U.S. v. Laville*, 480 F.3d 187 (3rd Cir. 2007).

[37] *Id.* at 191.

[38] *Id.* Other courts grappling with the same issue have simply given the "presence" requirement an extremely broad interpretation, such that an officer who acts quickly in response to an alert to arrest a noncitizen for a misdemeanor immigration violation still meets the "presence" requirement. *See, e.g., U.S. v. Daigle,* No. CRIM. 05-29-B-W, 2005 WL 1692648 (D. Me. Jul. 19, 2005).

[39] *Laville,* 480 F.3d at 193.

[40] 8 U.S.C § 1357(g) (2000).

[41] ICE, Partners, *Delegation of Immigration Authority Section 287(g) Immigration and Nationality Act,* April 18, 2008, www.ice.gov/partners/287g/Section287_g.htm.

[42] *Id.*

[43] Worker & Immigrant Rights Clinic, Yale Law School, http://islandia.law.yale.edu/wirc/287g_foia.html.

[44] *See, e.g.,* Memorandum of Agreement between the ICE and the Arizona Department of Public Safety, at 2-3, *available at* http://islandia.law.yale.edu/wirc/287g_foia.html.

[45] These include MOAs with the Arizona Department of Public Safety; with the Washington County, Arkansas, Sheriff's Office; with the Tulsa County, Oklahoma, Sheriff's Office; with the Springdale, Arkansas, Police Department.

[46] These include, for example, those MOAs signed by the State of Alabama (no serving warrants, but power arrest without a warrant); or the Sheriff's Office of Alamance County, North Carolina (no warrantless arrests).

[47] Memorandum of Agreement between the ICE and the Mecklenburg County, North Carolina, at 2-3, *available at* http://islandia.law.yale.edu/wirc/287g_foia.html.

[48] These include MOAs with the State of Florida (counterterrorism and domestic security); the Town of Herndon, Virginia, and the Herndon Police Department (be assigned and/or collocated as task force officers to assist ICE agents with criminal investigations); the Colorado Department of Public Safety/Colorado State Patrol (assigned or collocated as task force officers to assist ICE with criminal investigations, specifically human smuggling, human trafficking, and the exploitation of all persons); the State of Georgia Department of Public Safety (assigned or collocated as task force officers to assist ICE agents with criminal investigations, specifically transport of contraband, such as narcotics or proceeds from illegal activities, and identity theft and document fraud, especially involving state driver's licenses); the Hudson Police Department in New Hampshire (assigned and/or collocated as task force officers to assist ICE agents with criminal investigations, specifically assisting local authorities in urban areas who have requested assistance due to pervasive criminal activity occurring in hot spots within their communities); Benton County, Arkansas, Sheriff's Office (to identify and remove criminal aliens from Benton County); Shenandoah County, Virginia, Sheriff's Office (assigned and/or collocated as task force officers to assist ICE agents with criminal investigations, in particular illegal trafficking in narcotics investigations and gang investigations, or general criminal investigations of persons who are not authorized to be in the U.S.); the Collier County, Florida, Sheriffs' Office (assigned and/or collocated as task force officers to assist ICE agents with criminal investigations, in particular identifying high-risk felons wanted for crimes or offenses that represent a significant threat to public safety, illegal trafficking of narcotics, gang activity, identifying enterprises and other forms of criminal activity, arresting and prosecuting all subjects involved in criminal activity, and investigating identity theft and fraudulent use of Florida driver's licenses or identification cards); Maricopa County, in Arizona (assigned and/or collocated as task force officers to assist ICE agents with criminal investigations, in particular with identifying high-risk felons wanted for crimes that represent a significant threat to public safety, criminal enterprises and other types of organized crimes, gangs, illegal trafficking in narcotics, and assisting local authorities in urban areas who have requested assistance due to pervasive criminal activity; the Framingham, Massachusetts, Police Department (assigned and/or collocated as task force officers to assist ICE agents with criminal investigations); and the Rockingham County, Virginia, Sheriff's Office (assigned or collocated as task force officers to assist ICE with criminal investigations, in particular gangs and illegal trafficking in narcotics).

[49] Memorandum of Agreement between ICE and the State of Florida, at 2-3, *available at* http://islandia.law.yale.edu/wirc/287g_foia.html.

[50] These include MOAs with the Jail Board of the Prince William-Manassas Regional Adult Detention Center (Virginia); the Cabarrus County (North Carolina) Sheriff's Office jail/correctional facilities; the Barnstable County (Massachusetts) Sheriff's Office correctional facilities; the Arizona Department of Corrections; the Cobb County (Georgia) Board of Commissioners and the Cobb County Sheriff jail/correctional facilities; the York County (South Carolina) Sheriff's Office detention facilities; the Massachusetts Department of Corrections; El Paso County (Colorado) Sheriff's Office

detention facilities; the Gaston County (North Carolina) Sheriff's Office jail facilities; State of New Mexico Corrections Department; the Davidson County (Tennessee) Sheriff's Office jail and correctional facilities; the Los Angeles County (California) jail facilities; San Bernardino County (California) Board of Supervisors county jail facilities; County of Orange (California) jail facilities; and Riverside County (California) jail facilities.

[51] American Immigration Lawyers Association, Fact Sheet – "287(g)" Agreements, *available at* http://www.aila.org/search/default.aspx?searchterm=fact%20sheet%20287(g).

[52] Op. Ohio Att'y Gen. No. 2007-029 (2007), 2007 WL 2700588 (Ohio A.G.).

[53] Op. Va. Att'y Gen. No. 07-016 (2007), 2007 WL 1456159 (Va. A.G.).

[54] Kobach, *supra* note 4, at 220, Table 1.

[55] Press Release, U.S. Immigration and Customs Enforcement, Fact Sheet: Frequently Asked Questions About Worksite Enforcement (Oct. 15, 2007), http://www.ice.gov/pi/news/factsheets/worksite.htm.

[56] These include: Baltimore, Chicago, Denver, Detroit, Houston, Los Angeles, Minneapolis, New York City, Philadelphia, San Francisco, Seattle, and Washington, D.C. Orde F. Kittrie, *Federalism, Deportation, and Crime: Victims Afraid to Call the Police*, 91 Iowa L. Rev. 1449, 1466-74 (2006).

[57] Nat'l Immigration Law Ctr., Annotated Chart of Laws, Resolutions, and Policies, Instituted Across the U.S. Protecting Residents from Local Enforcement of Immigration Laws (2004).

[58] Kittrie, supra note 56, at 1455. *See also* Huyen Pham, *The Constitutional Right Not to Cooperate? Local Sovereignty and the Federal Immigration Power*, 74 U. Cin. L. Rev. 1373, 1388-91 (2006) (describing the characteristics of sanctuary policies as follows: no discrimination; no enforcement of civil immigration laws; no inquiry into citizenship status; and no notifying federal immigration authorities).

[59] *Id.* at 1474.

[60] This provision imposes criminal penalties on "[a]ny person who...knowing or in reckless disregard of the fact that an alien has come to, entered, or remains in the United States in violation of law, conceals, harbors, or shields from detection, or attempts to conceal, harbor, or shield from detection, such alien in nay place, including any building or any means of transportation." 8 U.S.C. § 1324(a)(1)(A)(iii) (2000).

[61] Kittrie, supra note 56, at 1493-95.

[62] *See id.*

[63] *Id.* at 1495.

[64] Pham, *supra* note 58, at 1384-85.

[65] 8 U.S.C. § 1373 (2000).

[66] 8 U.S.C. § 1644 (2000).

[67] 179 F.3d 29 (2nd Cir. 1999).

[68] *Id.* at 33.

[69] Kittrie, *supra* note 56, at 1498. *See also* Pham, *supra* note 58, at 1391-95.

[70] Kittrie, *supra* note 56, at 1499.

[71] *Id.* at 1487-93, 1499-1500.

[72] *Id.* at 1475-80.

[73] *Id.* at 1480-84.

[74] *See, e.g., Muehler v. Mena*, 544 U.S. 93 (2005) (involving the questioning of detainee about her immigration status during the execution of a gang-related warrant in a home); *Farm Labor Org. Comm. v. Ohio State Highway Patrol*, 991 F. Supp. 85 (N.D. Ohio 1997) (involving asking occupants in a car during a traffic stop about their immigration status); *U.S. v. Esparza-Mendoza*, 386 F.3d 953 (10th Cir. 2004) (involving the discovery of an outstanding immigration warrant during a community care-function encounter).

[75] *See, e.g., Flores v. Walla Walla Police*, No. CV-06-166-MWL., 2006 WL 2850010 (E.D. Wash. Oct. 2, 2006) (involving local police arrest based on a federal immigration warrant).

[76] *See, e.g., U.S. v. Vite-Espinoza*, 342 F.3d 462, 464 (6th Cir. 2003) (involving the execution of a home raid with a fed-

eral immigration search warrant during a joint federal, state, and local police task force investigating the counterfeiting of immigration and identification documents).

[77] *See, e.g., State v. Bolton*, 301 P.2d 98 (N.M. App. 1990) (involving participation of ICE agents in state road block).

[78] *U.S. v. Perez-Sosa*, 164 F.3d 1082 (8th Cir. 1998) (involving state trooper's consensual encounter that lead to probable cause based on report that person was transporting undocumented persons).

[79] *See, e.g., Arias, et. al., v. ICE*, Civ. No. 07-1959 ADM/JSM, 2008 WL 1827604 (D. Minn. Apr. 23, 2008). *See also* Original Complaint—Class Action Request for Injunctive Relief and Declaratory Relief and Damages, at 8-10, 12-14, *United Food & Commercial Workers Int'l Union v. Chertoff*, No. 07-000188 (N.D. Tex. Sept. 12, 2007), *available at* http://www.ailf.org/lac/chdocs/UFood-Complaint.pdf.

[80] *See, e.g.*, Randolph Capps, et. al., *Paying the Price: The Impact of Immigration Raids on America's Children*, Urban Institute, 2007, *available at* http://www.urban.org/url.cfm?ID=411566&renderforprint=1.

[81] *See, e.g., Arias*, 2008 WL 1827604 at 3.*See also* Complaint for Violations of the Fourth and Fifth Amendments to the United States Constitution, *Reyes v. Alcantar*, No. 07-02271 (N.D. Cal. Apr. 26, 2007), *available at* http://www.ailf.org/lac/chdocs/Reyes-Complaint.pdf.

[82] *INS v. Lopez-Mendoza*, 468 U.S. 1032, 1050 (1984). *See also* Joseph J. Migas, *Exclusionary Remedy Available in Civil Deportation Proceedings for Egregious Fourth Amendment Violations,* 9 Geo. Immigr. L. J. 207, 209 (1995).

[83] Daniel P. Blank, Note, *Suppressing Defendant's Identity and Other Strategies for Defending Against a Charge of Illegal Reentry After Deportation*, 50 Stan. L. Rev. 139,140-41 (1997).

[84] *U.S. v. Martinez-Fuerte*, 428 U.S. 543, 558 (1976).

[85] *INS v. Delgado*, 466 U.S. 210, 218 (1984).

[86] *See, e.g., U.S. v. Urrieta*, 520 F.3d 569 (6th Cir. 2008); *U.S. v. Pasillas-Castanon*, No. 06-CR-175-HDC, 2007 WL 43391 (N.D. Okla. Feb. 2, 2007); *U.S. v. Villanueva-Madriz*, No. 05-CR-60073-HO, 2006 WL 278160 (D. Or. Feb. 3, 2006); *U.S. v. Santana-Garcia*, 264 F.3d 1188 (10th Cir. 2001); *Farm Labor Org. Comm. v. Ohio State Highway Patrol*, et al., 991 F. Supp. 895 (N.D. Ohio 1997).

[87] *See, e.g., New Mexico v. Bolton*, 801 P.2d 98 (N.M. App. 1990).

[88] *Muehler v. Mena*, 544 U.S. 93, 100-01 (2005).

[89] *See* Raquel Aldana, *On Rights, Federal Citizenship, and the "Alien,"* 46 Washburn L. J. 263, 284 (2007).

[90] Geoffrey G. Hemphill, *The Administrative Search Doctrine: Isn't This Exactly What the Framers Were Trying to Avoid?*, 5 Regent U. L. Rev. 215, 128-220 (1995).

[91] *See, e.g., Blackie's House of Beef, Inc. v. Castillo*, 659 F.2d 1211, 1213 (D.C. Cir. 1981). *See also Int'l Molder's & Allied Worker's Local Union No. 164 v. Nelson*, 799 F.2d 547, 553 (9th Cir. 1986).

[92] *U.S. v. De Leon-Reyna*, 930 F.2d 396 (5th Cir. 1991).

[93] Immigration Reform and Control Act of 1986, Pub. L. No. 99-603, 100 Stat. 3359, 3359 (1986) (codified as amended 8 U.S.C. § 1324a (2000 & Supp. V 2005)).

[94] Nat'l Immigration Law Ctr., Basic Information Brief: DHS Basic Pilot Program 3 (rev. Mar. 2008), *available at* http://www.nilc.org/immsemplymnt/ircaempverif/e-verify_infobrief_2008-03-13.pdf.

[95] DHS, E-Verify, *available at* www.dhs.gov/xprevprot/programs/gc_1185221678150.shtm.

[96] *Id.*

[97] Raquel Aldana, *Of Katz and "Aliens": Privacy Expectations and the Immigration Raids*, 41 U.C. Davis L. Rev. 1081, 1098-99 (2008) (describing the IMAGE program under which employers voluntarily agree to annual audits and to report any violations or deficiencies of employee records to ICE and employer response to SSA so-called No-Match letters, which notifies employers of SSN discrepancies).

[98] 8 U.S.C. § 1324a(e)(2)(C) (2000).

[99] U.S. Citizenship & Immigration Servs., Report to Congress on the Basic Pilot Programs 4-5 (2004), *available at* http://www.nilc.org/immsemplymnt/ircaempverif/basicpilot_uscis_rprt_to_congress_2004-06.pdf.

[100] Office of the Inspector Gen. Soc. Sec. Admin., Congressional Response Report: Accuracy of the Social Security Administration's Numident File, at ii (2006) *available at* http://www.ssa.gov/oig/ADOBEPDF/audittxt/A-08-06-26100.htm .

[101] *Id.* at 11.

[102] *Id.*

[103] *See* Aldana, *supra* note 97, at 1109 for a description of ICE's absconder initiative.

[104] Memorandum from Larry Thompson, Deputy Att'y Gen., to the INS Comm'r, FBI Dir. U.S. Marshall Serv. Dir., and U.S. Att'ys, § A, at 1 (Jan. 25, 2002), *available at* http://fl1.findlaw.com/news.findlaw.com/hdocs/docs/doj/abscndr012502mem.pdf.

[105] 8 U.S.C. §§ 1326(a), (b) (2000).

[106] Seventh Public Hearing of the National Comm'n on Terrorist Attacks Upon the United States, Jan. 26, 2004, http://govinfo.library.unt.edu/911/hearings/hearing7/witness_ziglar.htm (statement of James W. Ziglar, INS Commissioner).

[107] Ernesto Londoño, *Database is Tool in Deporting Fugitives: Police Officers Find Illegal Immigrants in Warrant Searches*, WASH. POST., June 12, 2003, at A1.

[108] Kobach, *supra* note 4, at 188-192.

[109] Memorandum from Glenn A. Fine, Inspector Gen., U.S. Dep't of Justice, Review of the Immigration and Nationalization Service's Removal of Aliens Issued Final Orders I-2003-004 (Feb. 25, 2003), *available at* http://www.usdoj.gov/oig/reports/INS/e0304/memo.pdf.

[110] Office of the Inspector Gen., U.S. Dep't of Justice, Report No. 1-2003-004, The Immigration and Naturalization Services' Removal of Aliens Issued Final Orders 14 (2003) *available at* http://www.npr.org/documents/2005/mar/doj_alien_removal.pdf.

[111] *See* Ruth Morris, *U.S. Adding Fugitive Squads that Target Immigrants Who Ignore Expulsion Orders*, S. FLA SUN SENTINEL, Feb. 26, 2007, *available at* http://oneoldvet.com/?page_id=281#12.

[112] Michelle Wucker, *The Top Ten Ways America Gets Immigration Wrong*, AM. IMMIGRATION L. FOUND., June 19, 2006, *available at* http://www.visalaw.com/06oct2/12oct206.html.

[113] *U.S. v. Hines*, 564 F.2d 925, 928 (10th Cir. 1977) (finding that reliance upon NCIC to substantiate probable cause for arrest was acceptable. *See also U.S. v. Davis*, 568 F.2d 514, 515 (6th Cir. 1978).

[114] *Arizona v. Evans*, 514 U.S. 1, 16-17 (upholding use of evidence obtained from false arrest records that was the product of clerical errors).

[115] *Nat'l Council of La Raza v. Mukasey*, No. 07-0816-cv, 2008 WL 2630729 (2nd Cir. Jul. 3, 2008) and *Nat'l Council of La Raza v. Gonzales*, 468 F. Supp. 2d 429 (E.D. N.Y. 2007).

[116] 466 U.S. 210, 218 (1984).

[117] *Id.* at 212.

[118] *Id.*

[119] *Id.*

[120] *Int'l Molders' & Allied Workers' Local Union No. 164 v. Nelson*, 643 F. Supp. 884, 893-95 (N.D. Cal. 1986); *Ill. Migrant Council v. Pilliod*, 51 F. Supp. 1011, 1020-21 (N.D. Ill. 1982).

[121] *See* Aldana, *supra* note 97, at 1114-1115 (documenting several complaints on ICE execution of home warrants).

[122] *See* Daniel Kanstroom, *Deportation, Social Control, and Punishment: Some Thoughts about Why Hard Laws Make Bad Cases*, 113 HARV. L. REV. 1889, 1894 (2000).

[123] *See, e.g.*, Stephen H. Legomsky, *The New Path of Immigration Law: Asymmetric Incorporation of Criminal Justice Norms*, 64 WASH. & LEE L. REV. 469 (2007); Juliet Stumpf, *The Crimmigration Crisis: Immigrants, Crimes, and Sovereign Power*, 56 AM. U. L. REV. 367 (2006); Teresa A. Miller, *Citizenship and Severity: Recent Immigration Reforms and the New Penology*, 17 GEO. IMMIG. L. J. 611 (2003).

[124] Legomsky, supra note 123, at 521.

[125] *Id.* at 472.

[126] In 2005, the House of Representatives passed a bill that would have created several additional crimes, including criminalizing the presence of the undocumented. Border Protection, Antiterrorism, and Illegal Immigration Control Act of 2005, H.R. 4437, 109th Cong. (2005).

[127] Nicole Gaouette, *Federal Prosecution of Illegal Immigrants Soars,* L.A. TIMES, June 18, 2008, at A-8, *available at* http://articles.latimes.com/2008/jun/18/nation/na-immig18.

[128] *Id.*

[129] U.S. Immigration and Customs Enforcement, Fact Sheets: Frequently Asked Questions about Worksite Enforcement (last updated Aug, 12, 2008), http://www.ice.gov/pi/news/factsheets/worksite.htm.

[130] Stephen Lendman, *Civil Wrongs: Targeting Immigrants - The Largest Ever US ICE Raid,* BALTIMORE CHRONICLE & SENTINEL, *available at* http://baltimorechronicle.com/2008/081108Lendman.shtml.

[131] *See, e.g.,* Overview of State Legislation Related to Immigrants and Immigration, January-March 2008, National Conference of State Legislatures, Immigrant Policy Project, April 24, 2008, *available at* http://www.ncsl.org/print/immig/immigreportapril2008.pdf (reporting that in the first three months of 2008 alone, 24 bills on human trafficking and 198 bills on law enforcement were introduced).

[132] *Id.*

[133] Miller, supra note 123, at 614-15; Stumpf, supra note 123, at 391.

[134] Miller, supra note 123, at 648-49.

[135] *Id.* at 635-36.

[136] Consider, for example, DHS Secretary Michael Chertoff's remarks in defense of worksite raids:

> [Document fraud] is a serious problem not only with respect to illegal immigration, but with respect to national security. And that's precisely the point made by the 9/11 Commission a couple of years ago, because illegal documents are not only used by illegal migrants, but they are used by terrorists who want to get on airplanes, or criminals who want to prey on our citizens. And so, as part of this overall strategy of worksite enforcement, we've gotten very focused on the question of those who exploit illegal documents and identity theft in order to pursue illegal acts. So yesterday's enforcement action [the Swift and Co. raids] demonstrate another step in this worksite enforcement strategy. A tough stance against worksites that employ illegal aliens and against individuals and organizations that commit or facilitate identity theft or fraud.

Press Release, Dep't of Homeland Security, Remarks by Secretary of Homeland Security Michael Chertoff, Immigration and Customs Enforcement Assistant Secretary Julie Myers, and Federal Trade Commission Chairman Deborah Platt Majoras at a Press Conference on Operation Wagon Train (Dec. 13, 2006), *available at* http://www.dhs.gov/xnews/releases/pr_1166047951514.shtm.

[137] *See* Craig M. Bradley, *The Reasonable Policeman: Police Intent in Criminal Procedure,* 76 MISS. L. J. 339, 340 (2006).

[138] *Whren v. United States,* 517 U.S. 806, 811 (1996) (holding that ulterior motives need not invalidate police conduct that is otherwise justified by reasonable belief that a violation of law has occurred).

[139] *Id.*

[140] 531 U.S. 32, 50-51 (2000).

[141] Immigration and Nationality Act (INA) of 1990, 8 U.S.C. § 1253 (2000).

[142] *See* Kevin Lapp, *Pressing Public Necessity: The Unconstitutionality of the Absconder Apprehension Initiative,* 29 N.Y.U. REV. L. & SOC. CHANGE 573, 574 (2005).

[143] ICE Press Release, ICE Apprehends More Than 2,100 Criminal Aliens, Gang Members, Fugitives and Other Immigration Violators in Nationwide Interior Enforcement Operation, Jun. 14, 2006, *available at* http://www.dhs.gov/xnews/releases/press_release_0926.shtm.

[144] *See* Andrew Ryan, *Agency Nabs Illegal Immigrants Across U.S.,* WASH. POST, Jun. 14, 2006, *available at* http://www.washingtonpost.com/wp-dyn/content/article/2006/06/14/AR2006061401245.html.

[145] *See* Leticia M. Saucedo, *The Employer Preference for the Subservient Workers and the Making of the Brown Collar Workplace*, 67 OHIO ST. L. J. 961, 965-66 (2006).

[146] *See* Anthony E. Mucchetti, *Driving While Brown: A Proposal for Ending Racial Profiling in Emerging Latino Communities*, 8 HARV. LATINO L. REV. 1, 3 (2005)

[147] Carrie L. Arnold, *Racial Profiling in Immigration Enforcement: State and Local Agreements to Enforce Federal Immigration Law*, 49 ARIZ. L. REV. 113, 119-120 (2007) (discussing the "Chandler Roundup" operation which lasted five days and resulted in the arrest and deportation of 432 undocumented immigrants).

[148] ACLU Press Release, Sheriff Arpaio Sued over Racial Profiling of Latinos in Maricopa County, July, 7, 2008, *available at* www.aclu.org/immigrants/gen/36011prs20080716.html. A copy of the complaint is *available at* http://www.aclu.org/pdfs/immigrants/filedfirstamdcm071608(2).pdf.

[149] *Manuel de Jesus Ortega Melendres, et al., v. Arpaio*, First Amended Complaint, Class Actions, No. CV -07-02513-PHX-MHM, ¶ 16 *available at* http://www.aclu.org/immigrants/gen/35998lgl20080716.html.

[150] *Id.* at ¶¶ 3, 30-48.

[151] *See* David Harris, *"Driving While Black" and Other Traffic Offenses: The Supreme Court and Pretextual Traffic Stops*, 87 J. CRIM. L. & CRIMINOLOGY 544, 550-51 (1997).

[152] *See* DAVID COLE, ENEMY ALIEN: DOUBLE STANDARDS AND CONSTITUTIONAL FREEDOMS IN THE WAR ON TERRORISM 204 (2003) (discussing the Court's tolerance of ethnically selective targeting).

[153] *See* Alfredo Mirande, *Is There a "Mexican Exception" to the Fourth Amendment?*, 55 FLA. L. REV. 365, 372-74 (2003).

[154] *See, e.g., U.S. v. Brignoni-Pince*, 422 U.S. 873, 885-87 (1975).

[155] *Id.* A Pew Hispanic Center estimate of the size and characteristics of the undocumented population concluded that as of March 2004, of the 10.3 million estimated undocumented persons, 57 percent or 5.9 million were from Mexico, while 24 percent were from other Latin American nations. Jeffrey S. Passel, *Estimates of the Size and Characteristics of the Undocumented Population*, Report, Mar. 21, 2005, at 8 *available at* http://pewhispanic.org/files/reports/44.pdf.

[156] Consider, for example, ICE's enforcement statistics for 2006. ICE apprehended more than 1,206,000 foreign nationals that year, nearly 88 percent of whom were natives of Mexico. Moreover, of the 272,389 foreign nationals removed from the U.S., the leading countries of origin represented were: Mexico (67 percent); Honduras (10 percent); and Guatemala (7 percent). This record of removal does not consider the ethnic origin of the more than 1 million persons who accepted voluntary departure without a removal order. Office of Immigration Statistics, Immigration Enforcement Actions: 2006, Annual Report, May 2008, *available at* http://www.dhs.gov/xlibrary/assets/statistics/publications/enforcement_ar_06.pdf.

[157] U.S. Census Bureau News, U.S. Department of Commerce, U.S. Hispanic Population Surpasses 45 Million Now 15 Percent of Total, *available at* http://www.census.gov/Press-Release/www/releases/archives/population/011910.html.

[158] *U.S. v. Montero-Camargo*, 208 F.3d 1122 (9th Cir. 2000).

[159] *Arguelles-Vasquez v. INS*, 786 F.2d 1433 (9th Cir. 1986); *Gonzalez-Rivera v. INS*, 22 F.3d 1441 (9th Cir. 1994). *See also Orhordaghe v. INS*, 38 F.3d 488 (9th Cir. 1994) (holding that the INS's investigation of an individual based solely on his or her "foreign-sounding" name is also egregious).

[160] Rebecca Chiao, *Fourth Amendment Limits on Immigration Law Enforcement*, 93-02 IMMIGR. BRIEF. 1 (1993).

[161] 8 U.S.C. § 1302 (2000).

[162] *Id.*

[163] 542 U.S. 177 (2004).

[164] *Florida v. Royer*, 460 U.S. 491 (1983) (refusal to cooperate, without more, does not furnish the minimal level of objective justification needed for a detention or seizure). *But see Illinois v. Wardlow*, 525 U.S. 119 (2000) (rejecting that unprovoked flight upon sight of police per se offers ground for reasonable suspicion but allowing it as a factor to find reasonable suspicion).

[165] *See Wilson v. Arkansas*, 514 U.S. 927 (1995).

[166] WILLIAM E. RINGEL, EXECUTION OF WARRANTS, SEARCHES AND SEIZURES, ARRESTS, AND CONFESSIONS § 6:10 (2007).

[167] Nina Bernstein, *Hunts for "Fugitive Aliens" Leads to Collateral Arrests*, N.Y. TIMES, July 23, 2007, at B1 (reporting on DHS Secretary Chertoff's explanation that civil immigration warrants do not permit ICE to force entry); Jerry Seper, *Outnumbered in a Hunt for Aliens: Force of 200 Charged with Tracking 400,000 Criminals, "Absconders,"* WASH. TIMES, July 20, 2004, at A1 (describing same practice).

[168] Matter of Baltazar, 16 I & N Dec. 108, 1977 WL 39227 (B.I.A. 1977); *U.S. v. Valdez*, 917 F.2d 466 (10th Cir. 1990) (in conviction for re-entry after deportation, no right to or prejudice in absence of Miranda warnings).

[169] 8 C.F.R. §§ 1240.10, 1240.48.

[170] 8 C.F.R. §§ 1240.10(a)(1); 1240.48(a).

[171] Chiao, *supra* note 160, at 1 (describing requirements of lawsuit settlement (expired in 1995) against INS to allow foreign nationals access to counsel during post-arrest questioning).

[172] *Bustos-Torres v. INS*, 898 F.2d 1053, 1057 (5th Cir. 1990); Matter of Garcia, 17 I & N Dec. 319, 321 (B.I.A 1980).

APPENDIX D

Undocumented Immigration and Rates of Crime and Imprisonment: Popular Myths and Empirical Realities

BY RUBÉN G. RUMBAUT

Introduction

The perception that the foreign-born, especially "illegal aliens," are responsible for higher crime rates is deeply rooted in American public opinion and is sustained by media anecdote and popular myth. In the absence of rigorous empirical research, stereotypes about immigrants and crime often provide the underpinnings for public policies and practices, and shape public opinion and political behavior (Chávez 2001; Hagan and Palloni 1999; Lee 2003; Martínez and Valenzuela 2006). Such stereotypes, reinforced through popular movies and television programs and fueled by media coverage of singular events, project an enduring image of immigrant communities permeated by criminal elements.

The extent to which such views shape American public opinion was shown by the results of the National Opinion Research Center's 2000 General Social Survey, which interviewed a nationally representative sample of adults to measure attitudes toward and perceptions of immigration in a "multi-ethnic United States." Asked whether "more immigrants cause higher crime rates," 25 percent said "very likely" and another 48 percent "somewhat likely." Thus about three-fourths (73 percent) of Americans believed that immigration is causally related to more crime. That was a much higher proportion than the 60 percent who believed that "more immigrants were [somewhat or very] likely to cause Americans to lose jobs," or the 56 percent who thought that "more immigrants were [somewhat or very] likely to make it harder to keep the country united" (Alba, Rumbaut and Marotz 2005; Rumbaut and Alba 2003). A year later, the attacks of September 11, 2001, and the political and media reaction in the wake of a "war on terror," further exacerbated public fears of the foreign-born and conflated "illegal immigration" not only with crime but with potential terrorism.

But these perceptions are not supported empirically; instead, as demonstrated below, they are refuted by the preponderance of scientific evidence. Both contemporary and historical studies, including official crime statistics and victimization surveys since the early 1990s, data from the last three decennial censuses, national and regional surveys in areas of immigrant concentration, and investigations carried out by major government commissions over the past century, have shown instead that immigration is associated with *lower* crime rates and *lower* incarceration rates.

In what follows we examine the relationship of contemporary immigration, including undocumented migration, to crime and imprisonment. First, at the national level, we analyze changes in the rates of violent crimes and property crimes during the years of the surge in immigration. Next we look at the incarceration rates of young men eighteen to thirty-nine, comparing the foreign-born versus the U.S.-born by national origin and by education, and, among the foreign-born, by length of residence in the United States. The analysis compares the rates of incarceration of foreign-born young men from nationalities the majority of whom are undocumented

Rubén G. Rumbaut is Professor of Sociology at the University of California-Irvine.

immigrants with less than a high school education (Mexicans, Salvadorans and Guatemalans) versus the rates for other immigrant nationalities as well as for native ethnic majority and minority groups. Finally, we summarize the available empirical evidence from a wide range of other studies, compare it to prevailing public perceptions, and note their implications for criminological theory, research, and public policy.

The Conflation of "Undocumented Immigrant" and "Crime"

Periods of increased immigration have historically been accompanied by nativist alarms, perceptions of threat, and pervasive stereotypes of newcomers, particularly during economic downturns or national crises (such as the 2000-2002 recession and the "war on terror" of the post-September 11 era, which spiked public anxiety), and when immigrants have arrived *en masse* and differed substantially from the native-born in religion, language, physical appearance, and world region of origin (Fry 2006; Johnson 2005; Kanstroom 2007). The present period is no exception—with the twist that "illegal immigrants" are now singled out with added animus and framed as harbingers of crime.

Thus, California's Proposition 187, which was passed with 59 percent of the statewide vote in 1994 (but challenged as unconstitutional and subsequently overturned by a federal court), asserted in its opening lines that "the people of California...have suffered and are suffering economic hardship [and] personal injury and damage caused by the criminal conduct of illegal aliens in this state." Similarly, the "Illegal Immigration Relief Act Ordinance" passed in 2006 by the city council of Hazleton, Pennsylvania—the first of hundreds of such ordinances passed by local councils throughout the U.S. since 2006—declared in part that "illegal immigration leads to higher crime rates" and sought accordingly to secure for the city's legal residents and citizens "the right to live in peace free of the threat of crime" and to protect them from "crime committed by illegal aliens." (The Hazleton ordinance too was overturned in 2007 as unconstitutional.)

Such attitudes find support at the highest levels of political leadership. For example, in his May 15, 2006, address to the nation on immigration reform, President George W. Bush asserted that "illegal immigration puts pressure on public schools and hospitals, it strains state and local budgets, and brings crime to our communities." Two days later, CNN anchor Lou Dobbs, taking President Bush to task for what he termed "woefully inadequate" proposals, framed the issue as follows in his televised commentary: "Not only are millions of illegal aliens entering the United States each year across that border, but so are illegal drugs. More cocaine, heroin, methamphetamine, and marijuana flood across the Mexican border than from any other place, more than three decades into the war on drugs...If it is necessary to send 20,000 to 30,000 National Guard troops to the border with Mexico to preserve our national sovereignty and protect the American people from rampant drug trafficking, illegal immigration and the threat of terrorists, then I cannot imagine why this president and this Congress would hesitate to do so." About the only point of agreement between the president and Dobbs seemed to be the equation of "illegal immigration" and "crime."

The belief that immigration leads to increased crime is not solely an American phenomenon; we see similar trends at the international level. Kitty Calavita's (2005) recent study in southern

Europe, for example, reports that in Spain in 2002 a national poll found that 60 percent believed that immigrants were causing increases in the crime rate, while a survey conducted in Italy found that 57 percent of Italians agreed that "the presence of immigrants increases crime and delinquency." These notions in turn were fanned by media accounts. A content analysis of newspapers in southern Italy found that 78 percent of the articles regarding immigration were crime related, while another study found that 57 percent of television reports on immigrants dealt with crime.

The Coincidence of Mass Immigration and Mass Imprisonment

A new era of mass migration, accelerating since the 1970s, has transformed the ethnic and racial composition of the U.S. population and the communities where they settle. This time the flows have come largely from Latin America, the Caribbean, and Asia, not from Europe. Over the past fifteen years, the number of immigrants—in varying legal statuses[1]—coming to the United States has been the largest in history in absolute terms. In 2006 the foreign-born population surpassed 38 million, nearly 13 percent of the U.S. population.

In 1970, the U.S. census had found that the foreign-born population accounted for only 4.7 percent of the total population—the lowest proportion since 1850, when it first recorded the country of birth of U.S. residents. But by 1980, the foreign-born population had grown to 14.1 million, or 6.2 percent of the national total; by 1990 it had grown to 19.8 million (7.9 percent); by 2000, to 31.1 million (11.1 percent); and it has been growing by more than one million per year since. More immigrants came in the 1980s than in any previous decade but one (1901-10, the peak years of mass migration from Europe when the foreign-born population reached 14.7 percent of the U.S. total); and more immigrants came in the 1990s than in any other decade—a total that may be surpassed in the present decade, adding to the largest immigrant population in history (both legal and illegal). By 2008, over 70 million persons in the United States were of foreign birth or parentage (first or second generations)—about 23 percent of all Americans, including 76 percent of all "Hispanics" and 90 percent of all "Asians" (Rumbaut, 2008). Immigrants are heavily concentrated in metropolitan areas, are predominantly nonwhite, speak languages other than English, reflect a wide range of religious and cultural backgrounds, and arrive with a mix of legal statuses (Alba and Nee 2003; Portes and Rumbaut 2006).

More significant still is the diversity of their social class origins. By far the most educated *and* the least educated groups in the U.S. today are immigrants, a reflection of polar-opposite types of migrations embedded in different historical contexts—and inserted in a labor market increasingly polarized into high-tech/high-wage and manual/low-wage sectors, which attracts both immigrant professionals and undocumented laborers. They come through regular immigration channels, or without legal authorization, or as state-sponsored refugees—legal statuses which interact with their human capital to shape distinct modes of incorporation. One mode is exemplified by groups composed of a majority of legal permanent residents with college degrees or more advanced credentials (such as the Indians, Chinese, Koreans, and Filipinos); another is typified by groups composed of a majority of unauthorized laborers with less than a high school education (principally Mexicans, Salvadorans, and Guatemalans, who have the lowest levels of education in the U.S.); yet a third involves groups admitted as refugees (such as the Vietnamese, Laotians, and Cambodians, and the Cubans, who benefit from a 1966 law that applies uniquely to them) (Rumbaut 2008).

Unlike the Europeans who entered a rapidly industrializing society in the last era of mass migration a century ago, the incorporation of contemporary immigrants has coincided with a period of economic restructuring and rising inequality in income, wealth, and social well-being, during which the returns to education have sharply increased (Massey 2007). As the post-World War II era of sustained economic growth, low unemployment, and rising real wages ended for most workers by the early 1970s, men with only a high school degree or less were hardest hit. In this changing context, social timetables that were widely observed a half century ago by young people for accomplishing adult transitions have become less predictable and more prolonged, diverse, and disordered (Settersten, Furstenberg, and Rumbaut 2005).

This new era of mass immigration has also coincided with an era of mass imprisonment in the U.S., which has further transformed paths to adulthood among young men with low levels of education (Pettit and Western 2004). The number of adults incarcerated in federal or state prisons or local jails in the U.S. skyrocketed during this period, quadrupling from just over 500,000 in 1980 to over 2.2 million in 2006. Those figures do not include the much larger number of those on probation (convicted offenders not incarcerated) or parole (under community supervision after a period of incarceration); when they are added to the incarceration totals, over seven million adults were under correctional supervision in the U.S. in 2006 (U.S. Bureau of Justice Statistics 2007).

Among some racial minorities in the U.S., becoming a prisoner has become a modal life event in early adulthood: astoundingly, as Pettit and Western (2004) have noted, a black male high school dropout born in the late 1960s had a nearly 60 percent chance of serving time in prison by the end of the 1990s, and recent birth cohorts of black men are more likely to have prison records than military records or bachelor's degrees. In a cycle of cumulative disadvantage, young men with low levels of education are significantly more likely to become a prisoner than same-age peers with higher levels of education. Having a prison record, in turn, is linked not only to unemployment, lower wages, marital and family instability, and severe restrictions on social and voting rights (including lifetime disenfranchisement in many states) but also to stigmatized identities and pathways to criminal recidivism (Manza and Uggen 2006; Pager 2003; Sampson and Laub 1993; Western 2002; Western, Kling, and Weiman 2001; Visher and Travis 2003).

In the wake of both phenomena—the rise of immigration and the rise of incarceration, which have occurred rapidly and in tandem, extending deeply into the fabric of American life—the research literatures on both immigration and incarceration have burgeoned, but independently of each other. Surprisingly, with some exceptions (e.g., Butcher and Piehl 1997; Hagan, Levi, and Dinovitzer 2008; Hagan and Palloni 1999; Lee 2003; Lee, Martínez, and Rosenfeld 2001; Martínez 2002; Martínez, Lee, and Nielsen 2004; Rumbaut, 1997, 2005), there has been scant scholarly effort made to connect the respective literatures. Immigration scholars, focused on the incorporation of the latest waves of newcomers, have all but ignored the areas of crime and imprisonment—although those would be indispensable to tests of theories of segmented assimilation and modes of incorporation. And criminologists in turn have paid no attention to the surge in immigration (for instance, Zimring 2007). Contemporary criminology has focused largely on the stratifications of race (still largely framed in black and white terms) and place, class, age and gender, leaving out ethnicity, nativity, and generation (in part because official criminal justice statistics are not collected by national origin, immigration or generational status).

Undocumented Immigration 1993-2006

Today an estimated twelve million immigrants are unauthorized, or 30 percent of the foreign-born population of the U.S.; those figures are unprecedented. The number of undocumented immigrants has quadrupled since 1994. The U.S. Department of Homeland Security estimated their numbers at 11.6 million as of January 2006 (Hoefer *et al.*, 2007). According to the Pew Hispanic Center, two-thirds (66 percent) of the unauthorized population had been in the country for ten years or less, and the largest share, 40 percent or 4.4 million people, had been in the country five years or less. There were 1.8 million children who were unauthorized, or 16 percent of the total. In addition, 3.1 million children who are U.S. citizens by birth were living in households in which the head of the family or a spouse was unauthorized. About 56 percent of the unauthorized population was from Mexico, and another 8 percent from El Salvador and Guatemala, so that two-thirds of the total came from those three countries alone. Another 14 percent came from other Latin American countries, and 22 percent from Asia, Europe, Canada, Africa, and elsewhere (Passel 2006).

Since 1993, the militarization of the U.S.-Mexico border in four key sectors from San Diego to El Paso and the lower Rio Grande Valley, including a tripling of the number of Border Patrol agents and a quadrupling of the Border Patrol budget, has not deterred the flow of unauthorized migrants. Instead it has led to a booming industry of professional smugglers (*coyotes*) and redirected the flow of undocumented immigrants through more isolated and dangerous desert terrain, resulting in hundreds of deaths each year. Undocumented immigrants are now heading to new destinations across all fifty states, rather than just traditional destinations in California and Texas. Another unintended consequence of heightened border enforcement is that the largely temporary population of "sojourner" workers that predominated in the past has been transformed into a population of permanent "settlers" who bring their families and stay, since the risks and costs of dangerous border crossings have sharply increased. For instance, in recent years *coyotes* have charged Mexican migrants about $3,000 per person to cross the border (Cornelius 2006; Massey, Durand and Malone 2002).

Still, the undocumented immigrant population is disproportionately made up of poor young males who have recently arrived from Mexico, El Salvador, and Guatemala, and a few other Latin American countries to work in low-wage jobs requiring little formal education. These migrants are responding to the growing demand for their labor generated by the U.S. economy, which faces a demographic challenge to future labor-force growth as the fertility rate of natives declines and a growing number of native-born workers retire (IPC 2005). As the Congressional Budget Office put it in a recent report (2005: 25): "The baby-boom generation's exit from the labor force could well foreshadow a major shift in the role of foreign-born workers in the labor force. Unless native fertility rates increase, it is likely that most of the growth in the U.S. labor force will come from immigration by the middle of the century."

Conventional wisdom presumes a connection between the characteristics of workers who fill less-skilled jobs (i.e., young, male, poor, high-school dropout, ethnic minority)—which describe a much greater proportion of the foreign-born than of the native-born—and the likelihood of involvement with crime, all the more when those young male workers are unauthorized migrants. Federal Bureau of Investigation (FBI) statistics also show that late teens and young adult males exhibit the highest rates of violent and property crimes. But if immigration (legal or illegal) were associated with increasing crime rates, the official crime statistics would clearly reveal it. The opposite, however, is the case.

Crime Rates 1993-2006

Since the early 1990s, over the same time period as legal and especially illegal immigration was reaching and surpassing historic highs, crime rates have *declined*, both nationally and most notably in cities and regions of high immigrant concentration (including cities with large numbers of undocumented immigrants, such as Los Angeles and border cities like San Diego and El Paso, as well as New York, Chicago, and Miami). This is especially evident from national-level data on crimes and arrests reported by city, county and state law enforcement authorities to the FBI, as well as from the National Crime Victimization Survey (NCVS), an annual household survey ongoing since 1972 that interviews about 134,000 persons age twelve or older in 77,200 households about their victimizations from crime (whether or not they were reported to the police). Data from the latter provide a more precise estimate of crimes that often go unreported to the police (in 2005, for example, only 47 percent of all violent victimizations and 40 percent of all property crimes were reported to the police).

The Uniform Crime Reports released each year by the FBI demonstrate the decline of both reported violent crime and property crime at the same time that the foreign-born population has surged. *From 1994 to 2005, property crimes and violent crimes reached lows in the United States not seen in decades.* Over that period, the total number of reported *property* crimes declined significantly. Specifically, burglary rates stabilized after many years of decline, motor-vehicle theft rates were cut by more than half during the 1990s and leveled off after 2000, and theft rates reached the lowest level ever recorded in 2005. Even more significantly, in this same time period, the total number of reported *violent* crimes declined by 34 percent. In particular, homicide rates fell 38 percent to levels last seen in the late 1960s, robbery rates dropped 41 percent, and assault rates declined 32 percent; serious violent crimes committed by juveniles also decreased during this period. In fact, both overall property and violent crime rates reached their lowest levels in about thirty years, with rates for some reported crimes at all-time lows (U.S. Bureau of Justice Statistics 2007).

Data from the NCVS document even more impressive reductions in serious violent crime and property crime during the same period. Between 1993 (when the NCVS was redesigned) and 2005, the rate of every major violent and property crime measured—rape or sexual assault, robbery, aggravated assault, simple assault, burglary, theft, and motor vehicle theft—fell significantly. Overall, the violent crime rate decreased 58 percent, from fifty to twenty-one victimizations per 1,000 persons age twelve or older. Property crime declined 52 percent, from 319 to 154 per 1,000 households. Specifically, significant declines were measured in the rates of rape or sexual assault (down 69 percent), robbery (down 57 percent), aggravated assault (down 64 percent), and simple assault (down 54 percent). The household burglary rate fell 49 percent; the motor vehicle theft rate fell 56 percent; and the theft rate fell 52 percent (Catalano 2006).

Yet during these same years there was an unprecedented rise in the foreign-born and Hispanic populations. From 1994 to 2006, the foreign-born population grew from 22.6 to 38.6 million people in the United States (a 71 percent increase), and the Hispanic population increased from 26.6 to 43.2 million people (a 62 percent increase). "Hispanics" are often lumped together in both the media and official statistics without regard to generational differences, national or class origins, or immigration status, and are often categorically scapegoated for perceived increases in crime rates. While correlation is not causation, *it is telling that during a thirteen-year period when the immigrant population (and especially the undocumented population) was increasing sharply to historic highs, the overall rates of property and violent crimes in the United States decreased significantly, in some instances to historic lows.*

Incarceration Rates 1980-2006

On the other hand, paralleling the rise in immigration, the U.S. incarceration rate has become the highest of any country in the world. There are more people behind bars in the United States than in either China or India, each of which has a population roughly four times larger than that of the United States (Walmsley 2005). The U.S., with less than 5 percent of the world's population, now has almost a fourth of the world's prisoners. The U.S. incarceration rate, which had been relatively stable at some 110 prisoners per 100,000 people from 1925 to 1975, began increasing sharply thereafter. Between 1980 and 2006, the rate grew from 139 prisoners for every 100,000 people to 751 per 100,000. Of the more than two million people behind bars, two-thirds are in federal or state prisons and one-third in local jails. The vast majority are young men between eighteen and thirty-nine.

Although official statistics are not kept by nativity or immigration status, they show that imprisonment rates vary widely by gender (93 percent of inmates in federal and state prisons are men, most between eighteen and thirty-nine); by racial/pan-ethnic groups (there were 4,834 black male prisoners per 100,000 black males in the U.S., compared to 1,778 Hispanic males per 100,000, and 681 white males per 100,000, although since 1985 Hispanics have been the fastest group being imprisoned); and by level of education (those incarcerated are overwhelmingly high school dropouts) (U.S. Bureau of Justice Statistics 2007). According to the National Center on Addiction and Substance Abuse at Columbia University (1998), about 80 percent of those in prison either violated drug or alcohol laws, were high at the time they committed their crimes, stole property to buy drugs, had a history of drug and alcohol abuse and addiction, or some combination of those characteristics—reflecting the impact of mandatory-sentencing and "three strikes" laws during this period.

Incarceration Rates of Foreign-born vs. Native-born Men

Inasmuch as the incarcerated population is overwhelmingly composed of less educated young adult males from ethnic minority groups—a profile which, as noted, fits a much greater proportion of the undocumented immigrant population—it follows that immigrants would be expected to have higher incarceration rates than natives. And immigrant Mexican men—who comprise fully a third of all immigrant men in the U.S. between eighteen and thirty-nine—would be expected to have the highest rates. The hypothesis is examined empirically in Tables 1 and 2. The results shown there turn those expectations on their head. Data from the 2000 census are used to measure the institutionalization rates of immigrants and natives, focusing on males age eighteen to thirty-nine, among whom the vast majority of the institutionalized are in correctional facilities (Butcher and Piehl 1997).

As Table 1 shows, 3 percent of the 45.2 million males age eighteen to thirty-nine were in federal or state prisons or local jails at the time of the 2000 census (a total of over 1.3 million, coinciding with official prison statistics). However, *the incarceration rate of the U.S.-born (3.51 percent) was five times the rate of the foreign-born (0.68 percent)*. The latter was less than half the 1.71 percent rate for non-Hispanic white natives, and seventeen times less than the 11.6 percent incarceration rate for native black men. The advantage for immigrants *vis-à-vis* natives applies to every ethnic group without exception. Almost all of the Asian immigrant groups have lower incarceration rates than the Latin American groups (the exception involves foreign-born Laotians and Cambodians—two refugee groups with the highest levels of poverty in the country—whose incarceration rate of 0.92 percent is still well below that for non-Hispanic white natives). Tellingly, among the foreign-born the highest incarceration rate by far (4.5 percent) was observed among island-born Puerto Ricans—who are not immigrants as such since they have statutory U.S. citizenship and can travel freely to the mainland as natives.

Incarceration Rates by Education and Nativity

Of particular interest is the finding that *the lowest incarceration rates among Latin American immigrants are seen for the least educated groups, who are also the groups who account for the majority of the undocumented*: the Salvadorans and Guatemalans (0.52 percent), and the Mexicans (0.70 percent). However, those rates increase significantly for their U.S.-born co-ethnics. That is most notable for the Mexicans, whose incarceration rate increases to 5.9 percent among the U.S.-born; for the Vietnamese, whose incarceration rate increases from 0.5 among the foreign-born to 5.6 percent among the U.S.-born; and for the Laotians and Cambodians, whose rate moves up to 7.3 percent, the highest of any group except for native blacks. (Almost all of the U.S.-born among those of Latin American and Asian origin can be assumed to consist of second-generation persons—with the exceptions of Mexicans and Puerto Ricans, who may include among the U.S.-born a sizable but unknown number of third-generation persons.) Thus, *while incarceration rates are found to be extraordinarily low among the immigrants, they are also seen to rise rapidly by the second generation*: except for the Chinese, Indians, Koreans, and Filipinos (who as noted earlier are the children of mainly professional immigrants), the rates of all other U.S.-born Latin American and Asian groups exceed that of the referent group of non-Hispanic white natives.

For all ethnic groups, as expected, the risk of imprisonment is highest for men who are high school dropouts (6.9 percent) compared to those who are high school graduates (2.0 percent). However, as Table 2 elaborates, *the differentials in the risk of incarceration by education are observed principally among native-born men, and not immigrants*. Among the U.S.-born, 9.8 percent of all male dropouts age eighteen to thirty-nine were in jail or prison in 2000, compared to

Undocumented Immigration and Rates of Crime and Imprisonment: Popular Myths and Empirical Realities

TABLE 1. PERCENTAGE OF MALES 18 TO 39 INCARCERATED IN THE UNITED STATES, 2000, BY NATIVITY AND LEVEL OF EDUCATION, IN RANK ORDER BY ETHNICITY

Ethnicity	Males, ages 18-39:		Percent incarcerated, by nativity and by education:			
	Total in U.S.	Percent incarcerated	Nativity:		High school graduate?	
			Foreign-born	U.S.-born	No	Yes
	N	%	%	%	%	%
Total:	45,200,417	3.04	0.68[b]	3.51	6.91	2.00
Latin American Ethnicities:	**7,514,857**	**3.26**	**0.99**	**6.72**	**3.95**	**2.62**
Salvadoran, Guatemalan	433,828	0.68	0.52	3.01	0.71	0.62
Colombian, Ecuadorian, Peruvian	283,599	1.07	0.80	2.37	2.12	0.74
Mexican	5,017,431	2.71	0.70	5.90	2.84	2.55
Dominican	182,303	2.76	2.51	3.71	4.62	1.39
Cuban	213,302	3.01	2.22	4.20	5.22	2.29
Puerto Rican[a]	642,106	5.06	4.55	5.37	10.48	2.41
Asian Ethnicities:	**1,902,809**	**0.62**	**0.29**	**1.86**	**2.43**	**0.35**
Indian	393,621	0.22	0.11	0.99	1.20	0.14
Chinese, Taiwanese	439,086	0.28	0.18	0.65	1.35	0.14
Korean	184,238	0.38	0.26	0.93	0.93	0.34
Filipino	297,011	0.64	0.38	1.22	2.71	0.41
Vietnamese	229,735	0.89	0.46	5.60	1.88	0.55
Laotian, Cambodian	89,864	1.65	0.92	7.26	2.80	1.04
Other:						
White, non-Hispanic	29,014,261	1.66	0.57	1.71	4.64	1.20
Black, non-Hispanic	5,453,546	10.87	2.47	11.61	21.33	7.09

SOURCE: 2000 U.S. Census, 5% PUMS. Data are estimates for adult males, ages 18 to 39, institutionalized at the time of the census.

[a] Island-born Puerto Ricans, who are U.S. citizens by birth and not immigrants, are classified as "foreign born" for purposes of this table; mainland-born Puerto Ricans are here classified under "U.S.-born."

[b] The foreign-born incarceration rate is 0.68 percent when island-born Puerto Ricans (U.S. citizens) are excluded, 0.86 percent when included.

Undocumented Immigration and Rates of Crime and Imprisonment: Popular Myths and Empirical Realities

TABLE 2. PERCENTAGE OF U.S.-BORN AND FOREIGN-BORN MALES 18-39 INCARCERATED IN THE UNITED STATES, 2000, BY COMPLETION OF A HIGH SCHOOL EDUCATION, IN RANK ORDER BY ETHNICITY

Ethnicity	Males, ages 18-39:		Percent incarcerated, by education by nativity:			
	Total in U.S.	Percent incarcerated	If foreign-born: High School Graduate?		If U.S.-born: High School Graduate?	
	N	%	No	Yes	No	Yes
Total:	45,200,417	3.04	1.31	0.57	9.76	2.23
Latin American Ethnicities:	**7,514,857**	**3.26**	**1.11**	**0.81**	**12.42**	**4.22**
Salvadoran, Guatemalan	433,828	0.68	0.58	0.43	4.70	2.16
Colombian, Ecuadorian, Peruvian	283,599	1.07	1.54	0.54	7.01	1.58
Mexican	5,017,431	2.71	0.70	0.70	10.12	3.95
Dominican	182,303	2.76	3.99	1.24	8.67	1.82
Cuban	213,302	3.01	3.18	1.78	11.32	2.90
Puerto Rican[a]	642,106	5.06	9.01	1.96	11.54	2.66
Asian Ethnicities:	**1,902,809**	**0.62**	**1.03**	**0.18**	**9.66**	**1.00**
Indian	393,621	0.22	0.29	0.09	6.69	0.48
Chinese, Taiwanese	439,086	0.28	0.91	0.07	4.71	0.36
Korean	184,238	0.38	0.58	0.24	2.05	0.82
Filipino	297,011	0.64	1.73	0.23	4.73	0.81
Vietnamese	229,735	0.89	0.85	0.32	16.18	2.85
Laotian, Cambodian	89,864	1.65	1.72	0.52	9.11	5.80
Other:						
White, non-Hispanic	29,014,261	1.66	1.63	0.43	4.76	1.23
Black, non-Hispanic	5,453,546	10.87	7.08	1.32	22.25	7.64

SOURCE: 2000 U.S. Census, 5% PUMS. Data are estimates for adult males, ages 18 to 39, institutionalized at the time of the census.

[a] Island-born Puerto Ricans are U.S. citizens by birth and not immigrants, but are classified as "foreign born" for purposes of this table; mainland-born Puerto Ricans are classified under "U.S.-born."

2.2 percent among those who had graduated from high school. But among the foreign-born, the incarceration gap by education was much narrower: only 1.3 percent of immigrant men who were high school dropouts were incarcerated, compared to 0.6 percent of those with at least a high school diploma. The advantage for immigrants held when broken down by education for every ethnic group. Indeed, *nativity emerges in these data as a stronger predictor of incarceration than education*: as noted, native-born high school graduates have a higher rate of incarceration than foreign-born non-high school graduates (2.2 to 1.3 percent).

Among U.S.-born men who had not finished high school, the highest incarceration rate by far was seen among non-Hispanic blacks, an astonishing 22.2 percent of whom were imprisoned at the time of the census; that rate was triple the 7.6 percent among foreign-born black dropouts. Other high rates among U.S.-born high school dropouts were observed among Vietnamese (over 16 percent), followed by Colombians (over 12 percent), Cubans and Puerto Ricans (over 11 percent), Mexicans (10 percent), and Laotians and Cambodians (over 9 percent). Almost of all these can be assumed to consist of second-generation persons—with the exceptions of Mexicans and Puerto Ricans, who may include among the U.S.-born a sizable but unknown number of third-generation persons.

Incarceration Rates over Time in the United States

The finding that incarceration rates are much lower among immigrant men than the national norm, despite their lower levels of education and minority status, but increase significantly among their co-ethnics by the second generation, especially among those with lower levels of education, suggests that the process of "Americanization" can lead to downward assimilation and greater risks of involvement with the criminal justice system among a significant segment of this population. To explore this question further, we examined what happens to immigrant men over time in the United States. The results are presented in Table 3.

For every group without exception, *the longer immigrants had resided in the U.S., the higher were their incarceration rates*. Here again, the rates of incarceration for island-born Puerto Ricans are significantly higher—regardless of how long they have lived in the U.S. mainland—than the rates for all the immigrant groups listed in Table 3, underscoring the unique status of the former. In contrast, foreign-born Mexican men age eighteen to thirty-nine, by far the largest group (at over three million), have a *lower* incarceration rate than many other ethnic and racial groups—even after they have lived in the U.S. for over fifteen years. The Mexican incarceration story in particular can be very misleading when the data conflate the foreign-born and the native-born (as official statistics on "Latinos" or "Hispanics" routinely do). Rather than a story of upward mobility often mentioned in the "straight-line" assimilation literature, the data in Tables 1-3 suggest instead a story of segmented assimilation to the criminal norms of the native-born.

Incarceration Rates in California

We also examined the same census data for California, the state with by far the greatest number of immigrants, legal and illegal (over a quarter of the national total), and the state with the greatest number of persons in prisons and jails (in fact, California has one of the highest inmate populations in the world, behind China and a handful of other countries). California also has

Undocumented Immigration and Rates of Crime and Imprisonment: Popular Myths and Empirical Realities

TABLE 3. PERCENTAGE OF FOREIGN-BORN MALES 18-39 INCARCERATED IN THE UNITED STATES, 2000, BY LENGTH OF U.S. RESIDENCE, IN RANK ORDER BY ETHNICITY

Ethnicity	Total foreign-born males 18-39:		Years in the United States:		
	N	% incarcerated	0-5 yrs	6-15 yrs	16 yrs+
Total (foreign-born men 18-39):	8,079,819	0.68[b]	0.50	0.77	1.39
Latin American Ethnicities:	**4,535,269**	**0.99**	**0.57**	**0.89**	**1.70**
Salvadoran, Guatemalan	407,147	0.52	0.37	0.46	0.88
Mexican	3,082,660	0.70	0.46	0.66	1.12
Colombian, Peruvian, Ecuadorian	234,834	0.80	0.55	1.30	1.98
Cuban	127,399	2.22	1.28	1.99	3.07
Dominican	144,387	2.51	1.48	2.49	3.40
Puerto Rican[a]	240,713	4.55	2.57	4.01	6.06
Asian Ethnicities:	**1,510,298**	**0.29**	**0.14**	**0.25**	**0.50**
Indian	343,834	0.11	0.05	0.11	0.27
Chinese	347,029	0.18	0.07	0.22	0.27
Korean	152,785	0.26	0.10	0.15	0.50
Filipino	205,167	0.38	0.31	0.35	0.45
Vietnamese	210,331	0.46	0.46	0.41	0.51
Laotian, Cambodian	79,489	0.92	†	0.33	1.19
Other:					
White, non-Hispanic	1,266,100	0.57	0.36	0.41	0.88
Black, non-Hispanic	441,263	2.47	1.64	2.10	3.80

SOURCE: 2000 U.S. Census, 5% PUMS. Data are estimates for all foreign-born males, ages 18 to 39, institutionalized at the time of the census, regardless of age at arrival in the United States.

[a] Island-born Puerto Ricans (who are U.S. citizens by birth) are classified as "foreign born" for purposes of this table.

[b] The foreign-born incarceration rate is 0.68 percent when island-born Puerto Ricans (U.S. citizens) are excluded.

† There are too few cases for an accurate estimate.

one of the toughest mandatory-sentencing "three strikes" laws in the country (Domanick 2004). The results of the state-level analysis further reinforce those reviewed above.

Overall, native-born men age eighteen to thirty-nine in California have *higher* incarceration rates than the rest of the U.S., while the foreign-born have *lower* rates in California compared to the rest of the U.S. The total incarceration rate for the U.S.-born is more than 1 percentage point higher in California than in the rest of the U.S. (4.5 to 3.4). In contrast, the rate for the foreign-born in California was less than half the foreign-born rate in the rest of the country (0.4 to 1.0).

Survey Findings from Southern California

Those incarceration estimates were drawn from U.S. census data. We can get more direct evidence of actual lifetime experiences with the criminal justice system from comprehensive regional surveys of immigrant-origin populations. Consider, for instance, two major surveys of adult children of immigrants recently carried out in Southern California, the region with the greatest number of immigrants (and of undocumented immigrants): the Immigration and Intergenerational Mobility in Metropolitan Los Angeles (IIMMLA) survey, carried out in 2004 (Rumbaut *et al.*, 2003); and the third wave of the Children of Immigrants Longitudinal Study (CILS) in San Diego, a decade-long panel study whose last phase of data collection ended in 2003 (Portes and Rumbaut 2005).

By the year 2000 one of every five immigrants in the United States resided in the region's six contiguous counties (San Diego, Orange, Los Angeles, Ventura, Riverside, and San Bernardino), including the largest communities of Mexicans, Salvadorans, Guatemalans, Filipinos, Taiwanese, Koreans, Vietnamese, Cambodians, and Iranians outside of their countries of origin, and to sizable contingents of many others (Rumbaut 2004). For this analysis the two data sets were merged (n=6,135), since they are based on representative samples evenly divided by gender, of the same approximate age (the mean age was 27.5) and national origins (Mexicans, Salvadorans, Guatemalans, Filipinos, Chinese, Koreans, Vietnamese, Cambodians and Laotians make up 76 percent of the merged sample, and other Latin American and Asian nationalities 10 percent), and surveyed at about the same time in the same metropolitan region (the six contiguous Southern California counties). Our surveys collected data on criminal justice involvement of *foreign-parentage* (1.5- and second-generation) young adults, compared to *native-parentage* (third-generation and beyond) white, black and Mexican-American peers. (For details of the sampling and research design of each study, see Rumbaut 2008.)

We focus here on the arrest and incarceration histories of the males in the sample (n=2,971). Table 4 looks at whether they had ever been arrested or incarcerated (which in most cases involved being convicted and sentenced for the commission of a crime), broken down by ethnicity and generation. There are striking differences between ethnic groups and generations. Intergenerational differences are strongly significant overall, with the U.S.-born (second and third-plus generations) much more likely to become ensnared with the criminal justice system than the foreign-born (the 1.5 generation, who came to the U.S. as children), reflecting the national patterns noted earlier among young adult men age eighteen to thirty-nine. The patterns are linear,

TABLE 4. ARREST AND INCARCERATION AMONG YOUNG MEN IN SOUTHERN CALIFORNIA, BY ETHNICITY AND GENERATION
(MERGED IIMMLA AND CILS-III SURVEYS: N=2,971 MALES, AGES 20-39; MEAN AGE=27.5)

		Ever arrested			Ever incarcerated		
Ethnicity	Generation[a]	1.5	2nd	3rd+	1.5	2nd	3rd+
	N	%	%	%	%	%	%
Total sample (males 20-39):	2,971	13.2	20.7	36.3	7.8	12.1	23.8
Latin American Ethnicities:							
Mexican	787	22.3	29.8	39.6	11.9	20.4	26.6
Salvadoran, Guatemalan	187	21.3	36.7		11.2	17.3	
Other Latin American	107	17.4	21.3		15.2	11.5	
Asian Ethnicities:							
Chinese	245	5.8	7.4		2.9	1.9	
Korean	201	11.6	18.1		3.9	2.8	
Filipino	475	13.3	9.6		8.2	5.7	
Vietnamese	294	8.1	12.7		5.8	9.9	
Laotian, Cambodian	88	8.4	20.0		8.4	20.0	
All other nationalities	200	12.3	21.7		7.0	11.9	
Other:							
White, non-Hispanic	201			29.4			18.1
Black, non-Hispanic	186			40.4			27.3

SOURCE: Adapted from Rumbaut, 2008.
[a] 1.5 generation = foreign-born, arrived in the U.S. before teen years; 2nd generation = U.S.-born, one or both parents foreign-born; 3rd or higher generations = U.S.-born, both parents U.S.-born.

but with the outcomes worsening over time and generation—and acculturation—in the United States: among the 1.5ers, 13 percent had ever been arrested and 8 percent incarcerated, compared to 21 percent and 12 percent respectively in the second generation, and 36 percent and 24 percent in the third-plus generations. Indeed, the rates for all of the immigrants and U.S.-born children of immigrants in this sample are *lower* than the rates for native-stock majority-group *whites*. The rates of arrest and incarceration were highest by far for blacks (almost all of whom were fourth-plus generation African Americans), and lowest for Asians, with whites and Hispanics in between. Among native-parentage blacks, fully 40 percent had been arrested at some point by the police and 27 percent had been incarcerated; among both native-parentage whites and Hispanics, 29 percent had ever been arrested and 18 percent incarcerated; and among Asians, the respective figures were 10 percent and 6 percent.

For the large Mexican-origin subsample, the intergenerational patterns are clear: among the Mexican-born 1.5ers, 22 percent had ever been arrested and 12 percent incarcerated (significantly *lower* than the rates for native whites), compared to 30 percent and 20 percent respectively in the second generation (about the *same* as the rates for native whites), and almost 40 percent and 27 percent in the third-plus. The latter figures are virtually identical to those for African American men—the highest observed in this sample, as well as nationally. Given the huge size of the Mexican-origin second generation compared to other groups in the U.S., this is a finding fraught with implications for the future—not only for the downward mobility prospects of men caught in a cycle of arrest and imprisonment (who tend to have high rates of recidivism after release), but also for both the short-term and long-term effects on their ethnic communities.

In a multivariate analysis of the odds of having been convicted and jailed for a crime (among the men in this merged sample), incarceration was found to be most strongly predicted by poor educational attainment in adolescence *and* by the generational status variables: i.e., compared to native-parentage non-Hispanic whites, the *least* likely to be incarcerated were the foreign-born 1.5-generation children of immigrants, followed by the U.S.-born second generation with two immigrant parents, and more weakly by those with only one immigrant parent. Having been raised in a two-parent family *reduced* the odds of incarceration, while having grown up in dangerous neighborhoods (with major problems of drugs, crime and gangs) *increased* the odds. Ethnicity washed out of the logistic regression once the other predictor variables were controlled—that is, none of the ethnic group variables was significantly linked to incarceration, despite the fact that non-Hispanic blacks and Mexicans had the highest rates of arrest and incarceration, suggesting that those other variables rather than ethnicity as such accounted for the association.

Confirmatory Results from Other Empirical Studies

The evidence from the 2000 census demonstrating the lower rate of incarceration among immigrants is strongly supported by other studies conducted over the past century. For instance, a study by economists Kristin Butcher and Anne Morrison Piehl based on data from the 1980 and 1990 U.S. censuses yielded similar findings (1998). A more recent analysis by Butcher and Piehl (2005) demonstrates that lower rates are *not* the result of increased deportations of non-citizen criminals or the impact of harsher immigration laws in deterring immigrants from committing crimes. Rather, the authors conclude that during the 1990s, "those immigrants who chose to come to the United States were less likely to be involved in criminal activity than earlier immigrants and the native born." Taken together with the findings presented above, those studies provide consistent and compelling evidence over a period of three decades that incarceration rates are much lower among immigrant men than the national norm despite their lower levels of education and higher rates of poverty. In 2000, these patterns applied to every ethnic group without exception.

APPENDIX D

Undocumented Immigration and Rates of Crime and Imprisonment: Popular Myths and Empirical Realities

Other scholars have addressed similar questions concerning immigration and crime and concluded that increased immigration is a major factor associated with lower crime rates. In a study of 180 Chicago neighborhoods from 1995 to 2002, Robert J. Sampson and his colleagues found that Latin American immigrants were less likely than the U.S.-born to commit violent crimes even when they lived in dense communities with high rates of poverty. First-generation immigrants (foreign-born) were 45 percent less likely to commit violent crimes than were third-generation Americans (children of native-born parents), adjusting for family and neighborhood background. The second generation (those born in the United States to immigrant parents) was 22 percent less likely to commit violence than the third or higher generation (Sampson, Morenoff, and Raudenbush 2005; see also Press 2006). These findings clearly echo those reported above.

Recent empirical studies by sociologists Ramiro Martínez and Matthew Lee of homicides in three high-immigration border cities (San Diego, El Paso, and Miami) and of drug violence in Miami and San Diego came to similar conclusions, further refuting commonly presumed linkages between immigration and criminality (Martínez, Lee, and Nielsen 2004; Lee, Martínez, and Rosenfeld 2001). In addition, several other studies have examined homicide rates among the Cuban refugees who arrived in the United States as a result of the Mariel Boatlift of 1980. Although these *marielitos* frequently were depicted in the media as prolific criminal offenders, even murderers, they in fact were not overrepresented among either homicide victims or offenders. Moreover, after only a short time in the United States, they were much less likely to commit crimes than Cubans who arrived in Miami before the Mariel Boatlift. As with South Florida in general, Miami experienced a sharp spike in homicides *before* the Mariel Cubans arrived in the city. Homicide rates continued to decline throughout the 1980s despite a steady inflow of Latin American immigrants (see Martínez and Lee 2000).

Data from the National Longitudinal Study of Adolescent Health (Add Health) demonstrate the intra- and inter-generational differences in delinquency and other risk behaviors among adolescents. Add Health is a nationally representative longitudinal survey of adolescents conducted in several "waves" since 1994. Drawing upon this survey, sociologists Kathleen Mullan Harris (1999), and Hoan Bui and Ornuma Thingniramol (2005), have found that second-generation youth were significantly more prone than foreign-born youth to engage in risk behaviors such as delinquency, violence, and substance abuse—precisely the sorts of behaviors likely to lead to involvement with the criminal justice system and to cycles of arrests and incarceration. In their analyses, every foreign-born (first-generation) immigrant nationality engaged in significantly *fewer* risk behaviors than the comparison group of native-born non-Hispanic whites.

Similarly, John Hagan and his colleagues (2008) used scores from a delinquency and drug use scale of two cohorts near Toronto to examine delinquency and violent behavior among Canadian youth. They separated the first, 1.5, and second generations from third-generation Canadians. Controlling for gender, age, socioeconomic background, ethnic origin, and cohort, they found generational status to be the most significant predictor of youth delinquency. That is, the foreign-born first and 1.5 generations were significantly *less* likely than the native-born to engage in high-risk activities. As generational status increased, the odds of engaging in delinquent behavior also increased.

Undocumented Immigration and Rates of Crime and Imprisonment: Popular Myths and Empirical Realities

Survey research has consistently shown a striking relationship between acculturation and risk behaviors, for both Hispanic and non-Hispanic ethnic groups. For example, data from the Hispanic Health and Nutrition Examination Survey (HHANES), with a large regional sample, indicated that marijuana use is five to eight times higher among highly acculturated Mexican Americans compared to those (Mexican immigrants) who are not, controlling for demographic factors. Studies based on the HHANES and more recent survey data have also documented adverse effects of acculturation among Hispanic groups with respect to cocaine use and alcohol consumption (for a summary see Portes and Rumbaut 2006).

A recent study in Washington State (Akins *et al.*, 2008), with a rural and more dispersed Hispanic population, found that acculturated Hispanics were nearly thirteen times more likely to report current illegal drug use and more than four times as likely to report current hard drug use than non-acculturated Hispanics. Acculturated Hispanics were about twice as likely to report alcohol binge drinking (consuming five or more drinks in one day) and more than three times as likely to report bender drinking (drinking for two or more days in a row without sobering up). Such findings on substance abuse support the growing body of research indicating the negative consequences of acculturation—and help in part to explain the significantly higher rates of arrest and incarceration among acculturated U.S.-born groups as compared to the foreign-born. Increased exposure to the U.S. brings, among other things, increased opportunities and risks for substance use and abuse—particularly among the U.S.-born.

In a sense, these findings should not come as news, for they are not new—merely forgotten and overruled by popular myth. In the first three decades of the twentieth century, during the previous era of mass immigration, three major government commissions came to similar conclusions. The Industrial Commission of 1901, the [Dillingham] Immigration Commission of 1911, and the [Wickersham] National Commission on Law Observance and Enforcement of 1931 each sought to measure how immigration resulted in increases in crime. Instead, each found lower levels of criminal involvement among the foreign-born and higher levels among their native-born counterparts (see Tonry 1996). As the report of the Immigration Commission concluded a century ago (1911: 168): "No satisfactory evidence has yet been produced to show that immigration has resulted in an increase in crime disproportionate to the increase in adult population. Such comparable statistics of crime and population as it has been possible to obtain indicate that immigrants are *less* prone to commit crime than are native Americans." More than eight decades later, not surprisingly, the U.S. Commission on Immigration Reform concluded in a 1994 report that immigration is not associated with higher crime. The Commission compared crime rates in U.S.-Mexico border cities such as El Paso with cities elsewhere in the United States and found that crime rates generally were lower in border cities.

Conclusion and Implications

Because many immigrants to the United States, especially Mexicans and Central Americans, are young men who arrive with very low levels of formal education, popular stereotypes tend to associate them with higher rates of crime and incarceration. The fact that many of these immigrants enter the country through unauthorized channels or overstay their visas often is framed as an assault against the "rule of law," thereby reinforcing the impression that immigration and criminality are linked. This association has flourished in a post-September 11 climate of fear and ignorance where terrorism and undocumented immigration often are mentioned in the same breath. Thus in May 2007, as reported by the Associated Press, former U.S. Senator Fred Thompson, a star of the television series "Law & Order" and later Republican presidential candidate, blamed the Immigration Reform and Control Act of 1986 for illegal immigration, adding: "Twelve million illegal immigrants later, we are now living in a nation that is beset by people who are suicidal maniacs and want to kill countless innocent men, women and children around the world....We're sitting here now with essentially open borders."

But political scapegoating and hyperbole are no substitute for scientific evidence. Since the early 1990s, as the immigrant population (especially the undocumented population) increased sharply to historic highs, the rates of violent crimes and property crimes in the United States decreased significantly, in some instances to historic lows—as measured both by crimes reported to the police and by national victimization surveys. Moreover, data from the census and a wide range of other empirical studies show that for every ethnic group without exception, incarceration rates among young men are lowest for immigrants, even those who are the least educated. This holds true especially for the Mexicans, Salvadorans, and Guatemalans, who make up the bulk of the undocumented population. These patterns have been observed consistently over the last three decennial censuses, a period that spans the current era of mass immigration, and recall similar national-level findings reported by three major government commissions during the first three decades of the twentieth century, as did another U.S. commission in the 1990s.

Given the cumulative weight of this evidence, the rise in immigration is arguably one of the reasons that crime rates have *decreased* in the United States over the past decade and a half—and even more so in cities of immigrant concentration. A further implication of this evidence is that if immigrants suddenly disappeared and the U.S. became immigrant-free (and illegal-immigrant free), crime rates would likely *increase*. The problem of crime and incarceration in the United States is not "caused" or even aggravated by immigrants, regardless of their legal status. But the uncritical and evidence-optional assumption that the opposite is true persists among policymakers, the media, and the general public, thereby impoverishing a genuine understanding of complex phenomena—a situation that undermines the development of evidence-based, reasoned public responses to both crime *and* immigration.

APPENDIX D

Undocumented Immigration and Rates of Crime and Imprisonment: Popular Myths and Empirical Realities

Endnotes

[1] As used here, "legal" immigrants consist of Legal Permanent Residents (LPRs)—about 40 percent of whom had been in the United States in other statuses (refugee, temporary, or unauthorized) before becoming LPRs—as well as former LPRs who subsequently became naturalized U.S. citizens. "Illegal" or undocumented immigrants are those who entered the country without proper authorization, or who entered the country lawfully with non-immigrant visas but subsequently over-stayed or violated the terms of their visas. Visa overstayers and violators may make up as much as 40 percent of the "illegal immigrant" population (see Passel, 2006: 16).

References

Akins, Scott, Clayton Mosher, Chad L. Smith, and Jane Florence Gauthier. 2008. "The Effect of Acculturation on Patterns of Hispanic Substance Use in Washington State." *Journal of Drug Issues* 38, 1: 103-118.

Alba, Richard D., and Victor Nee. 2003. *Remaking the American Mainstream: Assimilation and Contemporary Immigration.* Cambridge, MA: Harvard University Press.

Alba, Richard D., Rubén G. Rumbaut, and Karen Marotz. 2005. "A Distorted Nation: Perceptions of Racial/Ethnic Group Sizes and Attitudes Toward Immigrants and Other Minorities." *Social Forces* 84: 901-919.

Bui, Hoan N., and Ornuma Thingniramol. 2005. "Immigration and Self-Reported Delinquency: The Interplay of Immigrant Generations, Gender, Race, and Ethnicity." *Journal of Crime and Justice* 28(2), 79-100.

Butcher, Kristin F., and Anne Morrison Piehl. 2005. *Why Are Immigrants' Incarceration Rates So Low? Evidence on Selective Immigration, Deterrence, and Deportation* (WP 2005-19). Chicago: Federal Reserve Bank of Chicago, November 2005.

_____. 1998. "Recent Immigrants: Unexpected Implications for Crime and Incarceration." *Industrial and Labor Relations Review* 51(4), July: 654-679.

_____. 1997. "Recent Immigrants: Unexpected Implications for Crime and Incarceration." *NBER Working Paper 6067.* Cambridge, MA: National Bureau of Economic Research.

Calavita, Kitty. 2005. *Immigrants at the Margins: Law, Race, and Exclusion in Southern Europe.* Cambridge: Cambridge University Press.

Catalano, Shannan M. 2006. "National Crime Victimization Survey: Criminal Victimization, 2005." *Bulletin,* September 2006. U.S. Bureau of Justice Statistics, NCJ 214644. At: http://www.ojp.usdoj.gov/bjs/pub/pdf/cv05.pdf

Chávez, Leo R. 2001. *Covering Immigration: Popular Images and the Politics of the Nation.* Berkeley: University of California Press.

Congressional Budget Office. 2005. *The Role of Immigrants in the U.S. Labor Market.* Washington, DC: U.S. Congress.

Cornelius, Wayne A. 2006. "Impacts of Border Enforcement on Unauthorized Mexican Migration to the United States." New York: Social Science Research Council. At: http://borderbattles.ssrc.org/Cornelius/

Domanick, Joe. 2004. *Cruel Justice: Three Strikes and the Politics of Crime in America's Golden State.* Berkeley: University of California Press.

Fry, Brian N. 2006. *Nativism and Immigration: Regulating the American Dream.* New York: LFB Scholarly Publishing.

Hagan, John, Ron Levi, and Ronit Dinovitzer. 2008. "The Symbolic Violence of the Crime-Immigration Nexus: Migrant Mythologies in the Americas." *Criminology & Public Policy* 7: 95-112.

Hagan, John, and Alberto Palloni. 1999. "Sociological Criminology and the Mythology of Hispanic Immigration and Crime." *Social Problems* 46: 617-32.

Harris, Kathleen Mullan. 1999. "The Health Status and Risk Behavior of Adolescents in Immigrant Families," in Donald J. Hernández, ed., *Children of Immigrants: Health, Adjustment, and Public Assistance.* Washington, DC: National Academy of Sciences Press, pp. 286-347.

APPENDIX D

Undocumented Immigration and Rates of Crime and Imprisonment: Popular Myths and Empirical Realities

Hoefer, Michael, Nancy Rytina, and Christopher Campbell. 2007. "Estimates of the Unauthorized Immigrant Population Residing in the United States: January 2006." Office of Immigration Statistics, Policy Directorate, U.S. Department of Homeland Security. Accessed at: http://www.dhs.gov/xlibrary/assets/statistics/publications/ill_pe_2006.pdf

Immigration [Dillingham] Commission. 1911. *Reports of the Immigration Commission*, 61st Congress, 3rd Session. Washington, DC: Government Printing Office.

Immigration Policy Center. 2005. *Economic Growth and Immigration: Bridging the Demographic Divide*. Washington, DC: American Immigration Law Foundation.

Johnson, Kevin. 2005. "The Forgotten 'Repatriation' of Persons of Mexican Ancestry and Lessons for the 'War on Terror.'" *Pace Law Review* 26, 1: 1-26.

Kanstroom, Daniel. 2007. *Deportation Nation: Outsiders in American History.* Cambridge: Harvard University Press.

Lee, Matthew T. 2003. *Crime on the Border: Immigration and Homicide in Urban Communities.* New York: LFB Scholarly Publishing.

Lee, Matthew T., Ramiro Martínez, Jr., and Richard B. Rosenfeld. 2001. "Does Immigration Increase Homicide? Negative Evidence from Three Border Cities." *Sociological Quarterly* 42:559–580.

Manza, Jeff, and Christopher Uggen. 2006. *Locked Out: Felon Disenfranchisement and American Democracy*. New York: Oxford University Press.

Martínez, Jr., Ramiro. 2002. *Latino Homicide: Immigration, Violence and Community*. New York: Routledge.

Martínez, Jr., Ramiro, and Matthew T. Lee. 2000. "On Immigration and Crime," in National Institute of Justice, *Criminal Justice 2000: The Nature of Crime, vol. 1* (NCJ 182408). Washington, DC: U.S. Department of Justice, Office of Justice Programs, July 2000.

Martínez, Jr., Ramiro, Matthew T. Lee, and Amie L. Nielsen. 2004. "Segmented Assimilation, Local Context and Determinants of Drug Violence in Miami and San Diego: Does Ethnicity and Immigration Matter?" *International Migration Review* 38: 131-157.

Martínez, Jr., Ramiro, and Abel Valenzuela, Jr., eds. 2006. *Immigration and Crime: Race, Ethnicity, and Violence.* New York: New York University Press.

Massey, Douglas S. 2007. *Categorically Unequal: The American Stratification System.* New York: Russell Sage Foundation.

Massey, Douglas S., Jorge Durand, and Nolan J. Malone. 2002. *Beyond Smoke and Mirrors: Mexican Immigration in an Era of Economic Integration.* New York, NY: Russell Sage Foundation.

National Center on Addiction and Substance Abuse. 1998. *Behind Bars: Substance Abuse and America's Prison Population.* New York: Columbia University.

Pager, Devah. 2003. "The Mark of a Criminal Record." *American Journal of Sociology* 108: 937-975.

Passel, Jeffrey S. 2006. *The Size and Characteristics of the Unauthorized Migrant Population in the U.S.* Washington, DC: Pew Hispanic Center.

Pettit, Becky, and Bruce Western. 2004. "Mass Imprisonment and the Life Course." *American Sociological Review* 69:151-169.

Portes, Alejandro, and Rubén G. Rumbaut. 2006. *Immigrant America: A Portrait.* 3rd edition. Berkeley: University of California Press.

_____. 2005. "The Second Generation and the Children of Immigrants Longitudinal Study." *Ethnic and Racial Studies* 28, 6: 983-999.

Press, Eyal. 2006. "Do Immigrants Make Us Safer?" *The New York Times Magazine*, December 3.

Rumbaut, Rubén G. 2008. "The Coming of the Second Generation: Immigration and Ethnic Mobility in Southern California." *The Annals of the American Academy of Political and Social Science* 620, 1: 196-236.

_____. 2005. "Turning points in the transition to adulthood: Determinants of educational attainment, incarceration, and early childbearing among children of immigrants." *Ethnic and Racial Studies* 28, 6: 1041-1086.

_____. 2004. "Ages, Life Stages, and Generational Cohorts: Decomposing the Immigrant First and Second Generations in the United States." *International Migration Review* 38: 1160-1205.

_____. 1997. "Assimilation and Its Discontents: Between Rhetoric and Reality." *International Migration Review* 31(4): 923-960.

Rumbaut, Rubén G., and Richard D. Alba. 2003. "Perceptions of Group Size and Group Position in 'Multi-Ethnic United States.'" Paper presented at the annual meeting of the American Sociological Association, Atlanta.

Rumbaut, Rubén G., Frank Bean, Leo Chávez, Jennifer Lee, Susan Brown, Louis DeSipio, and Min Zhou. 2003. *Immigration and Intergenerational Mobility in Metropolitan Los Angeles*. At: http://www.russellsage.org/programs/main/immigration/immigration_and_intergenerational_mobility_in_metropolitan_los__angeles

Sampson, Robert J., and John H. Laub. 1993. *Crime in the Making: Pathways and Turning Points Through Life*. Cambridge, MA: Harvard University Press.

Sampson, Robert J., Jeffrey D. Morenoff, and Stephen Raudenbush. 2005. "Social Anatomy of Racial and Ethnic Disparities in Violence." *American Journal of Public Health* 95, 2: 224-232.

Settersten, Jr., Richard A., Frank F. Furstenberg, Jr., and Rubén G. Rumbaut, eds. 2005. *On the Frontier of Adulthood: Theory, Research, and Public Policy*. Chicago: University of Chicago Press.

Tonry, Michael, ed. 1996. *Ethnicity, Crime, and Immigration: Comparative and Cross-National Perspectives*. Chicago: University of Chicago Press.

U.S. Bureau of Justice Statistics, Department of Justice. 2007. "Adult Correctional Populations in the United States, 1980-2006." At: http://www.ojp.usdoj.gov/bjs/glance/tables/corr2tab.htm, and "Crime and Victims Statistics." At: http://www.ojp.usdoj.gov/bjs/cvict.htm

U.S. Commission on Immigration Reform. 1994. *U.S. Immigration Policy: Restoring Credibility*. Washington, DC.

Visher, Christy A., and Jeremy Travis. 2003. "Transitions from Prison to Community: Understanding Individual Pathways." *Annual Review of Sociology* 29:89-113.

Walmsley, Roy. 2005. *World Prison Population List, 6th edition*. London: University of London, King's College, School of Law, International Centre for Prison Studies.

Western, Bruce. 2002. "The Impact of Incarceration on Wage Mobility and Inequality." *American Sociological Review* 67:1-21.

Western, Bruce, Jeffrey R. Kling, and David F. Weiman. 2001. "The Labor Market Consequences of Incarceration." *Crime and Delinquency* 47:410-427.

Zimring, Franklin E. 2007. *The Great American Crime Decline*. Oxford: Oxford University Press.

APPENDIX E

Why Integration Matters: The Case of Undocumented Immigrant Youth and Moving Beyond Enforcement

BY ROBERTO G. GONZALES

Today's immigration debates have brought to the fore conflicting visions within the United States over how to address a population of eleven to twelve million undocumented immigrants. In the absence of a comprehensive set of immigration policies at the federal level, individual states and localities are left to reconcile these problems on their own. Unfortunately, most of the proposed solutions, to date, fail to address the complexity and diversity of the undocumented population and have focused chiefly on enforcement and less so on integration. As such, they have largely ignored the particular needs of families and children. While immigration enforcement is certainly a necessary ingredient for any comprehensive strategy, enforcement alone creates a deeper set of problems, particularly when not combined with integration policies.

Of the more vocal complaints, have been those lodged against efforts to enlist community officials—educators, social service and health providers, teachers, and police—to carry out immigration enforcement. Opponents of these measures argue that immigration enforcement by the police or other community providers erodes community trust and compromises their ability to effectively carry out their jobs.

A relatively understudied segment of the undocumented population, the youth, provides policy makers and community officials, alike, a different lens through which to examine questions of immigrant reform and community responsibility. Undocumented youth represent a sizeable and vulnerable population.[1] These children grow up and are schooled side-by-side with American born youth. They experience childhood and early adolescence without many of the restrictions that impact their parents, as the Fourteenth Amendment guarantees their access to a free public education.[2] However, after high school they are excluded from participating in most forms of adult life. They cannot vote, participate in the labor force, and, in most states, drive. These young men and women are directly affected by a confusing and contradictory immigration system that leaves more questions than answers.

Because the transition to adulthood marks their entry into undocumented life, these young people find many of the defining roles of adulthood to be beyond their legal limits. As a result, they spend much of their late adolescence and early adulthood contending with blocked opportunities, stigma, and fear. However, many of these young people have to contribute to their families and take care of themselves. On a daily basis, they spend much of their time looking over their shoulders and worrying about what might happen to them and their family if they come in contact with their legal limitations.

While the particular circumstances of these young people may warrant a broader discussion on legalization, immediate integration efforts are of equal importance. Undocumented youth, particularly those transitioning to adulthood, are in need of a range of community services to ensure

Roberto G. Gonzales is an Assistant Professor at the University of Washington School of Social Work. Special thanks to Hubert Williams and the fine staff of the Police Foundation. All errors in fact or interpretation are my own. Address correspondence to Roberto G. Gonzales, University of Washington School of Social Work, 4101 15th Avenue, WA 98105-6299, or rggonzal@u.washington.edu. To protect confidentiality, all names of individuals have been replaced with pseudonyms.

they grow up healthy, receive the benefits of an education, and develop trusting relationships with community members. However, when they are in constant fear, they retreat into the shadows, do not seek the help they need, and become susceptible to engaging in illicit activities. The findings in this paper suggest that while enforcement efforts are counterproductive, police and other community officials have an important role to play in the integration process of undocumented youth.

Contemporary Immigration Enforcement

It has become the contention of most Americans that the current immigration system is no longer adequate and requires a major overhaul. However, there are diverging opinions on what immigration reform may entail. On one hand, many Americans favor guest worker programs, a pathway to legalization, and increased access to education. On the other hand, many others favor tighter enforcement, an expansion and fortification of a fence along the border, and stricter punishment for those in this country without proper authorization. However, Congress has failed to provide any solutions to the nation's complex immigration problems. And with efforts towards comprehensive immigration reform stalled in Congress, states and local jurisdictions have attempted to make their own reforms by drafting and passing piecemeal immigration legislation.

As a result, the last two or three years have witnessed huge increases in state- and local-level activity. In the first quarter alone of 2008, state legislators across the country considered more than 1,100 proposals related to immigration in 44 states. Twenty-six states have enacted 44 laws and adopted 38 resolutions or memorials. These numbers are comparable to those of 2007 at the beginning of the first quarter, and double those of 2006 (National Conference of State Legislatures 2008). While some states adopted measures to help immigrants by protecting them from exploitation and by extending education and health care to immigrant children, the political tide ran generally against immigrants (Olivas 2008). Many other states drafted a wide range of legislation to limit undocumented immigrants, including: education, employment, driver's licenses, law enforcement, legal services, public benefits, housing and rental, alcohol and tobacco purchases, gun and firearm permits, flag displays, and juvenile reporting requirements (Rumbaut and Menjívar 2008). Further, municipalities and counties considered hundreds of harsh provisions aimed at undocumented immigrant renters, use of English-only documents, the use of a public library card, and prohibition of the sale of Mexican food from trucks (ibid). Many of these local ordinances have been struck down in the courts, but many more are still pending.

Meanwhile, immigration enforcement efforts have increased. The Department of Homeland Security's Immigration and Customs Enforcement (ICE) initiated Operation Return to Sender in 2006. Since then, ICE agents have carried out removal efforts in homes, shopping mall parking lots, bus terminals, farms, meatpacking plants, and other public and work places across the country. As a result, thousands of unauthorized migrants have been deported, many more children have lost their parents due to deportation, and increasing numbers of students have been targeted.

In fact, since September 11, 2001, immigration enforcement has received a significant amount of attention. The contention by some that the federal government is not equipped with resources sufficient to enforce immigration law has prompted a discussion on state and local law enforcement's role in the enforcement of immigration law (Seghetti, Viña, and Ester 2004). To date, a handful of states and localities have entered into agreements to deputize officers and assist the federal government with enforcing certain aspects of immigration law. Georgia's law, for example, contains a provision that allows state and local law enforcement to detain arrestees for federal immigration law violations, and several other counties and local municipalities have followed suit.

Many other state and local enforcement agencies, however, contend that it is the federal government's role to enforce immigration law, in light of limited state and local resources and immigration expertise. Moreover, many police officials have expressed concern over proper training, finite resources at the local level, potential civil rights violations, and the overall impact on communities.

The stance that many police officials have taken is that immigration enforcement by local police, among other things, erodes community trust. Already, ICE raids and local measures against unauthorized immigrants have elevated a climate of fear within the immigrant community. A recent Pew Hispanic Center survey (2007) found that more than 50 percent of Latinos living in the U.S. fear that either they or someone they know will be deported. For many, the constant fear of deportation exacerbates physical and mental health problems. In San Pedro, California, "a school principal told reporters that the raids and presence of ICE agents near the school has created a climate of 'ongoing, relentless terror' with more students absent from school or distracted by the possibility of their parents being gone when they arrive home" (Rumbaut and Menjívar 2008).

Defining the Problem

Over the last three decades, however, dislocations in sending countries, increased labor recruitment, and dramatic changes in immigration policy have dramatically altered the complexity of international migration and the immigrant family. Until the 1980s, unauthorized immigrants were mostly seasonal labor migrants who left children and families home in their countries of origin. The unauthorized now consist of larger proportions of families and children who will grow up and be schooled in the U.S.[3] These unauthorized children, who come to the U.S. before the age of twelve, represent a relatively new and vulnerable population. Given the size and relative recency of this population, what happens to these children is of great scholarly and policy significance. To date, however, there has been a dearth of scholarly research on undocumented youth (Abrego 2008, 2006; Gonzales 2008; Perez-Huber and Malagon 2007; Seif 2004), and a scattered few notable policy reports and articles (Gonzales 2007; Batalova and Fix 2006; McGray 2006; Passel 2003).

The 1.5 Generation

Unauthorized children find themselves betwixt and between two worlds. Most of them only know their country of birth through their parents' stories. They may feel a nostalgic connection to their homeland, but with every year lived in the United States they feel a growing distance between them and their parents, as they speak more English and less of their parents' language. Ironically, though, each of these years also brings them closer to the realities of their parents' undocumented lives.

APPENDIX E

Why Integration Matters: The Case of Undocumented Immigrant Youth and Moving Beyond Enforcement

These children, born abroad and brought to the U.S. before the age of twelve, represent a relatively new but significant population. Their generation, referred to as the 1.5 generation, fit somewhere between the first and second generations (Rumbaut 2004). They are not of the first generation because they did not choose to migrate, but not of the second generation either, as they were born and spent part of their childhood abroad. While they have some association with their countries of origin, their primary identification is affected by experiences growing up American. They straddle two worlds and are often called upon to assist their parents in the acculturation and adaptation process. Their dual frames of reference provide both advantage and difficulty. Those of the 1.5 generation tend to be bicultural and attain linguistic characteristics similar to those persons born in the U.S. This unique positioning could provide them an advantage in the global economy, as they are equipped with bilingual and bicultural skills. However, many of these youngsters fail to experience these advantages.

Rumbaut and Ima (1988) explain that the 1.5 generation faces two challenges: adolescence and the transition from childhood to adulthood, and acculturation and the task of managing the transition from one culture to another. Similar to their parents, they must successfully acculturate to the values and norms of the host society. Many will find more ease in this process than will their immigrant parents. However, they must do so while simultaneously making transitions from childhood to adulthood. Because of their legal status, these dual transitions are often in great conflict.

From childhood to early adolescence, legal status has little meaning in the lives of undocumented youths. During this buffer period, undocumented children move through their own development and participate in community institutions, notably the school system, and are sheltered from the constraints their parents experience. Once undocumented youth reach late adolescence, however, the limits imposed by their immigrant status make themselves known. American culture creates various needs and thus defines what it means to successfully pass from one phase of development to the next: obtaining a library card, renting a movie, applying for a driver's license, obtaining a work permit, moving on to college, marrying, and buying a home. From about the ages of fifteen to sixteen on, these various turning points mark and define successful transitions from childhood to adolescence and adulthood. However, many of these important stages require important forms of state-issued identification and legal status. Without the ability to produce such forms of legitimizing identification, undocumented young adults are shut out of these important activities and distanced from their peers.

Exclusion from these important rites of passage circumscribes their limited roles within adult society and sets them apart from their peers. While certain avenues are closed, others are restricted. In order to help their families, support themselves, and pay for school, they must face the dilemma of whether or not to work. And, in order to get to and from work and school, they must make tough decisions about how to get around. In most states, the unauthorized cannot obtain a driver's license. Hence, they cannot purchase a car, buy insurance, or legally drive. In cities with good public transportation systems like New York and Chicago, this is a viable, yet limited, option as many of the manufacturing jobs have moved out to suburban areas. In metropolitan areas like Los Angeles, however, the prospects are dim. Given the limited public transportation options and the sprawling nature of the municipality, reliance on public transportation limits employment and school options severely. Taken together, these numerous barriers severely limit the mobility of these young adults. At every turn, daily decisions are tantamount to putting their lives on the line as any of these pursuits can place them face-to-face with immigration authorities.

Suddenly the world changes substantially for these youngsters, as does what it means to participate in society. Not only do undocumented youth experience exclusion, they are also unable to meet the demands of adult life and are forced to make important decisions that have consequences not only for the present but also for the future. This new status within society and their communities proves extremely difficult to overcome, both in terms of the numerous new barriers and the psychological effects.

What happens in the early years has a strong bearing on later life chances. Blocked opportunities early on can cause these youth to retreat underground and to seek illicit alternatives. However, the longer the buffer period, the stronger the opportunities to successfully compete in school, develop positive self-image, and prepare themselves for full and active participation in the legal world. By the time they reach adulthood, the impediments and opportunities faced as adolescents play strong determining roles in how their adult lives will unfold.

Without adequate education and requisite job skills, many undocumented youth will find difficulties securing steady work, as options with or without legal status are both limited and limiting. However, early opportunities in education and community-based mentorship can help them hold on to aspirations and ready themselves for the possibility of a change in status.

Data Section

The following discussion draws from more than three years of fieldwork in Southern California, seventy-eight in-depth life histories, and observations of more than 250 young adults, ages twenty to thirty-six, who migrated clandestinely with parents before the age of twelve.[4] While a portion of these young men and women have regularized their status, all of them began and spent most of their school years in unauthorized status. I have also stratified the interview sample so as to be able to compare diverse experiences. Half of the interviewees went on to graduate from high school and went to college, while the other half exited before college, either by dropping out of high school or ending their education upon completion of high school. This sampling choice helped me to draw out the various contexts and structural mechanisms that promoted upward trajectories and downward spirals.

Transitioning to Illegal Lives

Among my respondents, many described this period as one of great stress and anxiety. Because most of them were not required as children to produce forms of identification, when they attempted to insert themselves into the American mainstream, they found themselves without the proper credentials. And because their own status did not pose too many restrictions as they grew up, many of them simply did not think of legal status as an issue in their lives. In fact, many believed themselves to be just like their U.S.-born peers. However, their status came as a surprise to many who were unaware they were not legal citizens.

Rodolfo described to me this pivotal period and the moment he realized he was different.

> **Rodolfo: Well you know what, I never actually felt like I wasn't born here. 'Cause when I came here, I was like ten and a half. I went to school, I learned the language. But it was like, I first felt like I was really out of place when I graduated from high school, when I tried to get a job.**

Roberto: Why was that?

> **Rodolfo: Because I didn't have a social security number...Well I didn't even know. I mean, I didn't even know what it meant. You know social security, legal, illegal. I didn't even know what that was. I asked my mom and [she] said, "it's in the process." In the process? I didn't even know what that meant. I don't know why she would tell us that.**

Prior to this experience, Rodolfo was never required to produce his social security number for entry and acceptance and, as a result, his early life was not defined by his legal status. However, the process of looking for a job forced him to discover what he was missing and to confront the implications of not having legal status. This sudden discovery and hard lesson had immediate and severe consequences, as Rodolfo's plans were quickly diverted and his hopes for some level of intergenerational mobility were quickly derailed.

It took Rodolfo some time to come to terms with the meaning of his status, whether it was temporary or permanent, and what it meant for his day-to-day life. While his stepfather had gone through a local immigration attorney to try to sponsor his family, at the time of Rodolfo's job search there were no legal options.

I have talked to many adults who experienced similar discoveries of their limitations during this critical period, many blaming their parents for keeping them in the dark during their childhood. While it was true that in most of those cases parents withheld information about their legal status, a social security number was not the defining factor of childhood and early adolescence that it became for late adolescence and early adulthood. It was not the decisions made by parents on whether or not to disclose to their children, but the intersection of late adolescence, the cultural requirements of that particular period, and legal restrictions that make the experience of this transition so jarring and potentially traumatic. As one respondent described to me, "It's like living a nightmare, but not being able to wake up."

Indeed, the sudden and dramatic changes that accompany these transitions alter the lives of undocumented young adults in profound ways. As these young people come to grips with their new status, the recognition of their limitations sets in. Many of my respondents described a sense of hopelessness as they looked ahead to an uncertain future. Miguel explained to me that during most of high school he believed he had his whole future laid out, but when his mother alerted him to the reality of his status, everything was "turned upside down." As a result, his school work and attendance trailed off. When Cory found out, she ran away from home. Many other of my respondents concurred that their levels of productivity and optimism about the future fell considerably during their last year or two of high school.

This transition can also be quite stigmatizing, as it occurs during a corresponding period in which American-born peers and siblings are making similar, albeit unrestricted, transitions into adulthood. Until then, they sit in the same classrooms, participate in the same social functions and compete uniformly for the attention of school personnel. However, legal limitations during late adolescence separate many undocumented youths from their peers and siblings.

As the world of adulthood was opening up to their peers, a succession of doors was simultaneously being shut on them. My respondents recounted numerous instances whereby they also felt as though they were forced to explain why they did not drive, could not meet their friends at bars, or could not travel to local destinations that led them across immigration checkpoints.

The confusion and fear of unauthorized adult life leads many to a state of perpetual limbo. Many of the young people I met had gone through various processes of legalization, while others were waiting. Over my three-plus years in the field, I met many young people who were in the process of being sponsored by a family member or spouse for residency. However, many found the waits to be long and became discouraged and doubtful after long periods of waiting. However, the fear of something happening to jeopardize their immigration case renders many of these undocumented young adults immobile and afraid to invest time, money, or hopes in their future. Living their lives in a narrowly circumscribed present, several of these young men and women let go of their aspirations to have anything more.

While the consequences of being caught while working and driving are severe, the effects of inactivity can be numbing. Many of these young adults stay frozen in a state of limbo for long periods of time. They do not gain work experience and become increasingly dependent on others to meet their needs. Over time, many of them become so fearful, they stop holding on to things, such as material possessions, relationships, and aspirations. Living only for today, many of these young men and women lose a sense of the future, while only the past and present are their realities.

Nevertheless, many feel as though they do not have the choice whether to work or drive, as family and individual circumstances necessitate the entry of these young adults into the workforce. The act of working also sets into motion a myriad of other decisions that have equally grave consequences. Faced with such dilemmas of needing to take care of themselves and their families, but not being able to legally meet these needs, their circumstances require many to take the risk. However, in doing so, they place themselves in direct contact with their legal limits and in a perpetual state of fear.

Working without the proper authorization is always a precarious venture. The risks of getting caught include jail and deportation. However, many undocumented immigrants feel as though they have little choice. While some adult migrants have learned the ropes and are skillful at finding safer jobs and dealing with the consequences, for many of the undocumented 1.5 generation navigating the world of unauthorized work and the subsequent consequences is a daunting challenge.

Similarly, many take the risk of driving without licenses. Driving, like work, is a necessity for most. Public transportation is neither highly accessible nor convenient for many. Those with children explain that getting to daycare and then to work require commutes of up to three to four hours a day on the bus and waking up two hours early in order to get to work on time. Regardless of their situation, however, by driving they face potential legal trouble. Most of my respondents were well aware of the consequences, yet felt as though they had little choice. Nevertheless, even a minor traffic violation or accident can throw their lives into peril.

Over time, the jarring transition, the day-to-day efforts to conceal their status, and the constant stress and fear take their toll on these unauthorized young adults. Many of these young undocumented men and women in my sample experienced stress, fear, and worry, as a result. A common experience among most is the continual looking over their shoulders. Many of these young people, do not, however, have the luxury of time and space needed to pull their lives together. Faced with impending deadlines for colleges and economic pressures to work, few experience comfortable transitions. As a result, the corresponding entrances into adulthood and the constraints of undocumented life create numerous points of stress. Many find that the pressures of adulthood and the numerous decisions they needed to make in order to survive—with respect to working, driving, going to school, raising families—have tremendous consequences for their present and future lives.

Community Support and Divergent Paths

While the transition to adulthood and the accompanying constraints of unauthorized status are stressful and difficult, unauthorized youth do not experience them uniformly. A range of factors creates divergent outcomes, including family resources, individual choices, social ties, and mentorship. Of crucial importance, assistance from adults within the family and community can enable some unauthorized youth to seek out and access resources to alternative and legal avenues. However, without such resources and support, limited and limiting options place unauthorized young adults in more direct contact with their legal constraints and further expose them to stress, fear, and anxiety. Taken together, this confluence of unfavorable circumstances pushes many of these youth underground and more vulnerable to fringe elements within the community.

Above all sources of support, mentorship from adults provides these young people with distinct advantages with respect to information and resources. High school teachers and counselors, social workers, church officials, human service providers, and local police are important sources of information, advice, and support. Many of these community-level officials have the capacity to help youngsters access the needed financial support and continue their schooling.

For unauthorized youth, the ability to seamlessly move from high school to college is tremendously important. Because school is one of the few legal avenues accessible to the unauthorized, staying in school allows young people a productive and viable pursuit. Moreover, the college campus preserves a certain level of protection, sheltering unauthorized students from potential run-ins with hate groups or immigration officials.

César's story provides further insight into the benefits of mentors and a post-secondary education. Ever since he was young, science has been César's passion. At the end of his senior year of high school, he was accepted to the University of California, Berkeley. His excitement was short-lived, however, after receiving a phone call from the office of admissions asking for his social security number. At that time, there was not an allowance for undocumented students to pay in-state tuition, and César's family could not afford to send him to Berkeley. However, he had support from teachers and counselors who encouraged him to continue his schooling. The following fall, he enrolled in a community college and finished with a 3.8 grade point average and honors. Meanwhile, his parents took extra jobs and saved enough money to pay for his tuition at UCLA at nearly $25,000 a year.

César graduated two years later with a bachelor of arts in molecular, cell, and developmental biology. He was offered a job in a cytogenetics lab, analyzing chromosomes under a microscope, but lost out because of his undocumented status. Thanks to a tip from a leader within the community, however, he was able to take an internship in a similar lab (albeit without pay). César continued his schooling, finishing a master's program in public health at a California State University campus and a one-year post-baccalaureate program in medicine at a nearby University of California campus. Upon acceptance to the program, community leaders pooled money together to come up with his tuition costs.

César continues to pursue education, while waiting for a door to open to medical school. As he waits he tutors neighborhood children, runs a summer youth leadership program for low-income males, and speaks regularly at community events. To his advantage, he has a strong network of support and resources among his family, school personnel, and community members. Because of this extensive support system, César has successfully navigated obstacles at every step along his post-secondary educational journey. This important support has enabled him to find alternatives to work, access important sources of financial support, and actively pursue education while he waits for a change in his circumstances.

Among the young people in my study who went on to college, each of them had similar systems of support that enabled them to push over barriers, access needed resources and opportunities, and participate in community service. On the other hand, not having such sources of support proved to be the chief difference between young adults experiencing productive educational and career pursuits and those facing day-to-day constraints and troubled involvement with neighborhood countercultures.

Gabriel's late adolescent-early adulthood trajectory helps to provide a contrast to that of César, and an example of the potentially debilitating effects of unauthorized status on 1.5 generation youth. After Gabriel's family was evicted from an apartment in Anaheim, he decided to find a place of his own in order to alleviate the burden on his mother. He felt like a "dead weight," not being able to contribute financially to the family because of his legal status. On his own, Gabriel needed to work in order to support himself. He found factory jobs and used someone else's social security number in order to secure employment. However, he has twice received No-Match letters from the Social Security Administration stating that his social security number did not match the name he was using. He lost one job because of this and is fearful that future employers will also find out. Beyond being scared, Gabriel is frustrated and angry about his status. Moreover, Gabriel is increasingly turning to illicit means in order to support himself: he stopped taking the bus in lieu of driving after receiving a warning from an employer that his tardiness would cost him his job; when he could not buy a cell phone through regular channels, he bought one from a guy in his neighborhood only to find that the number had more than four hundred dollars of charges on it. To further weigh him down, Gabriel served a three-year probation sentence for an attempted robbery as an accomplice, after being pulled over with a group of guys with which he was hanging out. As Gabriel's situation indicates, restrictions due to immigrant status limit the scope of choices and structure decisions.

Based on my interviews and observations, Gabriel's situation is not uncommon. In fact, many others described to me similar limiting circumstances that they felt pushed them into illicit activity. For many years Josue made his money selling drugs. Contemplating the alternative of working clandestinely in a factory or restaurant, he chose the street, where he felt he had some power. As he looks ahead at his future, with little formal job training, he cannot help but to compare these different experiences and outcomes.

> **In a way it's hard to get a job, you know? Get paid the way we want to be paid. And back then I used to skip that you know? You know what I'm not gonna work for a job. I'm not gonna bust my ass for someone who can be yelling at me for like $5.75, $5 bucks an hour. Nah nah hell no. If I get a job, I wanna get paid $20 bucks an hour. Because I thought that man, I speak English, I do good, I do that, but actually I didn't have any experience and I decided to start selling drugs, you know, because I thought, this is easy. I got my own schedule, I can do whatever the hell I want to the whole day, I can scream at them, nobody is gonna scream at me. Nobody is gonna do nothing to me because I am the one in control.**

However, Josue's activities caught up to him and put him in a life-threatening situation. At twenty-six, he finds himself struggling to put his life together. He refuses to go back to selling drugs but is having a hard time competing with adult migrant workers for low-wage jobs.

Discussion and Conclusion

While undocumented young adults face limited choices and debilitating circumstances, some, in fact, find sources of support to bring them into mainstream institutions, provide them with safe and productive alternatives, and allow them to experience the transition to adulthood without undue stress and anxiety. Comparing César and Gabriel, whose stories provide important analytical contrasts, suggests some clues about community-level contextual factors. At 27, these two young men are the same age, both came to the U.S. before they were eight years old, grew up in Southern California, and neither has regularized his immigrant status. While they share many common characteristics, the differences between the two are several.

César has three degrees, including a master's in public health, and runs a successful private tutoring business. Gabriel, on the other hand, works in a factory with low-skilled immigrant coworkers. He has been laid off from several jobs and has received No-Match letters from two of them. Although he has community college credits, Gabriel is no longer in school after several interruptions. He lives on his own and from check to check.

APPENDIX E

Why Integration Matters: The Case of Undocumented Immigrant Youth and Moving Beyond Enforcement

None of the differences between César and Gabriel are coincidental. César's parents both work and, before he began high school, managed to move to a quiet neighborhood with an academically strong high school. With the constant encouragement of his parents to excel in school, he brought home good grades and attracted the attention of several teachers and counselors. His strong high school record earned him admission to several universities. The transition from high school was relatively smooth and without many of the constraints of his status. When he realized he could not attend his dream school because of family finances and had to attend community college, his network mobilized resources and raised enough money for him to attend the University of California. With his degree, he was able to continue to pursue education while he waited for a change in his status.

Gabriel, however, experienced the cumulative disadvantages of unauthorized status as he transitioned out of school. He was kicked out of high school for excessive absences and did not finish on time. Although he eventually earned his diploma at a continuing education school, his progress was slowed considerably. While his mom wishes for him to be successful and to go to college, she has very little means to support those endeavors. Her monthly income is often insufficient to meet monthly expenses. A few years ago, Gabriel felt as though he was a burden on his mom and moved out. Over the years, he has gained work experience in low-wage sectors and has become conditioned to the limitations and hazards of low-wage work. Because two of his employers were sent No-Match letters from the Social Security Administration, he is fearful of getting caught at work and being deported. He takes the risk of driving, relies on underground means for providing basic needs, and is surrounded by a peer group that has, more than once, brought trouble.

While parental experiences shape children's trajectories, educational attainment determines whether or not the transition to adulthood will be successful. Gabriel was one of the almost 50 percent of his entering freshmen class who left high school before completion. As a result, he did not have any mentors to guide him through the barriers that awaited. César went to a high school that was ethnically and economically diverse and enjoyed a range of honor's and AP classes. He accumulated a strong network of supporters in high school, was active in extracurricular activities, and carried his network and skills to college and community service. While he remained undocumented, he was, however, able to seamlessly move on to college and concentrate on his studies. As a result, he graduated within four years and moved on to attain two graduate degrees.

The divergent trajectories of César and Gabriel provide important illustrations of the key determinants of mobility and incorporation of the undocumented 1.5 generation into the community. There is good reason to be cautious attributing success to human characteristics alone, as family circumstances, quality of educational opportunities, the presence of adult mentors, and access to community resources structure opportunities for these young adults. Because of modest levels of family success, César was able to attend a stronger high school. His friends were of different ethnicities, and he experienced greater opportunity. He also benefited from a wide range of classes, teachers who advocated for him, and important school resources. Gabriel, on the other hand, went to a large, crowded high school that was over 80 percent low-income. His classes were large, and he had little contact with his teachers or school counselors. And when he left school, there was no one from his school reaching out to him. As a result, Gabriel was not able to enlist the support needed to develop resiliency and coping strategies.

The presence of adult mentors in the lives of unauthorized youth is of paramount importance. And because, in most states, college offers a legal and legitimate means to participate and compete in American life, moving on to post-secondary institutions is critical. Adults in the community can play an important role in not only helping these young people navigate these stressful transitions but also providing guidance and resources that will enable these young men and women to continue to play active and productive roles in communities.

While the immigration debate stalls in Congress, on the ground local-level decisions regarding health care, education, and law enforcement are shaping communities across the U.S. This paper is an attempt to contribute to localized conversations about today's immigrants and how we respond to them.

Contemporary immigration is taking shape differently than it did a century ago. The increased presence of unauthorized immigrants—young as well as old—compels us to make important decisions about their role in communities. However, in order to do so, it is important that we move beyond one-size-fits-all approaches to this complex set of issues.

Based on extensive observation in immigrant communities and in-depth interviews with unauthorized young adults, this paper has focused on a particular subset of the unauthorized population and their experiences of unauthorized adult life. As I have found in my research, these experiences prove to be quite difficult. Saturated with fear, stigma, paralysis, and physical and mental health problems, day-to-day life can be challenging and unpleasant. For a group of young people who grow into these limitations as they are acculturating, the net effect can be quite debilitating. These experiences, however, provide evidence for the potential benefits of integration efforts. To be sure, policies that criminalize the unauthorized fail to account for these unique circumstances. Moreover, increased enforcement efforts that keep these young people in fear and away from critical services they require are limited and limiting.

The transitions young people make from childhood to adolescence and to young adulthood are of critical importance. Because of the circumstances of unauthorized youth, these transitions are often traumatic. As a result, unauthorized youth require a range of services that cover education, occupation, and physical and mental health issues. Moreover, their unique circumstances require trusting relationships with institutions and mentors within their communities. However, when health care officials, social service providers, and community police perform immigration-related duties, the level of fear and anxiety in communities is ratcheted up and exacerbates mental and physical health problems. Moreover, unauthorized youth lose trust in community officials, do not seek out the help they need, and shy away from cooperating and participating in important community-level institutional efforts. This scenario is neither good for unauthorized youth nor the community.

The youth are the future of our communities. What we must decide is whether we want a healthy and productive generation of young people marching forward, or whether we are ready to deal with the consequences of an undereducated, underground, frustrated population of young men and women with limited access to mainstream opportunities.

By virtue of their status, unauthorized youth cannot work, vote, or drive in most states. However, they can go to school and make positive contributions to our communities. When they are presented with a narrow range of options, necessity forces them to move beyond the legal realm. Here is where they come in contact with increased exposure to fringe elements within the community. While channels of legalization are beyond the scope of this particular discussion and the purview of community-level decision makers, we can strategize ways to eliminate dangerous and illicit choices by broadening the range of possibilities for unauthorized youth to participate in productive activities.

This research suggests a need for increased community awareness and for adult stakeholders better educated on the issues these youth confront. By mobilizing community resources, schools, community-based organizations, chambers of commerce, and police districts can work together to provide alternative solutions, a broader range of activities, and increased educational access for the youth of the community.

Why Integration Matters: The Case of Undocumented Immigrant Youth and Moving Beyond Enforcement

Endnotes

[1] According to recent estimates, undocumented youth who are under the age of 24 and who have lived in the U.S. for 5 years or longer number 2.5 million. At 20 percent of the total undocumented population, these numbers are significant enough to warrant attention.

[2] The Supreme Court ruled in *Plyler v. Doe* (1982) that, because these children are "persons" under the Constitution and thus entitled to equal protection under the law according to the Fourteenth Amendment, they cannot be denied access to public elementary and secondary education on the basis of their legal status. This decision has enabled thousands of undocumented students to graduate from high school each year. See Michael A. Olivas, "*The Story of Plyler v. Doe, The Education of Undocumented Children, and the Polity*," in David A. Martin and Peter H. Schuck, eds., *Immigration Stories.* New York, NY: Foundation Press, 2005, pp. 197-220.

[3] As of 2005, there were an estimated 4.9 million children of unauthorized parents living in the U.S. Of these, about 1.8 million are unauthorized, while an additional 3.1 million are U.S. citizens (Passel 2006; Passel and Suro 2005).

[4] This paper is based on ongoing research with adult children of unauthorized Mexican migrants. The entire sample consists of 102 in-depth interviews with 1.5 and 2nd generation young adults in the five-county Los Angeles metropolitan area. For this paper, I am focusing only on the 1.5 generation respondents within that sample.

References

Abrego, Leisy J. 2008. "Legitimacy, Social Identity, and the Mobilization of Law: The Effects of Assembly Bill 540 on Undocumented Students in California." *Law & Social Inquiry,* 33(3).

——. 2006. "I Can't Go to College Because I Don't Have Papers: Incorporation Patterns of Undocumented Latino Youth." *Latino Studies*, 4: 212-231.

Batalova, Jeanne, and Michael Fix. 2006. "Estimates of Unauthorized Youth Eligible for Legal Status under the DREAM Act." *Immigration Backgrounder,* October 2006. Washington, D.C.: Migration Policy Institute.

Gonzales, Roberto G. 2008. "Left Out but Not Shut Down: Political Activism and the Undocumented Student Movement." *Northwestern Journal of Law and Social Policy*, 3(2).

——. 2007. "Wasted Talent and Broken Dreams: The Lost Potential of Undocumented Students." *In-Focus*, 5(13). Washington, D.C.: Immigration Policy Center.

McGray, Douglas. 2006. "The Invisibles." *Los Angeles Times Magazine*. April 23, 2006.

National Council of State Legislators. 2008. "State Laws Related to Immigrants and Integration, January 1-June 30, 2008." *Immigration Policy Project*, July 24, 2008, prepared by Dirk Hegan.

Olivas, Michael A. 2008. "Lawmakers Gone Wild? College Residency and the Response to Professor Kobach." *SMU Law Review* 99: 101-166.

Passel, Jeffrey S. 2006. "The Size and Characteristics of the Unauthorized Migrant Population in the U.S.: Estimates based on the March 2005 Current Population Survey." Washington, D.C.: Pew Hispanic Center.

——. 2003. *Further Demographic Information Relating to the DREAM Act*. Washington, DC: The Urban Institute.

Passel, Jeffrey S., and Roberto Suro. 2005. *Rise, Peak, and Decline: Trend in U.S. Immigration 1992-2004*. Washington, DC: Pew Hispanic Center.

Perez-Huber, Lindsay, and Maria Malagon. 2007. "Silenced Struggles: The Experiences of Latina and Latino Undocumented College Students in California". *Nevada Law Journal*, Vol. 7: 841.

Pew Hispanic Center. *2007 National Survey of Latinos: As Illegal Immigration Issue Heats Up, Hispanics Feel A Chill.* Washington, DC, December 2007.

Rumbaut, Rubén G. 2004. "Ages, Life Stages, and Generational Cohorts: Decomposing the Immigrant First and Second Generations in the United States." *International Migration Review,* 38: 1160–1205.

APPENDIX E

Why Integration Matters: The Case of Undocumented Immigrant Youth and Moving Beyond Enforcement

Rumbaut, Rubén G., and Kenji Ima. 1988. *The Adaptation of Southwest Asian Refugee Youth: A Comparative Study.* Washington, DC: U.S. Office of Refugee Resettlement.

Rumbaut, Rubén G., and Cecilia Menjívar. 2008. "Rights of Racial and Ethnic Minorities and Migrants: Between Rhetoric and Reality." *The Leading Rogue State: The United States and Human Rights,* Judith Blau, David Brunsma, Alberto Moncada, and Catherine Zimmer, eds. Boulder, CO: Paradigm Publishers.

Seghetti, Lisa M., Stephen R. Viña, and Karma Ester. 2004. "Enforcing Immigration Law: The Role of State and Local Law Enforcement." *Congressional Research Service,* The Library of Congress, March 11, 2004.

Seif, Hinda. 2004. "'Wise Up!' Undocumented Latino Youth, Mexican-American Legislators and the Struggle for Higher Education Access." *Latino Studies,* 2(2).

APPENDIX F

Local Enforcement of Immigration Laws: Evolution of the 287(g) Program and Its Potential Impacts on Local Communities

BY RANDOLPH CAPPS

Introduction

The Urban Institute has for years studied the unauthorized immigrant population, but for the most part our research has focused on demographic trends, the incorporation of unauthorized immigrants in the U.S. workforce, and the well-being of children with unauthorized parents. Until the last few years, there has been little enforcement of laws that make it illegal for unauthorized immigrants to live and work in the United States. But following the events of September 11, 2001, and the creation of the Department of Homeland Security in 2002, U.S. policy has moved rapidly toward increasing enforcement and criminalization of this population. While most of the legal foundation for the current uptick in enforcement was grounded in legislation enacted in 1996, if not before, there clearly was a sea change in the nation's immigration enforcement policies during the 2005-2008 period. With about twelve million unauthorized immigrants (including two million children) and an additional three million U.S.-born children of unauthorized immigrants, these enforcement policies put an ever greater number of families at risk of separation and other adverse consequences (Passel 2006).

The Urban Institute modified its research agenda somewhat to reflect the change in our nation's approach to enforcing immigration laws. Starting in 2005, the new Department of Homeland Security began investing substantial new resources in arrests of unauthorized immigrants at their workplaces, as well as using Fugitive Operation Teams (FOTs) to arrest immigrants with outstanding deportation orders. In 2007, we investigated three of the largest worksite raids Immigration and Customs Enforcement (ICE) had conducted to that point, and published a report that focused on the impact of parental arrest, detention, and deportation on children in unauthorized families in these locations (Capps, Castañeda, Chaudry, and Santos 2007). ICE arrested approximately 5,000 immigrants per year in worksite raids in fiscal years 2006-2008, about ten times the pace of arrests by the old Immigration and Naturalization Service in its last year of operation—2002.[1] These worksite raids have received a lot of attention in the media and in Congress recently, especially because of the large raids in May 2008 in Postville, Iowa, and in August in Laurel, Mississippi.

The 5,000 arrests in worksite raids, however, represent a small fraction of the now more than 275,000 arrests and deportations made annually by the Department of Homeland Security (including by Customs and Border Protection (CBP) as well as by ICE).[2] When compared to the number of immigrants arrested in worksite raids by ICE, far more have been arrested, detained, and deported by FOTs and by state and local law enforcement agencies (LEAs) that have signed formal agreements with ICE granting them immigration authority, as authorized by Section 287(g) of the Immigration and Nationality Act. It is these memoranda of agreement (MOA) between ICE and LEAs, known now as "287(g)s," that are primary addressed here.

Randolph Capps is Demographer and Senior Policy Analyst at the Migration Policy Institute in Washington, DC. Dr. Capps prepared this paper while at The Urban Institute in Washington, DC.

Local Enforcement of Immigration Laws: Evolution of the 287(g) Program and Its Potential Impacts on Local Communities

The balance of this paper begins with a brief timeline and overview of the 287(g) program and discusses some of the broad outlines of how it has been implemented to date. Then, for further background, population and political trends that underlie the adoption of 287(g) programs across the country are discussed. As part of our ongoing research, we are investigating the impact of immigration raids at worksites on children in some new locations (including Postville) but also taking a look at the impact of FOT raids in Miami as well as the 287(g) program now active in Northwest Arkansas. Next presented are preliminary findings about the implementation of 287(g) in Arkansas, based on a site visit there in June 2008. The paper concludes with policy recommendations and general observations about potential impacts of 287(g) operations on cities, immigrant communities, and children.

Overview of 287(g) Program

Section 287(g) of the Immigration and Nationality Act was enacted as part of the Illegal Immigration Reform and Immigrant Responsibility Act (IIRIRA) of 1996. The mid-1990s were a period of anti-immigrant sentiment that led to 1994 Proposition 187 in California (which denied unauthorized immigrants a range of public services) and of increasing enforcement along the U.S. border, beginning with Operation Hold the Line in El Paso in 1993. IIRIRA established the 287(g) program in order to help INS expand its resources for interior enforcement—resources which were at that time much more limited than they are today. It is important to remember also that the 1996 law greatly expanded the categories of crime for which immigrants—both legal and unauthorized—could be deported; reduced their appeal rights after arrest; and added lengthy bars on legal reentry into the United State for those who are deported (Espenshade, Baraka, and Huber 1997). The 1996 law was the primary legal foundation not only for the 287(g) program but also for many of the tools and strategies that ICE uses today in enforcement. However, other than expansions in CBP operations and some modest increases in interior enforcement, the 1996 law did not result in major immediate changes in immigration enforcement strategies.

If we turn specifically to the 287(g) program, the first agreement between the federal government and a LEA was not implemented until 2002, with the State of Florida (Figure 1).[3] The State of Alabama followed with an agreement in 2003, and there were a half dozen more agreements implemented in 2005 and 2006 in Arizona, California, and North Carolina. But the program really took off in 2007, with twenty-six LEAs signing on, and with twenty-eight more joining the program during the first seven months of 2008. According to ICE, in August 2008 there were sixty-two active 287(g) programs, and about seventy-five more LEAs were on a waiting list to execute agreements. By August 2008, more than 840 LEA officers had been trained under the 287(g) program, and over 65,000 individuals were identified as being in the country "illegally" between January 2006 and August 2008.

FIGURE 1 (1 OF 2). 287(g) PROGRAMS IMPLEMENTED AS OF AUGUST 2008

State	Memorandum of Agreement (MOA) Name	Type*	Signed
AL	AL State Police	TFO	9/10/2003
AL	Etowah County Sheriff's Office	JEO	7/8/2008
AR	Benton County Sheriff's Office	JEO/TFO	9/26/2007
AR	City of Springdale Police Department	TFO	9/26/2007
AR	Rogers Police Department	TFO	9/25/2007
AR	Washington County Sheriff's Office	JEO/TFO	9/26/2007
AZ	AZ Department of Corrections	JEO	9/16/2005
AZ	AZ Department of Public Safety	TFO	4/15/2007
AZ	City of Phoenix Police Department	TFO	3/10/2008
AZ	Maricopa County Sheriff's Office	JEO/TFO	2/7/2007
AZ	Pima County Sheriff's Office	JEO/TFO	3/10/2008
AZ	Pinal County Sheriff's Office	JEO/TFO	3/10/2008
AZ	Yavapai County Sheriff's Office	JEO/TFO	3/10/2008
CA	Los Angeles County Sheriff's Office	JEO	2/1/2005
CA	Orange County Sheriff's Office	JEO	11/2/2006
CA	Riverside County Sheriff's Office	JEO	4/28/2006
CA	San Bernardino County Sheriff's Office	JEO	10/19/2005
CO	CO Department of Public Safety	TFO	3/29/2007
CO	El Paso County Sheriff's Office	JEO	5/17/2007
FL	Bay County Sheriff's Office	TFO	6/15/2008
FL	Brevard County Sheriff's Office	JEO	8/13/2008
FL	Collier County Sheriff's Office	JEO/TFO	8/6/2007
FL	FL Department of Law Enforcement	TFO	7/2/2002
FL	Jacksonville Sheriff's Office	JEO	7/8/2008
FL	Manatee County Sheriff's Office	JEO	7/8/2008
GA	Cobb County Sheriff's Office	JEO	2/13/2007
GA	GA Department of Public Safety	TFO	7/27/2007
GA	Hall County Sheriff's Office	JEO/TFO	2/29/2008
GA	Whitfield County Sheriff's Office	JEO	2/4/2008
MA	Barnstable County Sheriff's Office	JEO	8/25/2007
MA	Framingham Police Department	TFO	8/14/2007

*TFO means that LEA officers were trained as Task Force Officers. JEO means that officers were trained as Jail Enforcement Officers.

APPENDIX F

Local Enforcement of Immigration Laws: Evolution of the 287(g) Program and Its Potential Impacts on Local Communities

FIGURE 1 (2 OF 2): 287(g) PROGRAMS IMPLEMENTED AS OF AUGUST 2008

State	Memorandum of Agreement (MOA) Name	Type*	Signed
MA	MA Department of Corrections	JEO	3/26/2007
MD	Frederick County Sheriff's Office	JEO/TFO	2/6/2008
MO	MO State Highway Patrol	TFO	6/25/2008
NC	Alamance County Sheriff's Office	JEO	1/10/2007
NC	Cabarrus County Sheriff's Office	JEO	8/2/2007
NC	Cumberland County Sheriff's Office	JEO	6/25/2008
NC	Durham Police Department	TFO	2/1/2008
NC	Gaston County Sheriff's Office	JEO	2/22/2007
NC	Henderson County Sheriff's Office	JEO	6/25/2008
NC	Mecklenburg County Sheriff's Office	JEO	2/27/2006
NC	Wake County Sheriff's Office	JEO	6/25/2008
NH	Hudson City Police Department	TFO	5/5/2007
NM	NM Department of Corrections	JEO	9/17/2007
OH	Butler County Sheriff's Office	JEO/TFO	2/5/2008
OK	Tulsa County Sheriff's Office	JEO/TFO	8/6/2007
SC	Beaufort County Sheriff's Office	TFO	6/25/2008
SC	York County Sheriff's Office	JEO	10/16/2007
TN	Davidson County Sheriff's Office	JEO	2/21/2007
TN	TN Department of Safety	TFO	6/25/2008
TX	Carrollton Police Department	JEO	8/12/2008
TX	Farmers Branch Police Deptartment	TFO	7/8/2008
TX	Harris County Sheriff's Office	JEO	7/20/2008
VA	City of Manassas Police Department	TFO	3/5/2008
VA	Herndon Police Department	TFO	3/21/2007
VA	Loudoun County Sheriff's Office	TFO	6/25/2008
VA	Manassas Park Police Department	TFO	3/10/2008
VA	Prince William County Police Department	TFO	2/26/2008
VA	Prince William County Sheriff's Office	TFO	2/26/2008
VA	Prince William-Manassas Adult Detention Center	JEO	7/9/2007
VA	Rockingham County Sheriff's Office	JEO/TFO	4/25/2007
VA	Shenandoah County Sheriff's Office	TFO	5/10/2007

SOURCE: U.S. Immigration and Customs Enforcement, *Partners: Delegation of Immigration Authority Section 287(g) Immigration and Nationality Act*, August 18, 2008, available at http://www.ice.gov/partners/287g/Section287_g.htm.

What are these 287(g) programs? Essentially they are memoranda of agreement between LEAs and ICE that allow LEA officers to enforce immigration laws. LEAs designate officers for training by ICE in, among other things, immigration laws, identification of potential unauthorized immigrants, procedures for verifying documents, and use of databases to validate identities. Once trained, the designated officers then return to their home jurisdictions where they continue their roles as state or local law enforcement officials but are supervised by ICE agents whenever conducting immigration enforcement activities. There are essentially two different types of 287(g) agreements—"Jail Enforcement" and "Task Force" models. They differ depending on the type of LEAs that enter into agreements. Through Task Force agreements, designated officers (and only designated officers) may check the legal status of arrestees at the scene of arrest or participate with ICE agents in joint enforcement operations. The Task Force agreements generally designate officers to check immigration status as part of their regular policing duties and spell out which officers will become part of the Task Force. Jail Enforcement officers check the legal status of inmates as they are booked into jail, and Jail Enforcement agreements are mostly between ICE and county sheriffs' offices.

As of August 2008, there were twenty-three LEAs with Task Force agreements, twenty-seven with Jail Enforcement agreements, and another twelve with joint Task Force/Jail Enforcement agreements (Figure 2). Forty-one county LEAs had adopted 287(g) programs, compared with just eleven city and ten state agencies. All of the joint models and almost all of the Jail Enforcement models were adopted by counties (as most of the jails in question are county jails), but the Task Force models were fairly evenly distributed among cities, counties, and states.

FIGURE 2: TYPES OF 287(G) PROGRAMS AND PARTICIPATING AGENCIES

Jurisdiction	Task Force Programs	Jail Programs	Joint Programs	Total
State	7	3	0	10
City	10	1	0	11
County	6	23	12	41
Total	23	27	12	62

SOURCE: U.S. Immigration and Customs Enforcement, *Partners: Delegation of Immigration Authority Section 287(g) Immigration and Nationality Act*, August 18, 2008, available at http://www.ice.gov/partners/287g/Section287_g.htm.

APPENDIX F

Local Enforcement of Immigration Laws: Evolution of the 287(g) Program and Its Potential Impacts on Local Communities

Demographics of 287(g) Program Location

Where are 287(g) programs located? As Figure 1 shows, a majority of jurisdictions with these programs (thirty-seven of them) are in southeastern states, with the greatest frequency in North Carolina and Virginia. The Southwest is the other region of the country with a substantial number (18), including programs in Arizona, California, Colorado, and Texas. There are only five programs in the Northeast (in Maryland, Massachusetts, and New Hampshire), and two in the Midwest (in Ohio and Missouri). It should not be surprising overall that the Southwest has such a high proportion of these programs, as that region of the country is closest to the U.S.-Mexico border, and so the proportion of unauthorized immigrants in the foreign-born and total populations is relatively high there. But why are there so many in the Southeast and so few in the rest of the country?

If we look at recent patterns of immigration, the 287(g) programs are mostly located in states with either substantial immigrant populations or with fast-growing immigration populations (Figure 3). In 2000, two-thirds of all immigrants were located in just six "major destination" states shown in blue: California, New York, Florida, Texas, Illinois, and New Jersey. These are the states with the nation's largest and most diverse cities; they also have a decades-long tradition of immigrant settlement. Half of these six major destination states—California, Florida, and Texas—had a combined total of thirteen 287(g) programs as of August 2008. In fact, these three states accounted for almost half (46 percent) of the estimated unauthorized population in 2005.[4]

On the other hand, there were twenty-two "new growth" states (shown in red in Figure 3) with foreign-born populations that grew faster than the major destinations between 1990 and 2000, led by North Carolina with a 275 percent increase. These states generally had very low or minimal immigrant populations in 1990, but by now all of them have substantial populations of newcomers.

There are several demographic factors about new growth states that may cause anti-immigrant backlash and lead to 287(g) implementation: relatively high shares of immigrants who are unauthorized and from Latin America, as well as a relatively low share who are citizens who can vote. North Carolina is among the nine new growth states that have 287(g) programs, and the state has eight such programs, more than any state except neighboring Virginia. There are forty-one programs overall in new growth states, far more than in the traditional states (all of which have much larger total populations). So clearly there is some correlation between rapid immigrant population growth and the implementation of 287(g). But there are also thirteen new growth states without 287(g) programs, and seven states with 287(g) programs that are neither main destination nor new growth states. It is worth noting that most of the southeastern new growth states have at least one 287(g) program, while none of the new growth states in the Midwest and Northwest have any programs.

There are also some interesting geographic and demographic features worth noting in the pattern of 287(g) location at the metropolitan level. There are just three major immigrant destination cities with 287(g) programs: Houston, Los Angeles, and Phoenix. The other large cities in the U.S. with longstanding immigrant populations (e.g., Dallas, Chicago, Miami, and New

FIGURE 3: 1990-2000 IMMIGRATION GROWTH PATTERNS AND LOCATION OF 287(G) PROGRAMS ACROSS THE STATES

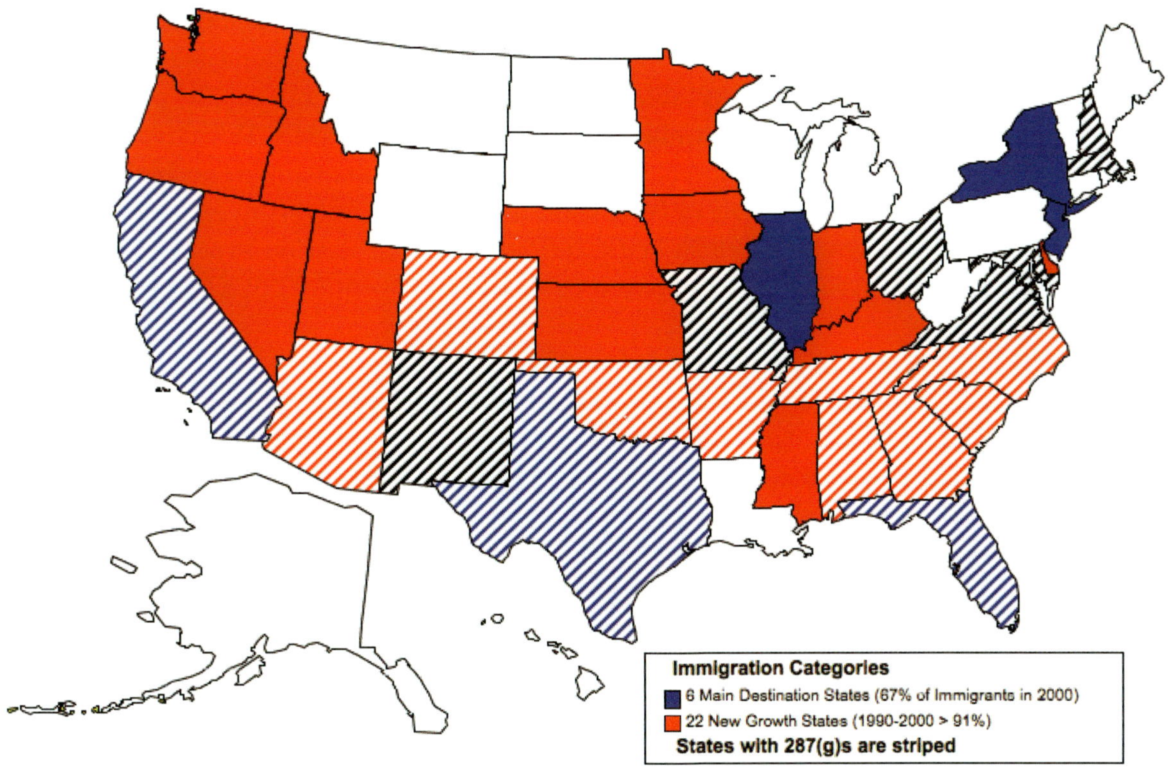

York) do not have 287(g) programs. Atlanta (Cobb County, GA) is the next largest city with a 287(g) program, but it has a relatively recent immigrant population (Singer 2004). Nashville (Davidson County, TN), along with Durham and Raleigh (Wake County) in North Carolina, represent other large southeastern cities with 287(g) programs. The four 287(g) programs in Arkansas are all located in the two northwestern-most counties in the state—Benton and Washington—which together include almost half of the state's immigrants (Capps, Henderson et al. 2007). Thus many of the southeastern 287(g) programs are in cities with substantial and rapidly growing immigrant populations; however, some are in very rural areas as well (e.g., Shenandoah and Rockingham Counties in Virginia). Closer to the nation's capital, the jurisdictions with 287(g) programs are all in suburbs of Washington, DC with small but rapidly growing immigrant populations (Frederick County, Maryland; Herndon, Manassas, Loudon County, and Prince William County, Virginia). The Dallas suburban areas of Farmers Branch and Carrollton County also have 287(g) programs.

Two political scientists, Paul Lewis and Karthick Ramakrishnan (2007), analyzed the factors that have led to the development of state and local legislation aimed at reducing the unauthorized population. While they did not specifically model the development of 287(g)s, their findings with regard to state and local legislation are informative. They found that immigrant population sizes and recent growth rates were correlated with the legislation, but that the political context was far more important. Republican Party affiliation was the single most important factor in predicting the passage of such laws. Thus it may be a combination of demographic and political factors that are at play in promoting the proliferation of 287(g) programs. It appears that the highest concentrations are in cities and suburban locations with new but rapidly growing immigrant populations in conservative states in the Southeast and Southwest. With the exception of a handful of programs in Maryland and New Hampshire, there are no programs in the more liberal areas of the Northwest, Midwest, or Northeast. In fact, almost half (fifteen out of the thirty-one) states that went for George W. Bush in the 2004 presidential election have 287(g) programs, compared with about a fifth (four out of nineteen) states that went for John Kerry.[5]

The 287(g) Program in Northwest Arkansas

Our field research in northwest Arkansas offers a little more detail with regard to the factors underlying implementation, implementation itself, and some preliminary possible impacts. Rogers and Springdale are located in the northwest corner of Arkansas, in Benton and Washington Counties respectively. They are the home bases of two large U.S. corporations—Wal-Mart and Tyson's—that have been on the receiving end of immigration raids in recent years. Their immigrant populations were small in the 1980s but grew rapidly starting in the 1990s, and currently Latino immigrants are about a quarter of total population and a third of the school-age population in both locations (Capps, Henderson et al. 2007).

The original motivation for the program came from the mayor of Rogers (located in Benton County), who campaigned on curtailing illegal immigration[6] and championed a restrictive ordinance targeting unauthorized immigrants. It was modeled after one in Hazleton, Pennsylvania, before that ordinance was struck down in the courts.[7] Once it became clear that a Hazleton-style ordinance (mostly restricting housing and government services for unauthorized immigrants) either would not pass or would fail on implementation, the mayor started to pursue a 287(g) agreement.[8] Due to lack of space to house unauthorized immigrants in Rogers' facilities, Benton County came on board. Around the same time, neighboring Washington County was building a large jail, which has since become the main holding facility for immigrants arrested through the program. Springdale also joined the agreement. In a somewhat unique arrangement, ICE negotiated the 287(g) program with all four jurisdictions (Rogers, Springdale, Benton County, and Washington County) simultaneously.[9] All four jurisdictions sent nineteen officers for training at the same time, and established a joint Task Force/Jail Enforcement model across all four jurisdictions.[10]

The mayor of Rogers was the driving force behind the creation of the program, but there was reluctant support from other quarters in the area as well.[11] Springdale proceeded somewhat more cautiously and established a Hispanic advisory committee for its program.[12] The primary rationale behind asking for the program was based on a perceived uptick in crime, which included several gang-related incidents and the non-fatal shooting of a Rogers police officer by an unauthorized immigrant.[13] Like the mayor of Hazleton and other local leaders who have promoted measures directed against unauthorized immigrants, the mayor of Rogers advocated the 287(g) program as means to combat crime. Local leaders in Springdale also used the anti-crime argument and, in public discussions with the Hispanic advisory committee, promised to focus solely on deporting immigrants who committed serious crimes. Thus the rapid increase in the Latino immigrant population, perceptions of a new crime wave among these recent immigrants, an increase in county jail capacity, and the personal leadership of the mayor were the major driving forces behind the pursuit of the 287(g) program in northwest Arkansas. Between October 2007, when the program there was implemented, and May 2008, over four hundred people had been arrested and identified as unauthorized immigrants to be deported.[14]

Because the 287(g) program is a joint Task Force/Jail Enforcement model, some of those immigrants were identified after they had already been arrested and booked at one of the county jails. But on the Task Force side, there were a variety of different operations. The Rogers Police Department has arrested a significant number of unauthorized immigrants through traffic violations, the most common of which is driving without a valid license. In some cases people were picked up during routine traffic stops, but the department has also operated some roadblocks to randomly check licenses.[15] This practice has been controversial because Rogers was sued by the Mexican American Legal Defense and Education Fund in 2001 for racial profiling against Latinos during traffic stops.[16] This suit was settled out of court, and the Rogers Police Department agreed to adopt language in its regulations to avoid racial profiling and set up an advisory committee to monitor compliance.[17] However, local advocates have accused the department of reverting to racial profiling during traffic stops since the 287(g) agreement was implemented. The Springdale Police Department has reportedly made far fewer arrests of unauthorized immigrants during traffic stops than has Rogers.

Police from both Rogers and Springdale have also participated in investigations and raids on worksites alongside ICE agents. The 287(g) Task Force there has concentrated heavily on identity theft and document fraud, much as ICE has across the country in recent large-scale worksite raids, including the one in Postville in May 2008. The Task Force has focused on small-scale investigations and, in the largest raid to date, arrested owners and about two dozen employees of a Mexican restaurant chain in the area.[18] ICE and other federal agencies had begun this investigation before 287(g) was implemented, but the designation of Rogers and Springdale police officers as immigration agents added manpower to the investigation and the raid, which took place in December 2007.[19]

Many local advocates and some within the local governments of Rogers and Springdale have questioned the implementation of the 287(g) program, as it has evolved from a focus on violent and other serious criminals toward more routine violations and worksite enforcement. Many local Latino leaders in Springdale were on board with the program originally, albeit reluctantly, because they approved of a focus on deporting serious criminals. But as the net widened to include traffic violations and it became clear that the designated Task Force officers were working on ICE worksite operations (such as the restaurant chain raid), many of the Latino leaders withdrew their support and began criticizing the program.[20] Relations between the police and the Latino community deteriorated further during spring 2008 following a few well-publicized abuses by a Task Force officer acting alone to question people about their legal status without probable cause for an arrest. Then Task Force officers arrested an unauthorized immigrant while he was at an elementary school picking up his son, which upset both the school district and the local Latino community.

One of the most troubling aspects of ICE's immigrant enforcement strategies generally, which we have observed both in worksite operations and in the 287(g) arrests in Arkansas, is the secrecy surrounding arrest and detention. Those immigrants arrested for a state or local violation were given the same rights as any other arrestee—to a phone call and a lawyer. Information about all of those arrested on state and local charges is available for immigrants, just as for any other inmates at the county facility. But those immigrants arrested on federal charges such as identity theft, or merely referred to ICE as an "administrative arrest" for deportation (because they committed no state or local crime), were generally not given access to a telephone, and often there was no information at all available about them.

ICE generally only releases the numbers they assign unauthorized immigrants in detention, not their names or locations. Many of those who were not charged with a state or local violation were moved out of Arkansas quickly, along with those who had served their sentence in the county jail and were remanded to ICE custody. Although the federal government had jurisdiction over this group of detainees, they were originally arrested by local police officers in most cases. When they disappeared into the federal system, their family members, lawyers, and others had difficulty locating and communicating with them. This increased the panic and sense of hopelessness among arrestees' families, as they did not know the whereabouts and could not verify the safety and health of their loved ones.

During June 2008 when we visited Rogers and Springdale, there was anecdotal evidence that the 287(g) program had led to strained relations between the police departments and local immigrant communities. There were anecdotes of crimes going unreported, though no hard evidence that crime rates had increased. The school districts in Rogers and Springdale saw their enrollments stabilize in 2007-08 for the first time following twenty years of rapid growth led by Hispanic immigrants, and there was anecdotal evidence that large numbers of Latinos were leaving the area for other parts of the U.S. Tax receipts began to decline and housing vacancy and foreclosures increased. But like so much of the rest of the country, the area was experiencing a housing bust (which in turn created a downturn in construction employment—a major source of immigrants' jobs), and so it is difficult to disentangle economic from enforcement effects. It is probably too early to tell, but many local leaders (within and outside the local governments) believe that the enforcement has taken an economic and social toll on the communities there.

Conclusions and Recommendations

Our research to date in Arkansas, though preliminary, suggests that LEAs should proceed cautiously in entering into 287(g) agreements with ICE. Perhaps the first caution is that there should be a broad base of local support for the program; too often it seems that one or a handful of local government leaders are promoting the program without broad-based support, as appeared to be the case in Rogers.

Second, local community leaders including immigrants may support a 287(g) program if it is directed at violent and other serious offenders, as they did initially in Springdale; however, their support is likely to erode and distrust to grow between the community and the police if immigrants are arrested for minor violations.

Third—and this is a very important factor for LEAs to consider—we were told that once trained, the Task Force officers were directly supervised by an ICE agent, and that all Task Force operations however minor had to be either initiated by or cleared by ICE. This means that in effect the Rogers and Springdale police departments were paying their staff to work for ICE, representing a cost transfer from the federal to the local government. On the other hand, we also heard that the Washington County Jail was reimbursed for housing those arrested on immigration charges, and thus 287(g) may have brought a fiscal benefit to the county.

Fourth, both because ICE initiated worksite operations and because one officer tested the boundaries of his authority, it appeared that the local police departments had lost some measure of control over the actions of their officers.

Fifth, because of the large numbers of arrests (several hundred) over just a short period of time (six months), a small wave of panic fell over the immigrant communities in Rogers and Springdale. While their fear was not as great as what we found in communities with large-scale single-day worksite raids (such as Postville, Iowa), nonetheless, this fear resulted in driving some families out of the area and others into hiding, thereby somewhat reducing overall economic activity.

Finally—and this was the major topic of our investigation—we have been documenting the impacts on families and children when parents are arrested in immigration raids, including those by the local police in Rogers and Springdale. In our previous work on ICE raids on worksites, we found that children suffer from separation from their parents (which may be prolonged if parents are detained for several months); economic hardship after parents are arrested (bearing in mind that unauthorized families, unlike most other families with incarcerated members, are by and large ineligible for or afraid to seek public assistance); social isolation as fear and panic grip immigrant communities and families go into hiding; and the social stigma associated with racial profiling and the labeling of parents as "illegal."

We have not yet investigated the longer-term impacts on children but are planning to do so both in Arkansas and in our other study sites. We anticipate we may also find that over time, these types of enforcement strategies not only sow distrust between law enforcement agencies and immigrants but also may lead immigrants' children to distrust authority and despise the laws that govern our country, which they may rightfully perceive as unjust. This is the greatest long-run danger of our current immigration enforcement regime—that it might create anti-social behaviors and increase crime among immigrants and their children—and it is no less a danger when the enforcement is conducted by local law enforcement than when conducted by federal authorities.

Given these tentative conclusions and the likelihood that the number, scope, and breadth of

287(g) activities will increase substantially in the near future, the following recommendations to state and local LEAs derive from our research:

- Establish a broad base of support for agreements before they are signed, and bring on board leaders from local immigrant communities. Seek the input of local immigrant leadership when drafting the agreement and setting the parameters on enforcement, and meet with local leaders regularly to monitor the program.
- Concentrate on deportation of immigrants already incarcerated (i.e., through the Jail Enforcement model) and those who are arrested for very serious crimes. Do not extend operations to include traffic and other routine violations.
- Avoid LEA involvement in potentially controversial worksite or other major ICE enforcement operations; leave the federal law enforcement side to federal officers.
- Work out a supervision arrangement with ICE that allows greater control over operations by the LEA, even if this requires tough negotiations with ICE or some overhaul of the program at the federal level.
- Maintain control over individual officers that receive Task Force designation and discipline those who step over the line.
- Establish and enforce prohibitions against racial profiling by designated Task Force officers and be sure that the public is aware that racial profiling will not be tolerated.
- Be transparent with local leaders and the public about the types of arrests and operations that Task Force officers are engaged in; provide data on numbers of arrests and allow family members to visit loved ones who have been incarcerated (which is sometimes difficult after people are moved into ICE custody). Providing accurate and timely information can avoid the spread of rumors and panic, which may be detrimental both to law enforcement and the local community.
- Provide resources for families whose members are arrested. Work with local schools, childcare providers, health and social service agencies, and faith-based organizations to ensure that they are aware of ongoing operations, get accurate and timely information about who is arrested, and are able to locate and assist families and children as necessary.

Acknowledgments

The author would like to acknowledge Urban Institute colleagues Ajay Chaudry, Rosa Maria Castañeda, Juan Pedroza, Robert Santos, and Katherine Matthews, who helped design and conduct the research that made this paper possible. A number of local elected officials, police officers, community leaders, and immigrant families were interviewed and gave their valuable input for this research project. The Urban Institute will release a full report on the impact on immigrant families and children of the 287(g) program in Arkansas—along with the impact of federal enforcement efforts—in early 2009.

Endnotes

[1] See U.S. Immigration and Customs Enforcement, "Frequently Asked Questions About Worksite Enforcement," *Fact Sheet,* August 12, 2008, available at http://www.ice.gov/pi/news/factsheets/worksite.htm.

[2] See U.S. Immigration and Customs Enforcement, "FY 2007 Accomplishments," *Fact Sheet,* January 2008, available at http://www.ice.gov/doclib/pi/news/factsheets/fy07accmplshmntsweb.pdf.

[3] See U.S. Immigration and Customs Enforcement, "Partners: Delegation of Immigration Authority Section 287(g) Immigration and Nationality Act," *Fact Sheet,* August 18, 2008, available at http://www.ice.gov/partners/287g/Section287_g.htm

[4] See Pew Hispanic Center, "Estimates of the Unauthorized Migrant Population for States based on the March 2005 CPS," *Fact Sheet,* April 26, 2006, available at http://pewhispanic.org/files/factsheets/17.pdf.

[5] For a map of states that went for Bush versus Kerry in 2004, see Gastner, Michael, Cosma Shalizi, and Mark Newman, "Maps and cartograms of the 2004 US presidential election results," University of Michigan, Department of Physics and Center for the Study of Complex Systems, November 17, 2004, available at http://www-personal.umich.edu/~mejn/election/.

[6] "Stephen Allen Womack Mayor with a mission," *Arkansas Democrat-Gazette,* November 25, 2001.

[7] "Ordinance on aliens hits snag," *Arkansas Democrat-Gazette,* November 2, 2006.

[8] "City's Immigration Plan Stretches to Nation's Border," *The Morning News* (Northwest Arkansas), November 29, 2006.

[9] "Regional Immigration Task Force Suggested, "*The Morning News* (Northwest Arkansas), July 4, 2007.

[10] "19 area lawmen begin immigration training," *Arkansas Democrat-Gazette,* August 22, 2007.

[11] "Alderman says crack down on illegals, cites Rogers' idea," *Arkansas Democrat-Gazette,,* November 15, 2006.

[12] "Council favors chief's bid for immigrant clout," *Arkansas Democrat-Gazette,* April 7, 2007.

[13] "Sides debate police training need," *Arkansas Democrat-Gazette,* March 4, 2007.

[14] "Information Scarce on 287(g) Program: Task Force Officers Arrest 419 in First Seven Months, "*The Morning News* (Northwest Arkansas), May 14, 2008.

[15] The Rogers MOA with ICE specifically allows Task Force officers to check immigration status during routine traffic enforcement operations, or after someone has been arrested for a traffic violation.

[16] "Rogers Police dealings with INS focus of profiling suit," *Arkansas Democrat-Gazette,* December 22, 2001.

[17] "Womack: Suit no issue in immigration enforcement training," *Arkansas Democrat-Gazette,* March 2007.

[18] "Restaurateurs before court deny harboring illegals," *Arkansas Democrat-Gazette,* January 15, 2008.

[19] "Prosecutor: Bad Employers Prompt Raids, Activists Question Move Against Smaller, Hispanic-Owned Businesses, *The Morning News* (Northwest Arkansas), January 28, 2008.

[20] "Hispanic leaders troubled by raids," *Arkansas Democrat-Gazette,* January 13, 2008.

APPENDIX F

Local Enforcement of Immigration Laws: Evolution of the 287(g) Program and Its Potential Impacts on Local Communities

References

Capps, Randy, Rosa Maria Castañeda, Ajay Chaudry, and Robert Santos. (2007). "Paying the Price: The Impact of Immigration Raids on America's Children." *Research Report*. Washington, DC: National Council of La Raza.

Capps, Randy, Everett Henderson, John D. Kasarda, James H. Johnson, Jr., Stephen J. Appold, Derrek L. Croney, Donald J. Hernandez, and Michael E. Fix. (2007). "A Profile of Immigrants in Arkansas." *Research Report*. Little Rock, AR: Winthrop Rockefeller Foundation.

Espenshade, Thomas, Jessica Baraka, and Gregory Huber. (1997). "Implications of the 1996 Immigration and Welfare Reform Acts for U.S. Immigration." *Population and Development Review* 23(4): 769-801.

Lewis, Paul, and Karthick Ramakrishnan. (2007). "Police Practices in Immigrant-Destination Cities: Political Control or Bureaucratic Professionalism?" *Urban Affairs Review* 42(6): 874-900.

Passel, Jeffrey S. (2006). "Size and Characteristics of the Unauthorized Migrant Population in the U.S." *Research Report*. Washington, DC: The Pew Hispanic Center.

Singer, Audrey. (2004). "The Rise of New Immigrant Gateways." *The Living Census Series*. Washington, DC: The Brookings Institution.

APPENDIX G

Immigration and Local Policing: Results from a National Survey of Law Enforcement Executives

BY SCOTT H. DECKER, PAUL G. LEWIS, DORIS MARIE PROVINE, MONICA W. VARSANYI

In the past several decades, the number of immigrants in the United States who lack legal documentation has grown to unprecedented levels—approximately twelve million, according to recent estimates (Passel 2006)—and so has controversy surrounding their settlement in American communities. Many immigrants are choosing new destinations. Cities, suburbs, and rural communities in parts of the country that have not traditionally hosted large numbers of immigrants are now more on par with traditional gateway cities like Los Angeles, New York, and Chicago (Zúñiga and Hernández-León 2005). As evidence of this dramatic shift, the Mexican immigrant population (both legal and undocumented) in "new gateway" states grew dramatically between 1990 and 2000: 200-400 percent in New York, Pennsylvania, Washington, and Wisconsin; 645 percent in Utah; 800 percent in Georgia; 1000 percent in Arkansas and Minnesota; and over 1800 percent in North Carolina, Tennessee, and Alabama (Zúñiga and Hernández-León 2005, p. xiv).

With immigrant settlement patterns shifting, undocumented immigration has become even more of a hot-button political issue. An increasing number of state and local governments are asking police to take a more active role in identifying and arresting immigrants for civil immigration violations. Two federal statutes adopted in 1996 created opportunities for this partnership between federal immigration agents and local police. The Antiterrorism and Effective Death Penalty Act (AEDPA) gives local police the authority to arrest previously deported non-citizen felons, and the Illegal Immigration Reform and Immigrant Responsibility Act (IIRIRA) authorizes training of local and state police to enforce federal immigration laws.

Federal Powers, Local Police, and Immigration

The devolution of immigration policing authority from the federal to local governments represents a sharp break with a long-established tradition of federal control over all aspects of immigration enforcement and is giving rise to what some observers are calling "immigration federalism" (Spiro 1997; Huntington 2007). Although federal authority over immigration has always involved a degree of cooperation and occasional conflict between local and federal officials, the federal government has historically been recognized to have plenary power in this area. Being present in the U.S. without authorization is a civil violation under federal law, not a prosecutable crime under the jurisdiction of localities. In the past, state and local police forces played only a supportive role, sometimes sharing information about those they had detained as criminal suspects or assisting in enforcement actions.

The federal government cannot require local governments to do immigration policing. Police powers are constitutionally reserved for the states and their jurisdictional subunits, an arrange-

Scott H. Decker, Professor, School of Criminology and Criminal Justice, Arizona State University; Paul G. Lewis, Assistant Professor, Department of Political Science, Arizona State University; Doris Marie Provine, Professor, School of Justice and Social Inquiry, Arizona State University; Monica W. Varsanyi, Associate Professor, Department of Government, John Jay College of Criminal Justice (at Arizona State University during preparation of this paper).

ment that provides localities with significant flexibility and autonomy. But with the AEDPA and IIRIRA, the federal government has created an opening for localities to ask their police officers to be trained by and to join the federal government in enforcing immigration laws within the interior of the United States.

Beginning in 2002, informal working relationships between local police and federal immigration agents have developed in some departments. Others are seeking formal training from federal immigration authorities under the 287(g) program (referring to the section of the IIRIRA which authorizes such collaboration). Federal agents also are embedded in some police departments to assist in enforcement of drug and human smuggling laws. A number of state prisons and local jails send the names of criminal suspects to federal authorities to be checked for immigration violations. And an increasing number of police departments are electing to do their own immigration status checks. Within the past several years, the number of law enforcement agencies that have asked for training to make these checks has increased from eight to more than sixty (Immigration and Customs Enforcement 2008). Other local governments and police departments, stating concerns for public safety and the importance of police-community relationships, have rejected local civil immigration enforcement entirely—a small number have declared themselves to be sanctuary cities, while others follow a kind of informal "don't ask, don't tell" policy regarding contacts with possible unauthorized immigrants.

This devolution of immigration policing to the local level presents police departments with several important challenges. One is the potential for conflict between commitments to community policing and active involvement in immigration control. Community policing practices emphasize close communication and collaboration between police and community. Engagement in identifying and removing unauthorized immigrants challenges these relationships in areas with large numbers of Hispanic residents. As the Immigration Committee of the Major Cities Chiefs (2006, p. 3) observed, "Local enforcement of federal immigration laws raises many daunting and complex legal, logistical and resource issues for local agencies and the diverse communities they serve." While stopping short of endorsing one approach for local law enforcement in the debate over how best to respond to unauthorized immigration, the recommendations highlight the many challenges to local law enforcement in carrying out its primary function, including loss of trust among immigrant groups, inadequate resources, complexity of federal laws, lack of local legal authority for intervention, and risks of civil liability.

A second concern is that immigration enforcement activities may discourage members of immigrant communities who are victims or witnesses of crime to come forward. Many new immigrant groups that may be vulnerable to high rates of victimization come from countries where distrust of authorities—particularly law enforcement—is a valid concern. In such cases, building community trust in the police is already a difficult task. A 2007 report by the International Association of Chiefs of Police notes that local immigration enforcement makes that task even more difficult. This report identifies eight specific areas of conflict between communities, elected officials, and federal and local law enforcement.

A third concern is that the core commitment to local concerns in policing will be lost in the process of developing stronger links with federal immigration authorities. American policing spent the last half of the twentieth century elaborating on and strengthening local control. During this period, the focus of police evolved from an emphasis on administrative and professional issues, to community relations and interaction. Problem solving and fear reduction and an emphasis on "zero-tolerance" have also been added to the policy mix (Greene 2001). Each of these re-conceptualizations of American policing, despite their differences, has a decidedly local character. Local communities have provided an important check on the expansion of police authority and jurisdiction, reflecting the historical antipathy of the American populace toward federalizing law enforcement (Mastrofski 1988).

Finally, police commitments to avoid racial profiling are put at risk by active involvement in immigration enforcement because the drive to eliminate unauthorized immigrants has focused on people who have crossed the nation's southern border from Mexico. Although many departments have developed antiprofiling policies, immigration enforcement subtly encourages officers to focus on people who "look Mexican" or who are heard to speak a foreign language. Also, enforcement efforts that target unauthorized immigrants will inevitably draw some naturalized citizens, legal permanent residents, and citizens into newly intrusive contacts with the police. The climate is reportedly becoming inhospitable for many people: as detailed in a recent Pew Hispanic Center report, over half of all Latinos in the United States fear that they or someone close to them may be deported in the current enforcement climate (Pew Hispanic Center 2007).

How, then, should police respond? Will enforcing civil immigration laws erode community policing ideals, particularly in towns and cities with significant immigrant populations? Are other essential elements of local police services at risk?

The growing involvement of local police in immigration enforcement has gained enormous momentum with almost no systematic research or information base (though see Waslin 2007 and www.trac.syr.edu). Law enforcement executives, public officials, and scholars seeking information on this topic have largely had to rely on media accounts, anecdotal information, and reports by advocacy groups of one stripe or another. To respond to the need for systematic information on this topic, the authors have launched a four-stage project, which includes two rounds of survey research and two rounds of local, in-depth, comparative case studies. Our research is geared toward describing the range of actions local police have taken in regard to unauthorized immigration and ultimately describing the context for these actions.

This report presents the initial results of our first nationwide survey of police executives in large U.S. cities. We report on several issues. These issues include the role of local politics in setting police policy, the relationship of local police departments with federal Immigration and Customs Enforcement authorities, the range of variation in local practices and policies, and community relations. The results indicate that local police play a critical role in the ways in which local communities relate to immigrants, particularly in their exercise of discretion with regard to immigration enforcement.

APPENDIX G

Immigration and Local Policing: Results from a National Survey of Law Enforcement Executives

Nature of the Sample

A national web/mail survey of 452 law enforcement executives was initiated in November 2007. We received 237 survey responses (a response rate of 52.4 percent). The sample chosen for this survey was large and medium-sized local (subcounty) jurisdictions. We began with a list of all U.S. cities and towns that were included in the Census Bureau's American Community Survey (ACS) in 2005; the Census Bureau aimed to include in the ACS all localities of 60,000 or higher population, although a few communities had slightly lower populations. We dropped from this list several communities that do not have their own police departments (such as certain townships, and some municipalities that contract with other local governments for police services). This list yielded our 452-community sample and ultimately the 237 responses reported here.

Most of these communities have a substantial number of foreign-born residents. Sixteen percent of the residents in the average locality represented in our survey were immigrants as of 2005 (according to the ACS data). The share of immigrants in the cities we surveyed ranged widely from 1 percent to 60 percent of the population.

Local Politics, Law Enforcement, and Immigration

One of the critical issues for law enforcement in responding to immigration is the extent to which the attitudes of personnel in their department may differ from those of residents or political leaders of the jurisdiction they serve. The nature of law enforcement and the situations officers encounter often cause the police to see their community from a somewhat different perspective than other community members. In this section, we contrast the views of law enforcement leaders with their perceptions of the attitudes prevailing in the jurisdictions their departments are responsible for protecting.

The responses suggest that on the issue of immigration, the difference between police departments and their community is significant. Figure 1 depicts the degree to which unauthorized immi-

Figure 1: Unauthorized immigration is a controversial topic...

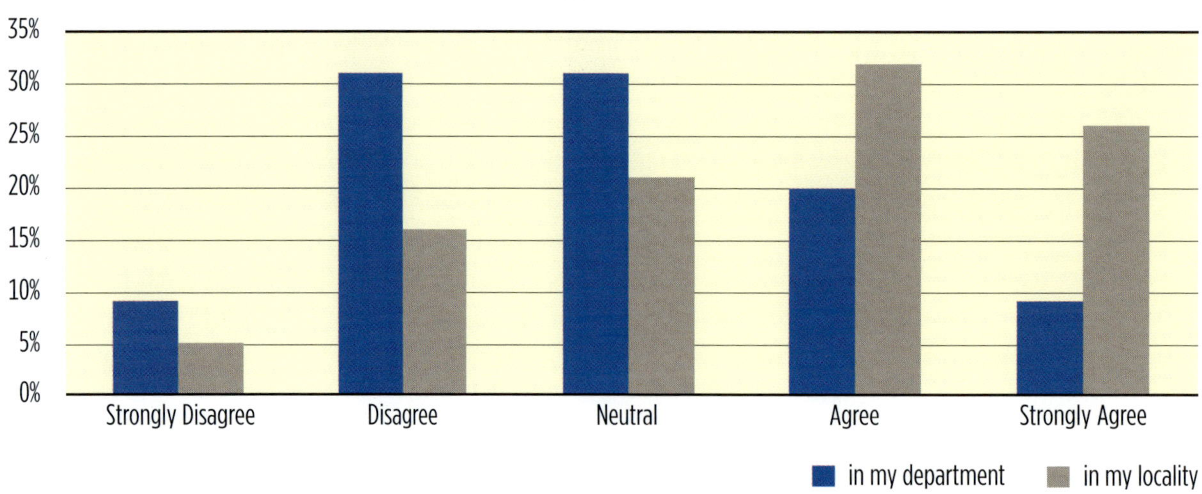

gration is viewed as a controversial topic in a comparative format. Police executives are more inclined to see unauthorized immigration as a controversial topic within their community than within their department. Indeed, the differences on this question are quite striking. This suggests a cleavage between the way that police and communities frame the immigration issue.

A related issue is whether people believe that it is easy to determine who is in the country without authorization. Figure 2 shows a contrast in views between departments and communities. Law enforcement officials see community members as more likely than police personnel to think that determining someone's immigration status is relatively easy. Chiefs also report that gaining the trust of unauthorized immigrants is a much greater priority for their department than for their locality. Fifty-two percent note that gaining the trust of unauthorized immigrants is a priority in their departments, as compared with 25 percent in their community. The difference may be attributable to the view, widespread among police departments, that effective police work depends on law enforcement's ability to gain the trust and communication of all segments of the local population.

Figure 2: People believe that it is relatively easy to determine who is in this country without authorization...

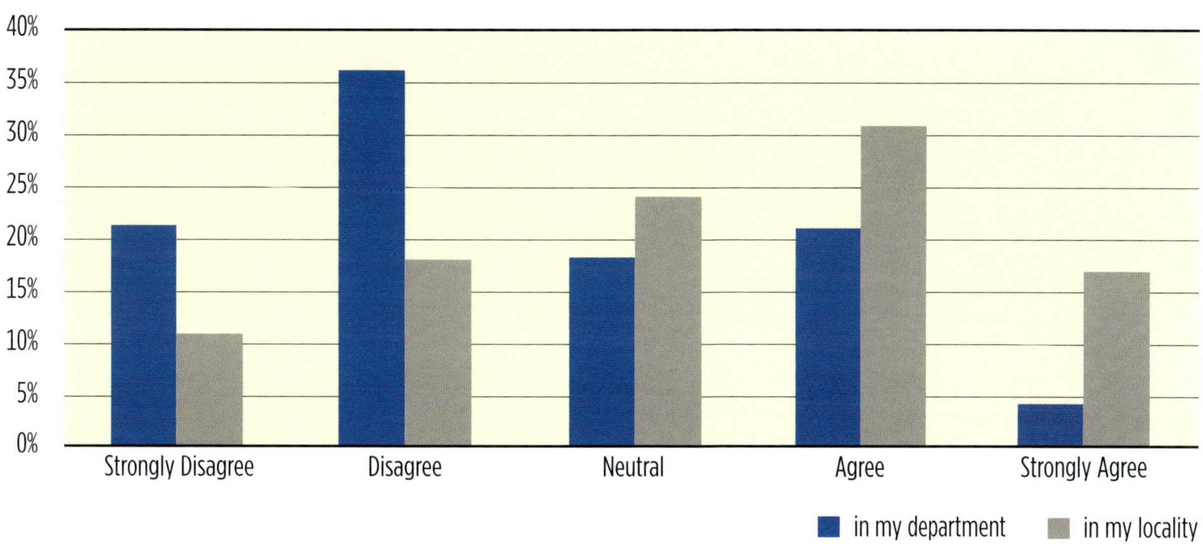

Figure 3 provides an additional perspective on the issue of trust in immigrant communities. The majority of chiefs believe that immigrants are less likely than the general population to report to the police situations in which they have been victims or witnesses of crime.

A related issue is the potential for victimization of unauthorized immigrants by criminals. Chiefs are split on whether unauthorized immigrants are more or equally vulnerable to street crime and domestic violence. But on this topic, chiefs tend to see their communities as somewhat less likely to appreciate the victimization of immigrants as a significant problem. Three in ten chiefs reported that their own departments consider victimization of immigrants to be a significant problem, compared to 23 percent who believe that the broader community feels the same way (see Figure 4).

Figure 3: How likely are immigrants in your community to contact law enforcement when they are victims or witnesses to crime, as compared with the general population?

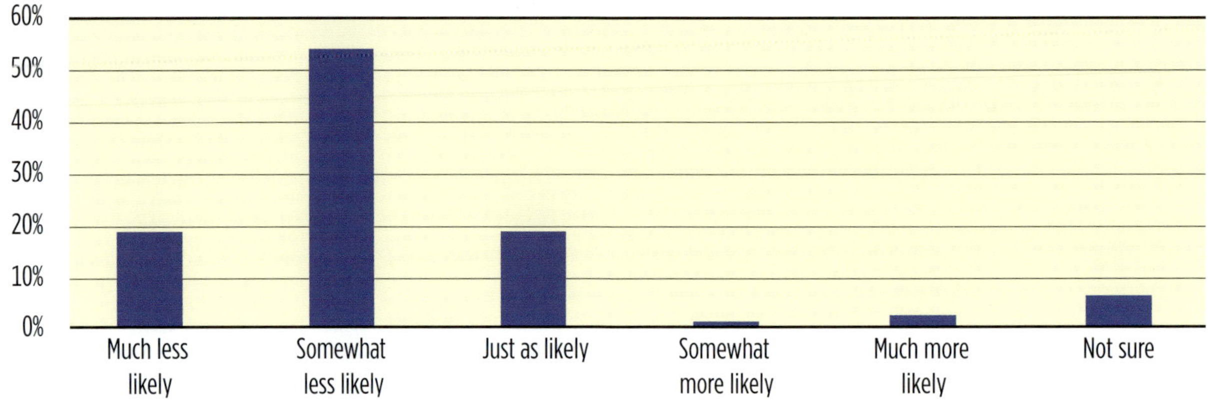

A majority of the chiefs responding (59 percent) report a relatively high level of satisfaction from elected officials with their current level of immigration enforcement. Chiefs report wide variation, however, in what local officials expect. Nearly half (46 percent) report that their local government has no official policy regarding unauthorized immigrants living or traveling through the jurisdiction. At the other end of the spectrum, 12 percent of chiefs report that their local governments expect their departments to take a proactive role in deterring unauthorized immigration. Only 4 percent of chiefs report that their local governments have openly declared themselves as "sanctuary cities" for unauthorized migrants who are not engaged in criminal activities, while another 15 percent report that their cities unofficially operate under a "don't ask-don't tell" policy.

Figure 4: Victimization of immigrants is considered a significant problem...

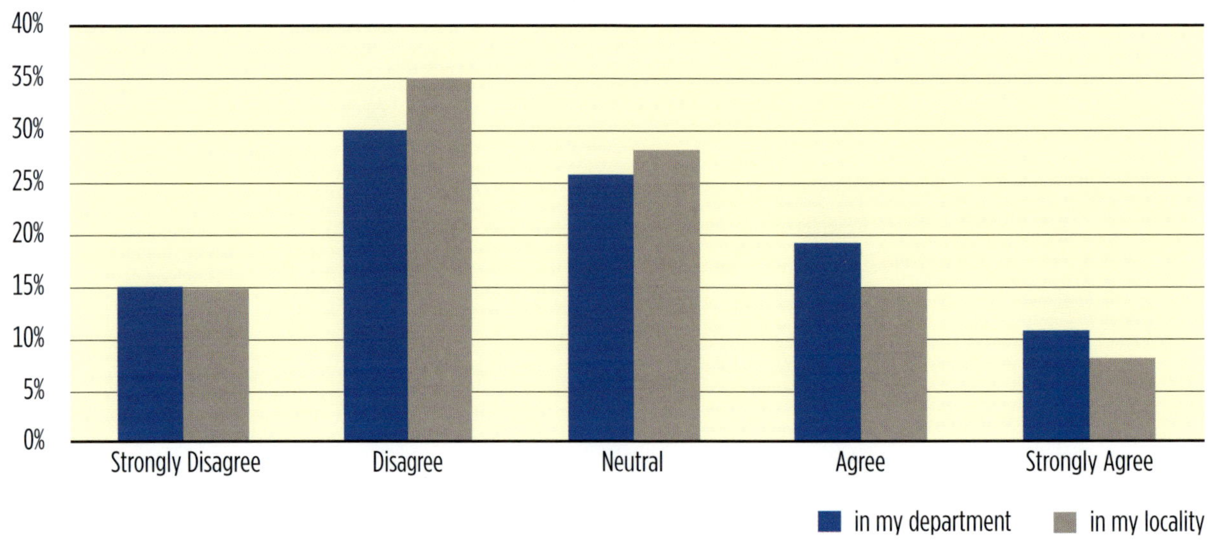

Relationships with U.S. Immigration and Customs Enforcement (ICE)

The relationship between local law enforcement and Immigration and Customs Enforcement, an agency of the U.S. Department of Homeland Security, is an important part of the local response to immigration issues. Our survey revealed interesting differences among local police chiefs in their views regarding the relationship between their department and ICE (see Figure 5).

Figure 5: Which of these statements best describes the direction of your department's current communication with ICE?

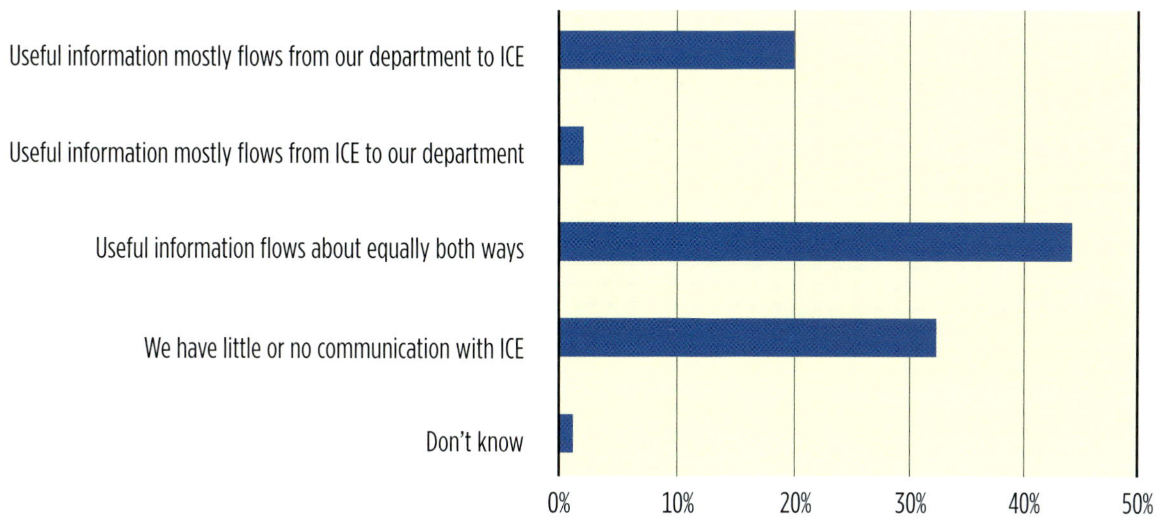

Although a plurality of chiefs (44 percent) believe that useful information flows equally between their department and ICE, 20 percent report that the flow of useful information is mostly in one direction—from their department to ICE. Another 32 percent report little or no communication with ICE at all.

Whether a department has a formal agreement with ICE or not, a large majority (74 percent) report that they contact ICE when a suspected unauthorized immigrant is held for a criminal violation. Formal written agreements with ICE are rare, however. Only 4 percent of departments report having a 287(g) Memorandum of Agreement (MOA) that provides for federal training of local law enforcement and cooperation in arrests and investigations of unauthorized immigrants, while 3 percent have an MOA to help manage unauthorized immigrants who have been incarcerated. A slightly larger share of departments (8 percent) have ICE officers embedded in one or more of their units. It should also be noted that 14 percent of chiefs responded that their departments do *not* participate or assist in ICE immigration-enforcement activities. (Note that respondents were allowed to choose more than one of the above responses, if appropriate.) A majority of those who work with ICE report satisfaction with this relationship.

The survey also asked chiefs how their department and their communities assess the responsibilities of the federal government in immigration control. The great majority of chiefs (72 percent) regard immigration enforcement as the responsibility of the federal government (see Figure 6). A significantly smaller majority (58 percent) perceive support for this view within their local communities.

Figure 6: Immigration enforcement is considered the responsibility of the federal government...

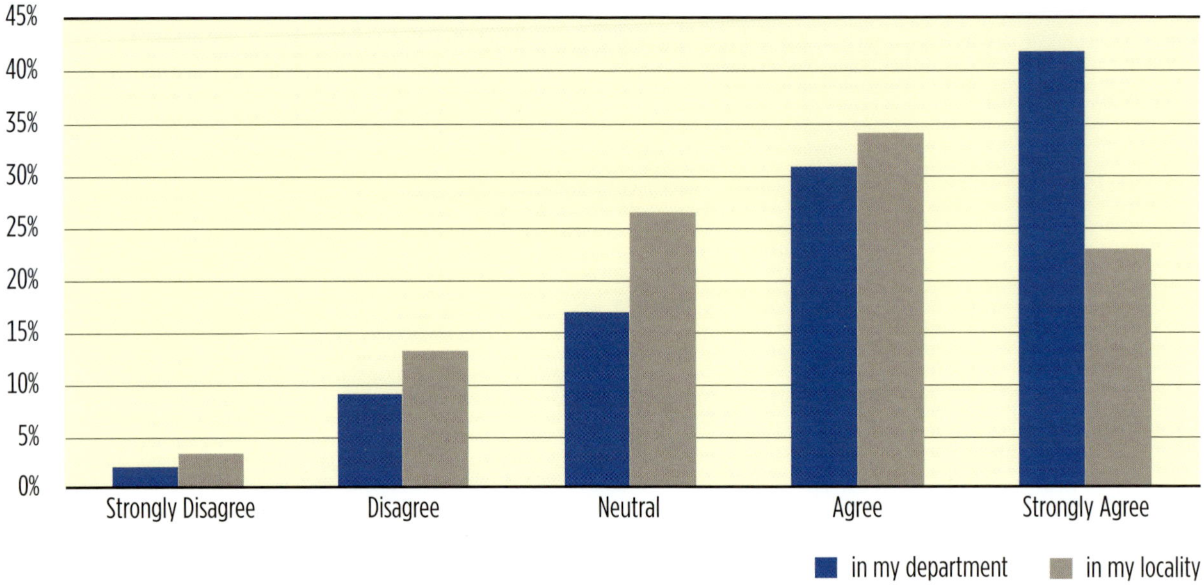

Practices and Policy of Immigration Enforcement

The survey probed police practices in situations involving immigrants whose residence in the U.S. was unauthorized. Chiefs were asked how their officers would respond when faced with a number of situations. In general, the more serious the violation, the more likely they believe that their officers are to check immigration status. Thus chiefs believe that in situations involving traffic violations and witnesses or victims of crime (except human trafficking), their officers are least likely to contact ICE or inquire of immigrant status. Chiefs believe that their officers are most likely to contact ICE in situations involving violent crime or a parole violation. Arrests for domestic violence and nonviolent crime fall somewhere between (see Figure 7).

In many cases, these decisions are made without clear policy guidance. Just under one-half of departments have a policy regarding interactions with immigrants, with 39 percent reporting that these are written policies and 9 percent reporting that these are unwritten policies. Fifty-one percent of departments do *not* have a written or unwritten policy regarding how officers are to deal with immigrants, and 1 percent reported that they do not know whether they have a policy regarding interactions with immigrants.

Furthermore, only 45 percent of departments offer training for sworn officers specifically related to incidents or calls involving unauthorized immigrants. This suggests that in many jurisdictions, local law enforcement is not well prepared to deal with the often complex and difficult decisions posed by unauthorized immigration and that decisions regarding immigrant-police interactions are more frequently made on an ad hoc basis.

Figure 7: Percentage of police departments that typically check immigration status, contact ICE, or both, when encountering possible unauthorized immigrants in these situations.

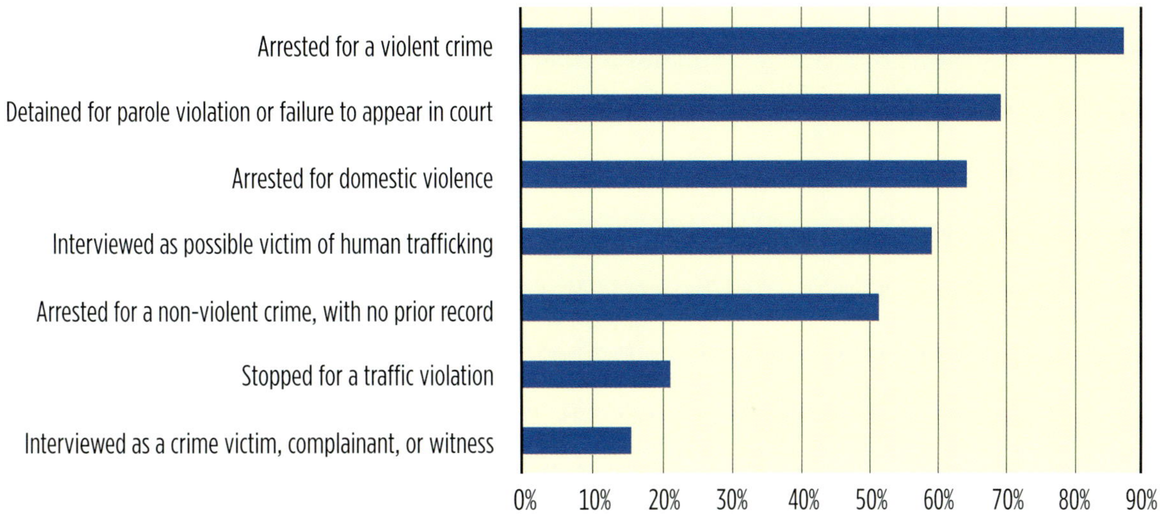

Most chiefs report that their response to the problem of illegal immigration is largely a product of their own departmental leadership, but some note the participation of local elected officials, the district attorney's office, federal officials, and the courts.

Community Relations and Local Law Enforcement

Good community relations was a priority in the departments surveyed. Chiefs report a variety of tools used to maintain relationships. A majority of chiefs rated the following activities as very effective: neighborhood meetings, visits to schools, churches and neighborhoods, bike patrols, cooperation with nongovernmental organizations, and officer proficiency in foreign languages.

Three-quarters of chiefs reported that their departments accept the Mexican consular ID card (*matrícula consular*) or other foreign IDs as forms of identification under some circumstances. However, only 17 percent of respondents said that their departments maintained a phone line for confidential reports of criminal activity by members of the immigrant community. Only 40 percent of chiefs report that their departments have enough officers proficient in foreign languages to work effectively in their immigrant communities.

Conclusion

The results of this survey suggest several important conclusions about immigration and local police departments.

First, chiefs perceive significant differences between their departments and the communities they serve on important dimensions of the immigration issue. In the view of law enforcement leaders, the community is more likely to view unauthorized immigration as controversial than is the department, somewhat more likely to see immigration as a local rather than federal enforcement problem, and more likely to see determining immigration status as relatively straightforward.

Second, in many cases the police lack guidelines for their officers in the area of immigration. While nearly every department (91 percent) has a policy prohibiting racial profiling, the potential for conflict between these policies and immigration enforcement remains unresolved in many departments. A majority of police departments in our sample lack an official policy on how to deal with unauthorized residents and do not provide training to their officers on this issue. Norms may be developing on an ad hoc basis. The survey responses suggested that officers make distinctions between types of crime in deciding whether to inform federal authorities, with less serious crimes being reported less often.

Third, while most departments have some relationship with ICE, the vast majority have no formal agreement, such as a 287(g) MOA. Nevertheless, ICE is viewed as an important resource by local law enforcement, and levels of satisfaction with ICE are reasonably high. It is noteworthy, however, that a significant minority of departments report no relationship with ICE.

Fourth, chiefs report varied levels of interest in their communities in the issue of immigration enforcement. Nearly half of the communities in this survey have so far remained silent on this issue, and opinion in the remainder is split on whether police should be more involved. Most chiefs report that local authorities are satisfied with the department's efforts in this area.

Taken together, these results suggest that the leaders of local law enforcement are at an early stage of the development of policies and training to respond to unauthorized individuals. Communities and departments are both in need of information. It is imperative that more information be gathered about the nature of challenges facing local police in immigration issues so that the police and community can work together more effectively. As in most areas of public safety, immigration enforcement requires effective engagement of the community in order to be successful. Policies, programs, and training that enhance such relationships are likely to pay dividends in this area.

References

Greene, Jack R. 2001. "Community Policing in America: Changing the Nature, Structure, and Function of the Police." In J. Horney (ed.) *Policies, Processes, and Decisions of the Criminal Justice System: Criminal Justice 2000*. Washington, D.C.: National Institute of Justice.

Huntington, Clare. 2007. "The Constitutional Dimension of Immigration Federalism," *University of Colorado Law Legal Studies Research Paper No. 07-06*. Available at SSRN: http://ssrn.com/abstract=968716.

U.S. Immigration and Customs Enforcement. 2008. *Partners: ICE ACCESS*. Retrieved http://www.ice.gov/partners/dro/iceaccess.htm.

International Association of Chiefs of Police. 2007. *Police Chiefs Guide to Immigration Issues*. Retrieved Jan. 3, 2008 from http://www.theiacp.org/documents/pdfs/Publications/PoliceChiefsGuidetoImmigration.pdf.

Major Cities Chiefs. 2006. *M.C.C. Immigration Committee Recommendations for Enforcement of Immigration Laws by Local Police Agencies*. Retrieved 3 Jan 2008 from http://www.houstontx.gov/police/pdfs/mcc_position.pdf.

Mastrofski, Stephen D. 1988. "Varieties of Police Governance in Metropolitan America," *Politics and Policy* 8, pp. 12-31.

Passel, Jeffrey S. 2006. *The Size and Characteristics of the Unauthorized Migrant Population in the U.S.: Estimates Based on the March 2005 Current Population Survey*. Last retrieved 15 July 2007 at http://pewhispanic.org/files/reports/61.pdf.

Pew Hispanic Center. December 2007. *2007 National Survey of Latinos: As Illegal Immigration Issue Heats Up, Hispanics Feel a Chill*. Last retrieved 3 January 2008 at http://pewhispanic.org/files/reports/84.pdf.

Spiro, Peter. 1997. "Learning to Live with Immigration Federalism," *Connecticut Law Review* 29, pp. 1627-36.

Waslin, Michele. 2007. "Immigration Enforcement by Local and State Police: The Impact on Latinos," *Law Enforcement Executive Forum* 7, pp. 15-32.

www.trac.syr.edu, "Transactional Records Access Clearinghouse: Comprehensive, Independent, and Nonpartisan Information on Federal Enforcement, Staffing, and Spending."

Zúñiga, Víctor, and Rubén Hernández-León, eds. 2005. *New Destinations: Mexican Immigration in the United States*. New York: Russell Sage Foundation.

APPENDIX H

Law Enforcement Executive Views: Results from the Conference Survey

BY KAREN L. AMENDOLA, KRISTIN N. WILLIAMS, EDWIN E. HAMILTON, AND VERONICA PURYEAR

Survey Respondents

The Police Foundation conducted a survey of law enforcement executives who attended the August 2008 national conference, The Role of Local Police: Striking a Balance Between Immigration Enforcement and Civil Liberties. Only those who were the top executive or his/her designee were asked to complete the survey. This report shows the findings for the surveys returned at the conclusion of the conference.

Respondents' Roles

A total of 54 attendees of the conference completed the survey as senior leaders in their respective agencies. As demonstrated in Figure 1 below, the majority of survey respondents (40) were police chiefs. The other respondents were deputy chiefs or assistant chiefs (9), sheriffs (2), a police superintendent (1), and two others (a major and one who indicated he/she was both a sheriff and a chief).

Figure 1: Survey respondents by agency role

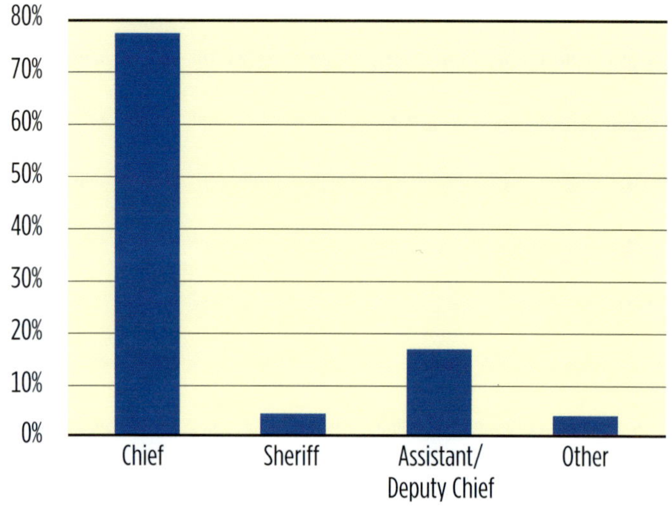

Respondents' Jurisdictions and Agency Types

Most of the participants were from urban agencies (n=29), while many were from urban/ suburban areas (n=19). The remaining six claimed to be from rural type areas. The size of the jurisdictions ranged from just under 15,000 to more than 4 million. Also, the majority of respondents (n=47) were from municipal or local law enforcement agencies while one was from a county police department, four were from sheriffs' offices, one was from an urban county met-

This survey was the work of the following Police Foundation staff: Karen L. Amendola, Chief Operating Officer, Research, Evaluation, and Professional Services; Edwin E. Hamilton, Professional Services Director; Veronica Puryear, Senior Research Associate; Kristin N. Williams, Research & Administrative Coordinator.

ropolitan area, and one was from both a sheriff's office and a municipal department. The sizes of the respondents' agencies ranged from very small (<10 officers) to very large (>20,000 officers).

Agency Concerns

Respondents were asked to list the five most critical issues facing them and their agencies. As Table 1 (below) shows, resource concerns topped the list, with violent crime and gangs following. Also among the top seven were community relations, drugs, and property crime, followed by immigration issues.

Impact of Immigration Issues

Almost three-fourths (74%) of respondents agreed that they were facing new demands and changing expectations as leaders as a result of the growing emphasis on immigration law enforcement, and almost half (44%) said they are responding to increasing political pressure in their communities as a result of this issue.

TABLE 1. HIGHEST RANKED AGENCY CONCERNS

In general, what do you consider to be the most critical issues facing you and your agency? Please list them in priority order, from highest to lowest.

1. Resources
2. Staffing
3. Violent Crime
4. Gangs
5. Community Relations; Drugs (tie)
6. Property Crime
7. Immigration Issues

Rankings were based on a weighted scoring system. Those ranked first were given a score of 5, second scored 4, third scored 3, and so forth.

While just 26% of these leaders felt that their resources were being diverted from activities that would better serve the community as a result of immigration enforcement, over three-fourths (78%) said that they were engaging the immigrant community more as a result of the growing emphasis on immigration law enforcement. They also expressed a high level of confidence in their understanding of immigration issues pertinent to their communities (76%).

Very few agencies were in favor of adopting a sanctuary policy (9%), whereas half (50%) were not supportive of sanctuary policies in their communities. At the same time, the remaining 41% had no opinion on that issue, perhaps indicating that they have not yet decided.

It is important to note that participants generally did not believe that *local* law enforcement should be even partially responsible for enforcement of immigration law (54%), whereas just 24% said they should. The remaining 22% neither agreed nor disagreed that local law enforcement had at least partial responsibility. However, the majority (62%) of law enforcement leaders believed that officers should ask for documentation of citizenship status when in contact with those who break the law (including those violating traffic laws), whereas only 17% agreed they should do so when in contact with crime witnesses, and even fewer (15%) when in contact with crime victims. While 13% of respondents felt such decisions should be at the discretion of officers, just 7% said that officers should *never* ask for proof of citizenship.

Strategies for Engaging the Immigrant Community

Respondents were asked to describe the strategies they have developed or would develop to engage the immigrant community. The most frequently cited strategies in the forty-five received responses were: organizing and/or attending community meetings, events, and forums (n=19), establishing community outreach programs or using community liaisons (n=17), attempting to educate the community through the media and bilingual pamphlets (n=13), or creating specialized department positions or programs to focus on the immigrant community (n=13).

Advantages and Disadvantages of Local Immigration Enforcement

Respondents were asked to summarize the advantages and disadvantages of enforcing immigration law at the local level. Some indicated that local enforcement would help to fight crime in general (n=9) and would appease supporters in the community (n=9). A few suggested that there would be little or no advantage (n=3).

Over one-third (n=22) of the respondents suggested that a potential disadvantage to local enforcement would be the corrosion of trust in the community, while almost one-third (n=16) said that it would put a strain on their resources, result in civil liability, or constitutional issues (n=7), as well as racial profiling (n=6), and reduce witness cooperation (n=5). These responses indicate concerns by local law enforcement about the complexity associated with enforcing federal law.

Impact of Immigrant Population on Crime and Victimization

Respondents were asked to indicate the likelihood of undocumented immigrants being crime perpetrators and crime victims. As Figure 2 shows, respondents believed that undocumented immigrants were more likely to be crime victims (81%) than crime perpetrators (39%). It should be noted that two respondents said they were not sure about the likelihood of immigrants to be perpetrators or victims.

While the aforementioned indicates that law enforcement leaders do not believe by and large that undocumented immigrants perpetrate crime, they have mixed views on the impact that undocumented immigrants have on various offenses. While less than half (44%) indicated that

Figure 2: Likelihood of crime perpetration and victimization

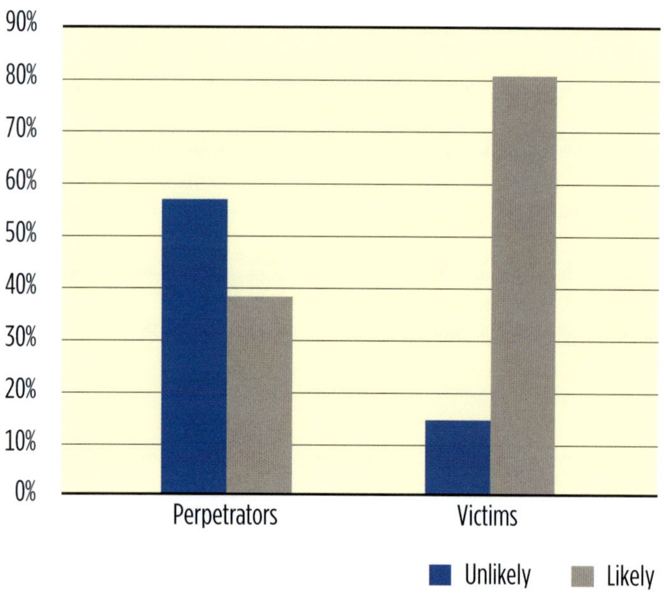

the presence of undocumented immigrants increases violent crime, youth crime (42%), or loitering (46%), half or more of the participants felt their presence increases traffic offenses (75%), drug-related crime (67%), gang-related crime (63%), and property crime (60%), followed by domestic assault and/or battery (52%) and public intoxication (50%).

Local Enforcement of Immigration Law

Nearly half (46%) of the survey respondents indicated that their department has decided not to enter into a partnership with the federal government to enforce immigration law, while almost a quarter (24%) of them considered such action. Conversely, 13% have implemented or are in the process of implementing this relationship, with another 2% planning on doing so. The remaining respondents indicated that their jurisdiction has done none of the above.

Fully 87% of respondents said that aggressive enforcement of immigration law would somewhat or significantly impact budgetary resources in their agencies.

The majority of respondents indicated that aggressive enforcement of immigration law would have a negative impact on community relationships by decreasing: the community trust of the police (74%), trust between community residents (70%), and reporting of both crime victimization (85%) and criminal activity (83%). These important findings underscore the problem local law enforcement would expect to face if they were to aggressively enforce immigration laws.

Adding to those concerns are beliefs that aggressive enforcement of immigration laws would weaken public trust initiatives (77%), community-policing efforts (77%), youth outreach (74%), intelligence/information gathering (63%), criminal investigations (67%), and even recruitment (31%), thereby impacting operations significantly.

At the same time, respondents felt that aggressive enforcement of immigration law would result in a *decrease* in various crimes (see Table 2). Crimes most likely to see a decrease according to the respondents were gang-related crimes (56.5%), while domestic assault and battery (21%) would be impacted the least.

The survey concluded with a request for policies that the respondents have developed or would develop for their agency in order to strike a balance between the enforcement of immigration laws and the protection of civil liberties. There were several respondents who said that they kept or would keep the local role to a minimum by only enforcing immigration law in the event of an arrest (n=11), by leaving the enforcement up to jail officials (n=2), or by not enforcing immigration law at all (n=3). Others offered a more general policy of 'treating everyone fairly' (n=6).

TABLE 2. IMPACT OF AGGRESSIVE ENFORCEMENT ON CRIME

	Expected to Decrease
a. Violent Crimes	37%
b. Property Crimes	37%
c. Gang-Related Crimes	56%
d. Drug-Related Crimes	45%
e. Loitering	46%
f. Domestic Assault/Battery	21%
g. Public Intoxication	38%
h. Traffic Offenses	46%
i. Youth Crime	25%

APPENDIX I

Unauthorized Immigrants: Trends, Characteristics, and Surprises

Jeffrey S. Passel
Pew Hispanic Center — Washington, DC

Unauthorized Immigrants: Trends, Characteristics & Surprises

Pew Hispanic Center
a PewResearchCenter project

Conference on *The Role of Local Police*
Sponsored by the Police Foundation
Washington, DC — August 21, 2008

Immigration as an Issue...

- ***Huge Increase in Immigration***
  - — Population Quadruples 1970-2008
  - — In-flows Increase 4-fold
  - — Undocumented Flows Begin in 1970s
- ***Geographic Dispersal***
  - — Top 6 States had 75% in '90 → 65% today
  - — 80% of Undocs in '90 → <60% in '06
  - — 7-fold increase in "New Destinations"
  - — Nationalized the issue
- ***Young, Working Unauthorized Families***
  - — <25% of Undocumented are "Solo males"
  - — 75% live in Families
  - — 3+ million U.S. Citizen Children in Families

Immigrant Numbers Keep Growing — Percent Approaches Historic Highs

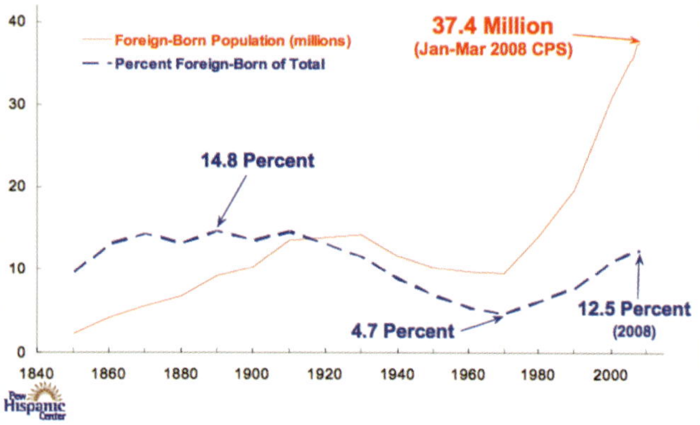

Unauthorized Number High — Trend Uncertain, but Slowing (?)

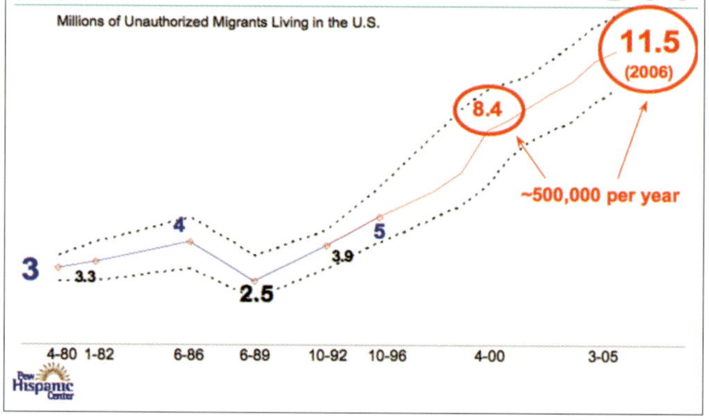

Very Large Recent Cohorts → Large In- & Out-Flows

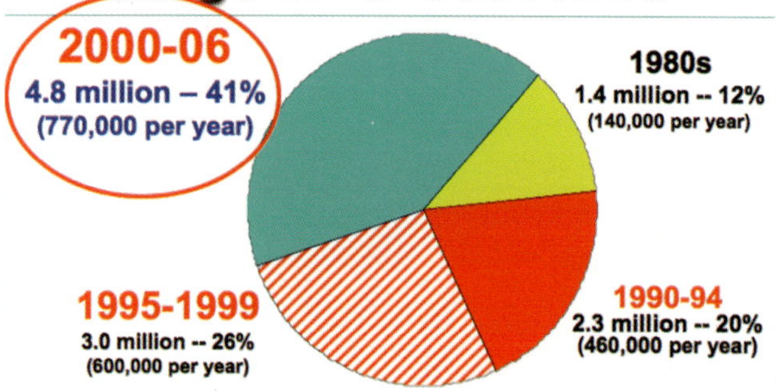

11.5 Million in March 2006
(Analytic estimates)

Legal Status of Immigrants

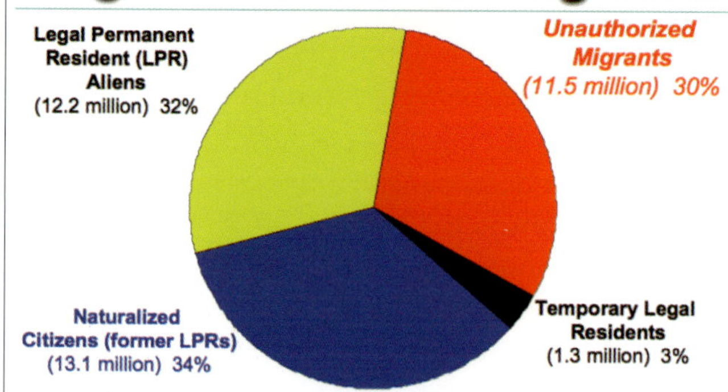

38.1 Million Foreign-Born in 2006

Jeffrey S. Passel is Senior Demographer of the Pew Hispanic Center in Washington, DC.

Unauthorized Immigrants: Trends, Characteristics, and Surprises

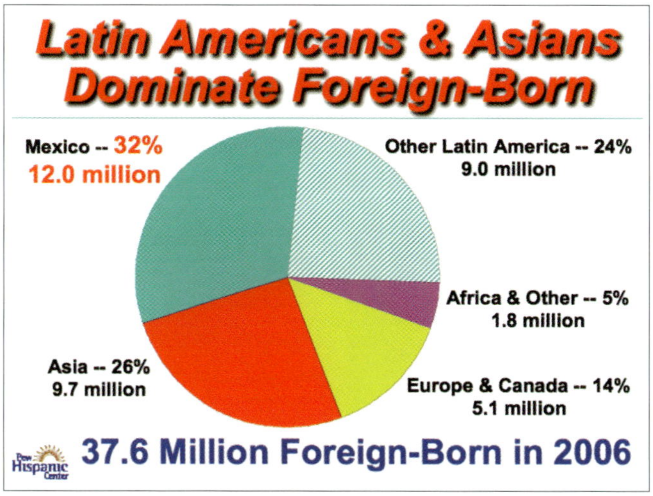

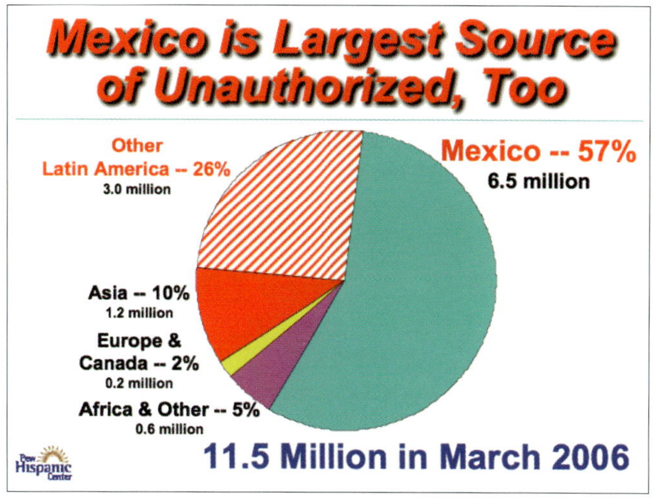

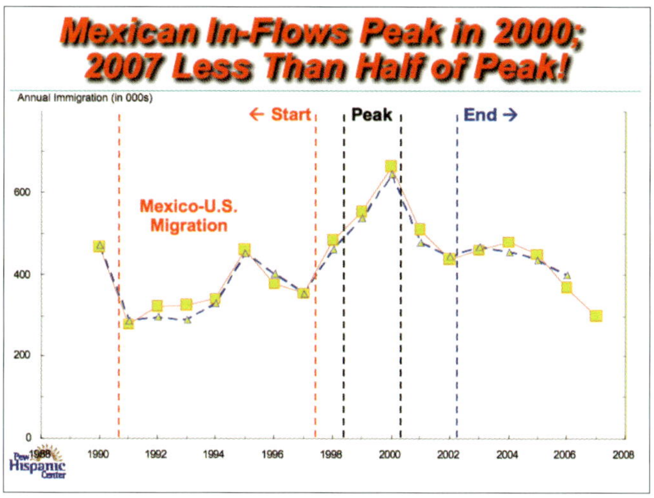

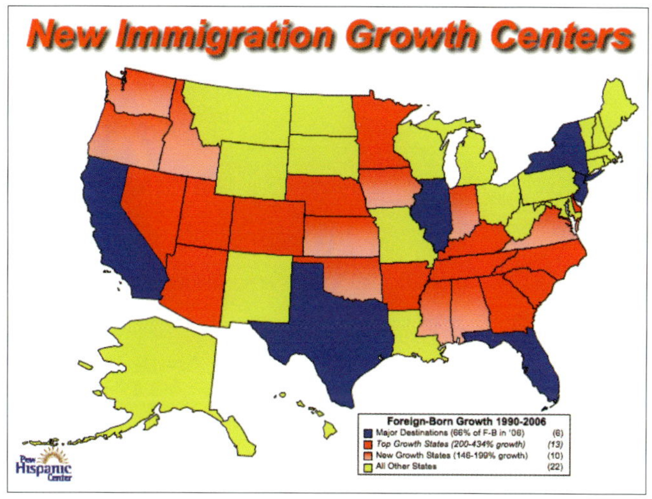

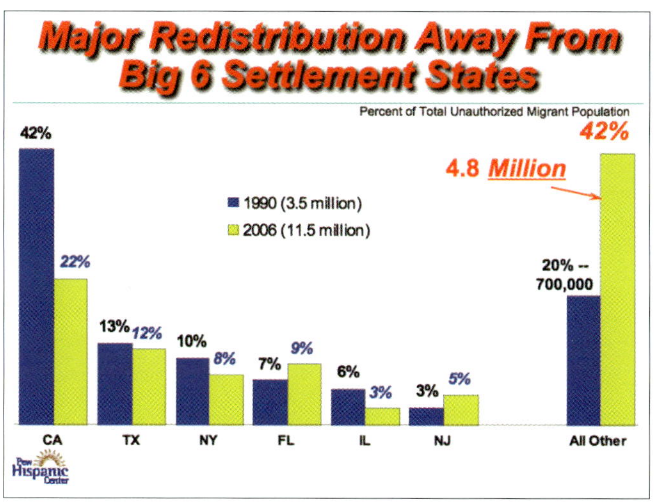

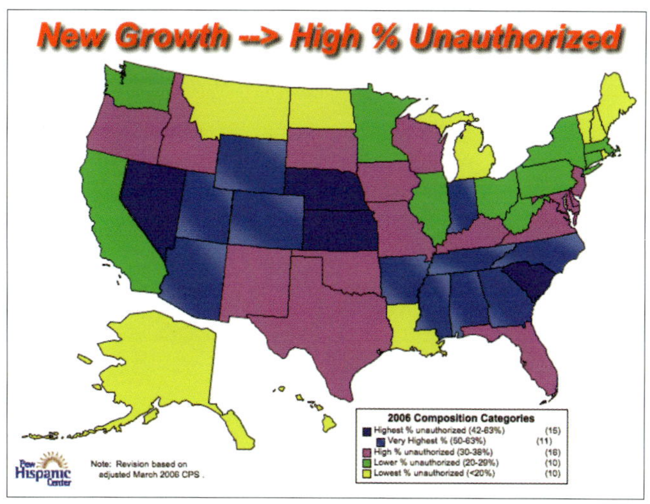

APPENDIX I

Unauthorized Immigrants: Trends, Characteristics, and Surprises

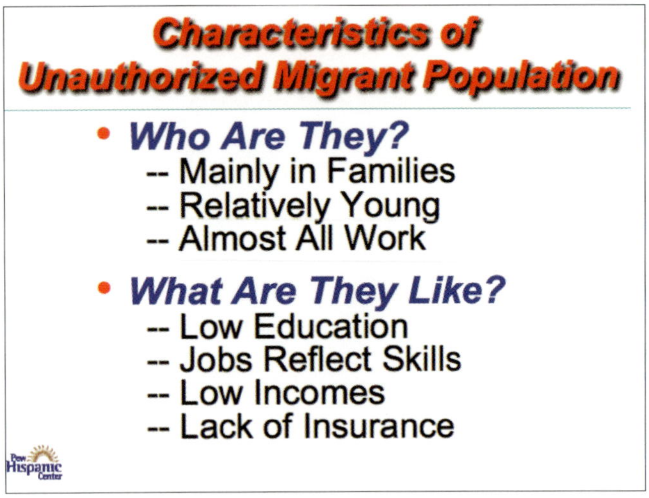

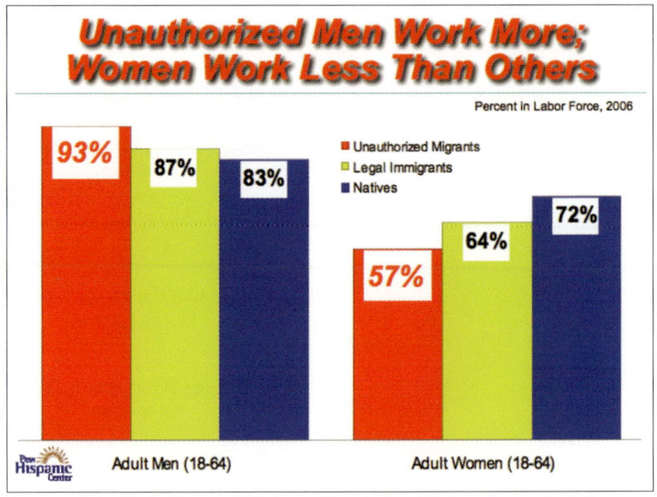

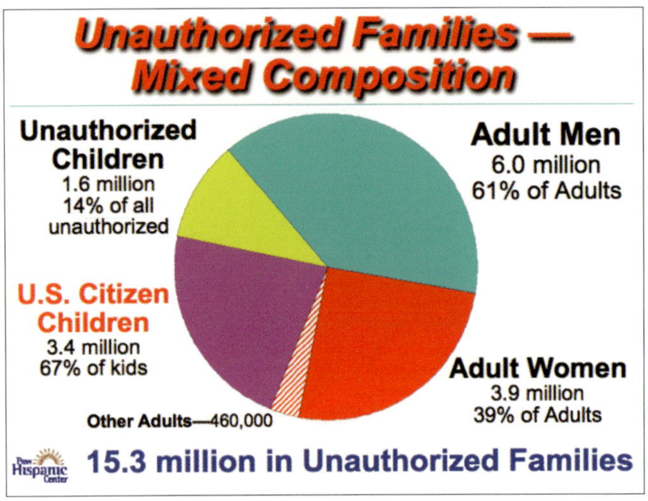

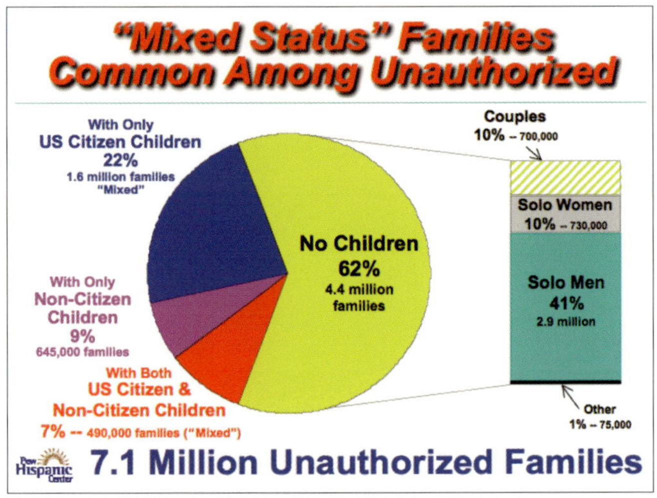

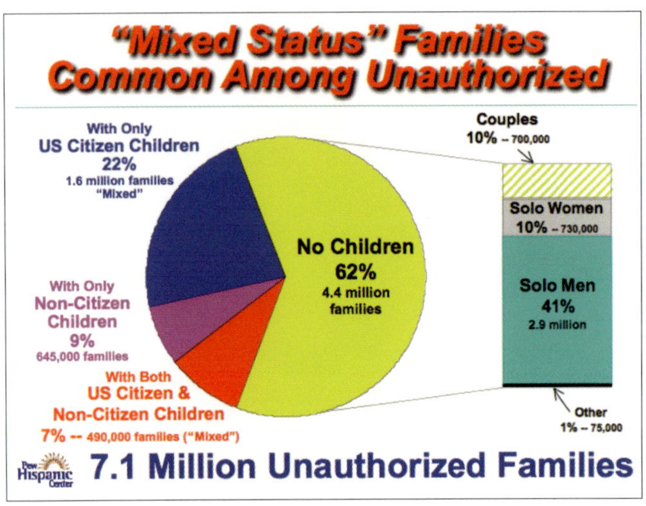

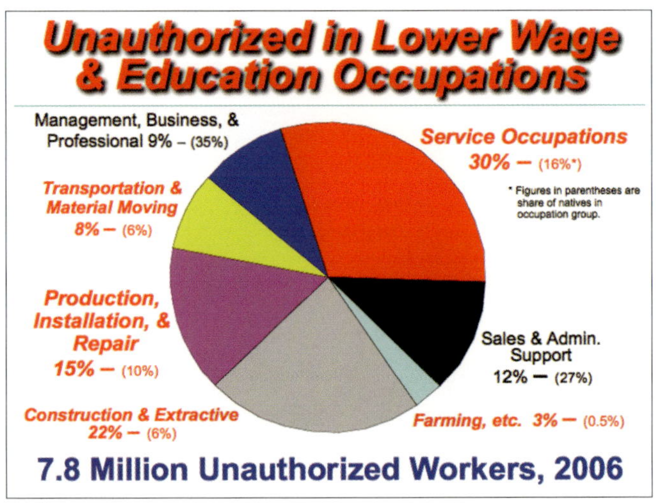

Unauthorized Immigrants: Trends, Characteristics, and Surprises

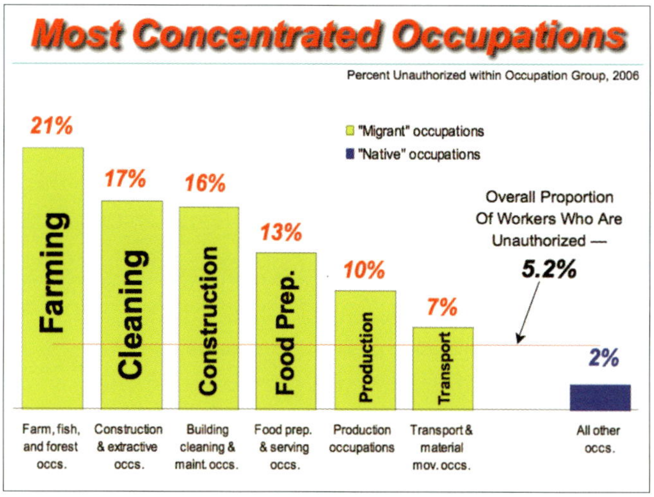

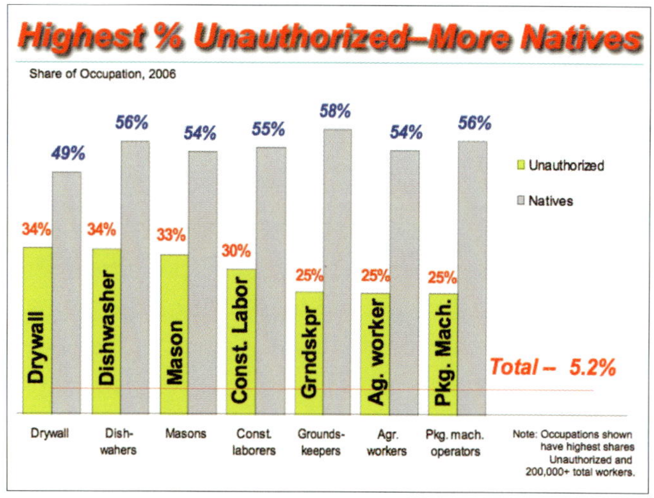

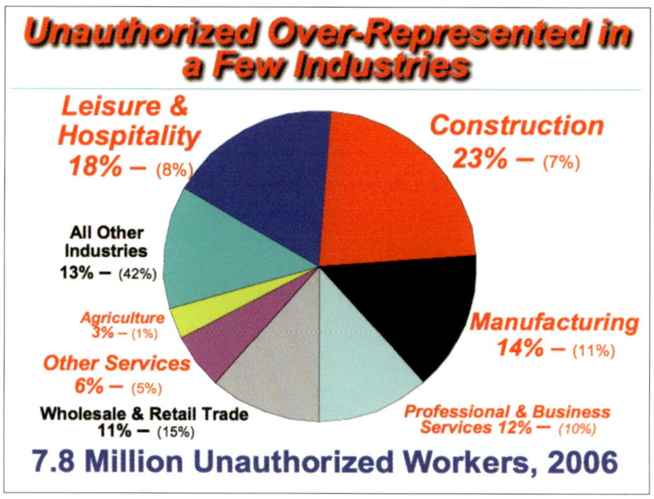

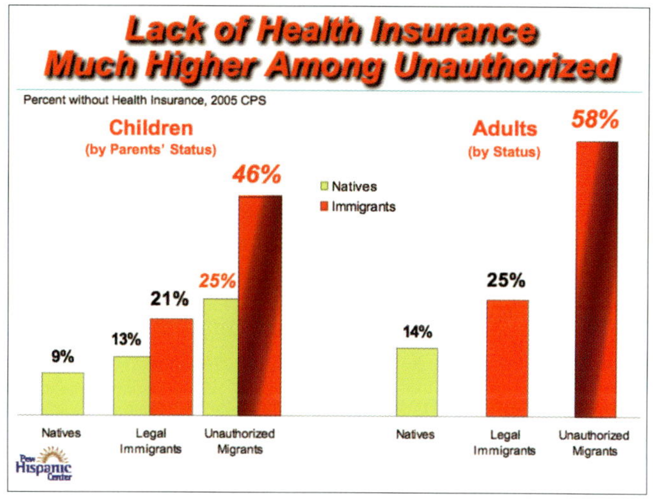

Unauthorized Migration to U.S.

- ***Very Large In-Flows***
  - — Steadily Increasing Population
  - — Slowing Growth (or Decline?)
- ***Largely Mexican & Latino***
  - — No Routes to Green Cards
- ***New Destinations Emerge***
  - — Job Availability in U.S.
  - — Conditions in Mexico & Elsewhere
- ***Majority in Families***
  - — Spouses & Families Follow
  - — 2/3 of Kids Born in U.S.

Pew Hispanic Center

For more information, contact:

Jeffrey S. Passel, Ph.D.
Pew Hispanic Center
Pew Research Center
1615 L St., N.W.
Washington, D.C. 20036

(202) 419-3625
jpassel@pewhispanic.org
www.pewhispanic.org

Pew Hispanic Center

APPENDIX J

Conference Keynote Address

BY MAYOR PHIL GORDON, PHOENIX, ARIZONA

August 21, 2008
JW Marriott Hotel
Washington, D.C.

Before I begin, I just want to recognize all of you—the men and women who risk everything, every single day—and to thank you for your service.

When this nation was founded, no one ever conceived or imagined that immigration enforcement was an issue that would ever fall to mayors and local police departments. But because of federal neglect, here we are. As the federal government continues to do *less* with more, cities are forced to do more with less. Not only are we being forced to step up our immigration efforts but we also have an increased burden when it comes to gun crimes and white-collar crimes connected to illegal immigration and formerly handled at the federal level.

In just the past two years, the Phoenix PD has arrested or turned over to ICE more than 13,000 illegal immigrants. Clearly, the lack of federal enforcement has a direct impact on cities like mine. And cities like yours.

Before I begin detailing that impact, let me give you just a little background on my city. Phoenix, Arizona, is the fifth largest city in the nation, the largest state capital in the United States, and continues to be the fastest growing major city in the nation. Slightly more than 42 percent of our population is Hispanic and, of the 3.4 million people in the greater Phoenix metropolitan area, about 275,000 persons are thought to be here illegally. That is a situation we did not create but it's a situation that we must contend with.

The question I have been asked to address this morning is an important one: What are the costs of enforcing immigration laws at the local level? Obviously, there are economic costs. But some costs go beyond dollars and cents. There are also public safety costs, social costs, and constitutional costs. There are human costs.

Not all can be easily quantified. But let's start with public safety personnel, which *can* be quantified. Quite simply, in order to deal with all the issues caused by our nation's failed immigration policy, local police resources in cities like mine are strained. At a time when our city budget is being otherwise reduced, at a time when we're eliminating positions and imposing hiring freezes in other departments, at a time when programs are being cut, we are hiring 600 new public safety personnel, mostly police officers. A large number of those new officers are the direct result of our growing population, but 100 of those new officers are directly related to the crimes associated with immigration, such as smuggling, kidnapping, and other felonies. And that equates to over $10 million a year.

Those are the basic costs of hiring new officers. But there are other hard costs. The City of Phoenix is paying about $2 million a year in booking costs to Maricopa County to house the illegal immigrants we arrest for committing crimes in our city. That number is growing—and doesn't include our sales and property taxes that help fund the increased jail costs—due to illegal immigration. I personally hand-delivered an invoice to the Department of Homeland Security last year seeking reimbursement for the hard costs directly tied to immigration. Do I expect to recover a single cent? I do not. But for cities like mine, immigration has turned into a de facto unfunded mandate and that's a point that needed to be made and still needs to be made.

Then there are operational costs. In my community, public protests and demonstrations are a regular occurrence, on both sides of the immigration issue. Some protestors on both sides are armed, sometimes with knives and guns, and sometimes with signs like these. For those of you who can't see it, here's what it says: *"Hooray for the slaughtering of the illegals. Boo to the Beaners !!"* And then it's got a swastika at the bottom. You may not yet see this in Des Moines, or in Fargo, or in Dover but you'll see them soon if the federal government doesn't act and act soon. It's hateful stuff and it's dangerous. That means the Phoenix Police Department is called upon to maintain law and order under extremely dangerous conditions and that also means hundreds of thousands of dollars of overtime.

Unique to the immigration issue is the proliferation of "Drop Houses." These are homes, in residential neighborhoods, where dozens of illegal immigrants are warehoused after being brought into the United States by various smuggling syndicates. Phoenix police rescue and turn over to ICE about 1,200 people a year from drop houses. We investigate, track, and break up the human smugglers known as coyotes. By the way, we are one of the very few police departments in the nation to have ten ICE agents embedded within our department on a full-time basis to go after violent criminals who are illegal. That, in terms of both cost and effectiveness, is a much better model for local police departments than taking police officers and turning them into full time immigration agents.

Hand-in-hand with the drop house operations are the kidnapping operations. Almost every night, Phoenix police will get one or more emergency calls with variations of the same story: "My wife is being held in a Phoenix drop house and she will be tortured and killed if we don't pay them thousands of dollars." That means Phoenix PD has to divert resources on the spot to find and protect these kidnap victims. And again, this happens routinely. The overtime hours are staggering and the personnel resources diverted from preventing or solving other crimes are massive.

Lastly, we have the cost of long-term, ongoing undercover and investigative operations designed to cut the head off big smuggling operations—humans, drugs, guns and money—and interrupt that activity, beginning at the top. We've taken down sophisticated syndicates, travel agents, and transportation providers who smuggle and transport humans and who launder millions of dollars in cash each month.

Smuggling operations are becoming more sophisticated and more dangerous, which means local police need more sophisticated intelligence and more strategic undercover work, which means more costs. And as the smugglers use more sophisticated and costly armaments and armor, so must we. Phoenix PD has just begun offering our officers 45-caliber Glocks and adding more rifles to our arsenal.

Then, we have another situation developing in Phoenix that is both difficult to describe and difficult to deal with. It has always been the rule of law enforcement that the victims of crimes and witnesses to crimes will be protected. If the witness to a homicide is in this country illegally, it is more important for us to catch the killer than to turn the witness over to ICE. If the victim of a sexual assault is in this country illegally, it is more important for us to catch the rapist than to turn the victim over to ICE. That makes sense and it's always been the rule. My police department absolutely protects innocent witnesses and victims, in order to catch the "really bad guys." But our job has been made tougher because of a sheriff who doesn't. Instead, he allows sexual assaults, homicides and other serious crimes to go unsolved, by arresting victims and witnesses and sending them to jail for violating immigration statutes. That's a direction that makes our community less safe. And that's a sad reality that creates public safety costs that are impossible to determine.

Targeting illegal immigrants who have not broken a single law since they crossed the border comes at too high a cost for our communities. In order, for example, to concentrate on these immigrants, the county sheriff's operations in El Mirage, Arizona, a city of just 32,000 people, failed to investigate at least thirty violent crimes, including a dozen sexual assaults last year. While crime rates are down in every category in Phoenix, in the parts of the county under the sole jurisdiction of the sheriff, crime rates soared in every category but one last year.

Lastly, the dearest costs we are incurring in our city are social, constitutional and human costs. And again, it centers around our sheriff and a broken federal system.

Maricopa County Sheriff Joe Arpaio has filled a political void created by the utter neglect and inaction on immigration issues by Congress and the president and he has exploited that void to suit his own political needs. Washington's inaction has caused frustration in cities like Phoenix. The sheriff's method is to profile people with brown skin and to ignore the civil rights we should all be enjoying. It is unconstitutional and wrong.

On April 4th, I called for an investigation by the United States Department of Justice for civil rights violations, a call that has yet to be answered. The sheriff, himself, says he doesn't need to engage in racial profiling because he can tell if someone is here illegally "by the way they dress and where they are coming from." That is, as you know, the very definition of racial profiling. One of his chief deputies admits that when it comes to enforcing immigration laws, their department does not follow federal civil rights requirements. *Citizens* are being stopped because they are brown. Immigrants here quite legally, carrying their paperwork, are detained. Street vendors with current visas and properly licensed mobile businesses are also being detained.

I'd like to tell you three quick but important stories that help to humanize these issues. The first is from an editorial in the *Washington Post* that was published earlier this month: *"Manuel Ortega, a Mexican citizen, entered the United States legally last fall, using a visa valid until 2016 as well as a permit from the Department of Homeland Security. Ortega had every reason to believe he was on the right side of the law, except for one small misstep: being brown in Maricopa County.*

"He had been in the United States for barely three weeks last September when Arpaio's deputies stopped the vehicle he was riding in. Despite showing the officers his documents, he was handcuffed, jailed (for 9 hours) and finally turned over to federal immigration officials, who promptly released him..."

That's shameful. And it's a cost no one should have to pay.

Very close to home—a member of my own staff and her husband went "off-roading" with five other couples a few months ago. Deputies pulled all six vehicles over. One by one each couple was approached, and let go—until they got to the last vehicle, the one driven by my assistant and her husband, third generation Americans. The sheriff's deputy didn't ask for a driver's license like he did the others. He asked for a social security card. And he didn't let them go like he did the others. He wrote a citation. Their first names are David and Jessika. And their last name is Rodriquez. And the only thing that made them different from the other five couples was the color of their skin.

Finally, as reported by a Phoenix radio station reporter, a United States Marine, in full uniform, was harassed, insulted, and called a traitor by a group of protestors posing as "Pretend Patriots." *"It's too bad you didn't die in the war; you're a disgrace to your uniform,"* they shouted at him. "*Go back to your own* country." Well, this American hero of Hispanic heritage *is* in his own country. He fought for this country.

These stories have nothing to do with green cards. They have everything to do with brown skin. They were about racism and nothing else. Yet despite these and other blatant violations—well documented in the Phoenix media—the Civil Rights Division of the United States Department of Justice, through its silence, continues to thumb its nose at both civil rights *and* justice.

And how do you assign a cost to that? How can you put a price tag on the very promise of America? Cemeteries here and around the world are filled with men and women who traded their lives for our rights and freedoms—the same rights we see perched at the top of that famously dangerous slippery slope.

Those are big prices to pay. And here's another one. Last September, one of Phoenix's finest—Police Officer Nick Erfle—was shot and killed by a man he was trying to arrest, a man who had been arrested before, found to be in this country illegally, and deported to Mexico by our federal government. Of course, because this Congress and this president have yet to find the time to secure our borders, this man had no problem re-entering the country, and crossing paths with Officer Erfle on that tragically fateful day.

My community paid too much on that day. But not as much as Officer Erfle's wife and children, who will continue to pay for our failed immigration policies and our do-nothing Congress for the rest of their days. Julie Erfle is here today, and will help lead the fight for a secure border and immigration reform so that, hopefully, no other officers and the people who love them will pay the consequences for the inactions of Washington. Julie, will you please join me at the podium as I ask everyone to join with me in thanking you for your service and the sacrifices you continue to make.

Julie, you said it best eight months after Nick's tragic death: *"We need comprehensive immigration reform that puts safety and humanity on equal footing."* And that's why I accepted the invitation to come to Washington today. It is time for the federal government to take responsibility for the situation they have created. They need to take responsibility today. They need to begin addressing each of these complex issues today.

But the good news is they *can* fix the problem. When, as a nation, we roll up our sleeves, focus on a goal, debate our options, outline a course, and act with conviction and principle there is nothing we cannot accomplish. America is a great nation and Americans always live up to that greatness. We have won freedom for much of the world. We have industrialized the world. We have fed the world. In so many ways, we have *changed* the world. And we have shown the ability to change our own nation when change was needed. During my lifetime, African Americans could not use public drinking fountains, sit at lunch counters, or ride in the front of a city bus. But thanks to the greatness of individual Americans like Rosa Parks, Martin Luther King, Jr., and Robert Kennedy, and thanks to a responsible and compassionate Congress and White House, we changed all that. We lived up to the very promise of America. And on the issue of immigration, this nation of immigrants will do it again.

I am calling upon this Congress and the next one—this president and the next one—to make the dual issues of border security and immigration reform their first order of national business. I don't believe that certain members of Congress understand what impact their neglect is having on cities. They don't see the hate. They don't see the division. They don't hear the rhetoric. They don't see the civil rights violations. And they don't understand the costs.

Phoenix is a good community, filled with good people. The many voices of compassion in our community have always prevailed over the voices of hate, racism, and violence. That's why I am calling upon this nation's investigative journalists and other members of the media to come to Phoenix and shine a light on the intolerant few. Let Congress and the White House finally see what their unconscionable neglect is costing us. Report on the racism and the hate. Turn your cameras into the eyes of American citizens whose civil rights don't seem to matter anymore. Help us tell this story to our national leaders and help them—no, *make them*—see the light.

It's been *seven* years since our nation was attacked by terrorists. It's been *four* years since the 9-11 commission made its recommendations. It's been *three* years since the United States House of Representatives debated the Border Protection, Anti-Terrorism and Illegal Immigration Control Act. It's been *two* years since the McCain/Kennedy Comprehensive Immigration Reform Act was defeated. And it's been *eleven months* since we said goodbye to Officer Nick Erfle.

And *still* there is no debate—meaningful or otherwise in House races, in Senate races, or between the two candidates for president of the United States. And that needs to change.

In just the past few days, I was asked by the U.S. Conference of Mayors to head up a Task Force on Immigration Reform, to study the problem and to make recommendations to the 111th Congress and the 44th president.

And I accepted that honor, with one important caveat: No more studying. No more hearings. No more task forces. No more white papers and executive summaries lining the shelves of Congress. This is an issue that has already been studied and studied and studied some more. Now it's time for action. Now it's time to implement.

My message is as simple as it is urgent: Do not wait another day to figure out a way to secure our borders. We need more personnel. We need to make better use of technology. I recently went to the State of Israel. They have, through sheer necessity, figured out how to best secure their own borders. For them, it's a literal matter of life and death. And I say to Washington, "If you can't figure out how to secure our borders, then ask the Israelis for their advice and counsel." I say to Washington, "If the greatest technological nation in the world can't do it, bring in someone who can."

Second, I call upon Congress to change our failed immigration policies. For our economy and for the foreign workers who need to support their families, let's use the technology that is available to match up the skills of these workers with jobs in this country that are going unfilled. Make the work visa program make sense. And because half the immigrants who are in our country illegally entered the United States quite legally but overstayed their visas, Congress needs to make this new visa system completely trackable.

Third, not everyone who comes here to work will want to become a citizen. But for those who do, we need a pathway to citizenship that doesn't stretch out for ten years or more, the way it does now. You wonder why so many ignore the system and come here illegally? It's because a ten year-plus process is no process at all. It is broken and it is ours to fix.

Fourth, we need to recognize the human side of immigration. Consider a grandmother who has lived here peacefully for decades, who has worked and raised a family, and paid taxes and contributed to our social fabric and our economy—treating *her* the very same way we treat a drug dealer who is in the United States illegally makes no sense at all. We should never paint with a brush that broad. We need to recognize different circumstances and treat them differently.

Two years ago, the Western Governors' Association, under the leadership of Arizona Governor Janet Napolitano, issued a policy resolution very much like the proposal I just outlined. It, too, is a reasonable proposal that a reasonable Congress should use as a road map. But here we are, two years later, and that map still sits folded in some Congressional cloakroom.

So one of the main reasons I'm here today is to force the Congress of the United States to face the two-headed monster of hate and racism it has created and turned loose 2,000 miles from this very room.

If you're a member of Congress, or the next president of the United States, you'll be hearing from me. And when you do, I'll be standing right next to Julie Erfle because I want you to look into her eyes and to see for yourself what the cost of your inaction has been.

So, again, the research has been done and the papers have been written. Our mission is to obtain the full backing of the US Conference of Mayors, law enforcement groups like this one, the United States Chamber of Commerce, the faith community and with the support of the Western Governors' Association march over to Capitol Hill, proposal in hand, and knock Congress upside its partisan head with it and tell them to fix... the damn...problem.

Thank you and God bless you.

Now, with the chair's permission, I'd be happy to take a couple of questions.

APPENDIX K

Collier County Sheriff's Office Criminal Alien Task Force An Overview of the 287(g) Program: Strategy, Outcomes and Benefits of the Partnership

BY DON HUNTER

Introduction and Background

There are an estimated 11.5-12 million illegal immigrants living in the U.S.[1] In January 2007, the Collier County Sheriff's Office determined approximately one-quarter of the jail population was comprised of illegally-present foreign nationals. At this time, the cost to house illegal immigrants committing crimes in Collier County totaled more than $9 million per year.[2] In addition, it was determined that approximately 40 percent of total felony warrants and 60 percent of murder warrants were for illegally-present foreign nationals.

The Sheriff's Office began formal efforts to address the problem of jail overcrowding and escalating costs associated with detaining criminal aliens. In June 2007, the Collier County Sheriff's Office entered into a Memorandum of Agreement (MOA) with the United States Immigration and Customs Enforcement (ICE), a component of the Department of Homeland Security (DHS). Among other things, the MOA outlines the purpose, authority, policy, training, ICE supervision and length of agreement.

Initially, in September 2007, 27 members of the agency graduated from extensive ICE training. In August 2008, another seven members of the agency graduated from ICE training. These members are authorized to perform certain immigration enforcement functions as specified in the MOA and Section 287(g) of the Immigration and Nationality Act. From this authority, the Collier County Sheriff's Office developed the Criminal Alien Task Force (CATF).

CATF Strategy

The agency designated members from various disciplines throughout the agency to receive the ICE training and certification. These members function under the authority and direction provided by the MOA. The various agencywide components are critical to the CATF strategy. In addition, the strategy outlines key concepts such as operational flexibility, and clear understanding and communication agencywide and with ICE.

CATF Agency Components

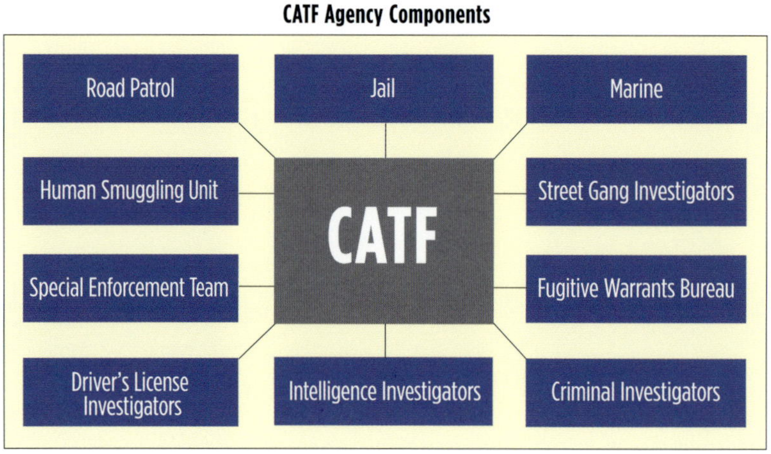

Don Hunter was elected sheriff of Collier County, Florida, in 1988 and served in that office for twenty years.

Collier County Sheriff's Office Criminal Alien Task Force An Overview of the 287(g) Program: Strategy, Outcomes and Benefits of the Partnership

Corrections Component and Process

- CATF members initiate contact with newly arrested and/or already detained inmates to determine legal status in the U.S.
- Fingerprints and identification documents are used to search several databases, including the ICE Identification System.
- Subjects qualifying for detainers enter the detention and removal process.
- A deportation file (including arrest report, criminal history, detain order, etc.) is sent to ICE.
- Upon final order from a Federal Immigration Judge, deportation orders are processed.
- Subject is removed from the country once all sentences have been served.

Law Enforcement Component

Phase 1: CATF members identify violent criminal aliens, including gang members, violent felony offenders, career criminals and sexual predators. The primary goal is to apprehend violent criminal aliens representing the greatest threat to residents in Collier County.

Phase 2: CATF members identify other felony criminal aliens, including those charged with identify theft, narcotics and fraud.

Phase 3: CATF members concentrate on lower level crime, such as DUI and driving without a license. In addition, the CATF educates the community, particularly assisting local employers to assure they are hiring authorized workers.

In all phases, no arrest is made until the subject is approved by ICE. Removing the most serious and violent offenders, as outlined in Phase I, will always remain a priority.

CATF — Descriptive Statistics and Program Activity

Corrections (October 1, 2007 – August 1, 2008)

Interviews Conducted – In the jail, a total of 4,147 inmate interviews have been conducted to determine legal status. Of those, 2,867 inmates (69%) were illegally present in the country and 1,271 (31%) were legally present.

Detainers Placed for Removal	No.
Entry without Inspection (EWI)	340
Final Orders	137
Re-Entries	102
Legal Permanent Resident (LPR)	32
Overstays (expired Visas)	11
Total Detainers Placed	622*

*25 lifted for various reasons for a total of 597 cases

Status of Detained Criminal Aliens	No.
Removed from the U.S.	344
In Collier County Custody	130
In ICE or U.S. Marshal Custody	74
Transferred to Other Facilities	38
Case Terminated or Posted Bond	11
Total Cases	597

APPENDIX K

Collier County Sheriff's Office Criminal Alien Task Force An Overview of the 287(g) Program: Strategy, Outcomes and Benefits of the Partnership

Detainers Placed for Removal

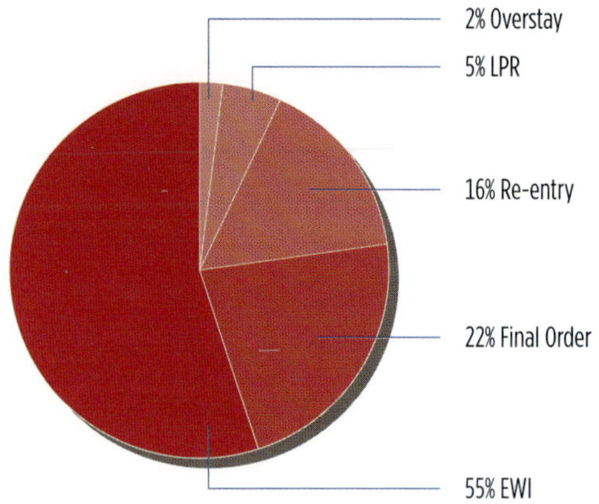

Status of Detained Criminal Aliens

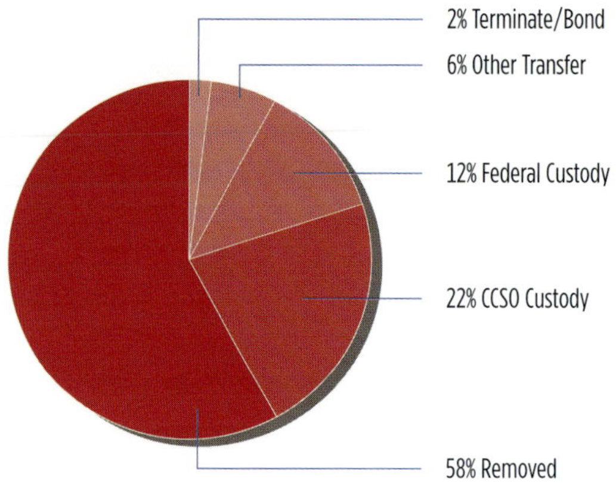

Prior Arrest History — The total number of arrest charges for criminal aliens identified in the jail and detained for removal is 3,993 (2,899 misdemeanor and 1,094 felony arrest charges). On average, each criminal alien has 1.8 prior felony and 4.8 prior misdemeanor arrest charges, for a total of nearly seven (7) prior arrest charges each.

Jail Population — Overall, in 2008, the jail population has been at lower levels when compared to the same month in 2007. The time period of January through July 2007 was prior to CATF implementation (the CATF was implemented in the jail in October 2007). So far, the largest drop by month has been in July 2008, with a 14 percent decrease in the jail population from the previous year.

Average daily jail population 2007-2008, monthly comparison.

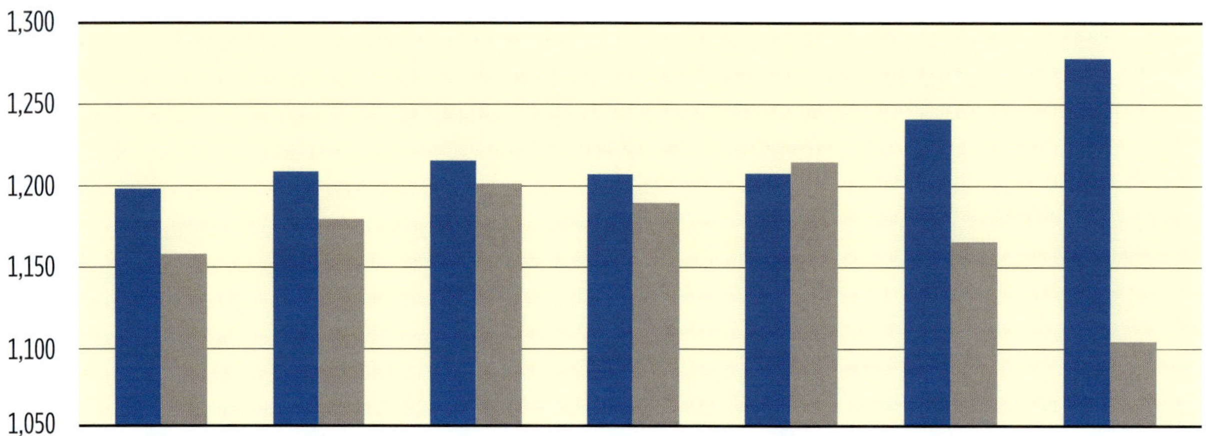

	Jan.	Feb.	Mar.	Apr.	May	June	July
2007	1,198	1,209	1,215	1,209	1,209	1,245	1,282
2008	1,159	1,180	1,202	1,192	1,214	1,170	1,107

APPENDIX K

Collier County Sheriff's Office Criminal Alien Task Force An Overview of the 287(g) Program: Strategy, Outcomes and Benefits of the Partnership

Law Enforcement (October 30, 2007 – August 10, 2008)

Investigations - Status	No.
Approved by ICE - detained by CATF	68
Approved by ICE - not yet located by CATF	35
Current Investigation	32
Pending ICE Approval	15
Detained by Other Agency	10
Total Investigations	160*

*CATF conducted 210 preliminary investigations; 50 did not meet standards to continue into formal investigations

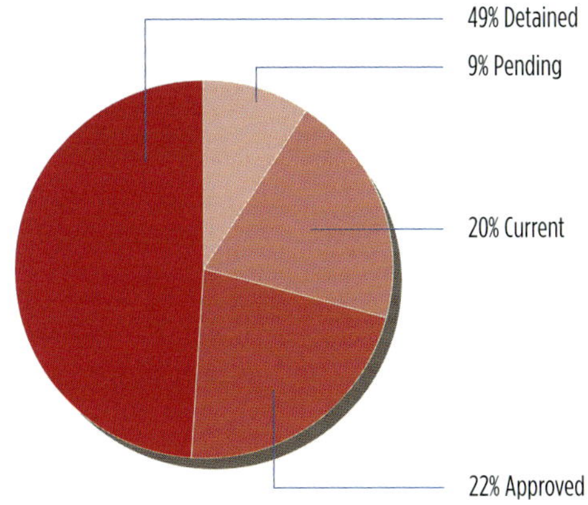

Prior Arrest Charges—Criminal aliens detained by CATF investigations have extensive prior arrest histories—a combined total of more than 1,300 prior criminal charges. On average, each criminal alien removed by CATF investigations has more than nine (9) previous arrest charges—with an average of 3.7 felony and 5.6 misdemeanor prior arrest charges each.

In this chart, person crimes include robbery, sexual assault, assault and battery, stalking and kidnapping. Property crimes include burglary and theft charges. Disorder crimes include disorderly conduct, disturbing the peace and resisting arrest. Traffic crimes include DUIs and all other traffic-related violations.

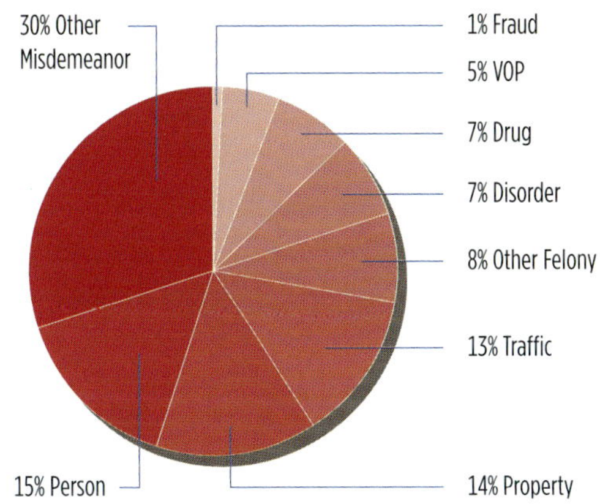

Examples of Phase I Cases—CATF investigations have apprehended and detained many violent, felony career criminals who otherwise would not have been identified.

- Subject with multiple prior arrests for robbery, burglary, drug/cocaine, and firearm charges was apprehended by CATF and charged federally. He used a false birth certificate to obtain US ID, including a passport and driver's license.
- Subject was previously arrested on multiple occasions for molesting children. He was apprehended by CATF investigations before he could reoffend.
- Subject had been previously deported and had a warrant in another state for rape of a child with a firearm. He is suspected of murdering his eight-month-old daughter and has been arrested by CATF on immigration charges.
- Subject is a documented MS-13 gang member previously deported from another state after a gang-related shooting. He traveled to Collier County and has been arrested and detained by CATF on immigration charges.

APPENDIX K

Collier County Sheriff's Office Criminal Alien Task Force An Overview of the 287(g) Program: Strategy, Outcomes and Benefits of the Partnership

Country of Origin — Due to geographic location, most illegally-present criminal aliens detained and removed by CATF are from Mexico (on average, 60 percent). However, the CATF has identified and interviewed aliens from more than 50 countries. These countries include:

Albania	Costa Rica	Iran	Russia
Argentina	Cuba	Israel	Scotland
Australia	Czech Republic	Jamaica	Slovakia
Bahamas	Dominican Republic	Jordan	South Africa
Bangladesh	Ecuador	Kazakhstan	South Korea
Belize	El Salvador	Mexico	St. Lucia
Bolivia	England	Nicaragua	Thailand
Brazil	Germany	Nigeria	Trinidad & Tobago
Bulgaria	Guatemala	Panama	Turkey
Canada	Haiti	Peru	Turks & Caicos
Chile	Honduras	Philippines	Uruguay
China	Hungary	Poland	Venezuela
Colombia	India	Romania	Vietnam

CATF Benefits

This program promotes community safety, reduces jail overcrowding, reduces victimization and provides cost savings for Collier County. Early outcomes and indicators are promising. Our jail population has been reduced and our crime rate continues to decline, a remarkable accomplishment particularly in this difficult economy.

Further, this program has greatly improved intelligence gathering and identification—a critical element in local enforcement in our country's post-9/11 environment. Through this program, the Collier County Sheriff's Office has been able to identify very violent criminal predators, including sexual offenders and gang members, using fraudulent identities to further their criminal careers. Without the necessary resources and support to pursue criminal investigations, these offenders would not be identified, arrested and removed from our country.

Endnotes

[1]Pew Hispanic Center, *Size and Characterisics of the Unauthorized Migrant Population in the U.S.*, March 2006.

[2]Cost was determined based on the number of self-admitting illegal immigrants, calculated at several times throughout the year. This does not include other justice costs such as court costs and victim services.

APPENDIX L

Fear, Crime, and Community Trust: Community Perspectives on Immigration Enforcement by Local Police

Statement by Kareem Shora, JD, LLM
National Executive Director
American-Arab Anti-Discrimination Committee (ADC)

August 21-22 2008
JW Marriott Hotel
Washington, DC

On behalf of the American-Arab Anti-Discrimination Committee (ADC), I wish to thank the Police Foundation for this valuable opportunity. As key stakeholders and community partners, we welcome the positive efforts already undertaken by the Police Foundation in coordination with key local law enforcement agencies in addressing the vital issues of trust, fear and crime prevention. My statement will highlight some of the challenges encountered by the Arab- and Muslim-American communities in the area of civil rights and liberties as a result of certain U.S. government policies that have involved local law enforcement agency enforcement of federal immigration law and the impact this has had on the ability of our communities to actively participate, as members of civil society, in reaching our full potential in assisting legitimate efforts aimed at combating crime in all its forms.

ADC is the largest grassroots organization in the United States dedicated to protecting the civil rights and liberties of Arab Americans. ADC was established in 1980 by a former U.S. senator and has grown into a national organization with headquarters in Washington D.C., fully staffed regional offices in Massachusetts, New York, New Jersey, Michigan, and California, as well as 38 volunteer-based chapters throughout the United States.

The unfortunate, ineffective, and cosmetic actions undertaken by the U.S. government in the days, weeks, and months following the horrific September 11, 2001, terrorist attacks on our nation left a bitter taste within the Arab, Muslim, and South Asian American communities and a mark of shame on the fabric of our American society. To be just, in the past several years some government agencies have undertaken constructive proactive steps at regular dialogue with the ADC and the Arab, Muslim, and South Asian American communities. Many local police agencies have taken the lead, utilizing the time proven method of "community policing" to build trust and work with the communities to protect and serve everyone regardless of race, religion, gender, age, or ethnicity.

Security cannot be assessed in a vacuum and must be addressed in light of the challenges encountered by members of most communities in the areas of civil and human rights and liberties as a result of some government domestic policies with mandates to combat terrorism. We also cannot ignore popular culture's and the media's portrayal of Muslims and Arabs, as well as some of the recent hateful rhetoric made by some of our elected officials. One cannot ignore practices which have involved some U.S. government agencies—practices that violate international human rights standards and U.S. constitutional standards—such as extraordinary rendition and secret detentions, the continuing controversy of the Guantanamo enemy combatant detentions, or the Abu Ghoraib torture scandal, all of which are factors in drumming up hate targeted against Arabs and Muslims.

The need for such an assessment is vital in understanding the negative perceptions and stigmas associated with anti-Muslim discrimination and the impact this has had on the relationship between these communities and local law enforcement. We must acknowledge and understand that some U.S. government policies designed to combat terrorism have both proven ineffective in fulfilling their mandates and have had a devastating impact on the ability of the Arab and Muslim communities to actively participate, as members of their communities, in reaching our full potential as full partners with the police.

Some of the policies the U.S. government undertook following the horrific September 11, 2001, terrorist attacks on our nation and some more recent decisions made in the name of combating terrorism have made it easier for those who promote hate, perpetuate violent extremism and radicalization, and others who engage in hate and anti-Muslim discrimination to operate regardless of the legal protections often afforded later to their respective victims.

I would like to highlight a few challenges that have involved local police and the enforcement of federal immigration law, challenges that have caused additional strain on already overburdened police agencies and, at the same time, served to negatively impact the trust and communication that is required to maintain a safe and law abiding community that is free of crime. These policies include targeted immigration enforcement measures such as the National Security Entry-Exit Registration System (NSEERS), also know as "special registration;" perceived racial profiling in the approach to conduct voluntary interviews by the FBI in partnership with local police agencies; the increased reliance on the "watch" and "no fly" lists (also known as the "terrorism watch list"); the Immigration Absconder Apprehension Initiative which, in 2002, targeted immigration absconders based specifically on national origin; and, most damaging to local police, the deeply flawed and now discredited reports by local law enforcement agencies, including the New York City Police Department (NYPD), advocating increased scrutiny of Muslims in the U.S. based on cultural affiliation and religious practices.

As you might have read or heard in recent high-profile media reports, some accounts have claimed that the U.S. government "terrorism watch list" now contains over one million names or records. Anecdotal examples suggest that Arab, Muslim, and South Asian Americans are more likely to be flagged by this watch list. Local police agencies are required to enforce this list when they conduct routine traffic enforcement, given that the list is maintained as part of the National Crime Information Center (NCIC) database operated by the FBI and accessed by all local law enforcement agencies. Although the U.S. government's position states that it does not profile individuals based on race, ethnicity, or religion, the "watch" and "no fly" list challenges, and the involvement of local police with this controversy, have created a tremendous level of mistrust and the perception of ethnic and racial profiling in Arab, Muslim, and South Asian American populations. It is clear that local police agencies have inherited, sometimes involuntarily, the mistakes born out of the federal government.

Another example is NSEERS or "special registration." NSEERS is a poorly constructed program that has outlived any constructive purpose it may have once served and is in need of replacement by the more extensive and reliable US-VISIT program. US-VISIT relies on biometric technology to obtain information about anyone entering the United States. While the port-of-entry phase of this program has been implemented, we are hopeful that the U.S. government, namely the United States

Congress, will provide the necessary funding for US-VISIT so that it can be fully implemented at ports of departure.

The U.S. Department of Justice (DOJ) created NSEERS, also known as "special registration," in 2002 allegedly as an anti-terrorism program that required male visitors from certain countries—and others whom an immigration inspector decides meet certain confidential criteria—to be fingerprinted, photographed, and questioned by immigration officers. The most controversial part of this program, known as the "domestic call-in" phase, required men from twenty-five predominantly Muslim and Arab countries to report to immigration offices around the country for fingerprints, photographs, and lengthy questioning by officers. There are criminal and civil penalties associated with NSEERS, including arrest, detention, monetary fines, and/or removal from the United States.

Although initially portrayed by the Department of Justice (and, in turn, understood by those who voluntarily complied with the program) as a tool to combat terrorism following the devastating terrorist attacks against our country on September 11, 2001, NSEERS has apparently become just another tool used in immigration law enforcement, and law enforcement more generally. NSEERS raises serious constitutional issues since the program discriminates on the basis of national origin and it further burdens local police with enforcing yet another federal program without receiving additional funding or resources.

Indeed, like the "watch list," NSEERS is also part of the National Crime Information Center (NCIC) database maintained by the FBI and routinely enforced by local police. A system designed to arrest those who are alleged to have committed serious crimes, such as bank robberies, murder, child molestation, and rape, is now using limited police resources to arrest or detain civil immigration violators. Ironically, it was those who complied with NSEERS that were subject to penalty. Nearly 14,000 men who complied with call-in registration were placed in removal proceedings. If a goal of special registration was to track possible terrorists, deporting those who complied with the program undermines this aim, by reducing future compliance and serving to destroy trust between the police and the community.

Because of the poor implementation of NSEERS, thousands of men who were required to register failed to do so—many no doubt due to lack of notice—and are therefore now vulnerable to NSEERS penalties. Although the NSEERS program was modified in December 2004, many elements remain and are subject to abuse, including departure registration, registration at ports of entry, as well as the potential for the re-initiation of domestic "call-ins" and enforcement action based on information collected through the program.

While some Bush administration officials have expressed apprehension about the continued use of NSEERS, the program is still being utilized. In fact, Asa Hutchinson, former Undersecretary of Border and Transportation Security at DHS, recognized the problems with NSEERS and has gone on record as saying "It is our hope to completely end this special registration program because our long-term goal is to treat everybody the same way and not based upon where you come from" (June 11, 2004, speech to ADC National Convention, Washington, D.C.).

It should be noted that the perceived injustice of singling out people based on national origin (and ultimately religion) and, in turn, penalizing them for their cooperation with a government program may have significantly harmed the relationship of trust between law enforcement and the Arab and Muslim American and immigrant communities—a relationship that is vital to the national security of the United States.

ADC has diligently sought to cast a public light on the NSEERS program and has maintained a dialogue with DOJ and DHS in hopes of curbing abuses of the program and ultimately seeing it retired. However, ADC's repeated efforts to obtain information on implementation and use of the NSEERS program and resulting databases have been rebuffed and multiple FOIA requests have gone unanswered, either under the guise of the "law enforcement exception" or have simply been ignored.

More recently, the U.N. Committee on the Elimination of Racial Discrimination (CERD) stated, in its February 2008 recommendations to the United States, that "Measures taken in the fight against terrorism must not discriminate, in purpose or effect, on the grounds of race, color, descent, or national or ethnic origin." The CERD urged the U.S. "to put an end to the National Security Entry-Exit Registration System (NSEERS) and to eliminate other forms of racial profiling against Arabs, Muslims, and South Asians."

I would like to describe a case example of the negative impact and fear the enforcement of federal immigration law by local police has had on the Arab, Muslim, and South Asian communities. In February of 2004, ADC was contacted by Mr. X. Mr. X is a United States citizen who lives in Tennessee and owns a small business. In February of 2004, Mr. X drove to a neighboring town in Mississippi to park one of his driver's cars and pick up his personal vehicle. When he arrived, Mr. X noticed a police car shining the lights on his vehicle. When Mr. X got out of the car while speaking on his cell phone, the officer pulled a gun and asked him not to move. The officer allegedly started screaming and asking Mr. X to put his cell phone down. Mr. X allegedly complied and within minutes three more sheriff cars arrived and with guns drawn the officers shouted, "Don't move or we will kill you. Any sudden moves, we will kill you!"

Complying with police orders, Mr. X got on the ground and placed his hands behind his back. The police handcuffed him and threw his money and wallet on the ground. Mr. X allegedly heard one of the officers using a cell phone, calling what appeared to be the FBI and saying, "We got him, we got him!" Mr. X alleged that while he was handcuffed and on the ground the other three officers continued to point their guns at him shouting, "If you move, we will kill you!"

Mr. X alleged that one of the sheriff deputies said, "I want to see your nose touching the ground. I know your kind of people; I worked for the CIA for ten years," all the while pointing his weapon at him and saying, "If you breathe wrong, I will kill you!" Mr. X alleged that the same officer said, "You need to go back to whatever Sand Ni**er country you came from," and he then allegedly called Mr. X a terrorist and a baby killer. Mr. X further alleged that the officer asked him if he was scared and then added, "Your kind of people don't care if they die. I want to see your nose touching the ground, you terrorist!" The officer allegedly kept walking back and forth, repeating his threats and racial epithets.

Mr. X reported that while this was taking place, the other officers were on their phones saying that his name came up on a terrorist watch list. The older officer who initially stopped Mr. X found a handgun permit in his wallet. He walked to Mr. X with his gun drawn and said, "I found a gun permit; don't let me find a gun or I will shoot you with it." Mr. X then alleged that a third officer walked to him and asked whether the car is "going to blow up in my face" if he turns on the ignition. Mr. X was then allegedly asked by the same officer whether Mr. X knew how to fly airplanes.

After over an hour on the ground, Mr. X saw his driver, the owner of the car approach. He later told Mr. X that he saw him on the ground and heard one of the police officers call him a baby killer. The driver also reported that he was asked by the police, "Why did you let him use your car? He is a well known terrorist. His information came up on our computer."

Finally, the officers took Mr. X's handcuffs off and permitted him to collect his belongings. One of the officers asked, "Do you know why we stopped you?" Mr. X said, "No, it doesn't make any sense to me, what you did does not make any sense to me." Mr. X then walked to the officer that called him a baby killer to ask why he was treated in this fashion, and the officer allegedly responded by yelling, "If you don't get out of (Mississippi) we will take you in!" and a second officer allegedly yelled, "If I see you back in Mississippi, I will personally kill you!"

Mr. X was permitted to leave with no federal agents being involved and without being read his Miranda rights or being arrested or charged with anything. When Mr. X got in his car he called the FBI in Memphis and gave them a description of the incident and the officers involved. He then called the FBI office in Jackson, Tennessee, and provided the same information. After a week, an FBI special agent interviewed both Mr. X and his witness and recommended that Mr. X file an internal affairs complaint with the same sheriff's department whose officers allegedly were involved in the incident. The sheriff's department failed to investigate the incident or address Mr. X's concerns. Unfortunately, when ADC filed a complaint with the DOJ Civil Rights Division, asking for an investigation, and when Mr. X followed up with the FBI on this matter, he received a letter from the DOJ Civil Rights Division, Criminal Section, stating that no further action would be taken by the DOJ and telling him he may wish to pursue the matter in civil court.

In conclusion, government agencies, including law enforcement agencies, have taken many proactive steps at constructive dialogue and communication in the past few years. These steps have gone a long way in improving trust and in turn effectively combating crime. However, the unfortunate policies I have mentioned here continue to reverberate with their negative and destructive effects on the Arab, Muslim, and South Asian communities and on the relationship between those communities and local police.

The lesson we have learned as a people is not to strip the most valuable treasure we have as a nation by ignoring the basic rights and liberties and inherently weakening the great American values of freedom, fairness, and equality we have championed for decades. With the exception of our friends in the Native American nations, we are indeed a nation of immigrants. Our African-American communities are primarily here as a result of another historical injustice, namely slavery, a form of cruel involuntary immigration. Most of the rest of us are here because of the great immigration tradition that has crafted this mosaic we hold so dear.

Thank you.

APPENDIX M
Remarks

By Julie Erfle

August 21-22 2008
JW Marriott Hotel
Washington, DC

It would have been easy to cling to hate when my husband was killed last September. I was certainly angry. Angry that my husband—a good man, a wonderful father, a two-time cancer survivor, a highly decorated officer—was killed by a street thug with a record almost as long as his life. It would have been easy to say, "Deport his family, deport them all!" They killed my husband, and they deserve no mercy. They showed no mercy for Nick, no mercy for me or my children, or the hundreds of other family members and friends and fellow officers left to pick up the pieces of their lives.

Except, "they" didn't kill Nick. A felon named Eric Martinez killed my husband, and Eric Martinez isn't a "they." But he certainly is a powerful example of a failed immigration policy, isn't he?

When Nick was killed, I knew deep in my heart that there had to be some greater purpose, some deeper meaning for his senseless death. I found that reason when just hours later, the media focus turned to the immigration status of his killer. It was then that the cries for deportation began, the lines were drawn, the political pundits on their game. They all had an opinion and they also had a great deal of anger and hate to go with it.

In some ways, I wished I could have joined in the yelling matches, screamed my way out of my pain, and found reasons as to why simple deportation was the answer. Except it wasn't that easy for me, and I knew better. I wanted the answer, the solution. So I did my research, read about the issue, talked to the real experts in the field like immigration attorneys and law enforcement officers—those dealing with this issue every day—and I listened to others like me who lived with the consequences of a failed system. And that's when I realized that it's a little more complex than some of our politicians and media would have us believe.

But I also realized that there were and are solutions out there. This issue has been researched very thoughtfully by people who are not seeking political office or hyped-up listeners to bolster their ratings. It isn't just a pro- or anti-immigration or Republican or Democratic solution. There *is* middle ground. We've just failed in our efforts to make that the focus of our discussions.

And so that's why I'm here today, to work with individuals, like Mayor Gordon, who have decided the time to move this discussion forward is now. I have asked the mayor and others to join me in supporting a comprehensive immigration policy outline put forth by the Western Conference of Governors. The mayor will address this policy in more detail shortly but know that this policy outline addresses all major areas of concern within the immigration debate. I hope you will join us in pushing this policy forward.

I will not stand idly by and wait for the day when our legislators finally decide, "Now is the time for action." That time has passed and, sadly, some of us have paid dearly because of it. Let's not wait any longer for a solution. The lives of our officers and their families are far, far too precious to just stand by and wait.

Julie Erfle is an advocate for immigration reform. The widow of Phoenix police officer Nick Erfle, she lives in Phoenix with her two children.

APPENDIX N

Conference Agenda and Presenters' Bios

WEDNESDAY, AUGUST 20		
4:00-7:00 pm	**Registration**	
THURSDAY, AUGUST 21		
7:00-8:00 am	**Registration/Continental breakfast**	
PLENARY **8:00-8:15 am**	**Opening remarks**	Hubert Williams, President Police Foundation
8:15-8:45 am	**Keynote address**	The Honorable Phil Gordon Mayor of Phoenix, Arizona
8:45-9:00 am	**Report of Police Foundation focus group findings**	Anita Khashu, Special Advisor, Center on Immigration & Justice, Vera Institute of Justice; consultant, Police Foundation
9:00-10:00 am	**Panel 1: Enforcing federal immigration law at the local level: why and why not?** States and local municipalities have been encouraged to participate in the enforcement of federal immigration laws. Some local law enforcement agencies have entered into a Memorandum of Agreement (MOA) with Immigration and Customs Enforcement (ICE) under Section 287(g) added to the Immigration and Nationality Act by the Illegal Immigration Reform and Immigrant Responsibility Act of 1996 (IIRIRA). MOAs authorize designated officers to perform civil immigration law enforcement functions, provide them with access to the ICE database, and enable them to fill out the necessary forms to initiate the deportation process. The purpose of this panel is to examine the challenges, problems, and opportunities encountered by local police and sheriffs engaged in the enforcement of federal immigration laws.	**MODERATOR:** Anita Khashu, Special Advisor, Center on Immigration & Justice, Vera Institute of Justice; consultant, Police Foundation **PANELISTS:** Sheriff Donald Hunter, Collier County, FL Chief Harold Hurtt, Houston, TX James Pendergraph, Executive Director, Office of State & Local Coordination, U.S. Immigration & Customs Enforcement
10:00-10:15 am	**Break**	
10:15-10:35 am	**Legal issues in local police enforcement of federal immigration law** As local police consider taking on enforcement of federal immigration law, they should carefully consider the legal complexity of their role and legal constraints on methods of enforcement in a legal and institutional system that operates quite differently from local criminal justice systems. Local police enforcement of federal immigration law must account for local, state, and federal laws that govern the rights of community residents and the obligations of localities. It must also account for the civil nature of most immigration violations. Most importantly, it must be conducted in a way that avoids several common misconceptions about the supposed targets of immigration law enforcement, including confusion over their rights,	Professor Nancy Morawetz, New York University School of Law

Time	Session	Presenters
	migration law enforcement, including confusion over their rights, status, and place in the community. The risk of error is high, and already several localities have been subject to lawsuits over unlawful arrests and detentions, the use of racial profiling in enforcement, poor conditions of confinement, and other violations of law. This panel discusses the legal complexities of federal immigration law enforcement in the local setting and the changing demographics of communities. Risks of liability provide yet another factor for police departments to consider before making a decision about whether to tread into this new field of enforcement.	
10:35-11:15 am	**Panel 2: A balanced perspective on the undocumented immigrant** The presentation will begin with a short summary of the issues raised, and some of the data, concerning the characteristics of the undocumented population in the United States. It will continue with a summary of the overall impact of this population. The presentation concludes by highlighting some of the most frequently debated policy responses, including enforcement, legalization, legal issues, and the bundle of more recent strategies that aim to encourage "self-deportation." It will seek to lay out, as objectively as possible, the pros and cons of the various strategies.	Professor Stephen Legomsky, Washington University School of Law Professor Raquel Aldana, William S. Boyd School of Law, University of Nevada, Las Vegas
11:15 am-12:15 pm	**Panel 3: Crime, violence, disorder, victimization: patterns and trends associated with the undocumented immigrant population** It has been estimated that there are 12 million undocumented immigrants in America and hundreds of thousands crossing our borders illegally each year or overstaying their visas. Americans are troubled by, and fearful of, the existence of such a large undocumented immigrant population. Shocking violent criminal acts committed by gangs such as MS-13 are frequently reported in newspapers, television, and the radio. This has heightened the anxieties and concerns about the undocumented community as a whole, and resulted in the passage of tough new statutes and more rigorous enforcement of immigration laws by some states and localities. The purpose of this panel is to examine research on crime within the undocumented community, discuss how the undocumented crime rate comports with that of other groups within the nation, and explore pattern and trends related to crime and victimization within the undocumented community.	**Moderator:** Professor William McDonald, Georgetown University **Panelists:** Professor Roberto Gonzales, University of Washington Jeffrey Passel, PhD, Senior Demographer, Pew Hispanic Center Professor Rubén Rumbaut, University of California-Irvine
12:15-1:15 pm	**Luncheon (Salon 1)**	
1:15-1:30 pm	**Break**	
1:30-2:30 pm	**WORKSHOPS (repeated at 5:00 pm)**	**Facilitator:**
	Workshop #1: How does law enforcement enhance cooperation with the undocumented and documented communities?	Chief (Ret.) Richard Wiles, El Paso, TX
	Workshop #2: What are the positive and negative impacts of 287(g)?	Chief Ron Miller, Topeka, KS

Time	Session	Presenters
	Workshop #3: How can law enforcement work within the undocumented community?	Chief (Ret.) Arturo Venegas, Sacramento, CA
	Workshop #4: What strategies should law enforcement executives employ to effectively manage the political pressures associated with the enforcement of federal immigration laws? *(chiefs and sheriffs only)*	Chief Theron Bowman, PhD, Arlington, TX
2:30-2:45 pm	**Break**	
2:45-3:45 pm	**Panel 4: What is the cost of enforcing immigration law at the local level? When state and local laws addressing undocumented immigrants are enacted, what are the social and economic impacts on: (1) police operations; (2) municipal budgets; (3) the quality of life of community residents?** Although the federal government has the primary role in directing overall policy regarding immigration and refugees, the effects of such policy on local communities present challenges that cannot be ignored by state and local governments. There is concern about the impact of local law enforcement of immigration law on already strained state and local resources, and particularly on the ability of local law enforcement to maintain its core mission of protecting communities and promoting safety. There is also concern about undermining law enforcement efforts to build trust and support in immigrant communities so that witnesses and victims are not fearful of reporting crime.	**Moderator:** Muzaffar Chishti, Director, Migration Policy Institute at New York University School of Law **Panelists:** Randolph Capps, PhD, Senior Research Associate, The Urban Institute Mayor John Cook, El Paso, TX Mayor Phil Gordon, Phoenix, AZ
3:45-4:45 pm	**Panel 5: Fear, crime, and community trust: community perspectives on immigration enforcement by local police** Although there are common threads that link fear, crime, and community trust, these issues are influenced significantly by public perceptions of the police, and differentiated by class, race, ethnicity, religion, culture, and national origin. Many of these differences are rooted in historical experiences or encounters with the police, directly or indirectly, that affect the way people view the police and the manner in which they respond to police authority. In an era of community policing, in which the police acknowledge public trust to be among their highest priorities, understanding these differences and developing constructive solutions to problems that separate the police from the public are essential for building and sustaining community partnerships that enhance public trust and public support for the police. The purpose of this panel is to consider the influence of immigration enforcement from the perspectives of different communities whose experiences may provide the police with insights into the impact of policy and practice at the ground level, and establish a new feedback loop that will facilitate improvement in both areas. It is our hope that the panelists' presentations, audience questions, and subsequent discussion will generate greater clarity and a more nuanced and in-depth understanding of the concerns and problems faced by diverse communities, as well as the types of policies and strategies necessary to effectively address them.	**Moderator:** Professor Rubén Rumbaut, University of California-Irvine **Panelists:** Tuyet Duong, Senior Staff Attorney, Immigration and Immigrant Rights Program, Asian American Justice Center Clarissa Martinez De Castro, Director, Immigration & National Campaigns, National Council of La Raza Kareem Shora, Executive Director, American-Arab Anti-Discrimination Committee

Time	Session	Presenters
4:45-5:00 pm	Break	
5:00-6:00 pm	**WORKSHOPS (repeat)**	**FACILITATOR:**
	Workshop #1: How does law enforcement enhance cooperation with the undocumented and documented communities?	Chief (Ret.) Richard Wiles, El Paso, TX
	Workshop #2: What are the positive and negative impacts of 287(g)?	Chief Ron Miller, Topeka, KS
	Workshop #3: How can law enforcement work within the undocumented community?	Chief (Ret.) Arturo Venegas, Sacramento, CA
	Workshop #4: What strategies should law enforcement executives employ to effectively manage the political pressures associated with the enforcement of federal immigration laws? *(chiefs and sheriffs only)*	Chief Theron Bowman, PhD, Arlington, TX
6:00-7:30 pm	Reception (Salon 1)	
FRIDAY, AUGUST 22, 2008		
7:30-8:15 am	Continental breakfast	
PLENARY 8:15-8:30 am	**Day 2: Opening remarks**	Hubert Williams, President, Police Foundation
8:30-9:45 am	**Panel 6: Immigration and local policing: results from a survey of local law enforcement executives** One of the most important challenges for law enforcement agencies in many communities is how to respond to immigration and the presence of undocumented residents. Departments often face conflicting pressures from local politicians, federal authorities, community groups, and the private sector. Yet they have little available information to help them make sound policy decisions. This panel reports on the results of a recent nationwide survey of police executives on several issues, including differences between departments and communities and their attitudes about immigration and local law enforcement; relationships with federal immigration and customs enforcement authorities; and the range of policies on immigration policing being developed by cities and departments. The survey also explores levels of commitment to community policing practices and the potential for conflict with enforcement of immigration laws by local police.	**MODERATOR:** Doris Marie Provine, Professor, Arizona State University **PANELISTS:** Scott Decker, Professor, Arizona State University Paul Lewis, Asst. Professor, Arizona State University Monica Varsanyi, Assoc. Professor, John Jay College, CUNY
9:45-10:00 am	Break	
10:00-11:00 am	**Open forum**	**FACILITATOR:** Chief William Matthews, Coatesville, PA, Police Department
11:00-11:30 am	**Conference summation**	Professor Stephen Legomsky, Washington University School of Law
11:30-11:45 am	**Closing remarks** **Conference evaluations**	Hubert Williams, President Police Foundation

APPENDIX N
Conference Agenda and Presenters' Bios

Raquel Aldana is professor of law at William S. Boyd School of Law, University of Nevada Las Vegas, where she teaches immigration law, criminal law and criminal procedure, international human rights, and international public law. She also co-teaches experiential learning courses, including a course in Nicaragua on domestic violence in a post-conflict society and a course on the criminalization of immigrants. Prior to coming to the Boyd School of Law, Professor Aldana worked for the Center for Justice and International Law, representing victims of gross human rights violations in the Inter-American System on Human Rights. She is the author of numerous books, articles, and other publications, including *Everyday Law for Latinos* (with S. Bender & J. Avila) (forthcoming 2008); Of Katz and "Aliens": Privacy Expectations and the Immigration Raids, ___ 41 U.C. Davis Law Rev. 101___ (forthcoming 2008); The Subordination and Anti-Subordination Story of the U.S. Immigrant Experience in the 21st Century, __ 7 Nev. L. J. 713__ (2007) (Lat Crit Symposium Cluster Introduction); On Rights, Federal Citizenship, and the "Alien", 46 Washburn L. Rev. 101 (2007). Professor Aldana earned her JD from Harvard Law School, where she served as articles editor of the Harvard Civil Rights-Civil Liberties Law Review.

Theron Bowman began his law enforcement career in 1983 as an officer with the Arlington, Texas, Police Department, and served in numerous positions before being appointed chief of police in 1999. A Fort Worth native, he received his bachelor's, master's, and doctorate degrees from the University of Texas at Arlington. Chief Bowman is a graduate of the Senior Management Institute for Police, the FBI National Academy, and the FBI National Executive Institute. He has served on the faculty of three local universities, teaching sociology, criminology, and criminal justice classes. He is a member of the International Association of Chiefs of Police, National Organization of Black Law Enforcement Executives, Police Executive Research Forum, and a host of other organizations. Dr. Bowman serves as chair for the Texas Intelligence Council and as a commissioner for the Commission on Accreditation for Law Enforcement Agencies.

Randolph Capps, a demographer with substantial expertise in immigrant populations, is a Senior Research Associate at the Urban Institute. He has a PhD in sociology from the University of Texas, and has analyzed data on immigrants from a wide variety of sources, at the national, state, and local levels. Dr. Capps recently published national-level reports on trends in the immigrant labor force, the health and well being of young children of immigrants, and the characteristics of immigrants' children in elementary and secondary schools. He is currently conducting a study of the impact of immigration enforcement operations on children of unauthorized immigrants and recently participated in an evaluation of employment services in the federal refugee resettlement program. His recent work at the state and local level includes a demographic profile of immigrants in Arkansas; a study of immigrant integration in Louisville, Kentucky; a description of the unauthorized population in California and Los Angeles; a study of tax payments by immigrants in the Washington, DC, metropolitan area; an assessment of immigrants' health care access in Connecticut; and an analysis of the involvement of children of immigrants in the Texas child welfare system.

Muzaffar Chishti, a lawyer, is director of the Migration Policy Institute's office at New York University School of Law. His work focuses on US immigration policy, the intersection of labor and immigration law, civil liberties, and immigrant integration. Prior to joining MPI, Mr. Chishti was director of the Immigration Project of the Union of Needletrades, Industrial & Textile Employees (UNITE). Mr. Chishti currently serves on the boards of directors of the National Immigration Law Center, the New York Immigration Coalition, and the Asian American Federation of New York. He has served as chair of the board of directors of the National Immigration Forum, and as a member of the Coordinating Committee on Immigration of the American Bar Association. His publications include: *America's Challenge: Domestic Security, Civil Liberties, and National Unity After September 11* (co-authored); "Guest Workers in the House of Labor" in the *New Labor Forum*; "The Role of States in US Immigration Policy" in the *NYU Annual Survey of American Law* (2002); "Employer Sanctions Against Immigrant Workers" in *WorkingUSA*; and "Rights or Privileges," in the special issue on the Promise of Immigration in *The Boston Review*. Mr. Chishti was educated at St. Stephen's College, Delhi; the University of Delhi; Cornell Law School; and the Columbia School of International Affairs.

John Cook was elected Mayor of El Paso, Texas, in 2005. From 1999 to 2005, he served on the City Council, representing El Paso's 4th district. Mayor Cook has lived in Northeast El Paso for most of his life where his family has owned and operated several Northeast businesses. He has been deeply involved in El Paso's community affairs, as a businessman, a teacher, coach, founder and member of the board of many civic and veterans' organizations. He served in the United States Army from 1966 to 1971, seeing service as a Special Agent Military Intelligence. He holds a business degree from the University of Texas at El Paso.

Alina Das is a supervising attorney and teaching fellow with the Immigrant Rights Clinic at New York University (NYU) School of Law. She works with clinic students to defend the rights of immigrants facing deportation and detention and to provide support for community organizations' immigrant rights campaigns. Prior to joining the Immigrant Rights Clinic, Alina was an attorney and Soros Justice Fellow with the New York

Biographical information current at the time of the Police Foundation conference, August 21-22, 2008.

State Defenders Association Immigrant Defense Project, where she engaged in a wide range of litigation and advocacy on immigration and criminal justice issues. Prior to joining the Immigrant Defense Project, Alina clerked for the Hon. Kermit V. Lipez of the U.S. Court of Appeals for the First Circuit. Alina's recent publications include *Immigrants and Problem-Solving Courts* in the *Criminal Justice Review* (forthcoming 2008) and *Addressing Unintended Consequences in Civil Advocacy for Criminally Charged Immigrants* in the *Clearinghouse Review Journal of Poverty Law and Policy* (July-August 2007). Alina is a graduate of Harvard University, NYU Wagner School of Public Service, and NYU School of Law.

Scott H. Decker is professor in the School of Criminology and Criminal Justice at Arizona State University. He received the BA in Social Justice from DePauw University and the MA and PhD in Criminology from Florida State University. His main research interests are in the areas of gangs, criminal justice policy, and the offender's perspective. His most recent books include *European Street Gangs and Troublesome Youth* Groups (winner of the American Society of Criminology Division of International Criminology Outstanding Distinguished book award 2006) and *Drug Smugglers on Drug Smuggling: Lessons from the Inside* (Temple University Press, 2008).

Tuyet G. Duong is a senior staff attorney for the Immigration and Immigrant Rights Program with the Asian American Justice Center (AAJC) in Washington, D.C. Previously, Ms. Duong led AAJC's language access and emergency preparedness program, advocating for Asian Americans impacted by Hurricanes Katrina and Rita, and as an immigration staff attorney for Boat People SOS, Inc. (BPSOS) in Houston, where she provided legal assistance on citizenship, human trafficking, family-based sponsorship, and domestic violence matters. During law school, she clerked at the Department of Justice Executive Office of Immigration Review in Los Angeles, California, and at the Texas Civil Rights Project. Ms. Duong is a frequent speaker and trainer on immigration and language issues. She currently chairs the Board of Directors of BPSOS, Inc. and is a founding board member of the Vietnamese American Bar Association in Washington, DC. Ms. Duong received her JD degree from the University of Texas Law School at Austin, and a bachelor's degree in English from the University of Texas at Austin.

Roberto G. Gonzales earned his PhD in the department of sociology from the University of California, Irvine, and in September 2008 will join the faculty of the School of Social Work at the University of Washington in Seattle. He received his undergraduate degree from Colorado College and an AM from the School of Social Service Administration at the University of Chicago. He combines fifteen years of direct service and formal training in social work and sociology to shape his research and teaching interests. His most recent research took place in Southern California and explores the effects of legal status on the adult children of unauthorized Mexican migrants. In particular, his doctoral dissertation, "Born in the Shadows: the Uncertain Futures of the Children of Unauthorized Mexican Migrants," examines the role of policy and mediating institutions in shaping the on-the-ground realities and options available for unauthorized Mexican youth as they move into adulthood. Gonzales' research and teaching interests include international and unauthorized migration, urban studies, the one-and-a-half and second generations, and Latino communities and families. He is the author of *Wasted Talent and Broken Dreams: The Lost Potential of Undocumented Students* published by the Immigration Policy Center and coauthor of *Debunking the Myth of Immigrant Criminality: Imprisonment Among First- and Second-Generation Young Men*. He has served on several local level and national boards, including the Crossroads Fund and the American Friends Service Committee.

Phil Gordon was elected Mayor of Phoenix, Arizona, on September 9, 2003, and was re-elected in September 2007. Gordon was recently appointed by the U.S. Conference of Mayors to chair its Comprehensive Immigration Reform Task Force. As Mayor, Gordon lists his three priorities for the city as public safety, education, and jobs. Phoenix invests more than 60 percent of its budget in public safety. A new crime lab is open, new precincts are under construction, and 600 new police officers and firefighters will be hired over the next two years. In education, a downtown Phoenix campus is a second home to both Arizona State University and the University of Arizona. Additionally, Phoenix has invested in small high schools to prepare students for immediate careers in specific areas like public safety and nursing. Phoenix has led the nation for three years straight, creating 45,000 new jobs each year. Before serving in elected office, Gordon was a leader in the movement to revitalize, preserve, and redevelop central Phoenix. Gordon has a bachelor's degree in education from the University of Arizona and graduated cum laude from Arizona State University School of Law.

Don Hunter has served as Sheriff in Collier County, Florida, since1988, when he was first elected. Prior to joining the Collier County Sheriff's Department in 1979, he served as administrator for the Southwest Florida Regional Planning Council. Hunter serves on the Commission on Accreditation for law Enforcement Agencies and is a member of the National Sheriffs Association and the International Association of Chiefs of Police. He has a BS and MS in criminology from Florida State University and is a graduate of the FBI National Academy. Sheriff Hunter is active in a number of community and civic organizations in Collier County.

Harold L. Hurtt, was appointed Chief of Police of Houston, Texas, in 2004. A veteran of the United States Air Force, he began his law enforcement career in 1968 as a patrolman in the Phoenix Police Department. During his tenure with the Phoenix PD, he attained many promotional achievements, including the ranks of patrolman, sergeant, lieutenant, captain/commander, major, assistant chief, and eventually executive assistant chief of police. In 1992, Hurtt retired from the Phoenix Police Department to become chief of police for the Oxnard, California, Police Department. In 1998, he returned to Phoenix as that city's chief of police. In 2002, and again in 2004, Chief Hurtt was selected by his peers as president of the Major Cities Chiefs Association, an organization of the 63 largest police departments in the United States and Canada. Chief Hurtt is a noted proponent of the "community policing" concept and has led efforts to increase the number of officers who speak Spanish, Chinese, and Vietnamese in the diverse Phoenix community. Chief Hurtt graduated from Arizona State University with a bachelor's degree in sociology, and earned a master's degree in organizational management from the University of Phoenix.

Anita Khashu was the first director of The Vera Institute of Justice's Center on Immigration and Justice, initiating and managing the Institute's various projects involving immigrants in the justice system. She currently serves as Senior Advisor to the Center. Anita is also currently working as a consultant for the Police Foundation on the project, The Role of Local Police: Striking a Balance Between Immigration Enforcement and Civil Liberties. Anita was a 2007-08 Fulbright Scholar in residence at Instituto Tecnologico Autonomo de Mexico in Mexico City, where she conducted research on Mexican policy and practice of detention and deportation of Central American unaccompanied migrant minors. She joined Vera at the Bureau of Justice Assistance in South Africa in 2002, where she managed Vera's technical assistance to the Legal Aid Board of South Africa. In 2003, Anita returned to New York and moved to the Institute's planning department, where she worked on projects involving immigrant relations with the police. Her publications include *Building Strong Police-Immigrant Community Relations: Lessons from New York City*, *Justice and Safety in America's Immigrant Communities*, and *Overcoming Language Barriers: Solutions for Law Enforcement*. Anita received her BA in economics, cum laude, from Tufts University and a JD, cum laude, from Boston University School of Law.

Stephen Legomsky is the John Lehmann University Professor at the Washington University School of Law in St. Louis. He is the author of *Immigration and Refugee Law and Policy* (now in its fourth edition), which has been the required text for immigration courses at 163 U.S. law schools. His other books, published by the Oxford University Press, include *Immigration and the Judiciary: Law and Politics in Britain and America*; and *Specialized Justice*. Legomsky founded the immigration section of the Association of American Law Schools and has chaired the Law Professors Committee of the American Immigration Lawyers Association and the Refugee Committee of the American Branch of the International Law Association. He has testified before Congress and has been a consultant to President Clinton's transition team, the first President Bush's Commissioner of Immigration, the UN High Commissioner for Refugees, and several foreign governments, on migration and refugee issues. Legomsky is an elected member of the American Law Institute. He has been a senior visiting fellow at Oxford University and a visiting fellow at Cambridge University. He has had other teaching or research appointments in the United States, Mexico, New Zealand, Switzerland, Germany, Italy, Austria, Australia, Suriname, and Singapore.

Paul G. Lewis is an assistant professor of political science at Arizona State University in Tempe, AZ. His area of research and teaching expertise is American local government, urban affairs, and public policy. With three ASU colleagues, Lewis has begun work on a national study of the responses of local police departments to unauthorized immigration. He also coauthored a prior study focused on such issues as California municipalities, "Policing Practices in Immigrant-Destination Cities," which appeared in Urban Affairs Review in July 2007. In addition to examining the relationship between immigrants and local governments, his research has focused mainly on issues of land-use policy and suburbanization. He is coauthor of a forthcoming book, Custodians of Place: Governing the Growth and Development of Cities, which will be published by Georgetown University Press in 2009, and his prior published work includes one book and numerous journal articles and policy reports. From 1996-2005 Lewis was a research fellow at the Public Policy Institute of California, a think tank focused on state and local policy issues, and from 2002-2005 he also served as program director for the Institute's governance and public finance program. He holds a PhD from Princeton University.

William F. McDonald is Professor of Sociology and Co-Director of the Institute of Criminal Law and Procedure at Georgetown University. Since 1995, his research has focused on the nexus between immigration and crime. He is currently editing a volume entitled Immigration, Crime and Justice and is beginning a survey of unauthorized immigrants to determine their experiences as victims of crime and their willingness to cooperate with the police. His work includes: "Immigrants As Victims of Crime: An Introduction," International Review of Victimology (1) (2007); "Police and Immigrants: Community & Security in Post-9/11 America," in Justice and Safety in America's Immigrant Communities: A Conference Report, Martha King, Ed. (Policy Research Institute for the Region at Princeton University: Princeton, NJ) "Crime and Illegal Immigration: Emerging Local, State, and Federal Partnerships," National Institute of Justice Journal, June 2-10, 1997. He has a doctorate of criminology from the University of California, Berkeley.

Clarissa Martínez De Castro is Director of Immigration and National Campaigns for the National Council of La Raza (NCLR), and oversees the organization's work on immigration and efforts to expand opportunities for Latino engagement in civic life and public policy debates. She previously managed NCLR's state policy advocacy efforts and civic engagement work, and in 2007 served as manager of the Coalition for Comprehensive Immigration Reform, a broad network of national, state, and local organizations committed to advancing policy solutions on immigration. Prior to NCLR, she served as public policy coordinator for the Southwest Voter Research Institute, as assistant director of the California-Mexico Project at the University of Southern California, as organizer with the Ladies' Garment Workers Union, and as union representative with the Hotel Employees and Restaurant Employees Union (HERE) Local 11. A Salzburg Seminar Fellow, she received her undergraduate degree from Occidental College, and her master's degree from Harvard University. A naturalized U.S. citizen, she was born and raised in the Mexican State of Sinaloa.

William H. Matthews is Chief of Police for the City of Coatesville, PA. Prior to his appointment in Coatesville, Matthews served as deputy director of the Police Foundation in Washington DC, and as executive director of the Community Policing Consortium, a national project of the Office of Community Oriented Policing Services of the US Department of Justice. Matthews' extensive criminal justice and policing background includes serving as director of community policing programs for the International City-County Management Association (ICMA); as executive director of the National Organization of Black Law Enforcement Executives (NOBLE); as chief of the Baltimore, MD, Housing Authority Police; and as CEO of a private firm that managed major law enforcement projects for national associations. He also assisted in the development of graduate courses at Howard University, and in the development of national standards for law enforcement agencies and the creation of the Commission on Accreditation for Law Enforcement Agencies. A native of New York and a military veteran, Chief Matthews is an experienced instructor, speaker, and group facilitator. He has a BS degree from Howard University and a MS degree from the American University of Washington, DC.

Ronald Miller was appointed chief of police in Topeka in 2006. He has served in law enforcement in the State of Kansas for thirty-six years, joining the Kansas City, Kansas, Police Department in 1972, rising through the ranks to serve as the chief of police for six years. Chief Miller holds a bachelor's degree from the University of Central Missouri and a master's degree from Wichita State University. He is a graduate of the FBI National Academy, the Southern Police Institute, and the Senior Management Institute for Policing at Harvard/Boston University. Chief Miller is active on several committees and boards in Topeka and also serves with national police organizations. He received the Clarence M. Kelley Award for Excellence in Law Enforcement Administration in the Kansas City Metropolitan area, and is a graduate of Leadership Greater Topeka.

Nancy Morawetz is a Professor of Clinical Law at New York University School of Law, where she has taught since 1987. She currently teaches in the Immigrant Rights Clinic (IRC). Professor Morawetz's recent writings include *Citizenship and the Courts*, 2007 U. Chi. Legal F. 447 (2007); *The Invisible Border: Restrictions on Short-Term Travel By Noncitizens*, 21 Geo. Imm. L. J. 201 (2007); *INS v. St. Cyr: The Campaign to Preserve Court Review and Stop Retroactive Application of Deportation Laws*, in David Martin and Peter Schuck, Immigration Stories (2005); *Determining the Retroactive Effect of Laws Altering the Consequences of Criminal Convictions*, 30 Ford. Urb. L. J. 1743 (2003); *Understanding the Impact of the 1996 Deportation Laws and the Limited Scope of Proposed Reforms*, 113 Harv. L. Rev. 1936 (2000); and *Rethinking Retroactive Deportation Laws and the Due Process Clause*, 73 N.Y.U.L. Rev. 97 (1998). Professor Morawetz is a graduate of Princeton University and NYU School of Law, where she served as Editor-in-Chief of the New York University Law Review. She is a former clerk to the Hon. Patricia M. Wald of the United States Court of Appeals for the District of Columbia Circuit.

Jeffrey S. Passel is the Senior Demographer at the Pew Hispanic Center in Washington, DC, which he joined in January 2005. His research interests include the demography of Hispanics and immigrants, measurement of immigration (particularly undocumented), integration of immigrants into American society, and the impacts (fiscal, demographic, and social) of immigrants. He also works on generational dynamics, population projections, defining racial/ ethnic groups, and measuring census undercount. Previous positions include principal research associate at The Urban Institute and various positions at the Census Bureau, where he directed programs of population estimates, projections, and demographic methods for measuring census undercount. Dr. Passel has served on committees of the Population Association of America, panels of The National Academy of Sciences, and on the Social Security Advisory Board's Technical Panel on Assumptions and Methods. He is a fellow of the American Association for the Advancement of Science and the American Statistical Association. In 2004, *American Demographics* magazine selected him as a "demographic diamond," one of the five demographers/social scientists most representative of influential work in the last 25 years. Passel has a bachelor's degree in mathematics from MIT, a master's degree in sociology from the University of

Texas at Austin, and a PhD in social relations from The Johns Hopkins University.

James Pendergraph is executive director of Office of State and Local Coordination, US Customs and Immigration (ICE). The first person to hold this position, Mr. Pendergraph heads an office responsible for coordinating U.S. Immigration and Customs Enforcement (ICE) participation in programs and activities that relate to state and local governments and their respective law enforcement entities. Mr. Pendergraph joined ICE in December 2007 after serving for 13 years as the sheriff of Mecklenburg County, N.C. During that time he was recognized for his innovative thinking and partnership with federal authorities on immigration enforcement. As Mecklenburg's sheriff, he spearheaded the use of the 287(g) program, through which ICE provides training and supervision that allow state and local authorities to provide targeted immigration enforcement. Mr. Pendergraph's law enforcement career began when he served as military policeman with the U.S. Army. Following his military service, he became a police officer with the Charlotte/Mecklenburg Police Department, where he served for 23 years, reaching the rank of deputy chief. He was first elected Mecklenburg County Sheriff in 1994 and was re-elected to three additional terms before joining ICE. Mr. Pendergraph is a graduate of Harvard University's John F. Kennedy School of Government. He also has an associate's degree in criminal justice and is a graduate of the FBI National Academy and FBI National Executive Institute. He has served in leadership positions with numerous law enforcement associations, including the National Sheriffs' Association and the International Association of Chiefs of Police.

Doris Marie Provine is a professor in the School of Justice & Social Inquiry at Arizona State University and a past director of the School (2001-2007). She is a lawyer and political scientist. Many of her publications explore the politics and practices of courts at various levels, from town and village justice courts *(Judging Credentials: Non-lawyer Judges and the Politics of Professionalism),* to the United States Supreme Court (Case Selection in the US Supreme Court) and courts at the international level. Her more recent work focuses on policy issues, including, most recently, racism in the war on drugs *(Unequal Under Law: Race and the War on Drugs)*. Currently Provine is studying policy responses to settled but unauthorized immigrants. With the support of a Fulbright North American Studies research grant, she spent the past academic year studying policies related to unauthorized immigration in Canada and Mexico. She is currently writing a book about these policies, from the vantage point of three cities, one in Canada, one in the United States, and one in Mexico. At the same time, with three Arizona State University colleagues, and with support from the National Science Foundation, she is examining how police departments are responding to calls from city officials to become more engaged in enforcing federal immigration laws.

Rubén G. Rumbaut is Professor of Sociology at the University of California, Irvine. He is the founding chair of the Section on International Migration of the American Sociological Association, a member of the Committee on Population of the National Academy of Sciences, and a former fellow at the Center for Advanced Study in the Behavioral Sciences at Stanford, and visiting scholar at the Russell Sage Foundation in New York. A leading authority on immigration in the United States, Dr. Rumbaut co-directs the landmark *Children of Immigrants Longitudinal Study*; and a large-scale study of *Immigration and Intergenerational Mobility in Metropolitan Los Angeles*. He is the author of more than one hundred scientific papers on immigrants and refugees in the U.S., and coauthor or coeditor of a dozen books, including *Legacies*, which received the Distinguished Book Award of the American Sociological Association and the Thomas and Znaniecki Award for best book in the immigration field. He recently completed work with a panel of the National Academy of Sciences on two volumes on the Hispanic population of the United States: *Multiple Origins, Uncertain Destinies*, and *Hispanics and the Future of America*. His doctoral dissertation, on "The Politics of Police Reform," was based on three years of research in the San Diego Police Department in the mid-1970s, supported by Police Foundation grants.

Kareem W. Shora is Executive Director of the American-Arab Anti-Discrimination Committee (ADC). Shora, who joined ADC in 2000, is a recipient of the 2003 American Immigration Lawyers Association (AILA) Arthur C. Helton Human Rights Award. He has testified before major international human rights bodies, including regular testimonies before the Organization for Security and Cooperation in Europe (OSCE) and the United Nations Human Rights Commission. He was selected by the Ford Foundation as a member of the Foreign Policy Task Force designing their 2008 Laboratory for New Thinking on Foreign Policy. He was selected by the Police Foundation in 2008 to serve on their advisory board on the study of the role of local police in immigration enforcement. Shora is also the civil society representative on the G8 Experts Roundtable on Diversity and Integration. He has been published by the National Law Journal, TRIAL Magazine, the Georgetown University Law Center's Journal on Poverty Law and Public Policy, the Harvard University JFK School of Government Asian American Policy Review, the American Bar Association (ABA) Air and Space Lawyer, and the Yeshiva University Cardozo Public Law Policy and Ethics Journal. Born in Damascus, Syria, Shora is a native of Huntington, West Virginia, is fluent in Arabic, and holds a JD degree from the West Virginia University (WVU) College of Law and the LLM specialty in International

Legal Studies from the American University Washington College of Law.

Monica Varsanyi will be an associate professor in the Government Department at John Jay College of Criminal Justice, City University of New York, beginning in the Fall of 2008, after a two-year tenure in the School of Justice and Social Inquiry at Arizona State University. She is an urban and political geographer whose research addresses the politics of unauthorized immigration in the United States. She is currently working on two related projects: one which explores growing tensions between local and state grassroots immigration policy activism and the federal government's plenary power over immigration and citizenship policy; and the second with Scott Decker, Paul Lewis, and Marie Provine, a national study which explores the growing involvement of city police in immigration enforcement and the impact this is having on the relationship of local police and (unauthorized) immigrant communities. Prior to joining the faculty at John Jay, she was a postdoctoral scholar at the Centers for Comparative Immigration Studies and US-Mexican Studies at the University of California, San Diego, an assistant professor at Arizona State University, and received her PhD in Geography from UCLA. Varsanyi's articles have appeared in academic journals such as *Urban Geography, Geopolitics, Annals of the Association of American Geographers, Citizenship Studies, Antipode*, and *Space and Polity*, and popular outlets such as the *Los Angeles Times*. She is currently editing a book on state and local immigration policy activism in the United States.

Arturo Venegas, Jr. was the chief of police in Sacramento, California, from January 1993 through February 2003. He instituted community-oriented policing during the difficult economic times of the 1990s and led the agency through a number of major financial reductions while maintaining a focus on community service and problem solving. He was credited with preventing the city from making detrimental cuts to the police and other city departments. He assisted in the delivery of training in various topic areas to communities and agencies across the nation for the national Community Policing Consortium. From August 1, 2006, through February 15, 2008, under a contract with the New Jersey Attorney General, he served as Supersession Executive over the Camden, NJ, Police Department, providing day-to-day oversight of the department. Chief Venegas has a BA degree from the University of San Francisco and a MS degree from California State University Polytechnic, Pomona. He is a graduate of the FBI National Academy, the FBI National Executive Institute, the California Law Enforcement Command College, and other California POST accredited studies. He is a member of IACP, PERF, HAPCOA, NOBLE, Cal Chiefs, and the Fresno Peace Officers Association.

Richard D. Wiles served as chief of police in El Paso, Texas, from 2003 through 2007. As chief, Wiles was committed to the implementation of a culture of integrity and honesty within the El Paso Police Department. During his 27-year public service career, he served with both the police and fire departments of El Paso. Wiles is currently the democratic nominee for Sheriff of El Paso County. He earned a bachelor of science in criminal justice from the University of Texas at El Paso and a master of science in criminal justice from Sul Ross State University. Wiles is a graduate of the Bill Blackwood Law Enforcement Management Institute of Texas, the FBI National Academy, and the FBI National Executive Institute.

APPENDIX O

Sample Police Department Policies on Immigration Enforcement

403.02 GENERAL RULES ON ARRESTS AND SEARCHES

(Title Effective 11-01-97)

A. **Probable Cause Required**. Arrest or search made without probable cause violates the Fourth Amendment to the U.S. Constitution and Art. 1. Sec. 9 of the Texas Constitution. (Re-numbered and **Revised 11-01-97**)

1. Probable cause **for arrest** exists when an officer has reason to believe that a person has committed an offense, although precisely what offense is not known, or that a person has committed a particular offense, the method of which is uncertain. (Re-numbered and **Revised 11-01-97**)
   - There is no difference in the amount of probable cause required to make an arrest without warrant, an arrest pursuant to warrant, or an arrest that ordinarily would require a warrant but because of exigent circumstances can be made without warrant.
   - The only difference in the three situations, from a probable cause standpoint, is the timing of the judicial scrutiny that will be given to the situation.
   - In the case of an arrest without warrant, a magistrate will review the arrest after-the-fact, and if the magistrate does not find that sufficient probable cause existed to make the arrest, the arrested person will be released and the officer may be subject to penalty for false arrest.
   - In the case of an arrest under warrant, a magistrate will review the affidavit to support issuance of the warrant, and if the magistrate finds that there is sufficient probable cause to justify the arrest, the magistrate will issue an arrest warrant.

2. Probable cause exists **for a search** when an officer has reason to believe that a person possesses seizable items or a place contains seizable items. (Re-numbered and **Revised 11-01-97**)
3. All facts and circumstances used to determine probable cause must be fully documented in writing. (Re-numbered 11-01-97)

   a. An officer shall employ the officer's training, skills, and experience as a peace officer in determining whether probable cause exists. (Re-numbered 11-01-97)
   b. All lawfully acquired information available at the moment of the arrest or search may be considered, regardless of its admissibility at trial. (Re-numbered 11-01-97)
   c. Mere suspicion, speculation, or reasonable suspicion, or generally suspicious conduct that does not suggest any specific kind of criminal conduct, is not probable cause but may be grounds for further investigation. (Re-numbered and **Revised 11-01-97**)
   d. Good faith, in the absence of probable cause, will not justify an invalid arrest or search. (Re-numbered 11-01-97)
   e. Probable cause for arrest requires only enough evidence to reasonably show that a particular person probably or most likely committed an offense. Probable cause for search requires only enough evidence to reasonably show that a particular person or place probably or most likely possesses or contains seizable items. It is not necessary to have sufficient evidence to prove these facts beyond a reasonable doubt. (Re-numbered 11-01-97)
   f. When probable cause is based on information from an informant, reliability of the informant, the underlying circumstances that form the basis for the informant's belief, and verification of the informant's information must be established. In most cases, all three are necessary. In some cases, informant reliability and verifying details together may be strong enough to overcome weak underlying circumstances that form the basis for the informant's belief. Similarly, strong underlying circumstances and observed details together may overcome weak or unestablished informant reliability. (Re-numbered and **Revised 11-01-97**)

g. Victim or witness information must be confirmed. Their ability to observe and remember what happened must be determined. Directly observable results of an offense can serve as partial confirmation of an offense. In cases of doubt, officers must investigate further. The more doubt an officer has about the victim or witness's veracity, sincerity, or ability to perceive, the more confirmation is needed. Particularly in cases of a citizen who is claiming to have made a citizen's arrest or security personnel or officers of other agencies who have taken a suspected violator into custody, officers will conduct an independent investigation to assure that sufficient probable cause exists for arrest and taking of the person into police custody. (Re-numbered and **Revised 11-01-97**)

h. An officer making an arrest at the request of another officer does not have to have probable cause as long as the requesting officer had probable cause. Where officers from another agency have made off-duty arrests, Arlington officers will not take the arrested person into Arlington police custody unless they are satisfied that sufficient probable cause for arrest exists and that the arrest is in the public interest and not just in furtherance of the off-duty employer's business. If officers do not believe the arrest was justified and in the public interest, they will tell the other agency officer, out of the hearing of the arrestee, that the other agency officer, must arrange transport to the Tarrant County Jail if they desire the person to be jailed. Where sufficient probable cause exists for the arrest, Arlington officers will take custody of persons arrested by off-duty officers from other agencies, transport the person to jail, and file appropriate charges, listing the other agency officer as a witness. (**Revised 11-01-97**)

B. **Arrest Awareness and Warnings**. Arrested persons must be made aware that they are being arrested. Unless in uniform, an officer must display badge and identification and state the officer's name and status as an officer with the Arlington Police Department, unless circumstances prohibit it. Persons will be told of the officer's intention to take them into custody and the reason for arrest unless they are in the act of committing the offense, are fleeing from the scene of the crime, the officer is endangered, or the arrest would be imperiled. An unconscious, insane, or injured person may be arrested even though the person is incapable of understanding that they are under arrest. If an arrest is pursuant to warrant, officers will so advise the arrestee and will exhibit the arrest warrant. If officers do not possess the warrant and the arrestee asks for a copy, officers will provide a copy of the arrest warrant confirmation as soon as possible. All arrested persons will be given standard Miranda warnings before questioning. (Re-numbered and **Revised 11-01-97**)

C. **Mistaken Identity/Alibi Claims**. At the time of arrest or thereafter, if an arrestee asserts mistaken identity or plausible alibi, mistake, or defense, a reasonable investigation will be made to clarify, confirm, or refute it. (Re-numbered 11-01-97)

D. **Prohibitions**. An officer shall not make an arrest: (Re-numbered 11-01-97)

- for conduct which the officer has provoked;
- when the department has administratively ruled that certain criminal laws will not be enforced. These will be specified in writing;
- based on the race, gender, religion, ethnicity, national original, or sexual preference or any other arbitrary classification of the offender or victim; or
- for investigation.

E. **Jurisdiction Limitations** (Re-numbered 11-01-97) (**A** 74.03.01)

1. **Arrest without Warrant**. An Arlington officer's authority to arrest without warrant is limited by department policy to Tarrant County unless the officer is in fresh pursuit or a felony or breach of peace has been committed in the officer's presence or view. See also directive on Off-duty Enforcement for off-duty enforcement limits. (**Revised 11-01-97**)

2. **Warrant Execution** is limited as follows:

   - Traffic or Class C misdemeanor arrest warrants may be executed anywhere in Tarrant County or adjoining counties. Execution elsewhere requires prior supervisor approval. (Re-numbered and **Revised 11-01-97**)
   - Search warrant executions are limited to Arlington except when a direct link of criminal activity can be demonstrated between the suspect and the Arlington community.
   - Arlington officers will not execute an arrest or search warrant outside Arlington without notifying authorities in the other jurisdiction. If resistance is anticipated or other high risk factors exist on any arrest warrant execution, and on all search warrant executions outside the City of Arlington, an officer of the jurisdiction where the arrest or search occurs is to accompany Arlington officers. (Re-numbered and **Revised 11-01-97**)

F. **Arraignments**: Code of Criminal Procedure Art. 15.18 requires that persons arrested under a warrant issued in a county other than the one in which the person is arrested are to be taken to a magistrate of the county where the arrest takes place. However, Art. 15.18 also provides that, if necessary to provide more expeditious magistrate's warnings, the arrested person may be taken before a magistrate in any county in the state in accordance with CCP Art. 15.17. (Re-numbered and **Revised 11-01-97**) (Revised 12-18-06)

G. **Immigration and Military Offenses**

1. **Aliens**. Texas Peace Officers have no authority to arrest individuals without a warrant for the federal misdemeanor of first offense illegal entry into the United States unless the officer observes the illegal entry. (Re-numbered 11-01-97)
2. **Federal Military**. Peace officers have no authority to arrest individuals without a warrant for federal military AWOL even if listed on NCIC. Peace officers may arrest those listed on NCIC as federal military deserters. (Re-numbered 11-01-97)
3. **State Military**. Peace officers may arrest state military deserters for whom an apprehension order or arrest warrant has been issued by proper state military authority. A sheriff or constable is the only authority permitted to arrest persons for state military AWOL or other non-desertion type offenses pursuant to an arrest warrant issued by proper state military authorities. (Re-numbered 11-01-97)

Dallas Police Department General Order
315.00 Arrests Requiring Special Handling

Revised 09/24/08

315.00 ARRESTS REQUIRING SPECIAL HANDLING

315.02 Arrests Made on NCIC, TCIC, and NCTCIC Checks

A. Arrests made on NCIC, TCIC, and NCTCIC (Regional) Hits will be in accordance with Communications Section, Detention Services Section, General Investigations Section, and Records Section Standard Operating Procedures.

B. No arrest or confiscation of property without a warrant will be made solely on an NCIC, TCIC, or NCTCIC hit on a computer or radio check. In all cases, the name of the confirming individual from the originating agency must be included in the report.

C. An NCIC or TCIC hit alone is not probable cause to arrest. A hit indicates a warrant has been issued and the date of the warrant. A hit is only one fact that an officer must add to other facts in arriving at sufficient legal grounds for probable cause to arrest. It is imperative that officers compare sufficient identifiers to verify that the person in custody is the same person named in the warrant.

1. To verify a person's identity, consider the following possible identifiers:
   a. Name.
   b. Race.
   c. Sex.
   d. Date of birth (DOB).
   e. Place of birth.
   f. Driver's License number (DL).
   g. Social Security number (SSN).
   h. Address.
   i. Complete physical description to include height, weight, hair, eye color, scars, marks, and tattoos.
2. Every effort must be made to verify an arrested person's identity prior to incarceration. When there is a doubt that an individual is the wanted subject, he/she will be fingerprinted prior to incarceration.
3. In instances where there is less than substantial evidence to identify the person in custody, a field supervisor must be contacted to make the final determination. An arrest will not be made if the field supervisor determines there are not enough significant identifiers to connect the individual to the warrant.
4. If a field release is made, comply with General Order 313.08 (Release of Erroneously Arrested Persons in the Field).

315.04 Illegal Immigrants

A. The U.S. Immigration Code denies us the authority to enforce its provisions; therefore, we do not enforce immigration laws. All other laws apply to illegal immigrants.

B. Officers will not stop or contact citizens for the sole purpose of determining immigration status.

C. Arrest reports will contain arrest elements only and not refer to immigration status.

D. INS agents have the sole responsibility for determining the immigration status of incarcerated persons.

E. The INS must confirm outstanding NCIC detainer hits for INS violations. Confirmed hits will be booked as Hold for INS.

F. Detention Services Supervisors will release city charges when requested by INS.

NOTE: Only relevant sections of General Order 315 are included by the Police Foundation for this publication.

Numbered Directives shall be retained by all members
Number: 07-04
Date: July 10, 2007

Detroit Police Department

Training Directive

SUBJECT: SOLICITATION OF IMMIGRATION INFORMATION BY POLICE DEPARTMENT PERSONNEL

The Detroit City Council has enacted an ordinance concerning the solicitation of immigration status by public servants and several provisions pertain directly to police officers. This Training Directive provides an explanation of the ordinance. The full text of the ordinance has been placed on the DPD Intranet.

BACKGROUND: The responsibility for enforcement of immigration laws rests with the federal government. Federal immigration laws are extremely complicated as there are several immigration status classifications and depending on the particular circumstances, the matter can be a criminal offense or a non-criminal matter handled through a civil deportation process. Under Michigan law, an officer's arrest powers do not extend to non-criminal offenses. Proper enforcement in this complex area requires specialized training beyond the training of members of this agency and improper enforcement could result in officers exceeding their authority and exposure to civil liability.

Additionally, persons whose immigration status prohibits their lawful presence in the country are nevertheless a significant part of the population that need police protection and service. Cooperation and assistance to the police in reporting crimes or coming forward with information to solve crimes require confidence and trust which can be undermined by unnecessary solicitation of immigration status, particularly if the only basis for inquiry is a person's surname or language fluency. It is with this background that Sections 27-9-1 through 27-9-7 of the Detroit City Code has been enacted.

1. What does the ordinance prohibit?

It prohibits an officer from soliciting information concerning immigration status in certain circumstances. The circumstances where solicitation of immigration information is prohibited are:

- If the solicitation of information concerning immigration status is **for the purpose** of ascertaining a person's compliance with federal immigration law.
- If the person from whom the immigration information is solicited is:
    1. A victim
    2. A witness
    3. A person who is seeking police services

This Training Directive is for internal departmental use only, and violations of the procedures outlined in this Training Directive may form the basis for Departmental administrative sanctions. This document is not intended for third-party use or benefit. No criminal or civil duty or standard of care is intended to be, or is, created by the issuance of this Training Directive.

Training Directive: SOLICITATION OF IMMIGRATION INFORMATION
Number: 07-04
Date: July 10, 2007

2. Under what circumstances does the ordinance permit police officers to solicit information concerning immigration status?

There are three circumstances in which the ordinance expressly authorizes the solicitation of information concerning immigration status. These are:

- A police officer is authorized to solicit information concerning immigration status if the officer is performing public safety functions while assisting federal law enforcement in the investigation of a criminal offense.
- A police officer is authorized to solicit information concerning immigration status from the subject of an investigation only when relevant to the investigation or prosecution of a criminal offense.
- A police officer is authorized to solicit information concerning immigration status when processing an arrested person.

3. What is the purpose of this ordinance?

As previously mentioned, the job responsibilities of a Detroit police officer do not include enforcement of federal immigration laws because, among other reasons, not all immigration violations are criminal offenses and police officers do not have the statutory authority to arrest or detain an individual in a non-criminal immigration matter. Further, the ordinance reflects the recognition that victims and witnesses may avoid contact with the police if they believe the consequence of cooperation is deportation. On the other hand, the ordinance recognizes that police officers at times have valid reasons for inquiring into immigration status and permits such inquiries.

4. What is an example where immigration status can be solicited from the subject of a criminal investigation?

During a proper investigative detention supported by reasonable suspicion (*Terry v. Ohio*), officers may properly make inquiries into a person's identity and run a name check in the LEIN system to determine if the person is wanted. In response to a possible hit, officers ask follow-up questions about his identity and the person claims that he is not the person named in the arrest warrant because he only recently came to the country. Because immigration status is relevant to the officer's investigation into whether the person is wanted, the officer is not prohibited from asking questions in that regard.

This Training Directive is for internal departmental use only, and violations of the procedures outlined in this Training Directive may form the basis for Departmental administrative sanctions. This document is not intended for third-party use or benefit. No criminal or civil duty or standard of care is intended to be, or is, created by the issuance of this Training Directive.

Training Directive: SOLICITATION OF IMMIGRATION INFORMATION
Number: 07-04
Date: July 10, 2007

5. Can a person be asked about immigration status during arrest processing?

Yes. The ordinance specifically permits questioning concerning immigration status during the processing of an arrestee. Members are reminded that federal law and department policy impose a duty to inform foreign nationals who are arrested, without delay, of their right to have a consular officer from their country notified of their detention. Furthermore, with regard to certain countries that are known as "Mandatory Notification Countries," the consular office must be notified by the law enforcement agency regardless of the wishes of the foreign national. This policy is delineated in Section 202.6 - 7 of the Detroit Police Manual. For purposes of consular notification, a "foreign national" is any person who is not a United States citizen, and includes lawful permanent resident aliens ("green card" holders) as well as persons in the country in violation of immigration laws.

6. Does the ordinance prohibit contacting or requesting assistance from federal agencies, such as Immigration & Customs Enforcement (I.C.E.) (formerly known as Border Patrol); concerning suspected violations of federal immigration laws or other law enforcement matters?

No. The ordinance only addresses the solicitation of immigration status and does not prohibit reporting suspected violations of immigration laws to appropriate federal agencies.

7. Should officers routinely ask that I.C.E. officers respond to the scene to translate when an individual does not speak English?

No. Members are advised that department policy is not to routinely request response by I.C.E. personnel solely to provide translation assistance. This policy does not prohibit the use of any law enforcement personnel already at the scene to assist in translating nor does it apply in emergency or serious situations requiring immediate action. Members requiring translation services should notify Communications for assistance.

8. Does the ordinance apply to city employees who are not police officers?

Yes. However, solicitation of immigration status by public servants is permitted if required by law as a condition of eligibility for a government program, for completing legally mandated employment forms, and with regard to the issuance of subpoenas.

Questions concerning the content of this Training Directive may be directed to Legal Affairs at 596-2161.

This Training Directive is for internal departmental use only, and violations of the procedures outlined in this Training Directive may form the basis for Departmental administrative sanctions. This document is not intended for third-party use or benefit. No criminal or civil duty or standard of care is intended to be, or is, created by the issuance of this Training Directive.

HPD Immigration Policy
Questions & Answers

1. Is it true that immigrants should now be afraid of reporting any crimes to HPD because if they do, they may be turned over to Immigration and Customs Enforcement (ICE)?

No. We hope and encourage immigrant communities to continue to call us when they need assistance from the police. Immigrants who are victims of crime or have information regarding criminal activity should contact the police. They should not fear that HPD will call federal immigration agents on them. HPD will contact ICE when the person is confirmed to have a deportation warrant or a notice that they are a previously deported felon.

2. Will HPD officers detain me simply because they think I am here illegally?

No. HPD officers are not authorized to arrest or detain a person solely on a belief that the person is in the country illegally. Officers are authorized to arrest and detain persons they have reasonable basis to believe have committed a criminal violation.

3. Is it true that HPD officers are going to ask all people they encounter for proof of legal residence/status?

No. Once a person has been arrested and taken to a jail facility, HPD jail personnel will then ask the person for his/her legal status. Jail personnel will ask the arrested person if they are a citizen of the United States or if they were born in the U.S.

4. Is it true that HPD will arrest any foreign person?

No. Officers are not authorized to detain or arrest a person solely on the basis of their nationality or ethnicity. Officers are authorized to arrest and detain persons they have a reasonable basis to believe have committed a criminal violation.

5. Is it true that HPD will run a background check on all people they encounter?

No. Officers will check the wanted status of all persons who are ticketed, arrested, or who have been jailed. Officers also have the discretion to check the wanted status of all persons they have legally detained.

6. Is it true that HPD will call ICE on all people they encounter?

No. ICE will be contacted if during a check of their wanted status, the person is confirmed to have a deportation warrant or a notice that they are a previously deported felon or have other criminal warrants issued by ICE.

7. If I am arrested or taken to jail by HPD will ICE be called?

HPD will contact ICE when a person is arrested and taken to jail and the person is confirmed to have a deportation warrant, a notice that they are a previously deported felon or any other criminal warrant with ICE. ICE officials will be allowed full access to HPD jail facilities.

8. If I am driving without a license and get stopped by HPD, will I get arrested? Will ICE be called?

If a person drives without a license and is stopped by HPD, that person will be asked to provide valid identification. If the person cannot provide valid identification and the HPD officer cannot verify their identity, the person will be taken to jail for driving without a license so the person can be can be positively identified and fingerprinted. ICE will be contacted only if the person is confirmed to have a deportation warrant, a notice that they are a previously deported felon or any other criminal warrant with ICE.

1

9. What forms of identification will HPD officers accept?

Officers will accept driver's licenses and identification cards issued by any state of the United States of America. Also, the officers will accept most other forms of government ID like a military ID, passport, etc. Additionally, officers are advised that a matricula consular card issued by the Mexican government is presumed valid unless the totality of the circumstances calls the validity of the card into question.

10. If I am a suspect in a crime or the HPD officer believes that I may be involved in a criminal episode, can he/she ask me for identification?

Yes. The officer is authorized to ask a person who the officer has a reasonable basis to believe has committed or was involved in a criminal episode for identification.

11. If I do not have identification, can I be arrested?

No. Not unless you have been suspected of committing a crime. If you have committed a crime or a traffic violation and cannot provide identification to the officer and the officer cannot verify your identity, the officer has the authority to take you into custody for the criminal violation and so that you can be identified and fingerprinted by AFIS (Automated Fingerprinting Identification System). For safety reasons, the HPD officer needs to know whom he/she is dealing with at the time.

12. If the officer stops me for a minor traffic violation, will I be arrested?

An officer has the discretion to arrest you if the officers cannot verify your identity. You will be arrested if it is confirmed that you have an NCIC and/or SETCIC warrant hit. Officers will check the wanted status of all persons arrested, ticketed or jailed. Officers have the discretion to check the wanted status of anyone legally detained, including persons detained on minor traffic violations.

13. If the officer stops me for a minor traffic violation, will I be deported?

If the officer's computer check verifies you have a deportation warrant or a notice that you are a previously deported felon, the officer will take you to a city jail facility and ICE will be contacted accordingly. The federal immigration authorities will determine whether or not you will be deported. HPD does not make decisions on deportation.

14. If I am found to have city warrants (like unpaid traffic tickets), will I eventually be deported?

If you have city warrants you are subject to arrest for those warrants. If during such arrest, you are also confirmed to have a deportati*on warrant, a notice that you are a previously deported felon or any other criminal warrant with ICE, the officer will take you to a city jail and ICE will be contacted. Only ICE will make decisions on deportation matters.*

15. If I am an illegal immigrant in possession of a firearm, can I be arrested and deported?

Yes! Illegal immigrants are prohibited from possessing a firearm and are s subject to arrest by HPD officers. If during such arrest, you are also confirmed to have a deportation warrant or are a previously deported felon, the officer will take you to a city jail and ICE will be contacted. ICE will decide on deportation matters. More importantly, you can be charged federally with a felony that carries a sentence of up to 10 years in prison and subject to deportation after serving that sentence. Should you return to the U.S. after being convicted of the felony of being in possession of a firearm, the federal authorities can prosecute you for illegal re-entry with a penalty of up to 20 years in prison. The Harris County District Attorney's Office has agreed to refer all cases of an illegal immigrant in possession of a firearm to the U.S. Attorney's Office for federal prosecution.

2

APPENDIX O

Sample Police Department Policies on Immigration Enforcement

LOS ANGELES POLICE DEPARTMENT

264.50 ENFORCEMENT OF UNITED STATES IMMIGRATION LAWS. Officers shall not initiate police action where the objective is to discover the alien status of a person. Officers shall neither arrest nor book persons for violation of Title 8, Section 1325 of the United States Immigration Code (Illegal Entry).

675.35 PLACEMENT AND DISPOSITION OF ILLEGAL ENTRY HOLDS. Supplemental holds charging illegal entry against persons in the custody of this Department for an unrelated criminal offense shall only be authorized by officers of the United States Immigration and Naturalization Service (INS). Arrestees against whom the INS has placed a hold shall be released to the custody of INS within 24 hours after:

- All local charges are dismissed; or,
- Bail is deposited on the local charges; or,
- The arrestee is determined to be eligible for release on his/her own recognizance on the local charges.

Note: Under no circumstances shall any person be held longer than 24 hours when an illegal entry hold is the only remaining charge. There is no extension of the 24 hour detention limit because of an intervening holiday or weekend period. Procedures governing the booking and detention of prisoners held enroute are unaffected by this section.

390. UNDOCUMENTED ALIENS. Undocumented alien status in itself is not a matter for police action. It is, therefore, incumbent upon all employees of this Department to make a personal commitment to equal enforcement of the law and service to the public regardless of alien status. In addition, the Department will provide special assistance to persons, groups, communities and businesses who, by the nature of the crimes being committed upon them, require individualized services. Since undocumented aliens, because of their status, are often more vulnerable to victimization, crime prevention assistance will be offered to assist them in safeguarding their property and to lessen their potential to be crime victims.

Police service will be readily available to all persons, including the undocumented alien, to ensure a safe and tranquil environment. Participation and involvement of the undocumented alien community in police activities will increase the Department's ability to protect and to serve the entire community.

APPENDIX O

Sample Police Department Policies on Immigration Enforcement

MESA POLICE DEPARTMENT

SPECIAL ORDER

George Gascón
Chief of Police

SO#:	Effective date:	Termination date:	Superseded Order(s):
2009-01	01/01/09	01/01/10	FLD 441

IMMIGRATION AND CUSTOMS ENFORCEMENT PROTOCOL

1. STATEMENT OF PURPOSE

The purpose of this protocol is to provide guidelines for the management of undocumented foreign nationals (UFN) that come in contact with law enforcement officers.

Where the contents of this special order conflict with earlier department statements, policies, procedures or rules, this order will control.

2. POLICY

The Mesa Police Department (MPD) is committed to improving the quality of life in our community by implementing strategies to reduce crime whether committed by citizens, visitors, and/or undocumented foreign nationals.

In 1996, the United States Congress passed the Illegal Immigration Reform and Immigrant Responsibility Act, 8 U.S.C. 1101, *et. seq* (IIRIRA). IIRIRA made many changes to immigration laws including adding immigration consequences to certain crimes and requiring mandatory detention of UFNs convicted of certain crimes. IIRIRA also addressed the relationship between the federal government and local governments by permitting certain designated officers to perform immigration law enforcement functions provided they receive the appropriate training and agree to function under the supervision of officers from Immigration and Customs Enforcement (ICE) to identify, process, and when appropriate, detain UFNs they encounter during their regular, daily law-enforcement activity.

Federal immigration laws are complicated in that they involve both civil and criminal aspects. Federal agencies such as ICE have the authority to determine if a person will be criminally prosecuted for their violations of immigration laws or be dealt with through a civil deportation process. Immigration violations are different from the typical criminal offenses that patrol officers face every day, whose law enforcement activities revolve around crimes such as murder, assaults, narcotics, robberies, burglaries, domestic violence, traffic violations and the myriad of other criminal matters. The immigration status of any particular person can vary greatly and whether they are in violation of the federal immigration regulations, civilly or criminally, can be very difficult to determine without a special expertise.

Page 1 of 6

SO#: 2009-01	Effective date: 01/01/09	Termination date: 01/01/10

The MPD is committed to partnering with federal agencies and others to the extent allowable under federal, state and local laws to address criminal activity within our community. This practice is consistent with our duty to ensure the safety and well-being of all persons, regardless of their immigration status.

3. PROCEDURES

The MPD provides law enforcement services and enforces the laws of the City of Mesa, the State of Arizona, and the United States Constitution impartially. While the investigation and enforcement of federal laws relating to illegal entry and residence in the United States is specifically assigned to ICE, the MPD commits to cooperating with ICE and others, to the extent permitted by law, on any criminal activity that threatens the safety and well-being of our community.

In enforcing the laws, officers may legally stop, detain or arrest anyone when reasonable suspicion or probable cause exists that a crime has occurred. Officers, however, shall not engage in bias-based profiling, also referred to as "racial profiling", when conducting stops, detentions, or arrests of any subject.

In order to combat state and local crime effectively the following policies apply:

Arrested - Booked

- Adults, not including juveniles (unless chargeable for a crime covered in ARS 13-501A 1-5, Persons under eighteen years of age; felony charging) who are arrested for committing a state or local crime **shall** be asked about their immigration status and, if the officer(s) develop information that the suspect is in the United States unlawfully, the information **shall** be detailed in the DR (Department Report). The detention supervisor **shall** contact ICE (Law Enforcement Agency Response Team (LEAR)), complete an ICE Inquiry (NLLQ) as needed, and **shall** notify the Support Services Lieutenant as soon practical. A copy of the NLLQ and any ICE response shall be forwarded to the Support Services Lieutenant.

Cite and Release Or Long Form

- If the person arrested is being cited and released or a long form complaint is being sought for a state or local crime he or she **may** be asked about their immigration status, and if the officer(s) develop information that the suspect is in the United State unlawfully, the officer(s) **shall** document it in a DR and **shall** refer the individual to ICE by completing an **ICE Request for Inquiry Form**, noting in the remarks sections that the person was cited and released, and forwarding the form to the affected District Coordinator/Metro Resources Lieutenant. The District Coordinator/Metro Resources Lieutenant is responsible for ensuring the notice to ICE (NLLQ)

Page 2 of 6

SO#:	Effective date:	Termination date:
2009-01	01/01/09	01/01/10

is completed. The **ICE Request for Inquiry Form**, NLLQ and any response from ICE shall be kept at the affected district.

NOTE: If an officer develops information that the individual is in the United States illegally without asking about his/her immigration status, the officer **may** complete the ICE Request for Inquiry Form and the District Coordination **shall** refer the information to ICE.

The officer should take into consideration the following factors in determining whether to cite and release or arrest:

ties to the community, including family ties and relationships, and length of residence, prior criminal activity, and any other facts bearing on the risk of nonappearance or danger to the public.

Unsolicited Information

- If the officer comes upon unsolicited information during the course of his or her enforcement efforts about a UFNs immigration status, of the person(s) being investigated, it **shall** be documented in a Field Interview Card (FI) and it **may** be detailed in the **ICE Request for Inquiry Form** and forwarded to the affected District Coordinator/Metro Resources Lieutenant.
- The **ICE Request for Inquiry Form shall** be routed to ICE through the District Coordinator/Metro Resources Lieutenant for investigation.

NOTE

Consistent with our efforts to protect the safety and well-being of the community and to encourage the public to report criminal activity, department personnel **shall not** ask a person about his or her immigration status who is:

- a victim of a crime,
- a witness to a crime,
- a juvenile, unless chargeable for a crime covered in ARS 13-501A 1-5, Persons under eighteen years of age; felony charging;
- stopped and/or cited for a civil traffic violation with a valid driver's license or evidence of identity pursuant to ARS 28-1595(B),
- seeking medical assistance,
- a victim of domestic violence incident, or
- a community volunteer in police service (including but not limited to police service based programs such as neighborhood watch, community forums, or community advisory board; youth programs, Making Every Student Accountable (MESA) Program or the citizens police academy or similar volunteer organization).

Page 3 of 6

SO#: 2009-01	Effective date: 01/01/09	Termination date: 01/01/10

Detention and Removal Order (DRO) Hold

The Detention and Removal Office is a unit of ICE that has the responsibility of detaining and transporting UFNs apprehended by ICE, Customs and Border Protection and local law enforcement.

- Once a person has been identified as being in the United States illegally, ICE issues a DRO hold, which can be for criminal or civil violations.
- This hold is similar to a hit from a warrant when a person's information is run through NCIC.

- If an Officer receives a DRO hit, the following **shall** be done:
  - Call the telephone number on the DRO hit to determine whether the DRO hold is criminal or civil.
- If an Officer receives a DRO hit, the subject may be detained for the length of time it takes to determine whether the DRO hold is criminal or civil.

DRO - Civil Hold

Arizona law authorizes police officers to enforce provisions of the criminal law. The authorization is limited to criminal and does not include civil. Therefore, officers shall not transport for civil violations or continue to detain if the only violation is a civil DRO hold.

- If the officers develop Information that the suspect is in the United States unlawfully, the information shall be detailed in the FI and forwarded to the affected District Coordinator/Metro Resources Lieutenant.
- The **ICE Request for Inquiry Form** shall be completed and routed to ICE through the District Coordinator/Metro Resources Lieutenant.
- Once the **ICE Request for Inquiry Form** has been completed, the subject may be released.
- An FI shall be completed containing all of the relevant information.

DRO - Criminal Hold

- Detain and transport for criminal DRO holds, if requested to do so by ICE.

Page 4 of 6

SO#:	Effective date:	Termination date:
2009-01	01/01/09	01/01/10

- A DR entitled "Possible Federal Immigration Violation" shall be completed for all arrests and transports for ICE on a criminal DRO hold or criminal violations of a federal immigration law.

- The questions and answers to the following shall be asked of all parties involved and documented thoroughly in the DR:

    - What is your country of birth?

    - Are you in the United States legally?

ICE Contact for Drop Houses, Human Smuggling and Load Vehicles

When dealing with drop houses, human smuggling, and/or load vehicles, the following steps **shall** be taken:

- A patrol supervisor **shall** contact the on duty shift lieutenant and provide a detailed account of the incident.

- The on duty shift lieutenant **shall** contact ICE to advise of the circumstances.

- The on duty shift lieutenant shall document each reported incident along with the response by ICE in a supplement to the DR.

- The on duty shift lieutenant **shall** advise the patrol supervisor of a response by ICE and/or other investigative details.

- Officers **shall** cooperate with ICE agents in ICE law enforcement activities consistent with the mandates of MPD policy.

- Officers may transport ICE prisoners at the request of an on-call ICE agent and with the approval of an on-duty supervisor when they come in contact with undocumented persons in regards to a smuggling operation/drop house, or a load vehicle.

- The command duty officer (CDO) or the affected division commander and the on-duty or on-call media relations officer (MRO) **shall** be notified as soon as possible for on scene assistance by ICE or other high profile incidents involving undocumented persons.

Community and Victim Services

Officers may refer community members to the Chicanos Por La Causa and/or Friendly House assistance; contact Communications or Victim Services for telephone numbers and locations.

For additional referral services contact Community Information & Referrals at (602) 263-8856.

Page 5 of 6

SO#:	Effective date:	Termination date:
2009-01	01/01/09	01/01/10

U-Visa Certification Forms

U-Visas are available through United States Citizenship and Immigration Services for immigrants who are current or former victims, witnesses, or affected family who are assisting or have assisted officials in the criminal justice system investigate or prosecute criminal activity.

If the applicant is requesting a U-Visa based upon past cooperation, the assigned detective may document specific details they believe merit consideration.

- All requests for U-Visas **shall** be forwarded to the affected Division Commander.

- The affected division commander **shall** determine if the applicant meets the conditions required on the U-Visa Certification Form in regards to type of crime committed and involvement (for example, the applicant is a victim, witness, or possesses relevant information for a successful resolution to the case).

- The affected division commander shall forward his or her written recommendation to the Chief of Police through the chain of command.

4. CONCLUSION

MPD recognizes its role in the community to fight crime and the fear of crime by implementing strategies and utilizing all available tools to do so. Our commitment to this mission extends to all persons that engage in criminal activity within our community irrespective of their immigration status.

This policy evidences our intent to cooperate with ICE and others, to the extent permitted by law, on any criminal activity that threatens the safety and well-being of our community.

APPENDIX O

Sample Police Department Policies on Immigration Enforcement

General Order 2008-39	FOREIGN NATIONALS – DIPLOMATIC IMMUNITY – RACIAL PROFILING – IMMIGRATION ENFORCEMENT	

MILWAUKEE, WISCONSIN, POLICE DEPARTMENT

130.25 RACIAL PROFILING POLICY

A. DEFINITION

Racial profiling is any police-initiated action that relies upon the race, ethnicity, or national origin of an individual rather than the behavior of that individual, or information that leads the police to a particular individual who has been identified as being engaged in or having been engaged in criminal activity.

B. POLICY

It shall be the policy of the Milwaukee Police Department that police members, during the performance of their duties, shall not engage in the practice of racial profiling. Police members shall not use racial or ethnic stereotypes as factors in selecting whom to stop and whom to search. Police members may use race or ethnicity to determine whether a person matches a specific description of a particular suspect.

130.30 IMMIGRATION ENFORCEMENT

A. POLICY

It shall be the policy of the Milwaukee Police Department to implement an immigration enforcement strategy that is consistent with the mission of reducing the levels of crime, fear, and disorder in the City of Milwaukee. However, this strategy must also be in balance with the jurisdictional responsibilities of the federal government and the corresponding jurisdictional limitations of local law enforcement. The following procedures not only achieve that balance but also comply with the Wisconsin Attorney General's law enforcement guide to immigration enforcement.

With a policing philosophy that is community-based, problem-oriented, and data-driven, we are committed to ridding the city's streets of violent offenders regardless of whether such offenders are in the United States legally or illegally. We are also committed to facilitating safe, sustainable communities where citizens are encouraged to report crime and provide the police with useful information and intelligence. However, proactive immigration enforcement by local police is inherently detrimental to our mission and policing philosophy when doing so ultimately deters some citizens from participating in their civic obligation to assist the police. It is therefore expected that each police member follow the procedures set forth below regardless of one's personal opinion or political ideology on the issue of immigration.

B. Enforcement of the nation's immigration laws is the responsibility of the federal government, particularly the United States Bureau of Immigrations and Customs Enforcement (ICE). Accordingly, the Milwaukee Police Department shall not unilaterally undertake immigration-related investigations and shall not routinely inquire into the immigration status of persons encountered during police operations. This prohibition does not preclude the Department from cooperating with federal immigration officials when requested, or from notifying those officials in serious situations where a potential threat to the public is perceived.

Note: Most immigration violations are civil and fall under the jurisdiction of the federal government. As such, local law enforcement officers have no right of arrest in these matters.

APPENDIX O

Sample Police Department Policies on Immigration Enforcement

General Order 2008-39	FOREIGN NATIONALS – DIPLOMATIC IMMUNITY – RACIAL PROFILING – IMMIGRATION ENFORCEMENT	

MILWAUKEE, WISCONSIN, POLICE DEPARTMENT

C. A person's right to file a police report, participate in police-community activities, or otherwise benefit from police services is not contingent upon their immigration status. Consequently, Department members shall not question any person about his or her immigration status unless that person is reasonably believed to be involved in one or more of the activities identified in (F) below.

D. Department members shall not request passports, visas, "green cards," or other documents relating to one's immigration status in lieu of, or in addition to, standard forms of identification such as a driver's license, state identification card, etc. Immigration related documents shall only be requested when standard forms of identification are unavailable, or when the member is proceeding under (F) below.

E. Police members shall not contact, detain, or arrest a person solely for a suspected immigration violation unless such contact, detention, or arrest is in cooperation with and at the direction of federal immigration officials.

F. Police members shall not inform federal immigration officials of the whereabouts or behavior of any suspected illegal immigrant or foreign visitor, except when the immigrant or foreign visitor:

1. Is arrested for a felony
2. Is arrested for a misdemeanor involving the possession or use of a dangerous weapon
3. Is arrested for a terrorism-related offense, or is otherwise reasonably suspected of involvement in terrorism and/or subversive activities
4. Is arrested for any offense involving the entry or fraudulent assimilation of undocumented foreigners into the country, or is reasonably suspected of participating in an organized venture to bring or fraudulently assimilate undocumented foreigners into the country
5. Is a previously deported felon
6. Is reasonably suspected of participating in criminal street gang activity

G. In the event a police member needs to contact ICE, they shall first attempt to contact the local office at (414) 297-1571. If the local office is closed or if an agent is unavailable, the police member shall contact the ICE Law Enforcement Support Center (LESC) at 1-802-872-6050.

H. <u>Only federal immigration officials can determine a person's immigration status</u>; therefore, citizens wishing to report immigration violations shall be referred to the local office of ICE at (414) 287-6326, fax (414) 287-6344.

EDWARD A. FLYNN
CHIEF OF POLICE

APPENDIX O

Sample Police Department Policies on Immigration Enforcement

State of New Jersey
OFFICE OF THE ATTORNEY GENERAL
DEPARTMENT OF LAW AND PUBLIC SAFETY
PO BOX 080
TRENTON NJ 08625-0080

JON S. CORZINE
Governor

ANNE MILGRAM
Attorney General

ATTORNEY GENERAL
LAW ENFORCEMENT DIRECTIVE NO. 2007-3

These guidelines shall establish the manner in which local, county, and State law enforcement agencies and officers shall interact with federal immigration authorities.

While enforcement of immigration laws is primarily a federal responsibility, State, county, and local law enforcement agencies necessarily and appropriately should inquire about a person's immigration status under certain circumstances. Specifically, after an individual has been arrested for a serious violation of State criminal law, the individual's immigration status is relevant to his or her ties to the community, the likelihood that he or she will appear at future court proceedings to answer State law charges, and the interest of the federal government in considering immigration enforcement proceedings against an individual whom the State has arrested for commission of a serious criminal offense. When there is reason to believe that the arrestee may be an undocumented immigrant, the arresting agency is responsible for alerting federal immigration officials, the prosecuting agency, and the judiciary.

The overriding mission of law enforcement officers in this State is to enforce the State's criminal laws and to protect the community that they serve. This requires the cooperation of, and positive relationships with, all members of the community. Public safety suffers if individuals believe that they cannot come forward to report a crime or cooperate with law enforcement. Moreover, Article 1, Paragraph 22 of the New Jersey Constitution mandates that "a victim of a crime shall be treated with fairness, compassion and respect by the Criminal Justice System." Consistent with that constitutional mandate, as well as basic

HUGHES JUSTICE COMPLEX • TELEPHONE: (609) 292-4925 • FAX: (609) 292-3508
New Jersey Is An Equal Opportunity Employer • Printed on Recycled Paper and Recyclable

principles of effective policing, victims, as well as witnesses and other persons requesting police assistance, should not be discouraged from approaching police officers out of fear of inquiry into their immigration status.

In 1996, Congress authorized federal authorities to delegate civil and criminal immigration enforcement authority to local, county and State agencies that enter into a written agreement with Immigration and Customs Enforcement (ICE).[1] Regardless of any additional enforcement powers granted pursuant to an agreement with ICE, however, the primary function of local, county and State agencies must be to enforce State law and to ensure public safety in the community. The exercise of federal immigration enforcement authority by State, county or local law enforcement officers must therefore be consistent with, and in support of, their State law enforcement mission. In addition, unlike federal task forces, to which participating officers are assigned on a full-time basis and are under direct and constant federal supervision, Section 287(g) officers need not obtain federal approval before taking enforcement actions in the name of the federal government.

To further the priorities of strong relationships between law enforcement and all members of the community, as well as other fundamental principles of equal protection and civil rights, New Jersey has taken a leadership position in eliminating racially-influenced policing, or racial profiling. In 2005, the Attorney General issued Attorney General Law Enforcement Directive 2005-1, which prohibits law enforcement officers from engaging in racially-influenced policing. In that directive, the Attorney General formalized and mandated the great advances that have been made in the State in eliminating racially-influenced policing practices. Additionally, the Legislature has affirmed that it is against the policy of this State for law enforcement officers to use race or ethnicity as a basis for initiating an investigation. See N.J.S.A. 2C:30-5. Consistent with public policy, statute, and Attorney General Directive, law enforcement agencies must refrain from any law enforcement strategies that risk undermining – or which create the impression of undermining – the prohibitions on racially-influenced policing.

Accordingly, by virtue of the authority vested in me by the Constitution and the Laws of this State, and in furtherance of securing

1 See Section 287(g) of the Immigration and Nationality Act, codified at 8 U.S.C. § 1357(g).

2

APPENDIX O

Sample Police Department Policies on Immigration Enforcement

the benefits of a uniform and efficient enforcement of the criminal law and the administration of criminal justice throughout the State, N.J.S.A. 52:17B-97 et. seq., I do hereby promulgate the following directives:

I. Arrest of Undocumented Immigrants for Indictable Offenses and Driving While Intoxicated (Applicable to all Agencies and Officers)

1. **When a local, county, or State law enforcement officer makes an arrest for any indictable crime, or for driving while intoxicated, the arresting officer or a designated officer, as part of the booking process, shall inquire about the arrestee's citizenship, nationality and immigration status. If the officer has reason to believe that the person may not be lawfully present in the United States, the officer shall notify Immigration and Customs Enforcement (ICE) during the arrest booking process. The only exception to this requirement shall be if the County Prosecutor or the Director of the Division of Criminal Justice determines, in writing, that good cause exists to refrain from notifying ICE during the arrest booking process.**

2. **Notification to ICE may be made telephonically, by facsimile transmission, or by such other means as ICE may provide. The officer shall document when and by what means notification to ICE was made and the factual basis for believing that the person may be an undocumented immigrant.**

3. **Whenever a law enforcement officer notifies ICE about a suspected undocumented immigrant, notification shall also be made to the prosecuting authority that will handle the matter (*e.g.*, the County Prosecutor in the case of an indictable charge), and to any court officer setting bail or conditions of pretrial release.**

4. **County Prosecutors shall on an annual basis report to the Director of the Division of Criminal Justice on the total number of notifications made pursuant to this Directive and the Director shall make the aggregate data public on an annual basis.**

3

II. Prohibition on Immigration Status Inquiries of Victims and Witnesses (Applicable to all Agencies and Officers)

5. No State, county, or local law enforcement officer shall inquire about or investigate the immigration status of any victim, witness, potential witness, or person requesting or receiving police assistance. An exception to this requirement shall exist if: (a) the County Prosecutor or the Director of the Division of Criminal Justice determines, in writing, that good cause exists to inquire about or investigate the person's immigration status; (b) the person has been arrested for an indictable offense or for driving while intoxicated as set forth in Section 1 above; or, (c) as may be constitutionally or otherwise legally required during the criminal litigation discovery process.

III. Standards for Agencies and Officers Who Enter Agreements to Exercise Federal Immigration Authority Pursuant to Section 287(g) (Applicable only to Section 287(g) Agencies and Officers)

Directives 6 through 12 apply only to those local, county, and State law enforcement agencies and officers performing functions of a federal immigration officer pursuant to an agreement with federal authorities under 8 U.S.C. § 1357(g). As used in this Directive, the term "Section 287(g) agency" means a State, county or municipal law enforcement agency that is a signatory to a written agreement with Immigration and Customs Enforcement (ICE) authorized by Section 287(g) of the Immigration and Nationality Act, 8 U.S.C. § 1357(g). The term "Section 287(g) officer" means a law enforcement officer employed by a Section 287(g) agency who has received the training required by Section 287(g) and is authorized by ICE to act as a federal immigration officer.

A. Provisions Applicable to Section 287(g) Officers in Detention Facilities

6. A Section 287(g) officer may invoke or exercise federal authority under Section 287(g) with respect to any undocumented immigrant who is being detained in a county jail or State detention facility.

4

B. Provisions Applicable to All Other Section 287(g) Officers

7. **A Section 287(g) officer may not exercise federal law enforcement authority under Section 287(g) unless and until the officer has arrested an individual(s) for violation of an indictable offense, or for driving while intoxicated, under State law.**

8. **Any law enforcement officer making inquiry or investigation into the immigration status of an individual arrested for an indictable offense, or for driving while intoxicated, shall document and report the inquiry to the officer's supervisor during the arrest booking process. The report shall include the individual's name, address, gender, date of birth, country/place of birth, race, ethnicity, location encountered, and shall specify the criminal offense that formed the basis for the arrest, the outcome of inquiry and investigation into immigration status, and indicate whether the individual was taken into custody or otherwise ordered detained based on immigration status. The officer shall attach the arrest report to the reporting document.**

9. **A Section 287(g) agency shall submit on a monthly basis to the Director of the Division of Criminal Justice all reports (with arrest report attached) produced pursuant to No. 8 of this Directive to ensure that immigration enforcement efforts are being performed in compliance with all applicable State laws, directives, and guidelines. The Director shall compile the information and shall make the aggregate data public on an annual basis.**

10. **A Section 287(g) agency shall enter into a written agreement with an appropriate ICE-approved detention facility or facilities to ensure that there is adequate space to hold potential federal detainees in addition to local, county, or State detainees. The agreement shall set forth the procedures established to ensure that the**

5

detention of any individual solely on the basis of immigration charges comports with the requirements of 8 C.F.R. § 287.7. No agency shall exercise the authority granted by Section 287(g) prior to reaching agreement with a detention facility that meets the requirements set forth in this paragraph.

11. **Nothing in this Directive shall limit the ability of local, county, or State law enforcement agencies to enter into written agreements authorized by Section 287(g) that impose greater restrictions on the agency's performance of functions under that agreement.**

12. **Directives 6 through 12 inclusive shall not apply to any officer who has been detailed on a full-time basis to a federal law enforcement agency or to a task force operated under the direct supervision of a federal law enforcement agency, provided that the officer is acting exclusively under the authority of federal law.**

IV. General Matters

13. **No law enforcement officer shall at any time engage in conduct constituting racially-influenced policing, as defined in Attorney General Law Enforcement Directive No. 2005-1. An officer or employee of a police agency in this State acting either under the authority of the laws of the State of New Jersey or pursuant to an agreement authorized by Section 287(g) shall not consider a person's race or ethnicity as a factor in drawing an inference or conclusion that the person may be an undocumented immigrant.**

14. **All questions concerning the interpretation, implementation or enforcement of this Directive shall be addressed to the Director of the Division of Criminal Justice, or his designee.**

6

15. This Directive shall take effect immediately and shall remain in full force and effect unless and until repealed, amended or superseded by Order of the Attorney General.

Anne Milgram
Attorney General

ATTEST:

John Michael Vazquez
First Assistant Attorney General

Dated: August 22, 2007

7